D1525930

Choosing the Chief

Choosing the Chief

Presidential Elections in
France and the United States

Roy Pierce

Ann Arbor

THE UNIVERSITY OF MICHIGAN PRESS

Copyright © by the University of Michigan 1995
All rights reserved
Published in the United States of America by
The University of Michigan Press
Manufactured in the United States of America
∞ Printed on acid-free paper

1998   1997   1996   1995   4   3   2   1

A CIP catalogue record for this book is available from the British Library.

Library of Congress Cataloging-in-Publication Data

Pierce, Roy.
    Choosing the chief : presidential elections in France and the
    United States / Roy Pierce.
        p.   cm.
    Includes bibliographical references (p.   ) and index.
    ISBN 0-472-10559-0 (acid-free paper)
    1. Presidents—France—Election.   2. Presidents—United States—
Election.   3. Comparative government.   4. France—Politics and
government—1981–   5. United States—Politics and government—20th
century.   I. Title.
JN2959.P54   1995
324.6′3′0944—dc20   95-3586
                                                              CIP

To the memory of Hervé LeLay

Preface

This book is meant to be a modest sequel to the larger volume, *Political Representation in France* (1986), that Philip E. Converse and I published almost a decade ago. That work discussed French electoral behavior in the context of legislative elections, the legislative behavior of the deputies in the French National Assembly, and the relationship between the voters' opinions on major political issues and the legislative decisions made by the voters' elected representatives. The central theme of the book was representation, as carried out in France by the quintessential representative body in any democratic political system, the popularly elected legislature. After having focused for so long on legislative elections and behavior, it seemed logical that I should shift my attention to that other great elective institution, the presidency.

It was apparent to me from the outset that this new project should be a comparative study of presidential selection in France and the United States, at the time the two most internationally prominent democracies whose chief executives were elected by popular vote. That signified a departure from the form of *Political Representation in France* which, as the title clearly states, was concerned predominantly with the *French* representational system. At various places throughout that book, when the availability of matching data permitted, comparisons were drawn between political phenomena in France and in other countries, including the United States. But systematic comparison between political behavior in France and elsewhere was ruled out by the lack of the kind of matching or even equivalent data that are required for cross-national comparative analysis. *Political Representation in France* was originally inspired by work done in and relating to the United States (by Warren E. Miller and Donald E. Stokes [1963]), but it rested on an extraordinary French data set of which there was no counterpart for any other country.

When I first generated the idea of comparing presidential selection in France and the United States, the relative situation with regard to the availability of data was the reverse of what it had been for Converse's and my work on representation in France. There was an enormous literature on the U.S. presidency, as well as the remarkable collection of sample survey data relating to all U.S. presidential elections since the middle 1950s that is archived and made available for scholarly research by the Inter-university Consortium for Political and Social Research (ICPSR), housed in the Center for Political Studies of the University of Michigan. Popular election of the president is a comparatively recent innovation in France, however, and related French literature is sparse. In addition, there were only limited French sample survey data available, most of it in forms that did not allow direct comparison with the U.S. data. I am, therefore, extremely grateful to the National Science Foundation for a grant (SES:8801639) that enabled me to remedy some of that imbalance by contracting with SOFRES, the prominent French survey research firm, to conduct a postelectoral national sample survey immediately after the French presidential election of 1988. Thanks to the sympathetic interest of Pierre Weill, the president of SOFRES, SOFRES underwrote a substantial portion of the data collection costs. Welcome support was also furnished by the French Consul for Cultural Affairs in Chicago and by the French-American Foundation in New York. My resources did not permit me to commission a French survey that matched the range and depth of coverage of the standard U.S. National Election Study (NES), but I was able to obtain enough relevant data to prepare the numerous comparative analyses that appear in this book.

The comparative approach enables me to try to bridge two separate analytic traditions. Students of the American presidency, on the one hand, and students of French politics, on the other hand, for the most part live in two different scholarly worlds. They have different preoccupations and different audiences; they ask different questions; and each group pays little or no attention to the other's work. French electoral scholars resolutely pass over the theory of elections that has been built over the last generation, mainly by scholars in the United States. American students of the presidency write as though the office were unique, without any counterpart elsewhere. There is more than a little irony to this pattern of scholarly insularity within the two countries that were the fields of observation for the greatest modern comparativist, Alexis de Tocqueville. It is as though his assertion of American "exceptionalism," a refrain that continues to be echoed a century and a half later (and has even been transposed to distinguish not the Americans but the French), has overshadowed the numerous ingenious and profound comparisons out of which de Tocqueville's notion of exceptionalism emerged and with which he repeatedly and variously illustrated it.

The chapters that follow deliberately reject any prior attachment to notions of exceptionalism. My application of the comparative method demands equal treatment of the presidential selection process in France and the United States. Whatever analytical perspective I apply, I apply to both countries. Whatever phenomenon I investigate, I examine in each of the two countries. The objective throughout is not to demonstrate some preconceived theme, but rather to determine in what ways the presidential selection processes in France and the United States differ and in what ways they appear to be very similar.

Comparative analysis heightens one's awareness of both the differences and the similarities between the objects being compared. Comparing anything as complex as modern political systems, one can expect to find numerous differences, even if the systems being compared are limited to the comparatively small class of democracies. So it is for France and the United States: there is no shortage of differences between the French and United States political systems. The main structural differences are set forth systematically in chapter 1, and other, operational differences are discussed in later chapters, as they pertain to or emerge from the comparative analysis. These differences are important, and awareness of them is essential to understanding how the two systems operate. At the same time, I have tried throughout this book, when the evidence warranted it, to emphasize the *similarities* between the two systems. My method is comparative, but my guiding principle is to highlight whatever analogies present themselves.

My interest in pursuing the analogies between politics in France and the United States was originally stimulated by the leading authority on the French Fourth Republic (1947–58), the late Philip Williams. In an article entitled "Political Compromise in France and America," published in the summer, 1957, number of *The American Scholar*, Williams (who, being neither French nor American but British, and therefore presumably immune to exceptionalist conceits of the kind described above) argued that despite obvious and perfectly intelligible differences, there were many similarities in the outlook and behavior of French and American politicians. Williams was writing about the French Fourth Republic, when the French legislature enjoyed great power and independence that made it more closely comparable to the U.S. Congress than is the case today, and it was the similarities in the behavior of French and American legislators in particular that impressed Williams. The constitution of the French Fifth Republic, adopted in 1958, reduced the independent authority of the French legislature, with the result that similarities between French and American legislators of the kind that Williams observed are less common today. But the advent of direct popular election of the French president in 1965 created a new institutional framework for comparison between France and the United States. Williams's fine intuition with regard to elected representatives applies at least as well to the pursuit of the presidency in the two countries.

This book, therefore, is a systematic comparative study of how presidents are chosen in France and the United States. It is divided into five parts. Each part is preceded by a brief introductory statement indicating its contents, so I will refrain from offering more than skeletal comments here. Part 1 consists of two background chapters that characterize the political environments in the two countries in contrapuntal fashion, both to furnish information that is critical to an understanding of everything that follows and to set familiar institutions, persons, and practices in sharper relief by means of cross-national comparison and counterfactual suggestion.

In Parts 2 and 3, the focus shifts from institutional factors and elite dynamics to the domain of the ordinary citizen. Part 2 charts the political orientations and perceptions of the French and U.S. electorates in common conceptual terms, giving due attention both to the phenomenon of party identification that is central to the theory of elections developed in the United States and to the left-right dimension that enjoys such prominence in France. Part 3 moves into the realm of mass political behavior. Chapter 6 deals with the preliminary necessities of voter registration and electoral participation. Chapter 7 then builds on the foundation established in Part 2 to apply a single model of the attitudinal bases of candidate choice to the closely matching U.S. presidential election of 1984 and French presidential election of 1988. Finally, in Part 3, chapter 8 deals with the group bases of electoral support for the leading candidates at the French and U.S. presidential elections of 1988. This leads to a discussion of the long-standing, historic social cleavages that underlie French and U.S. partisan conflict at the mass level, as well as the alternate strategies of political mobilization that are implied by the patterns of social group support that characterize each country.

Part 4 raises for both countries issues that have generally been salient in only one of them. Chapter 9 analyzes what voters do when they cannot vote for the candidate whom they prefer. The French two-ballot system makes forced choices at the runoff ballot a much-discussed phenomenon, but analogous situations in the United States are rarely investigated. I consider the French and U.S. cases in common terms. Conversely, in the United States, notions such as split-ticket voting, presidential coattails, and the midterm slump are common currency of political discussion and analysis, while their analogs have only recently begun to be explored in France. Again, I give France and the United States equal treatment under each rubric.

Finally, Part 5 offers some concluding reflections about how the two systems of presidential election operate, from multiple perspectives on the presidency as a representative institution. In an ascending order of abstraction, I move from considerations that highlight differences between the two systems to a discussion of some fundamental, and perhaps surprising, similarities in outcomes.

In addition to those benefactors whose support I have already gratefully acknowledged, other friends and colleagues have contributed in one way or another to the making of this book. My largest debt is to Philip E. Converse, without whose help in the formative stages of this project it would never have been undertaken, and who would have been a full partner in the enterprise if other considerations had not prevented him from doing so. In addition, much of what readers may find most interesting in chapter 3 was suggested to me by him.

Others, in the Center for Political Studies as well as other units of the Institute for Social Research of the University of Michigan, within which the Center is housed, have given me help along the way. Christopher H. Achen, Leslie Kish, and Laura Klem gave me valuable statistical advice. Indispensable technical assistance was provided by Peter M. Joftis, Marita Ann Servais, and David L. Oliver. Erik W. Austin, Gregory B. Markus, Michael W. Traugott, and Santa A. Traugott saved me enormous amounts of time by directing me to the best available sources for information that I needed.

Several students also contributed: James F. Adams, now of the University of California at Santa Barbara, worked with me on various aspects of chapters 8 and 9; Jeanne Bruns, Ken Goldstein, and Rodger Park prepared the aggregate data sets for chapter 10; and Nicolas Rose acted for a while as my middleman in Paris.

Others not directly affiliated with the University of Michigan also rendered valuable service. Nicholas Wahl of New York University was a sympathetic advocate at a time when prospects for carrying out this project were bleakest. At SOFRES, the cooperation of Jérôme Jaffré, vice president, and the attention to detail of Carine Marcé, ensured that my data requirements were properly reflected in the sample survey instrument. Richard A. Baker, the Historian of the U.S. Senate, Charles S. Bullock of the University of Georgia, and Carol A. Cassel of the University of Alabama, gave me the benefit of their expertise. Thomas D. Lancaster of Emory University and two anonymous reviewers made helpful suggestions for improving the original manuscript, which was cheerfully transformed from paper to a single disk by the successive efforts of Karen P. Russell and Judith A. Ottmar.

I am also grateful to the Plenum Publishing Corporation for permission to reprint (in chap. 3) material that was originally published under the title "Toward the Formation of a Partisan Alignment in France," in *Political Behavior*, 14, no. 4 (December 1992): 443–69, as well as to SOFRES for permission to reproduce the data from their surveys that appear in table 6.2, table 9.2, and figure 10.1.

Finally, the U.S. survey data utilized in this book were made available by the Inter-university Consortium for Political and Social Research. I have mainly reported data from the *American National Election Study, 1984*, and the *American National Election Study, 1988*, although I have made lesser use of data from studies conducted in earlier presidential election years as well. The 1984 data were originally collected by the Center for Political Studies of the Institute for Social Research, the University of Michigan, under the overall direction of Warren E. Miller; Santa Traugott was director of studies in 1984.

The data were collected under a grant from the National Science Foundation. The data for 1988 were originally collected by Warren E. Miller and the National Election Studies. Neither the collector of the original data nor the Consortium bears any responsibility for the analyses or interpretations presented here.

That last disclaimer must be generalized to include all the people and organizations cited above. I appreciate their generosity, but I alone am responsible for the use I have made of it.

Contents

Part 1
The Political Environments

The choice of a president takes place within an environment of political institutions and practices that govern, shape, influence, and condition every step in the selection process. The purpose of Part 1 is to portray those elements of the French and U.S. political environments that are directly relevant to presidential selection, and to illustrate their effects through a brief canvas of presidential elections in France and the United States between the middle 1960s and the early 1990s.

Chapter 1 discusses the institutional frameworks within which presidents are chosen in the two countries, in all their aspects: constitutional, electoral, and partisan. The chapter is mainly descriptive, and readers closely familiar with such background information may prefer simply to skim it, but the content is rigorously selective in that it refers only to arrangements that have a direct impact on the elite or mass behavior that characterizes presidential selection in each country.

The groundwork established in chapter 1 will be relevant for virtually all of the analyses that follow in later chapters, and it is particularly important for understanding the patterns of presidential candidate recruitment that are discussed in chapter 2. The impact of institutional forces is nowhere displayed more clearly than in the definition of the field of credible candidates—the "*présidentiables*" in France, those "available" in the United States.

In France and the United States, two different sets of institutional arrangements and political habits create different channels of presidential candidate recruitment, with the result that different types of people emerge at the top in the two countries. In particular, the French practice of multiple-office holding, which is virtually unknown in the United States, serves to reduce the size of the elite population that is presidentially available. But if different institutional frameworks produce different recruitment patterns, common political situations can also lead to similar elite strategies. The political background and experience of the presidential elites differ in the two countries, but the behavior of the top contenders in one country becomes more fully intelligible when set against that of the main players in the other.

CHAPTER 1

Institutional Frameworks

The U.S. presidential system was established 200 years ago in order to provide energy in the executive branch of a new nation. The French presidential system was created some 35 years ago in order to accomplish the same purpose in an old nation. The selection of the president did not, in either case, originally assign a central role to the popular electorate. In the United States, prior to 1824, the voters played only a limited part in the election of the president, and the same may be said of the first modern French presidential election, in 1958. But by 1832 in the United States, and beginning in 1965 in France, the suffrage became preeminent, if not—in the United States—always decisive, in the process of presidential selection. Today, in both countries, national politics revolves around presidential elections.

While presidential elections provide the focal point of national politics in the United States and France and display many and sometimes surprising similarities in the two countries, they take place within very different institutional frameworks. The basic constitutional structures of the United States and France are different. The mechanics of presidential elections in the two countries are very different. And the party systems out of which the contending candidates emerge also differ widely. Each of these institutional factors—constitutional, electoral, and partisan—shapes the overall process of presidential selection in important ways and contributes toward what is distinctive about the process in each country.

Constitutional Structures

The main features of the U.S. Constitution are the separation of powers, federalism, and equal representation of the states in the Senate. Both the president and the legislative chambers enjoy fixed terms of office, at the same time as they are dependent upon each other in the policy-making process. Federalism, which confers important areas of policy responsibility on the states, creates 50 opportunities at a time for politicians to acquire experience as chief executives, in some cases involving territories, populations, and budgets larger than those of many sovereign nations (Kallenbach 1966). Equal representation of states in the Senate, with only two senators for each state, has created a small legislative elite that is chosen (along with governors) by statewide electorates, and which, because of the Senate's constitutional role in confirming major presidential appointments and ratifying treaties, has a special interest in monitoring executive affairs. Congress may be the "keystone of the Washington establishment" (Fiorina 1989), but the Senate is the preeminent chamber of the bicameral U.S. legislature.

The French political structure is quite different. The constitution of the French Fifth Republic, adopted in 1958 and amended in 1962 with specific regard to presidential election, created what has been called, variously, a semi-presidential system (Duverger 1980) or a premier-presidential regime (Shugart and Carey 1992). In effect, the French constitution grafted a powerful presidency on to the traditional form of parliamentary government.[1] The result is that the popularly elected French president has numerous and important constitutional powers, but operates through a prime minister and a cabinet that must always have the support of a majority in the National Assembly, the popularly elected house of the two-chambered French legislature.[2] If the prime minister and cabinet (referred to, as in all parliamentary systems, as the "government") lose their legislative support, they must resign and be replaced by another government, unless the president dissolves the National Assembly in the hope that new elections will resolve the situation more favorably for his supporters.

There are, therefore, always two major executive figures in France; the president and the prime minister (whom the president appoints), and each prime minister is a potential presidential candidate. The two executives are usually not equal in seniority, but they may eventually approach peerage in experience and share more or less equally in the national political spotlight. Indeed, during the routine conduct of political affairs, the prime minister is likely to be in the national news more often and more regularly than the president.

Even when the president and the prime minister come from the same political party or coalition, which is normally the case, there can be tensions between the two. It is in the president's interest for his prime minister to be successful in winning popular and legislative support, but not if the result is the creation or strengthening of a rival, or the enactment of policies of which the president does not wholly approve.

When the two top executive officials come from opposing political forces, the potential for conflict is much greater. Under the French constitutional system, it is possible for the presidency to be occupied by a representative of one coalition while the assembly is controlled by a majority from an opposing coalition. In those circumstances, the president has no choice but to appoint a prime minister who is acceptable to the legislative majority. Such a situation arose for the first time in 1986, ushering in a period of "cohabitation" between leftist president François Mitterrand and right-wing leader Jacques Chirac. Both men were planning to be candidates at the presidential election scheduled for 1988, and for two years the executive was "divided against itself" (Pierce 1991) as the opposing leaders conducted what amounted to a presidential election campaign.

A second period of cohabitation opened in the spring of 1993, when the rightist parties again won control of the legislature while François Mitterrand was president. This time, no one expected Mitterrand to run for the presidency again, and the new conservative prime minister, Edouard Balladur, had never expressed presidential aspirations. But the two executive leaders, representing opposing political forces, could not fail to be in a competitive relationship during what inevitably was the run up to a presidential election that could be held no later than the late spring of 1995.

The French dual executive has no counterpart in the United States, where the second highest executive official, the vice president, is entirely subordinated to the president and has no independent opportunity to acquire either status or popularity. While vice presidential hearts may vibrate with presidential aspirations, and American vice presidents have obviously used their office as launching pads to the presidency, the French constitutional system institutionalizes rivalries within the executive in a way that the U.S. Constitution does not.[3]

The French constitutional system, therefore, has the customary characteristics of a parliamentary system, in which the top tier of the political elite consists of the government and their opposite numbers among the opposing parties, along with a powerful president who has a major and sometimes decisive role in determining who will populate the government. It is important to add that the French political system has traditionally been highly centralized, and serious decentralization efforts began only in the 1980s. France is honeycombed with municipal councils, and there are also 96 departmental councils,[4] but these are too small and numerous to exercise significant autonomous authority. A layer of regional government was created in the mid-1960s, and popular election of regional councils was introduced in 1986, but the 22 metropolitan regions do not have strong mass attachments and are not particularly attractive electoral targets for most French political leaders.

Terms of Office

The U.S. presidential term is four years. George Washington established the informal norm that no president should serve more than two terms. The norm operated until Franklin D. Roosevelt ran successfully not only for a third term in 1940 but also for a fourth in 1944. The two-term rule was reintroduced and given constitutional status by the Twenty-second Amendment, adopted in 1961.

The French presidential term is seven years, and there are no restrictions, formal or informal, on reeligibility. In the United States, a two-term president becomes a lame duck at the time of the second inauguration. In France, a president is always, at least legally, a potential candidate to succeed himself. But declining political fortunes can inflict the same loss of power on a French president that the two-term limit imposes on a U.S. president. François Mitterrand won reelection handily in 1988, but within a year the political tide began to turn, and in 1993 his supporters suffered a devastating defeat at legislative elections, which ushered in a period of cohabitation that provoked editorial questions about why he chose to remain in office (*L'Express*, April 1, 1993).

Among both the electorate and the political elites, the seven-year term is regarded as excessive.[5] In 1973, the constitutional amendment procedure was launched in order to reduce the term to five years, but as the outcome of the complex procedure appeared in doubt midway through the process, the effort was abandoned.

In the United States, the four-year presidential term is fixed; a presidential election is held regularly every four years. One can mark future presidential election dates on the calendar into perpetuity, or at least for as long as the current constitutional system endures. If a president dies in office, the remainder of the unexpired term is filled by the vice president, with further provision for filling the office according to an order of succession established by the Twenty-fifth Amendment to the Constitution, adopted in 1967.

Not so in France. The presidential term there is not fixed. There is no vice president. If a president resigns before his term expires (as Charles de Gaulle did in 1969), or if a president dies in office (as Georges Pompidou did in 1974), the president of the Senate, France's second legislative chamber, becomes acting president and is constitutionally empowered to exercise only the routine functions of the presidency. A presidential election must be held between 20 and 35 days after the incumbent ceased to exercise the office. The constitutional rule means that there is no respite from presidential campaigning in France. American presidential aspirants know with certainty when the next election day will be. French would-be presidential candidates do not. Moreover, there is always the risk that the campaign period will be short if not sweet. There is no time for outsiders to build support and gain visibility if the incumbent dies in office. In France, a serious candidate must be perpetually prepared to muster resources instantly, or the chance may be lost for seven years.

In the United States, presidential elections occur simultaneously with legislative elections, in that the entire House of Representatives and one third of the Senate are renewed every four years, at the same time as a presidential election is held. There is no constitutional requirement that this be so, and it has not always been the case. Throughout most of the nineteenth century, presidential elections and congressional elections were held at different times in most states, and it was not until the early twentieth century that the practice of electoral simultaneity was voluntarily adopted by all the states.

In France, a presidential election has never been held at the same time as a legislative election. Just as the seven-year presidential term is not fixed, the legislative term, which cannot exceed five years, is not fixed either. The president has the constitutional power to dissolve the National Assembly once during any 12-month period and, since 1958, that has happened four times, with the result that on four occasions the National Assembly did not sit for a full term.

Two of those four occasions followed closely upon presidential elections and were the direct result of the outcome of the elections. Both in 1981 and 1988, the victorious presidential candidate dissolved the National Assembly almost immediately after his election, in order to try to bring the legislative political balance into harmony with his own political outlook. The presidential and legislative elections were not simultaneous, but the latter followed the former in quick succession. From time to time, it is suggested that France move to a system of electoral simultaneity, in order to tie the two strands of the electoral process—presidential and legislative—into a common framework (Duhamel 1991). For the moment, however, the formal separation remains, with the regular possibility that, through use of the dissolution power, the president can bring about an approximation of electoral simultaneity when he believes it is desirable to do so.

Electoral Systems

The central feature of the U.S. presidential election system, and one that arouses the most curiosity among interested observers in France, is that the president is not directly elected by the voters. In the United States, the voters cast their ballots for electors from their state of residence, and it is the resulting electoral college that actually selects the president and vice president. Each state is allocated a number of electors equal to the number of senators and representatives to which the state is entitled. The electors from each state cast all of their votes, in a block, for the candidate who carried the state.[6] The candidate who receives a majority of the electoral votes is elected.

This system has two potential dangers. One is simply that it is possible for a candidate to win a majority of the electoral votes while receiving fewer popular votes than his opponent(s). This happened unambiguously once, in 1888, when Benjamin Harrison was elected president because he won a majority of the electoral votes even though Grover Cleveland, his opponent, won a majority of the popular votes. While that situation did not arouse a great deal of indignation at the time, sensitivity to the importance of the suffrage was not as strong a century ago as it is today. A president who actually "lost" the election would, other things being equal, take office with substantially reduced legitimacy.

At least equally disturbing is the possibility that several candidates can divide the popular vote so that no one of them receives a majority of the electoral votes. In such a case, the U.S. Constitution prescribes that the selection of the president devolves upon the House of Representatives, which must make its choice with each state delegation casting a single vote. That procedure has not been invoked since 1824, and most observers hope that it will never have to be employed again, as it would bring into play a large number of considerations that are not normally involved in presidential selection.

Various reforms of the U.S. presidential electoral system have been proposed to avoid the risks of the present one. One proposal is that the United States employ a system of direct election in conjunction with some sort of runoff procedure to ensure that the winning candidate has a majority or at least some minimum proportion of the popular vote. That particular proposal is among those least likely to be adopted in the United States. It is, however, essentially the electoral system that is used for the election of the president in France.

The constitution of the French Fifth Republic originally provided for the election of the president by a large electoral college (of some 80,000 members) consisting mainly of delegates selected by the local councils of France's more than 36,000 municipalities. It was by this agency that Charles de Gaulle was first elected president in 1958. In 1962, the constitution was amended to provide for the direct popular election of the president, according to a system that has remained in force since that time.

The French presidential electoral system allows for two ballots. At the first ballot, as many candidates as satisfy the eligibility requirements may compete, and election requires a majority of the valid ballots cast. If no candidate wins such a majority of the votes, there is a second, runoff ballot two weeks later, at which only the two front-runners at the first ballot may compete.[7] Reducing the number of contestants to two ensures that the winner receives a majority of the votes cast. This two-ballot runoff system is an adaptation to presidential elections of the electoral system that was used for most of the legislative elections during the Third Republic (1870–1940) and the Fifth Republic. Although popular presidential elections are a comparatively new phenomenon in France, the electoral method employed is familiar to the voters.

In the United States, it is notoriously difficult for presidential candidates other than those of the two major parties to gain places on the ballot throughout the entire nation. Each state has its own ballot access legislation. Virtually everywhere, the basic requirement is that the prospective candidate file a petition signed by a comparatively large number of citizens, defined according to various formulas ranging from some set figure to a proportion of the number of registered voters in the state or of the number of voters who cast a ballot at the previous election for some designated office, such as the governorship, the presidency, or Congress. In the state of Michigan, for example, Ross Perot submitted a qualifying petition in the spring of 1992 containing more than 25,000 signatures, in satisfaction of the requirement that he be endorsed by a number of voters amounting to at least 1 percent of the vote cast for governor in 1990, including at least 100 in each of at least half of the state's 16 congressional districts.

In France, access to the first ballot is almost ludicrously simple to gain. When the system of popular election was established in 1962, a place on the ballot required only the endorsement of at least 100 citizens who were either members of Parliament, members of the Economic and Social Council (a constitutional advisory body for economic matters), departmental councillors (of whom there were some 3,000), or elected mayors (of whom there were about 38,000). Those 100 sponsors had to be distributed across at least 10 of the some 100 departments and overseas territories. In order to prevent candidates from exploiting the names or positions of their sponsors for electoral purposes, the names of the sponsoring officials were not made public.

This low electoral threshold was not unduly abused in 1965 or 1969, when there were six and seven candidates, respectively, but it produced a dozen candidates for the election of 1974. In 1976 the required number of sponsors was raised to 500, the population of officials entitled to sponsor candidates was slightly amended (by dropping members of the Economic and Social Council and adding those of the Paris City Council and the assemblies of the overseas territories), and the geographical distribution was made harder to satisfy. After 1976 a candidate needed support from at least 30 departments or overseas territories, and no more than 10 percent of the sponsors could come from a single department or territory. Moreover, the earlier concern about candidates exploiting the reputations of their sponsors for campaign purposes gave way to concern that unscrupulous politicians might sponsor candidates in order to splinter their opponents. While sponsorship originally remained confidential, it had to be made public after 1976.

The new, presumably more constraining system of requirements for a place on the ballot did little to reduce the number of candidates, which was almost as large in 1981 (10) and 1988 (9) as it had been in 1974.[8]

Party Systems

The U.S. party system is old, small, stable, and weakly organized at the national level. Political parties operated for both electoral and legislative purposes in colonial times. The Democratic party is one of America's oldest continuing institutions, and the younger Republican party is itself more than a century old. The two main parties have sometimes been challenged by third parties or would-be founders of new political movements, and they are occasionally torn by factionalism that produces threats of partisan secession, but in the end the dissidents have either been defeated or absorbed by one major party or the other.

The most recent challenge to the monopoly of the two major U.S. parties was launched in 1992 by Ross Perot, an extraordinarily rich businessman who exploited television, both paid and free (as the invited guest on talk shows and eventually during the presidential candidate debates), to try to undermine confidence in both the major parties and their candidates. In terms of popular support, Perot turned out to be the most successful independent candidate in U.S. history, winning almost 20 percent of the votes. But Perot did not come close to carrying a single state and earned no electoral votes.[9] Perot succeeded in focusing public attention on certain issues, notably the size of the public debt, and he may well survive politically to fight additional electoral battles, but for the moment his spectacularly successful foray has left no visible marks on the U.S. party system.

The deeply rooted two-party system enables the U.S. presidential system to operate as well as it does. It does not, of course, guarantee either that the presidential candidate who receives the majority of the electoral votes also wins a majority of the popular votes or even that any single candidate will win a majority of the electoral votes. But the strength of mass attachments to the two major parties has been sufficient to ensure that third-party candidates and even dissident major-party candidates will not win large fractions of the popular vote, large blocs of electoral votes, or both. That, in turn, has reduced the incentives for third-party or dissident major-party candidates to challenge the major parties. In that respect, the party system has helped the United States to avoid the worst consequences to which its antique presidential electoral system can potentially lead: a president who received fewer popular votes than his opponent(s) or a president selected by a majority of the state delegations in the House of Representatives.

U.S. political parties are highly decentralized. Politics is basically local in any democratic society, but the United States is distinct in that while political activity percolates upward from towns, cities, and counties to the states, there is virtually no regular national-level organization for either major party. There are national committees for both parties that perform various housekeeping functions, but these are neither policy-making nor nominating bodies. The main national party organizations are the quadrennial national presidential nominating conventions, but while these remain final arbiters of presidential election platform drafting and may, if necessary, actually play a decisive role in presidential nominations, the increased use of state primaries has virtually eliminated the conventions' role as nominating bodies for the presidential candidates. Indeed, the growing use of primaries for nominations for statewide office has contributed to sapping the strength of the state party conventions as well. There are few state party machines left in the United States; such machines as exist are purely local.

Compared to the American one, the French party system is new, large, unstable, and oriented organizationally toward the national level. Modern parties, organized both to garner votes and to give coherence to like-minded candidates and legislators, did not appear in France until the turn of the twentieth century. Of the four main French parties today, the Socialist party is the oldest; it is the latest version of a party that was formed in 1905. The Communist party was founded in 1920. The Rassemblement pour la République (RPR) is a neo-Gaullist party that was established in 1976. The Union pour la Démocratie Française (UDF), which is itself a federation of several smaller parties, was founded even more recently, in 1978, as a counterweight on the conservative side of the political spectrum to the RPR.

These four main political formations (or, for the RPR and UDF, their predecessors) have accounted for the lion's share of popular votes cast and seats won at legislative elections since the mid-1960s, but other parties have also competed in the kaleidoscopic French political field. The continuity of political nomenclature is periodically interrupted. Parties not only change their names; sometimes they literally disappear. Even the major parties experience a great deal of electoral volatility. Since the mid-1960s, the French Communist party has seen its electoral strength decline from more than 20 percent of the legislative vote to less than 10 percent, while Socialist party electoral support ranged from more than 35 percent in 1981 to less than 20 percent in 1993. The Gaullist predecessor of the RPR won almost 40 percent of the votes in 1968, but the RPR won less than 20 percent in 1988. UDF electoral support is impossible to measure with precision, as the UDF fields candidates jointly with a wide variety of ephemeral groups as well as under its own umbrella-like banner. Its electoral support moves within a narrower range than does that of the other major groups, but even the UDF's proportion of the vote waxes and wanes.

French legislative elections rarely produce parliamentary majorities for a single party. Single-party majorities have occurred only twice in French democratic history: in 1968, when the Gaullists were swept to an unprecedented electoral victory on a conservative backlash to the mass upheaval of May 1968, and in 1981, when a similarly large Socialist party majority was returned to the National Assembly on a combined wave of enthusiasm among leftist voters and discouragement among conservative ones at the election of François Mitterrand as president. Even in 1993, when the rightist parties combined won a massive parliamentary majority, neither of the two main right-wing parties held a majority of the seats by itself. Most of the time it is necessary to build coalitions in order to produce the parliamentary majorities that are essential in a parliamentary system.

French political parties are not only more numerous and more volatile than U.S. parties; they are also more highly structured and centralized. The particulars of French party organization vary from party to party. Some parties, including the main leftist parties, the Socialists and the Communists, seek a mass membership and are organized to take comparatively large memberships into account, while some small groups are little more than frameworks for supporting a handful of members of Parliament. But the typical French party structure includes a hierarchy of committees, including national-level executive committees, that meet frequently, as well as national congresses that normally meet once a year or every second year. These various party organs adopt policies, decide on electoral and parliamentary strategies, give expression to internal factions and leadership rivalries, and—occasionally—endorse presidential candidates.

French party structures, which funnel partisan activities toward the national level, ensure that there is a continuous, active partisan presence, distinct from the parliamentary institutions, on the national scene. This is in marked contrast with what one finds in the United States, where parties are—as in France—active on the various grassroot levels, but where there are virtually no national partisan entities apart from the congressional parties.[10] French partisan agendas at the national level are usually crowded with items that are related to the formal constitutional machinery, but they also often seem to reflect a set of political dynamics with its own rhythms, conventions, and goals.

One important factor that greatly increases the role of parties in France compared with those in the United States is that parties control nominations for elective office at every level of government. In contrast to the United States, there are no party primaries in France for any elected office, with the result that there are thousands of nominations at the disposal of the parties. Conflicts over nominations, which are usually settled by party primaries in the United States, carry over into the various tiers of party organization in France, and sometimes have to be arbitrated at the national party level.

Multiple-Office Holding in France

The hierarchy of subnational elective offices in France is linked to politics at the national level through the practice of multiple-office holding (*cumul des mandats*). French members of Parliament, including the prime minister and members of the cabinet, have traditionally also held one or more local elective offices. Local officeholders who won seats as deputies or senators always retained their local offices, and members of Parliament without local offices regularly sought them. It was not unusual for a deputy to be simultaneously the mayor of a large city as well as a member or even the president of a departmental council.

One of the most impressive illustrations of the operation of the *cumul* is provided by the career of Jacques Chaban-Delmas. Chaban-Delmas, who became a deputy in 1945 and mayor of Bordeaux in 1947, continued to serve as mayor of that city while he was president of the National Assembly from 1958 to 1969, as well as while he was prime minister from 1969 to 1972. Later, from 1986 to 1988, when he was again president of the National Assembly, he not only retained his post as mayor of Bordeaux but also was president of the Bordeaux metropolitan region and of the regional council of Aquitaine. Leading political figures even sometimes simultaneously hold elective offices in more than one department. Former prime minister Michel Debré, who was a critic of the practice of the *cumul* (Debré 1955), was nevertheless for many years a deputy from Réunion, an island in the Indian Ocean, at the same time as he held local office in the metropolitan department of Indre-et-Loire. From 1986 to 1988, Jacques Chirac was simultaneously prime minister, mayor of Paris, and a departmental councillor in the southern department of Corrèze, where he has familial roots and where he is regularly elected a deputy.[11]

Prior to the 1980s the practice of multiple-office holding, while widespread, was still more or less contained by limits on the number of separate elective offices worth pursuing simultaneously. These were, basically, a seat on the municipal council or, better yet, the mayoralty, and/or a seat on the departmental council, or its presidency (Reydellet 1979; Mény 1992, chap. 2). But in 1979, popular election of the members of the European Parliament was introduced, and in 1986, membership on France's regional councils was also made elective. Moreover, the departmental councils had gained responsibilities as a result of decentralization measures introduced after 1981. These developments multiplied the number of tempting electoral targets at which French members of Parliament could (and did) aim. The pursuit of multiple offices became so frenzied that the Socialist government felt compelled to act, and in 1985 it persuaded a reluctant Parliament to phase in a limit of no more than two major elective offices. By 1993, deputies and senators were not allowed to hold more than one other important office.[12]

When Debré (1955) wrote his critique of multiple-office holding, his main complaint about the practice was that it inappropriately elevated local political considerations to the national level. The central institutions that Debré thought should be governed by a national perspective—the government, the parliament, and the parties—were, in his view, subordinated to local interests. Multiple-office holding meant that national office had become essentially the means of reinforcing the local position of the French member of Parliament.

Whatever the merits of this interpretation, it is surely incomplete. A major consequence of multiple-office holding in France is that it restricts the size of the political elite, and that was as true when Debré wrote as it was in 1985, when the French government moved to curtail its effects.[13] At the same time as it augments the status, power, and resources of certain top-level political leaders, it reduces the number of important posts that would otherwise be filled by others, who would—given the geographical proximity of the seats of power involved—naturally be their rivals.[14] In France, there are fewer powerful elected officials than there are potentially powerful offices, because many of those officials hold more than one such office. This has important implications for the recruitment of top political leaders, including viable presidential candidates. The number of genuine contenders is very small; their political resources are enormous; and their challengers are both limited in numbers and comparatively powerless.

Some sense of the effects of multiple-office holding on French presidential politics may be gleaned by imagining what U.S. presidential politics would be like if there were multiple-office holding in the United States.[15] Imagine, for example, that the senior senator for Massachusetts was also the governor of the state or the mayor of Boston. Imagine further that—at the same time—the governor of the state of New York, or the mayor of the city of New York, was also a U.S. senator. And so on, in various combinations, not excluding county offices, across, say, Pennsylvania, Illinois, and Kansas to California. Those comparatively few powerful political figures would have tremendous advantages if they chose to pursue the presidency, among them the virtual absence of any real regional opposition. And even if they did not seek office themselves, their accumulation of important regional offices would choke off the possibility of others getting handholds on local power bases from which they might launch their own presidential bids. In France, Chaban-Delmas did not pursue the presidency again after an unsuccessful bid in 1974, but his monopoly of the powerful posts in the Bordeaux area effectively prevented the emergence of any other major figures in the same region who might have developed independent presidential aspirations. Gaston Defferre, the longtime Socialist mayor of Marseille until his death in 1986, played the same dominant and chilling role in the Midi. So did Pierre Mauroy, the first Socialist prime minister of the Fifth Republic and, simultaneously, mayor of the northern city of Lille.

Before concluding this discussion of the implications of multiple-office holding in France, we may make a final effort at counterfactual thinking, and speculate on what French presidential politics might be like if there were no *cumul*. Deputies, presidents of departmental councils, possibly even mayors, from the same area could compete with one another on something approaching equal terms. Each of those posts might well be monopolized by a single person for long periods of time, but no one would hold more than one of them. The presidencies of the regional councils might even assume more importance, as ambitious politicians sought such roles and tried to exploit them for further political advancement. Seats on municipal and departmental councils might become less appealing if they could not be combined with seats in Parliament. The French elite would be more open, and while the constitutional structure would remain quite different from that of the United States, presidential politics in France would more closely resemble U.S. politics than it does today. As things stand, the French political elite is extraordinarily broad at the base, but unusually narrowly funneled upward at the apex.[16]

In the light of subsequent developments, in particular the establishment of the presidency that Michel Debré worked so hard to create, his verdict on multiple-office holding needs to be considerably amended. The *cumul des mandats* is far less important as a means by which members of Parliament can strengthen their local positions than as a device to limit political competition by reducing the number of competitors. Not all multiple-office holders choose to seek the presidency or are in a position to do so, but for those who do, the *cumul* puts local office at the service of presidential ambition.

Concluding Comments

The fluid, highly fractionalized, unstable, and volatile French party system, combined with the pursuit of multiple offices by ambitious politicians, are at once the causes and consequences of perpetual elite-level political maneuvering. Politics everywhere is a game of bargaining for positions, policies, and patronage in which the players exploit every opportunity to advance their fortunes and to frustrate those of their rivals and opponents. In France, however, this war of maneuver is more intense and variegated than in the United States. The U.S. system channels political conflict both within and between parties more narrowly and predictably than the French system does. In France there is always movement, which both reflects and exacerbates the instability of the party system.

Yet in one ultimate sense, the French constitutional requirements for presidential election apply more constraints to the divisive French party system than the U.S. presidential election system applies to the simpler U.S. party system. For the French constitutional system was established precisely with the disintegrative potential of the French party system in mind. Whatever the configuration of parties may be, the presidential race necessarily narrows to only two candidates in France.

The American system of presidential election was designed before the U.S. party system took shape. Indeed, according to one authority, it rested on the assumption that George Washington would live forever (Corwin 1948, 62). The U.S. constitutional procedures for presidential election were altered only once in order to bring them into harmony with the developing party system, early in the nineteenth century, when the Twelfth Amendment was adopted to ensure that the president and vice president chosen by the electoral college would be of the same party. It is not the Constitution but the simple two-party system that limits the number of major presidential candidates and helps the victorious one to win a majority of the popular vote as well as of the electoral vote. But there is no guarantee the electoral field will always remain uncrowded, and third-party candidates with the potential to deprive the others from winning an electoral vote majority have not been particularly rare. There is a mild irony in that in the United States, which has a predominantly two-party system, more than two candidates may compete for the presidency, while in France, which has a complex multiparty system, only two candidates may compete at the decisive, runoff ballot. At the decisive point of conflict, the U.S. two-party system is susceptible to fragmentation, while the range of choice in France is reduced to Cartesian simplicity.

CHAPTER 2

Dramatis Personae: 1964–92

Between 1964 and 1992, there were eight presidential elections in the United States and five in France.[1] Some 25 people contended more or less seriously for major-party nomination in the United States, and a round dozen received it. Adding George Wallace and Ross Perot, the main third-party candidates of the period, we arrive at 14 major U.S. presidential candidates.[2] The low eligibility threshold for first-ballot candidacy at French presidential elections led to a proliferation of candidates across the same time span: in all, 34 different people were officially candidates between 1965 and 1988. Of those, however, only 6 survived to the second, decisive ballot at one or more elections. Two first-round candidates who were eliminated from the second ballot must also be counted as major contenders (Jacques Chaban-Delmas and Raymond Barre) because they were widely perceived when they ran as having a real chance of qualifying for the second ballot. We have, therefore, 8 French candidates who were the counterparts of the 14 U.S. presidential candidates of the same era. Fourteen candidates at eight U.S. elections; 8 candidates at five French elections; 22 persons competing seriously for the biggest political prize their countries have to offer (see table 2.1). What were the political origins of those top-tier presidential contenders?

The typical sources of candidate recruitment tend to differ within both France and the United States, depending on whether one is considering the incumbent's own party (or supporting coalition) or the opposition party (or parties). For both classes of candidate, however, recruitment patterns differ between the two countries as well, as these depend on each country's particular constitutional structure and characteristic mode of party organization.

For the party(ies) in power, the norm in both countries is for the incumbent to seek a second term, while third terms are constitutionally prohibited in the United States and rendered problematic in France by the seven-year length of the presidential term. Once incumbents are ruled out by law or circumstance, in-party candidacy is conditioned by constitutional arrangements. In the United States, the main spawning ground of presidential candidates in recent years has been the vice presidency. In France, it is high ministerial office, particularly the prime ministership. This has meant that in both countries the departing president is in a position to affect the choice of his successor. The U.S. president lit-

TABLE 2.1.   Twenty-Two Major Presidential Candidates, 1964–92, France and the United States

United States		France
1964	Lyndon *JOHNSON* vs. Barry Goldwater	
		1965 Charles *DE GAULLE* vs. François Mitterrand
1968	Richard NIXON vs. Hubert Humphrey vs. George Wallace	
		1969 Georges POMPIDOU vs. Alain Poher
1972	*NIXON* vs. George McGovern	
		1974 Valéry GISCARD D'ESTAING vs. Mitterrand (Jacques Chaban- Delmas defeated at first ballot)
1976	Jimmy CARTER vs. Gerald *Ford*[a]	
1980	Ronald REAGAN vs. *Carter*	
		1981 MITTERRAND vs. *Giscard d'Estaing*
1984	*REAGAN* vs. Walter Mondale	
1988	George BUSH vs. Michael Dukakis	1988 *MITTERRAND* vs. Jacques Chirac (Raymond Barre defeated at first ballot)
1992	Bill CLINTON vs. *Bush* vs. Ross Perot	

Note: Winners are in capital letters, incumbents in italics.

[a] Succeeded to the presidency in August 1974 on the resignation of Richard Nixon.

erally does appoint his successor if his nominee for vice president is in that post and the incumbent president dies in office (as John Kennedy did in 1963) or resigns (as Richard Nixon did in 1974) or becomes disabled. The presidency, however, is not normally within the gift of any incumbent, although it is within the power of the president to confer an advantage on someone of his choice. Before he is even elected, the next president of the United States appoints the vice president at one or the other of the two presidential nominating conventions, and the president of the French republic both appoints (and removes) the prime minister and can play a decisive role in the appointment of other high-ranking ministers.[3]

For opposition parties, the recruitment base is different and wider. The immediate past vice president is of course ruled out in the United States, although earlier vice presidents are not. Former prime ministers may still populate the field in France. But challenging parties or coalitions may also turn to other sources for candidate recruitment. These include senators and state governors in the United States and party leaders in France. Here again, as in the case of the in-parties or coalitions, the channels for advancement to the presidency are created by the constitutional structure and patterns of party organization.

In-Party Behavior

The beginning of the period of the parallel series of elections we are considering, 1964 for the United States, 1965 for France, was marked by the reelection of incumbent presidents, neither of whom held office at the time as the result of popular election. In the United States, Lyndon B. Johnson, who as vice president had succeeded to the presidency when John F. Kennedy was assassinated in the fall of 1963, won an overwhelming victory over the Republican party candidate, Barry Goldwater. In France, Charles de Gaulle, who had been elected the first president of the Fifth Republic in 1958 via the cumbersome electoral college system that was initially employed, defeated François Mitterrand and was reelected to the presidency in 1965 at the first election conducted under the new rules providing for direct popular election of the president (see app. D for presidential election results from 1964 to 1992).

Neither Johnson nor de Gaulle ran for reelection. Johnson withdrew from the 1968 race soon after the New Hampshire primary, at which—as a write-in candidate—he defeated the anti–Vietnam War candidate Eugene McCarthy by a lesser margin than many observers thought safe. De Gaulle resigned from the presidency in 1969, three years before the expiration of his second term of office. The circumstances were formally quite different from those surrounding Johnson's renunciation in the United States one year earlier, but the underlying causes of the two chief executives' departures were similar (Cerny 1970). Johnson's authority had been sapped by mass discontent, particularly among Democrats and the young, with his conduct of the Vietnam War. De Gaulle's authority had similarly been shaken by mass demonstrations throughout France in May and early June of 1968 (Converse and Pierce 1986, chap. 14–15; Pierce and Converse 1989, 1990). At the time of the May 1968 upheaval, de Gaulle had proposed holding a referendum on the broad issue of diffusing political power in France, but the idea fell on deaf ears and, in any case, de Gaulle and his government were momentarily helpless to carry out a referendum in the face of the near-general strike of the period. In 1969, de Gaulle returned to his earlier notion and proposed a complicated plan to the voters for revising the constitution in order to establish regional councils and a new representational basis for the Senate. The plan met with widespread indifference and even some opposition among de Gaulle's customary supporters, and the proposal was rejected by the voters. Interpreting the referendum result as a popular repudiation of his rule, de Gaulle promptly resigned. After Johnson in the United States, and after de Gaulle in France, every president in both countries who completed his first term ran to succeed himself.[4]

Vice Presidents and Senior Ministers

In the United States, it is becoming the practice, if the incumbent does not choose to run for a second term or, having already served two terms, is not eligible to run again, for his party to nominate the vice president. From 1964 to 1988, there were only three elections at which the incumbent did not run, and at two of those elections the vice president was a candidate: Hubert Humphrey in 1968 and George Bush in 1988. Only two persons who have served as vice president since 1964 failed to run for the presidency. One was Spiro Agnew, Richard Nixon's running mate both in 1968 and 1972, who was forced to resign the vice presidency in 1973 when he was under investigation for alleged extortion and bribery.[5] Gerald Ford, the minority leader of the House of Representatives, was then appointed vice president under the terms of the Twenty-fifth Amendment to the Constitution.

Ford's appointment as vice president marked the first time that the Twenty-fifth Amendment was applied. It was employed a second time, not long afterwards, for the appointment of the second recent U.S. vice president who did not later become the presidential candidate of his party: Nelson Rockefeller. Ford succeeded to the presidency when Richard Nixon resigned from the office in August 1974, and the United States was left once again without a vice president. Ford appointed Rockefeller, who served until the end of Ford's presidential term, but Rockefeller was anathema to his party's conservative wing, and he announced well in advance of the 1976 Republican party nominating convention that in the interest of party unity he would not again be on the party ticket.

While the road to presidential candidacy in the United States frequently runs through the vice presidency, in France it passes through high cabinet office in general and the prime ministership in particular. Georges Pompidou, who was elected in 1969 following de Gaulle's resignation, had been de Gaulle's prime minister from 1962 to 1968. Jacques Chaban-Delmas, who had been Pompidou's prime minister from 1969 to 1972, was the Gaullist candidate to succeed Pompidou in 1974, although he did not survive into the runoff ballot. Instead he was outdistanced by Valéry Giscard d'Estaing, who had been his minister of finance. Jacques Chirac had the distinction of competing for the presidency with two different incumbents, from opposite sides of the political fence, both of whom he had served as prime minister. Chirac had been Giscard's prime minister from 1974 to 1976 and then unsuccessfully challenged his former boss at the 1981 election. He was also prime minister during the first Mitterrand cohabitation administration from 1986 to 1988 when, once again, he failed to outscore the sitting president. Raymond Barre, who had succeeded Chirac as Giscard's prime minister from 1976 to 1981, opposed Chirac at the latter's second bid for the presidency in 1988.

When Edouard Balladur was appointed prime minister in the spring of 1993, he was at first widely regarded as a kind of stalking-horse for his friend and former political chief Jacques Chirac. The two men had known each other at least since the 1960s, when Balladur worked in the office of then prime minister Georges Pompidou and Chirac was a junior minister in the latter's cabinet. Balladur continued to serve Pompidou when he became president, eventually becoming the senior civil servant in the president's office. Chirac went on to occupy various ministerial positions, eventually becoming prime minister under Pompidou's successor, Valéry Giscard d'Estaing. During the first cohabitation administration, Prime Minister Chirac named Balladur as his senior minister, in charge of the economy, finance, and privatization, and he was a key figure in making the cohabitation experiment with a divided executive operate tolerably well. The accepted view early in 1993 was that Chirac would run once again for the presidency at the expiration of President Mitterrand's second term and that Balladur would not stand in his way. Balladur gained considerable popularity during 1993 and 1994, however, and journalistic interest in commissioning public opinion polls of the "horse race" kind indicated that Balladur would be a formidable candidate in his own right.

Only two prime ministers of the Fifth Republic prior to 1981 failed to run for the presidency: Maurice Couve de Murville and Pierre Messmer.[6] Although both men enjoyed considerable national visibility because of the high office they had held, neither was really an electoral politician. Both men had been senior civil servants, Couve de Murville in the ministry of foreign affairs and Messmer in colonial affairs and as a reserve officer, when de Gaulle brought them into the cabinet early in the Fifth Republic. Each served as a skillful executor of policy in a domain that de Gaulle personally controlled: Couve de Murville as minister for foreign affairs from 1959 to 1968, and Messmer as minister of the armed forces from 1960 to 1972. Each man won election to the National Assembly, Messmer from a district in eastern France and Couve de Murville from one in Paris, but in 1969 Couve de Murville ran at a well-publicized special election in another district and lost to a radical young upstart named Michel Rocard, who had already launched what was to become a long-term pursuit of the presidency by running for the office at the 1969 election, as a token candidate on behalf of the participatory themes advanced during the student upheaval of 1968.

Out-Party Candidates

The recruitment of out-party presidential challengers in the United States in recent decades has followed well-established patterns, regardless of party. The major candidates have been former vice presidents (Nixon in 1968 and Mondale in 1984), senators (Goldwater in 1964 and McGovern in 1972), and governors or ex-governors (Wallace in 1968, Carter in 1976, Reagan in 1980, Dukakis in 1988, and Clinton in 1992). This triadic recruitment base reflects the structure of the highest levels of the U.S. political elite. Unless the 1992 intrusion of independent candidate Ross Perot transforms the U.S. political system in some durable fashion, those traditional channels of candidate recruitment can be expected to operate indefinitely.

The French political system, being of more recent vintage in its presidential aspects than the U.S. system, had no traditions of out-party recruitment on which to draw when popular election of the president was introduced. The French right, consisting of the Gaullists and their Giscardian allies, dominated Parliament and occupied the executive branch from 1965 to 1981, with the result that they had no trouble producing a succession of presidential candidates with prime or other high ministerial experience. The leftist opposition, however, had to feel its way more gradually, and candidate recruitment reflected the play of competing coalition strategies and the weight of obsolete political traditions, as well as more prosaic institutional factors.

The Emergence of François Mitterrand

The problem facing the left-wing parties—the Socialists and the Communists—before the 1965 presidential election was not only to find a suitable candidate to compete with Charles de Gaulle, who was expected to run, but also to devise a strategy that would maximize anti-Gaullist support. One strategy, advocated by Gaston Defferre, the mayor of Marseille and leader of the Socialist group in the National Assembly, was to try to form a centrist coalition in opposition to the Gaullists which would include anti-Gaullist conservatives but not, explicitly, the Communists. Unfortunately for Defferre, his party rejected his strategy and opted instead for the formation of an unambiguous leftist coalition consisting of the Socialists and the Communists. Those two parties, however, had been bitter rivals throughout almost all of the postwar period, and selecting a joint presidential candidate was a delicate task. Neither party would probably have supported a candidate from the other party. Moreover, it is not certain that either of the two main leftist parties even wanted to field a presidential candidate from its own ranks, as the prospects for a leftist electoral victory did not appear to be good at the time. Neither the

Socialists nor the Communists would have wanted to bear the stigma of having produced an unsuccessful candidate. The two parties, however, could and did agree on someone from outside their ranks who had appropriate anti-Gaullist credentials. That person was François Mitterrand.

It was a classic case of the right man being on hand at the right time. Mitterrand was not a major party leader. He was not even a member of the Socialist party, which he eventually was to head, but rather belonged to a small splinter group of uncertain political orientation. But he had been on the national scene since early in the postwar period, he had held ministerial offices during the Fourth Republic, and—most important of all—he had been a consistent and outspoken opponent of de Gaulle since the critical year of 1958, when the Fourth Republic crumbled as a result of the Algerian War and Charles de Gaulle returned to power and inaugurated a new constitutional system.

Mitterrand made an excellent, if losing, showing. He was the only leftist candidate at the first ballot and easily won eligibility for the second round of voting, at which he did better than either his own supporters or his Gaullist opponents probably thought he would. Capitalizing on his strong performance, Mitterrand formed an umbrella organization embracing the Socialist party and some smaller leftist groups, led those federated groups into an alliance with the Communist party for the 1967 legislative elections, and came very close to producing a left-wing parliamentary majority.

Mitterrand and his supporters, however, suffered severe setbacks in 1968. The student-ignited upheaval in May produced a right-wing backlash at legislative elections during the summer. The Warsaw Pact's invasion of Czechoslovakia in August made an electoral alliance with the Communists equivalent to the kiss of death. When de Gaulle resigned the presidency in 1969, Mitterrand's strategy of leftist unity was inoperable for the ensuing presidential election, and the Socialists reverted to the centrist strategy they had rejected for the 1965 election, although they were divided over who should be their preferred candidate. Gaston Defferre had a valid claim, and he did indeed try his luck at the first ballot, but most of his party's leaders thought that a centrist candidate would produce more anti-Gaullist votes. Accordingly, centrists, anti-Gaullist conservatives, and many Socialists encouraged the intriguing but unsuccessful candidacy of Alain Poher.

The Poher Experiment

Poher was the president of the Senate and, therefore, the closest formal French equivalent to the U.S. vice president. When de Gaulle resigned the presidency, Poher became acting president during the brief interval between de Gaulle's resignation and the presidential election. But that is where any similarity between Poher's term as interim president and the U.S. vice presidency both begins and ends. In the United States, an incumbent vice president must serve the sitting president, while a vice president who accedes to the presidency upon the death or resignation of the president will be of the same party as the departed president.

Poher, exactly to the contrary, was a political opponent of the incumbent president, Charles de Gaulle, and he did everything he could to bring about the referendum defeat that led to de Gaulle's resignation. The relationship between Poher and de Gaulle was more like that between a highly partisan Speaker of the U.S. House of Representatives and a president from the opposing party than that between vice president and president. One of the issues involved in the complex referendum of 1969 concerned the reorganization of the Senate in ways that would have diluted the influence of its sitting members. As president of the Senate, Poher spearheaded a national campaign in favor of a "no" vote among the local elites at what in the United States is referred to as the court-house level, who play the major role in electing the Senate. Poher's contribu-tion to de Gaulle's referendum defeat gave him a valid claim to presidential candidacy among the political elites, but he lacked both organized partisan support and well-established national visibility and he was beaten easily by Georges Pompidou.

Poher's defeat not only demonstrated that the essentially ceremonial post of acting president cannot easily serve as a springboard to the presidency. It also undermined any lingering attachments to a century-old belief that senior sena-tors have a special advantage in the race for the presidency. The French Senate does not enjoy the power or prestige within the French political system that the U.S. Senate does within the U.S. system. Senators are not directly elected by the voters, but rather by departmental electoral colleges populated by mayors and other local elected officials. Reasoning purely by analogy with the U.S. sys-tem, one would not expect the French Senate to be a major source of presiden-tial candidates. During the French Third Republic, however, from 1875 to 1940, when the president was elected by the two legislative chambers sitting jointly, the Senate was a more commanding institution than it became after World War II, and 5 of the 12 presidents elected in that fashion were president of the Senate at the time of their election. This particular strand of French senatorial courtesy even spilled over into the Fourth Republic, the second (and last) of whose 2 presidents had been the senior vice president of the upper chamber. The Poher experiment made it clear that direct popular election of the president had deci-sively altered earlier political conventions. When President Pompidou died in office in 1974, Alain Poher again became acting president during the interim prior to the ensuing election, but there was no suggestion that he should also again pursue the presidency. Indeed, after 1969 no senatorial hat was thrown into the French presidential ring.

François Mitterrand and Richard Nixon

After the failure of the Poher experiment, which demonstrated the futility of trying to dislodge the Gaullist hold on the presidency by following a centrist strategy and laid to rest the notion that the interim presidency could be used as a springboard to the real thing, François Mitterrand returned to the pursuit of the presidency through uniting the left-wing parties. He joined the dispirited and divided Socialist party and when, in 1971, the party was again ready to lean leftward, he became the party's leader. He revived the alliance between the Socialists and the Communists, restored much of the left's parliamentary strength at legislative elections in 1973, and again became the joint standard bearer of a united left at the 1974 presidential election.

Mitterrand's long, frustrating, and ultimately successful drive for the French presidency, is matched in recent U.S. experience only by Richard M. Nixon's comeback from his 1960 defeat to his 1968 renomination and victory. Nixon's preelectoral ordeal did not last as long as Mitterrand's, but the two men displayed remarkably similar skill, determination, and strategic sense in seeking the presidential office.

Mitterrand pursued his goal after 1971 from a position that has no direct counterpart in the United States, that of a major-party leader. From 1971 to 1974, and in later years as well, Mitterrand was favored by both the factionalism within the Socialist party and the dearth of other credible rivals for the presidential nomination. In these and other ways, his situation was similar to that of Nixon.

Although Mitterrand was the agent and symbol of a united left, there was a faction within the Socialist party that was to *his left*, with the result that he could plausibly appeal to his party's moderates. Nixon was in a similar situation among Republicans. Just as the French Socialist party was torn during the 1960s between proponents of a centrist electoral strategy and advocates, such as Mitterrand, of building an alliance with the Communists, so was the U.S. Republican party torn between its early postwar leadership, largely based on moderate, eastern business and financial elites, and the more conservative, western disciples of rugged individualism. That conflict came to a boiling point at the Republican nominating convention of 1964, which booed Governor Nelson Rockefeller of New York and nominated Senator Barry Goldwater of Arizona.

Nixon was able to straddle these two factions. He was nominated for the presidency in 1960 because he had been Dwight D. Eisenhower's vice president, but he had been chosen for that role in order to give geographical and ideological balance to Eisenhower who was sympathetic to the moderate, eastern Republican establishment. Nixon returned the courtesy in 1960 by naming Senator Henry Cabot Lodge of Massachusetts as his running mate, but he was also the only leading Republican who campaigned for Goldwater in 1964, and he devoted considerable effort to cultivating and aiding Republican senators and congressmen who had lost narrowly in the 1964 Democratic landslide and who could be expected to return to office soon (Ambrose 1989).

Nixon, therefore, supported the Goldwater forces and stood for many of their policies, but he was not actually one of them, and could appear to be a middle-of-the-roader because he did not attract the same kind of deep antagonism within Republican party ranks that the Goldwater people almost willfully engendered. Similarly in situation if not in ideology, Mitterrand maintained the leftward tilt of his party with the support of moderates who thought that he was more likely than anyone else to keep the party's more extreme leftists under control.

Like Nixon in 1968, Mitterrand benefited in 1974 from the absence of any real rival for his party's nomination. Rockefeller had lost the 1964 Republican party nomination to Goldwater, but Goldwater had lost the election, leaving the field clear for Nixon. In the late 1960s, the only Socialist with the kind of national standing necessary to compete with Mitterrand was Gaston Defferre, the longtime mayor of Marseille. But Defferre's alternate strategy had been tried unsuccessfully in 1969, so there was no one to stand in Mitterrand's way for the 1974 nomination.

Mitterrand's 1974 defeat left him a two-time loser,[7] but he had lost only by a whisker, and with Defferre sidetracked, he was still without rivals among his senior colleagues. The factionalism within the Socialist party required him to engage in virtually ceaseless maneuvering, but a serious challenge to his leadership could come only from a promising younger contender in circumstances that cast doubt on the viability of Mitterrand's leftist strategy.

Mitterrand and Michel Rocard

This conjunction of a rising star and an ostensibly faltering Mitterrand came after the 1978 legislative elections when, despite favorable preelection polls, the combined left failed once again to win a parliamentary majority. During the campaign the leftist alliance had become badly frayed, and its very existence had been put into doubt by the Communists until the last possible moment. Against this background, Michel Rocard presented himself as a more moderate alternative to François Mitterrand.

Rocard had been the leader of a small, radical party popular mainly with Parisian intellectuals during the 1960s. He ran as a minor-party candidate at the 1969 presidential election, thereby gaining some name recognition, although few votes. In 1974, he and his followers entered the Socialist party where, abandoning many of his earlier notions, he gradually emerged as a spokesman for moderate economic policies.

Rocard did not directly challenge Mitterrand for the Socialist party's presidential nomination in 1981, preferring instead only to make it clear that he was available in the event that Mitterrand did not choose to run.[8] But Rocard's availability, combined with poll results showing that he was more popular than Mitterrand both with the voters at large and with Socialist party supporters in particular, gave some impetus to a dump-Mitterrand movement. But Rocard did not have organizational support within the Socialist party to match his general appeal to the electorate, and the party nominated Mitterrand for his third candidacy.

While Mitterrand's earlier position within the French Socialist party had resembled that of Nixon within the Republican party in the United States, there is more than a touch of similarity between the rivalry between Rocard and Mitterrand and the contest between Gary Hart and Walter Mondale for the Democratic party's presidential nomination in 1984. Both Rocard and Hart tried to project images of youthful vitality; they claimed to be injecting fresh ideas into old debates; they were encouraged by the fascination of the media (television in the United States, the press in France) with novelty. But neither could match his rival's organized party support. Rocard, after all, had only been a member of the party since 1974. Mitterrand had helped to elect dozens of deputies, to say nothing of local officeholders. Rocard had embarrassed a former Gaullist prime minister, Couve de Murville, at a special election in 1969, but that was before Rocard had even joined the Socialist party, and in the same year he had competed with Defferre at the presidential election. Rocard would have to serve his newly acquired party in more conspicuous ways before the party's congress delegates would elevate him to a more exalted position than leader of a faction. That was difficult to do, because high office in the regime depended on the favor of the president whom Rocard had been so willing to challenge and who was not interested in giving Rocard the kind of posts he believed he deserved. Moreover, Rocard never abandoned either his interest in the presidency or his willingness to proclaim it publicly. Eventually, after his triumphant reelection in 1988, President Mitterrand made Rocard his prime minister, an office that he filled with competence if not éclat until Mitterrand removed him in May 1991.

As the end of François Mitterrand's second presidential term approached, the most formidable potential Socialist candidate to succeed him was Jacques Delors, another figure in the pool of top-level political executives who gravitate toward candidacy for the French presidency. Delors never ran for a major office, but he had been Gaullist prime minister Jacques Chaban-Delmas' advisor on social affairs and was minister of the economy and finance in the Socialist governments from May 1981 to July 1984. He became president of the Commission of the European Community in January 1985 and completed two four-year terms by the end of 1992, when he was reappointed for two additional years. Delors' reputation was to some extent hostage to the fortunes of the European Community, but he remains a highly visible European statesman who normally ranks high in the various presidential straw-vote polls commissioned by the French press.

Concluding Comments

We can now conclude our presentation of the major players in the high-stakes game of presidential politics in France and the United States. We will move on to a close examination of that game, with special reference to how it looks from the vantage point of the voters, those other and more numerous players, whose collective role is decisive for the outcome. Several themes that will appear with some regularity as we proceed have already been introduced. There are obvious institutional differences between the French and the U.S. political systems, and these differences can lead to different consequences, of which the most apparent is the difference in political experience of the presidential contenders of the two countries, a difference that is directly linked to different constitutional structures. But we have also seen that even within those different institutional contexts, candidates and parties may find themselves in similar situations and act in similar ways, because their strategic goals suggest it (as in the case of candidates Mitterrand and Nixon) or their resource base compels it (as in the analogy between Rocard and Hart). We will continue to pursue and seek to explain other differences and similarities. We will also return, in our overall conclusion, to the cast of characters we have introduced here, and present them in new and broader perspectives. In that fashion, we will give our players another stroll before we drop the final curtain.

Part 2
The Mass Electorates

Having described the institutional frameworks governing presidential elections in France and the United States, and briefly sketched the nature of the political elites who compete for the presidential office in the two countries, we now move on to a close examination of the French and U.S. electorates, which make the decisive choice among the elite contenders.

Our analysis of how the French and U.S. electorates make that choice, which will appear later, in Part 3, rests on a theory of elections that distinguishes between long-term and short-term forces. The long-term forces, which include partisanship and, in some circumstances, ideological positioning, tend to be stable across time. While they are not immutable, they do contribute toward the inertial character of the distribution of the vote at successive elections in the same country, even as there may be enough changes from one election to another to bring another candidate, party, or coalition to power.

The sources of change, according to this view of electoral behavior, are the short-term forces. These include those factors that may induce voters to depart from their customary partisan attachments, or even to abandon some ideological preconception, because of prevailing circumstances. The most prominent short-term forces include the electorate's responses to current issues and the attractiveness of the candidates. The long-term forces, therefore, tend to stabilize the vote while the short-term forces are the engines of electoral change. In Part 2, we will discuss partisanship, ideological positioning, and the role of issues, postponing until Part 3 our treatment of candidate appeal.

We begin Part 2 with a discussion of partisanship. This is the force that orients U.S. voters toward their political system in general, and their choice of presidential candidates in particular. We discuss how it operates in the United States, and how U.S. voters were aligned in partisan terms in 1988.

Partisanship has been only infrequently examined in France in terms that directly match those employed in U.S. electoral analyses, so we pay especial attention to discussing the growth of partisan attachments in France and the political composition of the French partisan alignment in 1988. Two points in particular are emphasized. One is the similarity between the origin of the New Deal alignment in the United States during the early 1930s and the emergence of the leftist alignment in France following the upheaval of May 1968. The other is the extreme fragility of the leftist partisan predominance that emerged in France during that recent era.

Following the discussion of partisanship, we examine the extent to which the electorates of the two countries may be viewed in terms of ideological categories. Using the left-right dimension as a surrogate for ideology in France, and the liberal-conservative dimension as the indicator of ideology in the United States, we find evidence to suggest that the U.S. electorate is much less susceptible to ideological classification than the French one, although we take pains to note that the power of ideological positioning to orient the French voter can easily be exaggerated.

Finally, we examine the distribution of opinion in the two countries on basic political issues, as well as the electorates' perceptions of where the candidates at the 1988 presidential elections stood on those issues. A principal finding here is that the French electorate is more sharply polarized than the U.S. one, both in its own issue positions and its perceptions of the candidates' issue positions. Throughout, however, we are attentive to the fact that the extent to which issues have electoral relevance is strongly affected by political involvement, and that there are severe limits to the degree to which issues are likely to have an independent effect on the voters' choice of a presidential candidate. In considering the broad question of the electoral relevance of issues, we examine whether simple measures of "which side are you on" are more likely to uncover voter sensitivity to issues than more complex measures that try to determine how close a voter's position on an issue is to those of the candidates. This comparison of directional models with proximity models of issue voting concludes that the simple directional model is no more likely than the proximity model to explain mass electoral choices in issue terms.

CHAPTER 3

Partisanship

The theory of elections that serves as the framework for much of this book has its origins in the work of V. O. Key, Jr. (1955) and was set forth in its most complete form in two classic works by Campbell, Converse, Miller, and Stokes (1960, 1966). In its simplest, skeletal form, this theory holds that the electorate's choice of a candidate is a function of two sets of forces. On the one hand, there is a long-term force in the form of abiding partisan attachments, whose distribution, discounted by the propensity to vote of each competing party's identifiers, governs what one would normally expect the distribution of votes to be at any given election (Converse 1966). On the other hand, there are also short-term forces. These too move the electorate and operate to prevent electoral outcomes from being merely the reflection of the momentary distribution of long-term partisan attachments, by affecting turnout and attracting the identifiers of any given party toward the candidates of a competing party.

The two most powerful short-term forces are the conditions out of which the issues that agitate the voters emerge and the character of the competing candidates. Voters with more or less stable partisan attachments may vote for the candidate of another party if they associate their own party's candidate with issue positions that they consider intolerable or if they associate an opposing party's candidate with issue positions that strike them as particularly appealing. In the United States, the kinds of issues that have played such a role relate to patriotism, national security, war and peace, the economy, racial equality, and corruption. The impact of issue positions on the presidential candidate choices of French partisans has not been closely investigated, but there are indications that economic issues played an important role in incumbent Valéry Giscard d'Estaing's defeat (and challenger François Mitterrand's victory) in 1981 (Cayrol 1988).

Similarly, more or less long-standing partisan attachments can be temporarily subordinated to personal evaluations of the candidates. Some political leaders, such as Charles de Gaulle in France and Dwight D. Eisenhower in the United States, were so highly esteemed for their personal traits that, at least in the early phases of their presidential careers, they were barely perceived in political terms at all, and they were rated negatively only by people strongly attached to the parties that opposed them (Converse and Dupeux 1966a). Even with regard to less stirring personalities than de Gaulle and Eisenhower, voters may be motivated by differential evaluations of the competing candidates to depart temporarily from their abiding partisanship by voting for the candidate of an opposing party.

The key concept on which this electoral theory rests is party identification, the sense of psychological attachment to a political party. Party identifications are normally established by the time a citizen is about 30 years of age and they tend to be strengthened by continuing participation in the electoral process. Party identification is not, of course, immutable. Depending on how strongly attached they are to a given party in the first place, people may—in certain circumstances—shift their loyalty to another party. But mass conversions of party identification occur rarely, usually as the result of major convulsive events, such as war or depression.

At the aggregate level, there may be a secular trend among newcomers to the electorate away from a party that has predominated in the distribution of partisan loyalties toward a different party. In such a case, the result can be a more or less silent shift in the underlying partisan basis of the electorate with few if any actual shifts in party loyalties among the older citizens. Such a movement among younger voters toward the Republicans may have occurred in the United States during the 1980s, thereby diminishing the perennial Democratic edge among party identifiers for the previous half century.

While the distribution of party identifications across an electorate can change, it is important to remember that once formed, partisan loyalties can become very powerful. They are among the most stable political attitudes temporally. People are more likely to remain constant in their attachment to parties than they are to the attitudes that relate to the most prominent short-term electoral forces, their positions on issues or their evaluations of political leaders (Converse and Markus 1979). While people may be motivated by considerations relating to issues or to candidate appeal to depart from the urgings of their long-standing party and vote for the candidate of an opposing party at any given election, they are more likely than not to return to their party of origin at the next election (Converse and Pierce 1986, 93–96).

Partisanship, in the form of party identification, is not unalterable, and it is not wholly controlling in the choice of a candidate, but it is both an individual and a collective mooring that powerfully affects the voter's choice of a candidate and accounts for the normally inertial distribution of the partisan vote at successive elections in the same country, even when power passes from one party or coalition of parties to another.

That is, in brief compass, the theoretical framework that governs most scholarly analyses of elections in the United States and, to varying degrees, in other countries as well. It is not a theory, however, that has gone unchallenged. Some scholars, basing their arguments on empirical data suggesting that party identifications are less temporally stable in other countries than they are in the United States, have raised doubts about whether such a phenomenon actually operates in those sites (Butler and Stokes 1969; Crewe 1976; Thomassen 1976; Klingemann and Taylor 1978). Others have noted that in some countries it is difficult to separate the effects of party identification from those of social class affiliation (Campbell and Valen 1966). Still others have argued that in some societies social class or other basic group attachments, such as religion, are the primary sources of electoral behavior (Shively 1972; Baker, Dalton, and Hildebrandt 1981). Finally, it has been suggested that, especially in multiparty systems, the principal mechanism by which ordinary citizens orient themselves to the political process is not party identification but rather their sense of the distance between their perceived self-location on an ideologically based left-right dimension and their perceptions of the locations of the various competing parties on the same dimension (Deutsch, Lindon, and Weill 1966; Inglehart and Klingemann 1976). From this perspective, people consider themselves as well as the competing candidates or parties as some degree of leftist or centrist or rightist, and then vote for the candidate or party they perceive to be closest to their own left-right position.

One general and three more specific points must be made with regard to these direct or indirect criticisms of the theory of elections that rests on the concept of party identification.

The general comment is simply that none of these criticisms or alternate approaches represents a credible general theory of electoral choice. None of them explains or even suggests how the particular factors they emphasize can account simultaneously for both the overall aggregate electoral stability that characterizes most democratic elections and the smaller shifts in partisan support that more or less regularly produce changes in the balance of political power. This is not to say that one might not, perhaps, be able to construct an alternate electoral theory on a foundation of social class, religion, or other social groups, or on the basis of left-right locations, that could then be set against the theory resting on party identification and tested for its relative explanatory power. It is, rather, only to say that no one has yet done so.

The more specific comments relate to the claim that party identification is not a phenomenon that appears in all democratic societies, the suggestion that social groups are the underlying electoral force, and the notion that left-right locations constitute the foundation of popular political orientations.

With respect to the generality of party identification, we may say at the outset that the countries where its existence has been doubted include Great Britain, the Netherlands, and West Germany. No one has suggested that the phenomenon does not exist in France. But that would be little comfort if it could be shown that party identification was not a general phenomenon but rather only system specific. If that were the case, we could not safely assume its existence anywhere.

Fortunately, we are not in that dire situation, and for two principal reasons. First, the doubters have never successfully answered the question of why a phenomenon that rests ultimately on simple psychological processes of group identification should exist in some countries but not others. No general cultural or institutional forces that might override what appear to be basic psychological processes have been unambiguously identified. Second, there is good reason to believe that the early criticisms of party identification theory that rested on perceived instability of what should have been a highly stable attitude reflected inappropriate data collection and measurement techniques (Converse and Pierce 1985, 1992; Heath and Pierce 1992). Without for a moment denying that party identifications may be more stable across time in some countries than in others, we may also say that the range of variation has been exaggerated, that such variation as appears in no way demonstrates that the phenomenon exists in some countries but not in others, and that there is no reason to believe that the phenomenon does not govern electoral behavior in the same fashion everywhere.

With regard to the suggestion that the primary correlate of electoral choice is class or religion or some other group identity rooted in a country's social structure, the main point to be made is that the theory of elections based on party identification in no way conflicts with the notion that partisanship itself can be anchored in social cleavages. The issue is simply which comes first in the causal chain that links social divisions with electoral choices. The critics of party identification theory argue that the connection is direct from class or religion or other social group status to partisan choice. Party identification theorists hold that the sequence is from social group to party identification to partisan vote, with the latter being affected by short-term forces as well.

Having said that, it may quickly be added that there is an honorable tradition in virtually every democratic country of thinking of electoral outcomes in terms of variously constituted voting blocs. The old "New Deal coalition" referred to such a bloc, for example, and it is routine for French scholars and the French press alike to discuss electoral results in terms of various demographic groups. We have no desire to repudiate such informative practices. On the contrary, after applying the theory based on party identification to elections in France and the United States in chapter 7, we will devote chapter 8 to a discussion of the group basis of electoral choice in the two countries.

In broad terms, the argument that the electorate orients itself politically by means of perceived left-right locations is analogous to the position that social group status is the fount of electorally relevant political attitudes. While group analysts believe that electoral choices emerge directly from social group identity, adherents of the left-right school see them as the result of ideological positioning, expressed in shorthand terms by perceived locations on a left-right dimension. We might, therefore, treat ideology in the same light as group status, as a force that may precede party identification but does not replace it, and one whose direct electoral impact may be measured and set against that of party identification itself.

At the same time, it is important to recognize that the operational properties of the two forces, group status and left-right positioning, are quite different. Group identity is essentially a nominal category. In some circumstances, it may take on a hierarchical or vertical character (upper vs. lower class, more vs. less religious attachment, and the like). It is doubtful, however, that many citizens spontaneously think of a country's party system as occupying a vertical space, with some parties resting on the lower rungs of a class or religious ladder, others positioned somewhere midway up the steps, and still others at the top. Ideological positioning expressed by means of left-right locations, however, is not only spatial in conception but is also instinctively acceptable to the democratic citizen (Laponce 1972). The electorates of modern democracies perceive themselves and the political parties of which they have cognizance as occupying locations along a horizontal dimension, and the degree of affect that they feel for each visible party is a function of the perceived distance of that party from the party with which the voter identifies (Converse and Pierce 1992).

Whatever the importance of ideological considerations may be in directly affecting electoral choices, it is quite clear that the spatial character of the left-right dimension by which they are expressed is highly relevant to how voters orient themselves to the party system within which they must act. For multiparty systems where left-right terminology is widely employed in political discourse, the left-right dimension constitutes an instrument with which party identifications themselves can be measured and expressed. The left-right locations assigned to the various parties by the electorate are highly stable temporally, and while there is some dispersion of perceived locations for any given party, the distributions of those perceptions typically reveal large modes (Converse and Pierce 1986, chap. 4). This considerable consensus among the electorate with regard to where each party stands on the left-right scale enables us to assign to each party the mean left-right score attributed to that party by the electorate. That consensus score represents the spatial location of the particular party for the average voter. The set of locations for all the parties within a particular multiparty system such as the French one, with which we are concerned here, constitutes a mapping of the party system along a pseudo-interval scale. Such a scale is a powerful instrument for the analysis of electoral behavior in multiparty systems. It enables us to measure the temporal stability of partisan identifications and electoral choices in multiparty systems, as well as the interrelationship between those two variables and the relationship between each of those variables and others (such as social class or other group status).

We will, of course, employ such scalar measures later in this book, just as we have done earlier (notably in Converse and Pierce 1986), to represent party identifications and electoral choices in France. Sometimes left-right locations, intended to represent ideological positions, will be set against partisan attachments or electoral choices that are themselves expressed in left-right terms. These operations will all be legitimate, but it is important to remember that all measures presented in left-right form within a single system constitute a family with a common ancestry.

Partisanship in the United States

The incidence and political composition of party identification in the United States have been recorded by the remarkable series of national election studies at which the same questions designed to elicit the distribution of such identifications have been asked biennially since 1952. These questions, long familiar to students of U.S. electoral politics, are three in number. The first elicits whether the respondents have any enduring sense of personal attachment to one or the other of the two major American parties: "Generally speaking, do you usually think of yourself as a Republican, a Democrat, an independent, or what?" Then, if the reply is either "Republican" or "Democrat," the respondents are asked "Would you call yourself a strong Republican (or Democrat) or a not very strong Republican (or Democrat)?" If the reply is "Independent" or some other party, the respondents are asked "Do you think of yourself as closer to the Republican or Democratic Party?" The replies to these three questions produce a seven-point scale, including strong Democrats, weak Democrats, independent Democrats (or Democratic leaners), independent Independents (or pure independents), independent Republicans (or Republican leaners), weak Republicans, and strong Republicans. The few off-scale cases, which include people who cite a third party, or who are so apolitical that their inability to understand the question is apparent, have not amounted to more than 4 percent of the sample electorate since the series of questions was first begun in 1952.

The aggregate proportions of people who fall within one or another of the seven categories of the U.S. party identification scale have been remarkably constant throughout the entire series of measurements. There have been some short-term deviations from the underlying longer-term pattern of stability. An almost monotonous regularity prevailed from 1952 until 1964, when the turmoil associated with the Vietnam War disillusioned many people with routine political processes and alienated them from the political parties. The proportion of U.S. citizens who declared themselves to be strongly attached to one or the other of the major parties dipped abruptly and then gradually descended even further for more than a decade. The proportion of U.S. citizens who claimed to be independent of either party rose sharply in 1966 and remained at historically high levels through 1980. Those shifts, away from intense partisanship and toward independence, led many commentators to talk about a "dealignment" of the U.S. electorate that could be expected to lead, in turn, to greater electoral volatility than had previously been the norm.[1]

The dealigning trend, however, was not only checked but actually reversed during the 1980s. The proportion of self-declared independents declined and the proportion of strong identifiers increased. By 1988, there were still fewer party identifiers (strong plus weak Democrats and Republicans) than there had been during the decade of the 1950s, but there was also a more or less compensating shift in the proportions of leaners. The overwhelming message of the measurements is that a large proportion of the U.S. electorate identifies to some degree with one or the other of the two major parties. During the 1980s, between 60 percent and 70 percent of the sample electorate were pure party identifiers, and if one also includes the leaners, those figures rise to between 80 percent and 90 percent. Furthermore, the relationship between party identification (excluding leaners) and the presidential vote between 1952 and 1988 has not only remained strong throughout the entire period but has also trended slightly upward. The mean bivariate correlation between the two measures for the whole period is .67, while the mean for the three presidential elections during the decade of the 1980s is .74 (Miller 1991, table 2).

The Composition of the Partisan Alignment

By and large, there was little change in the incidence of party identification in the United States between the 1950s and the 1980s. There was somewhat less overall continuity in the intensity with which the electorate experienced those long-term partisan attachments, but the deviations hardly merited being described as a dealignment.

During the same period, however, there was a noticeable movement in the composition of the partisan alignment. Specific estimates of the partisan balance vary depending on whether one counts only pure party identifiers or also includes leaners in the computation, but on either basis, the underlying partisan alignment was much less favorable to the Democratic party in the mid-1980s than it had been earlier, and among certain categories of voters, Republican identifiers outnumbered Democratic identifiers for the first time in half a century. While there had been discussion during the 1970s of a possible dealignment of the U.S. party system, scholars began speculating during the 1980s about the possibility of a major realignment of the system representing a shift from a Democratic to a Republican majority.

The prospect of a major realignment of the underlying balance of partisan attachments excited scholars and pundits because realignments, like earthquakes in large cities, are rare but of major importance. Moreover, while there is a broad scholarly consensus about how realignments occurred earlier in the history of the United States, those realignments antedated the development of scientific survey sampling techniques, and the precise patterns of events have had to be reconstructed indirectly. It is generally agreed that following the Civil War, there was an underlying majority of Republican party identifiers in the United States, and that this majority was enlarged and crystallized further with the panic of 1893 during the administration of Democrat Grover Cleveland and the subsequent election of Republican William McKinley in 1896. This Republican majority was greatly reinforced in 1920, when the Nineteenth Amendment to the Constitution made possible an infusion of new, women voters who overwhelmingly supported the Republican party, by which they were actively recruited (Brown 1991, chap. 6). Republican dominance continued until the Great Depression of the 1930s. New voters and former Republicans in farm areas flocked to the Democratic party and helped to sweep Franklin D. Roosevelt into the presidency in 1932, and a new Democratic majority was strengthened and consolidated by urban and working-class voters between 1932 and 1936 (Brown 1991, chap. 4). These depression-induced developments, which carried over into the wartime years, were the foundation for the postwar Democratic majority that prevailed conspicuously until the 1980s.

It is apparent that what some observers during the 1980s thought might be a partisan realignment would have been a different kind of phenomenon than the earlier Republican alignment of 1896 and the Democratic realignment of the 1930s. The conventional interpretation has always been that partisan realignments are the result of large-scale, convulsive events such as wars or depressions. One cannot single out any such decisive occurrences that might have contributed to a realignment during the 1980s. Instead, what appeared to be taking place was a gradual erosion of Democratic dominance. Democrats could win majorities in the House of Representatives and the Senate with great consistency, but between 1952 and 1988 they won the presidency only three times, in 1960 with John F. Kennedy, in 1964 with Lyndon Johnson, and in 1976 with Jimmy Carter. The rest of the time, Republican presidential candidates prevailed, and—after the election of Ronald Reagan in 1980 and his triumphant reelection in 1984—political observers could reasonably ask themselves (and one another) how long the Democratic margin of party identifiers could withstand the growing inroads being made by winning Republican presidential candidates. But if realignment there was, it would have been much more in the nature of a creeping realignment than the kind of cataclysmic realignments that had occurred earlier.

In point of fact, the changes in the distribution of basic partisan identifications in the United States during the 1980s were both complex and subtle. Across the nation as a whole, Democratic party identifiers continued to outnumber Republican identifiers in 1984 and 1988, but their marginal advantage shrank considerably from what it had been earlier. Miller (1991) has shown that this narrow Democratic majority was smaller among people who actually cast ballots than among nonvoters. The main trend away from the Democrats, again according to Miller (1991), was among southern male voters and among both male and female voters outside the South. Southern women, whether voters or nonvoters, conspicuously resisted the drift away from the Democratic party and contributed disproportionately to the small overall advantage that the Democrats still enjoyed in 1984 and 1988.

The distribution of party identification in the United States shifted across the decades from the early 1950s to the 1980s, but not in ways that are captured by the main conceptual categories that observers brought to bear on events. There was no long-term dealignment, in the sense of mass alienation from the two major parties. Nor was there a realignment, in the sense of a decisive shift in the underlying distribution of partisan attachments away from an advantage for one party to an advantage for the other. Rather, there continued to be a diminished but comparatively healthy Democratic majority across the nation as a whole, but a much narrower one, approaching a partisan equilibrium, among the active electorate.

Albert Camus (1956, 292) once compared the effectiveness of typhoons with that of sap. The vocabulary of party theory, including such terms as dealignment and realignment, is adapted more to the drama of the political typhoon than the gradual sapping of political superiority. There is no catchy concept to describe what happened to the composition of the partisan alignment in the United States between 1950 and 1988. Nor was there any basis in the nuanced pattern of partisan developments for predicting what the future course of events might be. The older Democratic dominance in abiding partisan attachments could be restored, the gradual Republican gains could continue and eventually result in a basic realignment, or a more or less stable near-equilibrium could continue to prevail.

The Formation of a Partisan Alignment in France

The historic role of partisanship has been quite different in France from what it has been in the United States. We pointed out, in chapter 1, that the U.S. party system is old, small, and stable, while the French one is comparatively new, large, and unstable. The stability of the U.S. party system is at once a cause and the result of the high incidence of party identification that prevails. Because the partisan objects in the United States retain their names and symbolism for generations, partisan attachments can be transmitted intergenerationally and are given the opportunity to harden with the passage of time (Converse 1969). At the same time, the incidence and intensity of partisan identifications are high enough to contain the partisan vote within comparatively narrow limits and virtually to preclude the emergence and growth of new parties.

The French partisan experience has been very different. A comparative study of electoral volatility (Mair 1989) reported that France not only experienced more high-volatility elections during the post-World War II period than any other country surveyed, but also had the most high-volatility elections during the entire century between 1885 and 1985. This characteristic electoral volatility is less the result of inconstancy in the partisan choices of French voters than of the propensity of French political elites to alter the terms of what Lancelot (1986, 20) has labeled the "political supply" (see also Grunberg 1985, 429). Converse and Pierce (1986) have shown that despite the French record of high net aggregate instability, when one controls for the constancy of partisan (or candidate) offerings from one electoral period to the next, French voters do not appear to be any more fickle in their electoral choices than their U.S. counterparts, and in some situations they are actually more loyal politically than comparably situated U.S. voters.[2]

The high-volatility postwar elections identified by Mair (1989) were the legislative elections of 1951, 1956, 1958, and 1962. There were surely some large gross shifts in electoral support for the same party during those years, such as the drop in the proportion of the vote for the Communist party from 1956 to 1958, and the gain in the vote for the Gaullists in 1962 relative to 1958. But the period also witnessed numerous changes in the terms of electoral choice presented to the voters, of which the most destabilizing were almost surely the successive incarnations of the Gaullist party, but also including the formation of such purely temporary electoral organizations as the Poujadists and Pierre Mendès-France's Republican Front.

The implications of this unceasing tinkering by the elites with the nature of the electoral alternatives offered to the voters for the breadth and depth of mass linkages with the parties were only tangentially appreciated during the early part of the period. Williams (1964, 151–52) raised the issue of the electoral worth of the party label during the Fourth Republic, but only in the context of maintaining party discipline among conservatives in Parliament. An Institut Français d'Opinion Publique (IFOP) poll conducted in 1952 (*Sondages* 1952) highlighted the limited confidence that French voters had in the parties for which they reported voting at the most recent election. Another IFOP poll (Fougeyrollas 1963, 180) carried out in 1956 indicated that more than 40 percent of the electorate either would not or could not name a party or political group that answered their needs. It was not until Converse and Dupeux (1966b) reported on the comparatively low incidence of party identification in France, as revealed at surveys conducted in connection with the 1958 legislative elections, and linked it with the potentiality for mass electoral support for "flash" parties, that the reciprocal relationship between the instability of the French party system and the comparatively underdeveloped nature of French partisan attachments began to be understood.

During the late 1950s, the mass-elite electoral connection in France was confined in a circuitous pattern from which there could be no quick or easy escape. Only about one half of the electorate was relatively firmly anchored to an existing political party. The remaining half was accessible to whichever parties were most attractive to individual voters at any given electoral moment.[3] New parties, which were rarely in short supply, could count on a large pool of potential supporters, and existing parties—particularly but not exclusively those on the right and in the center of the spectrum—were constantly under threat. The reserve army of new voters, combined with unattached older ones, produced a continuing supply of electoral recruits for France's political entrepreneurs. These, however, did not always give their newfound followers the opportunity to vote for their parties twice in a row, with the result that a party's electoral gains at one election were dissipated at the following one. Charles de Gaulle's Rassemblement du Peuple Français (RPF) halved the electoral strength of the Mouvement Républicain Populaire (MRP) in 1951 but no longer existed in 1956, while the Poujadists won almost 12 percent of the votes in 1956 but fielded only a handful of candidates in 1958.

At the same time as the large number of unattached French voters provided mass support for new parties, the unstinting efforts of the political elites to create them undermined the likelihood that the incidence and intensification of party identification would grow at more than a snail's pace. The kaleidoscopic character of the party system meant that there were few stable partisan referents. Only the traditional leftist parties, the Communists, Socialists, and Radical-Socialists, had the longevity and continuity of nomenclature and symbolism to be enduring objects of psychological attachment. Except for those parties, the possibility of intergenerational transmission of partisanship was virtually suspended. The endemic discontinuity of partisan offerings weakened the probability that freshly acquired partisan identifications would become reinforced through repeated expression. The underdeveloped status of party identification in France rewarded the efforts of partisan innovators, and those efforts in turn ensured that partisan identifications would not easily multiply or intensify.

At the outset of the French Fifth Republic, therefore, the incidence of party identification was so limited and the party system so fluid that it hardly makes any sense to speak of the existence at that time of some partisan alignment based on enduring party allegiances. The electorate was so heavily populated with citizens without any abiding party attachments that electoral outcomes could be expected to be affected as much by other factors as they were by partisan loyalties. Party identifications would have to become more numerous and more firmly implanted before it would be possible to talk about a partisan alignment in France.

The main condition for the diffusion and intensification of partisanship at the mass level was modification of the party system in the direction of simplification and stability. Developments consistent with those outcomes did in fact occur during the Fifth Republic. As a result, the incidence of party identification increased, at first slowly, and later, almost surely, more rapidly. By the late 1980s, the incidence of party identification in France had risen to the level that Converse (1969) had determined to be characteristic of a mature party system. With approximately the same proportion of the electorate identifying with a party in France as normally do in the other developed democracies for which we have the relevant data, it became possible to speak of the existence of a given partisan alignment. While U.S. pundits and political scientists asked themselves during the 1970s whether and, if so, why there was a dealignment of the U.S. party system, and during the 1980s whether and, if so, why there was a realignment of that system, we will ask here how and why a partisan alignment developed in postwar France in the first place. The remainder of this chapter will chart the rise in the incidence of party identification in France, analyze the political composition of the partisan alignment that had formed by 1988, and specify that alignment's particular vulnerabilities.

The Emergence of a Partisan Alignment

There is no longitudinal record of abiding partisan attachments in France comparable to the series of measurements of party identification contained in the U.S. National Election Studies (NES) or the equivalent studies that have been conducted elsewhere, notably in the Scandinavian countries. There are numerous studies that purport to measure party identification in France, but these invariably provide the respondents with a list of parties from which they are asked to choose. This interviewing technique inflates the proportion of respondents claiming to identify with a party, at the same time as it prevents expression of the idiosyncratic responses that an open-ended question permits. Converse and Pierce (1986, 58–61) have shown that in 1967 the median number of parties that the French electorate could spontaneously recall was less than 4. When respondents were shown a list of 10 parties, however, the number that they could recognize was larger. It does not seem to be unreasonable to count as true identifiers only those people who can spontaneously recall the name of the party to which they claim to be habitually close.[4]

In order to ensure the maximum degree of cross-time continuity in measurement of party identification in France, we will rely only on three studies: the Converse-Dupeux study of 1958, to which we have already referred; the Converse-Pierce study conducted during the late 1960s (Converse and Pierce 1986, chap. 3); and the postpresidential election survey conducted by SOFRES in France for the author in 1988. The basic question employed in 1958, which was formulated by Georges Dupeux, was "Quel est le parti dont vous vous sentez le plus proche?" [Which party do you feel closest to?] For the Converse-Pierce surveys of the late 1960s, the word *habituellement* was inserted, so that the question read "Which party do you usually feel closest to?" That same question wording was retained for the 1988 survey. The questions were completely open-ended. The respondents were given the opportunity to cite any party or group they wished, in their own words, without prompting or the use of aids of any kind.[5]

We have already recalled that in the late 1950s, the incidence of party identification in France was so low—some 20 percentage points less than it was at the same era in the United States (Converse and Dupeux 1966b)—that it would be futile to think in terms of there being some partisan alignment operative at the time. By the late 1960s, that comparatively low level had risen slightly, although the convulsive events of May 1968 produced some sharp discontinuities between the levels registered at the legislative elections of the spring of 1967 and the summer of 1968. Nevertheless, the direct indications that the incidence of party identification had increased over the previous decade, combined with ancillary evidence indicating that more French children were being socialized politically than had previously been the case, led Converse and Pierce (1986, chap. 3) to the cautious conclusion that the incidence of partisanship would increase still further in the future.

Our postelectoral survey of 1988 furnishes decisive evidence that such a development did in fact occur during the intervening two decades. Some 71 percent of the respondents reported a discrete partisan identification, a value that fully matches those reported for strict party identifiers (i.e., excluding leaners) in the United States during the 1950s and 1960s, against which the earlier French levels had seemed paltry, and even slightly exceeds U.S. proportions during the decade of the 1980s.

The incidence of party identification recorded in 1988 suggests strongly that France had by then, and possibly even earlier, reached the equilibrium level of mass partisanship that Converse (1969, 146) had estimated to be slightly more than 70 percent of the electorate.[6] This result is doubly satisfying. On the one hand, it can be taken as a confirmation of the validity of Converse's model of the intergenerational transmission of partisanship. On the other hand, it reinforces our confidence in the findings of our 1988 survey. The level of partisanship recorded for France in 1988 was just about what it should have been.[7] Between 1958 and 1988, therefore, the incidence of partisanship in France rose to a level typical of democracies with mature party systems, in effect embracing as large a proportion of the electorate as can probabilistically be expected to identify with a party.

At the same time as the incidence of partisanship rose, the contours of the political alignment it reflected underwent significant change. If it is not realistic to conceive of a basic partisan alignment during the late 1950s, it is reasonable to think in such terms for the late 1960s, when party identifications were more widespread than they had been earlier. The underlying political balance at that time was such that leftist and rightist party identifiers were virtually equal in numbers. A decade of Gaullist rule after 1958 had made the Gaullist party the beneficiary of more identifiers than any other single party enjoyed, but the Communist and Socialist parties combined, in more or less equal proportions, attracted more support than the Gaullist party did. The distribution of partisanship throughout the electorate was such that it could not be said, in 1967, that either leftists or rightists enjoyed any underlying, long-term electoral advantage. The closeness of the 1967 legislative elections reflected the even balance of left-right partisan attachments.

The configuration of partisan attachments was very different in 1988, when, as we have seen, these were also more numerous than they had been two decades earlier. In 1988, the underlying partisan alignment strongly favored the leftist parties in general and the Socialist party in particular. More than 40 percent of our 1988 sample electorate identified with a left-wing party in 1988, while only some 30 percent identified with a rightist party. The leftists, however, were overwhelmingly attached to the Socialist party, while the rightists divided their allegiances between the neo-Gaullist RPR and the neo-Giscardian UDF. Some two-thirds of the French voters who identified with a left-wing party (and almost half of the citizens who identified with *any* party) identified with the Socialist party. The largest right-wing party, the RPR, attracted the loyalties of less than half of the rightist identifiers, while the UDF enjoyed the allegiance of less than a third of them.

Between the late 1960s and the late 1980s, the underlying pattern of party identification in France was transformed. The incidence of party identification rose to the level characteristic of other democracies with well-established party systems. And the balance of professed partisan attachments shifted markedly from a virtual left-right standoff to the advantage of the leftist parties in general and the Socialist party in particular.

In the absence of comparable measures of party identification in France between those two limiting dates, it is impossible to reconstruct in detail how the partisan alignment of 1988 came about. But guided by the cluster of theory surrounding the concept of party identification, and relying on our soundings of the French electorate in 1967 and 1988, we can put the main pieces of the puzzle together in a way that renders the development intelligible. The puzzle itself contains two elements. One is why the incidence of partisanship rose. The other is why the balance of partisan orientations moved to the advantage of the Socialist party.

Why the Incidence of Party Identification Increased

It is necessary to distinguish between two main routes toward the acquisition of a partisan attachment: one that passes through familial political socialization and another that does not. In the former case, children develop some sort of political consciousness in response to messages they receive from their parents. Later, when these children become adults and make an independent entry into political life, they show a high propensity to acquire an abiding partisan identification. Children who receive no such familial political initiation can, of course, also develop long-term partisan attachments, but—at least in France and the United States during the late 1950s and 1960s—they did so at a considerably lower rate. Powerful forces were at work in France during the two decades preceding the presidential election of 1988 that almost surely augmented the number of French citizens who acquired partisan attachments via one route or the other.

During the 1950s and 1960s, the incidence of partisan identification was low in France not only because of the size and complexity of the party system, but also because a comparatively small proportion of the adults of those years experienced familial political socialization when they had been children. French families appear to have operated under a reticence norm relating to political matters that impeded the development of the kind of political orientations that contribute to the acquisition of partisanship in young adulthood. This norm was still clearly operative as late as 1970, but there was also evidence in the late 1960s to indicate that it was weakening.[8] By 1988, the French electorate contained a larger proportion of people who had received some sort of familial political socialization than had been the case in earlier years.[9] As those people tend to acquire a party identification more frequently than people who come from families that are noncommunicative politically, the proportion of party identifiers also rose.

This silent but inexorable impact of changing familial mores was related to other, more obvious forces at work between the late 1960s and the late 1980s that in all probability contributed to the increase in the incidence of party identification, among both people who had enjoyed the benefit of prior political socialization and those who had not. The most important of these is that the level of political interest rose enormously between 1967 and 1988. Three times as many people professed having "a lot" of interest in politics in 1988 as did so in 1967, while only about one-third as many indicated that they had no interest in politics at all. Expressed in terms of mean scores, political interest rose by about one-fifth across the entire electorate between 1967 and 1988.[10]

Some of this increase in political interest was due to the increased education of the 1988 electorate compared with the 1967 one. In 1967, almost three-fourths of the electorate had received only a primary school education, while well under 10 percent had gone to a university or other institution of higher learning. In 1988, about the same proportion of the population (some 25 percent) received a higher education as received only a primary school education. But greater educational opportunities are not the whole story. Interest in politics increased within every stratum of the population in educational terms. If the degree of political interest by educational level had remained the same in 1988 as it had been in 1967, overall political interest would have increased only by somewhat more than 10 percent over the 1967 mean, as compared with the 20 percent increase actually recorded.

Other factors conducive to increasing political interest had to be at work also. Almost surely, one of these was increased exposure to television. The decade of the 1970s was the period when French homes became saturated with television sets. These conveyed political information in an attractively packaged form that gained the attention of people for whom the other mass media were either unappealing or unavailable.

But even more important than the increased flow of information, in our opinion, was the simplification of political conflict in France between the late 1960s and the late 1980s, as the result of the creation of two broad competing electoral coalitions that regularly opposed each other at every presidential and legislative election (except the presidential election of 1969).

The neatness and clarity of this two-bloc system was a far cry from the extremely complicated form that French politics had displayed prior to the mid-1960s. Earlier, the party system was highly fractionalized; unstable coalition governments reduced political accountability; and even after the establishment of the Fifth Republic in 1958, the dimensions of political conflict were multiple and varied. French citizens thought that there were too many political parties; the political scene was too crowded and confusing to engage the attention of a large fraction of the electorate.

This situation began to change in the early 1960s, and was completely transformed at the presidential election of 1965, when the stark second-ballot confrontation between Charles de Gaulle and François Mitterrand symbolized a new kind of politics that was easy for ordinary citizens to understand. The creation of a Gaullist bloc, on the one hand, and a leftist bloc, on the other hand, produced a pseudo-two-party system that simplified the political alternatives facing the public.

Naturally, it took time for this new and more transparent political structure to become clearly established in the mass electorate's perceptions. Inevitably, however, the consistency with which conflict between two coalitions characterized political competition across the presidential elections of 1974 and 1981, and the legislative elections of 1973, 1978, and 1981, made politics more intelligible and attracted the attention of people who would have been discouraged by more complex patterns of the kind that de Gaulle had referred to as "the games, the poisons and the delights" of the system. French political elites continued to allow themselves the indulgence of a multiparty system, but its regular division into two competing electoral blocs, corresponding to a governing majority and a more or less united opposition, conferred a meaning to partisanship that had been lacking before. Individual parties could have particular policy preferences and distinctive leaders, but each party occupied a clearly visible position within one major bloc or the other. For two decades, the French political system not only permitted the more involved voters to pick and choose among multiple parties on the basis of complex policy formulations but also enabled the great majority of less sophisticated voters to know where the parties stood in the down-to-earth practical sense of whether they were in or out of office and whether they were in favor of or opposed to the highly visible national leaders who competed for the presidency.

The smaller size and the greater simplicity of the French party system of the late 1980s compared with that of 20 years earlier are captured neatly in the detailed reports of party identification furnished by the respondents at our 1988 survey as compared with those of 1967, in response to an identical open-ended question. In 1967, 24 categories were required to designate the entire universe of discrete parties mentioned by the sample electorate; 15 categories were adequate to record the partisan field of 1988.[11]

Furthermore, and related to the smaller number of parties claimed by the 1988 respondents as objects of identification, there was less fractionalization of party identification in 1988 than in 1967. On the basis of the Rae (1967) formula for computing party fractionalization, the fractionalization index for party identification in France dropped from .78 in 1967 to .70 in 1988. That is much higher than the level for the United States, with its two-party system, but it is not much higher than the levels for Great Britain during the 1980s, when the appearance of the Social Democratic party disturbed the hitherto more or less settled contours of the British party system.[12]

The Composition of the Partisan Alignment

We have seen that while the incidence of party identification in France was rising, the political composition of the partisan alignment was shifting. For 1958, at the founding of the Fifth Republic, one cannot even talk about a political alignment. In 1967, the Gaullist party was the dominant political movement but the balance between leftist and rightist identifiers was more or less equal. By 1988, the Socialist party was the dominant political group and leftist identifiers together outnumbered right-wing identifiers by a ratio of four to three.

Traces of this dual chronological development, in the incidence and composition of party identification, show up clearly when we break down the 1988 distribution of party identification by age. Figure 3.1 presents that fundamental information, as well as additional data about vaguer forms of political positioning (including references to left-right locations and to political leaders) than literal party identifications, so that we can account for all the political orientations, however expressed, of each age category represented. The age categories themselves are mainly delimited in conventional decade form, without partic-

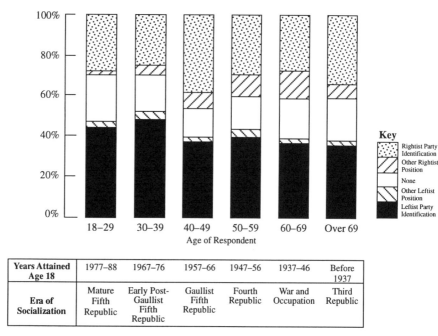

Fig. 3.1. Basic political orientations, by age, France, 1988

ular regard to the proportion of the total population represented by each category.[13] At the same time, these age categories broadly match the generational layering that is relevant for an understanding of the development of party identification in France.

As Butler and Stokes (1969, 59) succinctly put it, when seeking to understand the profile of party identification by age, one should not ask how old the voters are but rather when it was that they were young. It is during one's early, impressionable years that the seeds of political orientations are planted. National politics can be dominated by vastly different events, conflicts, and personalities from one generation to another, with the result that the basic political orientation of one generation will be quite distinct from that of another. It is in this context that there is a fortunate coincidence between the conventional age categories employed in figure 3.1 to indicate how old the voters were in 1988 and the coherence and distinctiveness of the political characteristics of the years when the respondents falling within each of those age categories were young.

It is, of course, largely in a poetic sense that we speak here of generations. These are normally thought of as 30-year spans, and not as decades. The term *cohort* might be more appropriate. Whatever label we use, we should be aware that while Butler and Stokes (1969, 50 n) could make do nicely with four cohorts, we have found it most convenient for our purposes to employ six. That simple difference in analytical categories, as between France and Great Britain, serves to underscore the more frequent underlying discontinuities in political life in France. In defining our cohorts in terms appropriate to when they were young, we have chosen—as Butler and Stokes did—to do so in terms of "coming of age." Even in this regard, there is a slight discontinuity for France: the voting age was reduced from 21 to 18 in 1974. We have ignored that change, and simply taken the years when the respondents in the cohort reached age 18 as the era of socialization for each cohort, whether the years involved were before or after 1974. As the labels on figure 3.1 indicate, each age category represents a distinctive generation in terms of the defining characteristics of the period when the respondents within that age bracket came of age.

The Incidence of Party Identification by Age

Confining ourselves first to the incidence of party identification, it is clear that the highest level occurs for the generation that came of age during what we have labeled the Gaullist Fifth Republic. These are the people whose political initiation took place during the years that encompassed the collapse of the Fourth Republic, the return to power of de Gaulle, Algerian independence, battles over the constitution, and the first modern French popular election to the presidency. The voters who were from 40 to 49 years of age in 1988 constitute the "founding generation" (Carmines 1991) of political conflict in contemporary France, as it is reflected in mass partisan attachments. We will return to this generation in a slightly different context later. Here we will add only that when one takes other expressed political locations into account as well as discrete party identifications, the generation of the Gaullist Fifth Republic is the one with the fewest people, proportionately, who have no sense at all of their political location.

The lowest levels of partisanship occur among the older age groups.[14] These generations, whose coming of age occurred during the Fourth Republic, World War II and the German occupation, and even the Third Republic, are cohorts that, along with their elders of the time, contributed to the very low rate of party identification recorded by Converse and Dupeux (1966b) for 1958. Their overall incidence of party identification in 1988, although less than the average, was still well above the mean level of 1958, a clear indication that adult French citizens were taking on partisan identifications at a higher rate during the Fifth Republic than they had done earlier.

The intermediate cohorts, in terms of the incidence of party identification, are those that came of age during the early post-Gaullist Fifth Republic and what we have labeled the mature Fifth Republic. The formative political experiences of these two generations naturally differed in their specifics, but they had in common the strong and eventually victorious efforts of the leftist forces to oust de Gaulle and his successors from power. These are the voters whose political environment was characterized most consistently and exclusively by the clarity and simplicity of the two-bloc, pseudo-two-party system that emerged during the middle 1960s. Indeed, the younger of the two cohorts in this category, the one born between 1959 and 1970, includes *children* of people from the cohort that came of age during the battles of the Gaullist Fifth Republic. The respondents in our youngest cohort not only had the opportunity to absorb the neat and clear political atmospherics of the mature Fifth Republic, but they also were likely to have experienced parental partisan pushes from the people who constitute the founding generation of contemporary French mass partisanship. In that fashion, the intensity of the political conflicts that were the hallmarks of the Gaullist Fifth Republic are wedded to the greater ease of situating oneself in partisan terms that was characteristic of the years of the mature Fifth Republic.

The Composition of the Partisan Alignment by Age

Leftist party identifiers outnumber rightist identifiers in four of our six age cohorts. Leftists are most numerous in the generation of the early post-Gaullist Fifth Republic, and next most prevalent among the youngest of the cohorts, that of the mature Fifth Republic.[15] In terms of formative political experience, therefore, the years of leftist challenges and defeats during the late 1960s and the 1970s spawned more left-wing party identifiers than the more recent period of leftist electoral victories. The lesser, although still substantial, lead of the left over the right in party identification among the respondents who were in their 50s and 60s at the time of our survey in 1988, reflects the close balance of left and right party identifications that we recorded in 1967. People in those age groups would have been in their 30s and 40s in 1967 and, therefore, contributing to the dead heat as between leftist and rightist party identifiers at that time (within a lower overall incidence of party identification than in 1988). The recorded 1988 levels of leftist party identification among those cohorts may be understood as a reflection of the left-right standoff of 1967, plus an increment of some 5 percent in favor of the left in harmony with the ongoing leftist surge of the last decade.

It should be noted that if we take into account not only discrete party identifications but also the other expressions of political positions that are recorded in figure 3.1 (and that overwhelmingly include references to left-right locations), the left-right balance is very close among the respondents who were in their 50s or 60s in 1988. The relatively large proportions of rightist respondents who designated themselves in these broader terms reflects the absence in 1988 of surviving partisan referents from the eras during which they came of political age.

The only cohort in which rightist party identifiers outnumbered leftist ones in 1988 is the 40–49 year old group, which came of age during the Gaullist Fifth Republic. This finding is noteworthy for two reasons. On the one hand, this is the generation that contains most of the people who were young adults in 1968, the year of the now legendary anti-Gaullist mass upheaval that ranks with the Paris Commune and the sit down strikes of 1936 in the mythology of the French left. The people in this cohort were between 20 and 29 years of age during the events of May 1968. On the other hand, there is a sharp difference in the ratio of leftist to rightist party identifiers as between the 40–49 year old cohort and the next younger cohort (aged 30–39 in 1988). The 40–49 group is the most rightist generation, while the 30–39 cohort is the most leftist. At least the oldest members of the latter cohort had also been young adults in 1968. These two aspects of our data raise the question of what the legacy of the 1968 events was in the context of French mass partisanship 20 years later.

To find the answer to that question, we pursued the traces of 1968 more finely than figure 3.1 alone permits by examining the distribution of basic partisan identifications within the relevant age groups on an annualized basis. This distribution appears in figure 3.2, in the form of the proportion of true identifiers with leftist parties less the proportion of true identifiers with rightist parties, by age in 1988, among all respondents in each annual cohort. In order to compensate for the thin case numbers that annualization produces, as well as to smooth out the curve slightly, we employed a three-year moving average. Each annual cohort, therefore, is the mean of three adjacent annual cohorts. This procedure yields 3-year case totals that are mainly in the 60s and 70s, and always more than 50, for respondents aged 30 to 43 in 1988. The case numbers for respondents aged 44 to 50 are all less than 50, and include some that are in the low 30s and high 20s.

Despite the risks of sampling error, particularly among the older cohorts displayed, one cannot fail to be impressed by the steep slope of the curve that occupies the middle third of figure 3.2. The implications of that slope and its location are so consistent with party identification theory, the local French historical facts, and comparable phenomena that have been reported for the United States that we feel justified, at least provisionally, in setting aside concerns about sampling error and concentrating our attention on the conspicuously coherent display of data.

Let us be clear about where figure 3.2 fits into our discussion about the development of party identification in France, and what, more exactly, it tells us. We know that in the past there have been two broad types of partisan configuration. One, which was measured during the late 1960s, showed leftist and rightist party identifiers to be in a more or less equal balance; the other, cap-

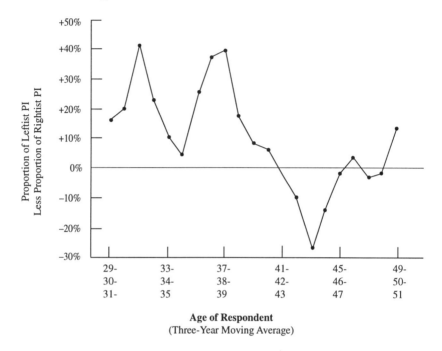

Fig. 3.2. Trends in balance of party identification (PI), among respondents aged 30–50, France, 1988

tured in 1988, was characterized by a clear predominance of leftist identifiers over rightist ones. These may be thought of as two plateaus, of different heights.

The residues of these two plateaus, in the form of current (1988) party identifications, appear quite clearly in figure 3.1. What does not appear in figure 3.1 is the nature and timing of the connection between the two plateaus. Figure 3.2 supplies us with that information, and it does so with uncommon clarity. The two plateaus are present there in somewhat ragged form, but now we see that they are connected to each other by a steep cliff that was chiseled into the French partisan landscape by people who were between 18 and 24 years of age in 1968. The importance of the 1968 upheaval as a great realigning event is strikingly affirmed. The central role of the youngest voters as the avant-garde of the new alignment is also unambiguously displayed.

These findings mesh admirably with analogous results reported long ago for the United States. In their classic work, *The American Voter*, Campbell et al. (1960, 154) charted the direction of party identification, by year of birth between 1900 and 1930, for some 10,000 cases from seven U.S. NES surveys conducted between 1952 and 1958. That chart similarly displayed two plateaus of unequal heights joined by a steep cliff (in the Democratic direction) centering on voters born between 1905 and 1912, indicating strongly that the New Deal realignment had been spearheaded by voters who were between 21 and 27 years old in 1932.

Converse (1976) later developed that analysis more powerfully and elegantly. On the one hand, he enlarged the case numbers and extended the time frame of the display of party identification by year of birth, and on that basis showed that the age-localization of the depression-era realignment in the United States increasingly lost sharpness of definition with the passage of time, even though it remained apparent from traces into the 1970s that something important had happened among people who entered the electorate during the 1930s (Converse 1976, 132–35). On the other hand, by correlating party identifications, by annualized age, with aggregate electoral outcomes for biennial U.S. elections, he showed that the optimal correlations for the period 1952–58 (the same years charted in *The American Voter*) occurred for voters between 21 and 22 years of age (Converse 1976, 132–37). For the years between 1964 and 1972 the optimal fit would still have been for age 22, although for that later period the range of variation was such that any age between 22 and 26 would have been almost as good.

These findings are directly relevant to the interpretation of our French data. Given that the clarity of earlier realignments progressively deteriorates in later expressions of partisanship, our 1988 portrayal of the 1968 French realignment should be more sharply etched than the rendition of the U.S. realignment that appears in *The American Voter*. While our analysis suffers by comparison with respect to case numbers, it gains in immediacy with regard to the lapse of time between the realigning event and the later distribution of partisan identifications by age. Our 1988 measurements of partisanship occurred a mere 20 years after the realigning upheaval of 1968. The original graph in *The American Voter* was based on pooled data gathered from 20 to 26 years after the realigning depression, with the result that the contours of the cliff rising upward to the new Democratic plateau were already becoming blurred. The best estimate that one can make simply by eyeballing the graph is that the realignment centered on the 24-year-olds of the era. We know from Converse's later analysis, however, that the cutting edge of change was the 21- and 22-year-olds. Our finding for France is that the age range that took the lead in scaling the new leftist rampart was from 18 to 24, which of course centers on 21. It is worth recalling in this connection that during the late 1960s and early 1970s the minimum voting age in France was still 21.

Having placed our French data within a larger, comparative perspective, we are in a position to give a clear answer to the question about the political legacy of the May 1968 upheaval with which we opened this section of our analysis. The 1968 revolt was a realigning event in France analogous—at least within a term of 20 years—to the Great Depression of the 1930s in the United

States. The leftist dominance in partisan attachments that we found in 1988 had its origins in the May days of 1968, just as the longer-term Democratic party ascendancy in the United States emerged from the Great Depression.[16]

The residues of that new French alignment that we find in the distribution of partisanship, measured 20 years after the aligning event itself, indicate that the shift in the partisan balance that occurred was led by the youngest cohort of voters, just as the youngest voters had spearheaded the New Deal realignment in the United States some 35 years earlier. That is exactly what we would expect on the basis of the theory of partisanship. The youngest voters are, other things being equal, less firmly anchored in the party system than their elders, and they are, consequently, more susceptible to change in reaction to destabilizing shocks to the ongoing party system.

Before we leave figure 3.2, there is one more comment to be made, albeit with added caution, as it refers to the right-hand third of the figure, where case numbers are perilously thin. While our 1988 respondents who had been between 18 and 24 years old in 1968 form the cliff that rises to the leftist plateau, there are indications that the slightly older voters, those who had been between 24 and 27 were actually moving *rightward* at the same time. That might be merely a trick played by sampling error, but it is in no way inconsistent with the actual events of 1968. There were, after all, two sides to the 1968 revolt. On the one hand, deep hostility toward the Gaullist regime produced weeks of near-general strikes and massive demonstrations. But there was also a sharp backlash against the disorders associated with the anti-Gaullist demonstrations that produced a right-wing landslide at the legislative elections of 1968. We know that in the immediate wake of the May events, more voters shifted rightward than moved leftward (Converse and Pierce 1986, 431–36).

It is not out of the question that while the 1968 revolt put an indelible stamp on the cohort that was between 18 and 27 years old at the time, it did so in internally contradictory ways, with the younger elements of that thin population slice being imprinted by an impulse toward radicalism and the older ones by the backlash. Such an interpretation gains plausibility by the fact that the older segment of the cohort would have been approaching the age when young adults begin to take on responsibilities that require order and a stable environment. But this subplot, even if sustained, is only a refinement alongside the central message that emerges from figure 3.2: the 1968 upheaval was a realigning event of historic proportions that centered on the youngest voters.

It is important to add, in any case, that the youngest cohort could not alone be responsible for the new leftist predominance in partisanship that was registered in France in 1988, any more than the youngest U.S. voters alone produced the post-1932 Democratic majority. The youngest voters, in both countries, were only the leading edges of what were broad period effects. The leading edge in France remained finely honed and optimally centered after a lapse of two decades. But the increase in leftist partisanship after 1968 was distributed broadly throughout the entire electorate, and particularly among voters who were too young to have been *soixante-huitards* (sixty-eighters).

The 1968 upheaval was a major turning point, but other forces also had to be operating on popular political orientations. The most important of these were the decline of Gaullism as the principal pole of attraction on the right, and the growth of the Socialist party into the main magnet on the political left. These dual developments were directly linked to the strategic roles played by the two presidential protagonists of 1965, Charles de Gaulle and François Mitterrand.

Contrasting Leadership Styles

De Gaulle's defeat at the referendum of 1969, followed immediately by his res-ignation from the presidency and by his death the following year, left the Gaullist party that had been founded by his supporters in 1958 disoriented and dispirited. The party was surely not leaderless, but its habit of dependence on and obedience to de Gaulle had left it without the experience, temperament, or even mechanisms, to produce a new leadership from its own ranks whom the party's numerous heavyweights could support. Pompidou became de Gaulle's immediate heir because he had been his prime minister, and not because he was the choice of calculating party leaders. When Pompidou's death opened up the succession once again, the Gaullists could not find a candidate capable of unit-ing their party. The candidate who formally ran under the Gaullist banner— Jacques Chaban-Delmas—did not outdistance Valéry Giscard d'Estaing at the first ballot of the 1974 presidential election. Gaullist dominance of the right came to an end.

After Giscard's electoral victory, the French right reverted to the splintered state it had been in before it was quasi-unified under the aegis of de Gaulle. Gaullist electoral fortunes ebbed during the 1970s and 1980s, while those of their Giscardian rivals gained, until the two right-wing groups were of about equal voting strength. Hardly distinguishable from each other in broad pro-grammatic terms, they were constantly jockeying for preeminence over each other. The Giscardians themselves were a loose federation of rival groupings. The salience that the Gaullist party once enjoyed as the lodestone of the right evaporated.

Even if the Gaullist party had fared better electorally after de Gaulle's departure than it actually did, there is reason to believe that mass attachments to the party would have dissipated at more than a random rate. De Gaulle's with-drawal from the political scene was far more than the passing of a popular party leader. De Gaulle's personal appeal was greater than that of the party that formed to support him. Large numbers of the general's admirers flocked to the Gaullist party because it was identified with him. When de Gaulle left the scene, his party was vulnerable to the loss of that vast conditional element of its foundation. French voters could, did, and still do identify with the Gaullist party for a variety of reasons, but the personal appeal of de Gaulle could not survive him indefinitely.

Even when he was active, de Gaulle did virtually nothing to contribute to the permanence of a Gaullist party. De Gaulle despised parties, and there is no reason to believe that he made any exception for the Gaullists when they behaved like a party, as opposed simply to supporting his positions, which he always presented as expressions of the national interest. De Gaulle regularly took a stance "above parties," which was hardly conducive to encouraging long-term attachments to any party, even the one that claimed to be his own. It was, in part, de Gaulle's above-parties posture that helped him to build personal popular support that was broader and deeper than that earned by the Gaullist party, but that aspect of his appeal made it all the more difficult for his admirers to transfer their allegiance to the Gaullist party, which in any case was bound to emerge diminished once the general was no longer there as a source of reflected glory.

While de Gaulle's disappearance ended the Gaullist hegemony on the right, François Mitterrand's advent to the leadership of the Socialist party set it on a course that culminated with that party's domination of the French left. The Gaullists, at the end of the 1960s, had succeeded in becoming virtually synonymous with the right, only to lose that status during the 1980s, when they found it difficult even to maintain parity of popular support with their Giscardian rivals. The Socialists, by way of contrast, began that same period weaker than the Communists, who were the major political force on the left, but they ended up barely a decade later not only as France's main left-wing party but as its largest party of any kind.

This outcome was the result of the appropriateness of Mitterrand's political strategy for a period when the appeal of the right was waning and anticommunist sentiment was intensifying. Mitterrand's strategy was to identify the Socialist party unmistakably with the left by allying with the Communists under an agreement according to which each party would throw its support at the second ballot of France's two-ballot elections to the candidate of the leftist party that was best placed to win.[17] This strategy required a Communist party that was sufficiently respectable not to make such a leftist alliance out of the question (as had been the case in 1969, in the wake of the Warsaw Pact countries' invasion of Czechoslovakia), but still frightening enough to give opposition-minded voters a real incentive to support the Socialists instead. The Communists providentially obliged, by taking only superficial steps to distance themselves from the characteristic features of Russian policy. They remained organizationally in the Stalinist mold and manifested only a slow, incomplete, and grudging acceptance of the "Eurocommunist" principles that were rapidly acquiring standing in other Western European Communist parties. In these circumstances, the Socialist party became the main point of attraction for voters who sought radical economic and social reforms but who also distrusted the Communist party.

As the main beneficiary of discontent with right-wing rule, the Socialist party regularly outdistanced its Communist allies at the first ballot of legislative elections, and the terms of the alliance became increasingly favorable to the Socialists. What was in principle a system of mutual assistance became mainly a conduit for the flow of Communist votes in support of Socialist candidates at the second ballot, as the proportion of districts in which Communists ran ahead of Socialists at the first ballot decreased during the 1970s and 1980s.

Furthermore, Mitterrand had no reservations about trying to convert whatever personal appeal he could muster to the advantage of the Socialist party. While de Gaulle styled himself as above parties, Mitterrand was unremittingly partisan. He worked and schemed tirelessly, not only in his party but also for his party. In this regard, Mitterrand's behavior could hardly have been more different from that of de Gaulle, and the results in terms of personal as compared with partisan political identifications were strikingly different as well. In 1968, shortly after the Gaullist party won the greatest electoral victory of its history, almost half as many respondents in the Converse-Pierce survey claimed to be "Gaullists" or identified with "de Gaulle's party" as professed an identification with some nominal variant of the Gaullist party. At our 1988 sample survey, conducted in association with Mitterrand's triumphant reelection to the presidency, a mere handful of respondents replied that they identified with "Mitterrand" or "Mitterrand's party," as compared with the more than one-third of them who claimed an attachment to the Socialist party.

The Socialist party had the good fortune of being in the ascendancy when the level of political interest was rising, partisan choices were becoming simpler and clearer, familial political socialization was widening, and the overall incidence of party identification was increasing. During the late 1960s, the French Socialist party was somewhat less visible than the Gaullist party and considerably less visible than the Communist party (Converse and Pierce 1986, 62). By 1988, the Socialist party was almost surely the most visible party on the French political horizon. Exercising the widest field of attraction, the Socialists were in a position to profit most from the increasing proportion of citizens that were receptive to partisan persuasion. The main source of Socialist party identifiers was, of course, the successive younger generations, but the data in figure 3.1 show that the left had also won at least the temporary allegiance of voters from older generations that had been immune to partisan appeals in their youth.

The Fragility of the Partisan Alignment

The two most prominent characteristics of the 1988 French partisan alignment were that it was comparatively new, having been formed only during the two decades between 1967 and 1988, and that its political composition was shaped mainly by the partisan identifications of the younger citizens. These two features, which are related to each other, meant that the foundation of the alignment was less than solid and its duration uncertain. The gradient in strength of party identification by age was the same in France in 1988 as it normally is in a developed system: party identification was weakest among the young and generally intensified with age, except for the most elderly cohort.[18] The probability that people would abandon or switch their partisan attachments was, therefore, highest for the voters under 40 years of age who contributed so heavily in 1988 to both the new equilibrium level of party identification in France, and its sharply leftist orientation. Furthermore, inasmuch as it is not biological age per se but rather length of systemic experience that affects the intensification of party identification, the predominantly leftist party identifications recently acquired by older members of the electorate were similarly more susceptible to change than they would have been if they had been of longer duration.

The political alignment that we measured in 1988, therefore, was highly vulnerable to destabilization by outside shocks. These could be of two kinds. One was simply the kinds of economic, social, or international developments that lead people to reconsider or alter their political orientations in any country. The other was that set of largely elite-driven factors, endemic to France, that for so long had been major impediments to the formation of any stable partisan alignment at all: inconstancy, complexity, and obscurity in the political supply. Shocks of both kinds reverberated throughout the French political system between 1988 and 1993, with effects on the distribution of partisanship that have not been measured but that were surely reflected in the sharp electoral losses sustained by the French Socialists during that period and, particularly, at the legislative elections of 1993. The French Socialist party, which had gained the most during the years when the party system stabilized and the incidence of party identification rose, was also the party that suffered the most when the destabilizing forces of the late 1980s and early 1990s were unleashed.

The most powerful conventional factor to affect the distribution of political outlooks was the sluggishness of the French economy. France was not alone in suffering economic ills during those years. All the countries of the Organization for Economic Cooperation and Development (OECD) experienced more or less severe economic difficulties during the same period. Indeed, from at least one point of view, it may be said that French policymakers shielded their citizens from some of the more demoralizing consequences of economic weakness better than others did, at least through 1984. Inequality in family income (after transfer payments and adjusted for family size) grew less between 1979 and 1984 in France than in any other country examined except Sweden (Gottschalk 1993).[19] However, perhaps because of the tax effort required to provide the transfer payments that sustained equality, disposable household income as a proportion of gross domestic product trended downward in France from 1981 to 1989, when it rose slightly but plateaued at about the 1987 level into 1992 (*L'Année politique 1992*, 626). And the statistics concerning unemployment were unrelievedly gloomy. The unemployment rate hovered around the 10 percent level from 1984 to 1992, comparing unfavorably with the average rates of France's natural points of reference: the countries of the European Community, the four largest European economies (those of Germany, the United Kingdom, Italy, and France), or the Group of Seven (the four large European economies plus those of Canada, Japan, and the United States). The unemployment figures were particularly embarrassing to the Socialist party, which had come to power in 1981 condemning a lower unemployment rate as intolerable.

Economic distress contributed greatly toward turning voters away from the Socialists, who had been the dominant party only a few years earlier, just as it played the major role in George Bush's defeat at the U.S. presidential election in 1992.[20] From the perspective of this chapter, however, which has traced the development of an original political alignment in France based on a normal incidence of partisan identifications, the critical shocks to the French party system were not economic, as important as those might be for the French people and the electoral fate of particular parties, but rather those that affected the basic properties of the entire party system. The main argument of this chapter is that the generation of a partisan alignment in France by 1988 was the result of a set of systemic factors having to do with the simplification, clarification, and stabilization of the entire party system. For 20 years there had been symmetrical electoral alliances on both left and right, and comparatively homogeneous governments faced similarly united oppositions. By 1988, when we took the reading of the distribution of partisan identifications that both reflected and contributed to that partisan structure, the pseudo-two-party system was already unraveling, and it continued to do so.

The Socialist-Communist alliance began to become undone almost as soon as it emerged triumphant in 1981. By 1988 it was no more than a least-of-evils electoral convenience. The Communist party had splintered, and if it was not already clear that any effort to restore a united left was doomed to failure, it became obvious soon thereafter, when the Soviet Union collapsed in abject failure. The right-wing bloc similarly lost much of the cohesion that it had displayed earlier in the face of Socialist domination. Elements of the old rightist coalition associated with the loose Giscardian grouping moved from the opposition into a coalition with the Socialists after the 1988 legislative elections.

The erosion of the dominance of the two-bloc system opened up space for political entrepreneurs across the political spectrum, who nibbled away at the fragile equilibrium that had been two decades in the making. The gross number of competing political categories is less important than the degree of solidity of the coalitions of major groups, but it is at least illustrative of the fragmentation of the French political system that *Le Monde* required, for its detailed summary of the results of the legislative elections of 1993, no fewer than 60 abbreviations to give proper treatment to all the political labels used by the candidates in metropolitan France (*Elections Législatives de Mars 1993*, 86).

This return to confusion at the elite level was bound to affect the voters' perceptions of their party system. The risk was not that the incidence of party identification would recede to its lower levels of two or three decades earlier. That was not impossible, but it was highly unlikely, given that party identification had already reached the equilibrium level, and in view of the weakening of the reticence norm that formerly impeded the intergenerational transmission of partisanship (Percheron 1989).

The more likely outcome, which was already reflected in the volatility of French electoral results after 1988, was an increase in the instability of individual-level partisan identifications beyond the expected rate for a party system of the size of the French one. As new parties emerged, old ones splintered, fractious leaders complicated the partisan field, and complex coalition strategies obscured the meaning of electoral choices for ordinary citizens, it could be expected that movements into and out of partisan identifications would accelerate, along with switches from identification with one party to identification with another. And as older identifications were abandoned and new ones adopted, the latter, because new, would inevitably be weak.

The fact remains, however, that a distinct partisan alignment was in place at the time of the presidential election of 1988. It was fragile, and it may well have given way to a dealignment or realignment of the kind that so agitated U.S. political observers during the 1970s and 1980s. But however temporary it may have been, it was operative in 1988. In chapter 7, we will show that it affected the electoral choices of the French voters in ways that directly paralleled the impact of the more stable U.S. pattern of party identification on presidential electoral choices in the United States.

CHAPTER 4

Ideological Orientations

The seating arrangements in the French parliamentary chambers of the revolutionary era, which placed the advocates of radical change on the left (facing the speaker), and the partisans of conservatism or reaction on the right, gave birth to political terminology that not only spread in varying degrees across continental Europe but also endures to this day. Simultaneously ideological shortcuts and political epithets, the terms left and right are the organizing concepts by which French politicians, political commentators, and scholars alike classify the political parties and establish historical continuities among them. These politically attentive groups may be intensely interested in some particular political party at any given moment, and from one or more points of view, but that party will inevitably be situated in relation both to the other parties of the same moment and to its historical ancestors in left-right terms.

Given the kaleidoscopic character and temporal instability of the French party system, some such principle of classification is a virtual necessity. One is tempted to say that if the left-right imagery did not exist, some analogous concept would have to be invented to bring order to the restless components of the French party system. The age and stability of the U.S. party system make it possible to say that one state or another has been predominantly Republican since the Civil War, or to refer to the solid (Democratic) South for a century after the Civil War. Partisan discontinuities rule out such nominal references in France. One can, however, refer to long-term political constancy in France, as Siegfried (1913) did early in this century, and as countless others have done since, in terms of left-right tendencies. Any modestly competent student of French politics can identify regions that have been leftist or rightist at least since 1848, but few even of the ablest can specify the particular parties that triumphed there at successive elections.

The regional stability of French electoral patterns in broad left-right terms, along with a gross overall regularity of support at the national level throughout the Third Republic for what Goguel (1946) preferred to call the party of "movement" and the party of the "established order," gave impulse to the notion that what was fundamental to French electoral politics was not the ephemeral parties but rather the enduring left-right sentiments that they represented. There still remained, however, the problem of determining just where each of the finer shades of political opinion that existed on one side or another of the left-right divide stood in relation to one another and in relation to the numerous, if transient, groups that purported to express them. Goguel (1946), who was interested mainly in the electoral history of the Third Republic, which for the most part rested on a two-ballot electoral system that required electoral alliances to be effective, could insist not only that his two categories reflecting "movement" and "order" were not merely adequate but wholly appropriate for discussing the nature of electoral conflict during the period. As late as 1930, Siegfried (1930) thought that three tendencies—left, center, and right—sufficed to exhaust the political field. But even early in the twentieth century, other commentators thought that more categories were required. Five was the most commonly suggested number, which Siegfried (1948) also came to accept in the early postwar period, ranging from left, across the center-left (or moderate left) and center to the center-right (or moderate right) and the right. The postwar prominence of the Communist party suggested that the term *extreme left* would be a more appropriate label for anchoring the end of the scale that represented radical change, while the wartime experience with the Vichy regime stretched the scale in the other direction to include the *extreme right*.[1]

In that fashion, the simple left-right dichotomy was stretched conceptually into a hypothetical seven-point scale, even before techniques were developed to measure the left-right perceptions of political objects.

The Limitations of the Left-Right Dimension

The establishment of the left-right locations of parties and political leaders was exclusively a subjective exercise of elite political actors and observers until the middle 1960s, when Deutsch, Lindon, and Weill (1966) began to employ sample survey techniques to elicit people's perceptions of their own locations on a hypothetical seven-point left-right scale. Converse and Pierce (1986) employed a metric scale in the late 1960s to determine not only the survey respondents' self-locations but also where the respondents placed the various political parties of the era on the same scale. Since that period, the measurement of people's self-perceived left-right locations has become routine throughout Western Europe, although assessing the locations of parties and candidates in those terms is still comparatively rare.

As a result of these empirical studies, it quickly became clear that the extent to which left-right positioning operated to orient French voters to their political environment was a lot more limited than many people had earlier assumed. Deutsch, Lindon, and Weill (1966) discovered that while the modal point at which people located themselves on their seven-point scale was the center, fully two-thirds of these centrists had little or no interest in politics and had chosen that neutral location because they had no conception of what being some distance to the left or to the right of center actually meant. The Deutsch, Lindon, and Weill (1966) baptized those uninvolved centrists, along with the people who could not or refused to place themselves on the scale, the *marais*, which amounted to almost a third of the sample electorate. The Converse and Pierce (1986) measures of the next few years suggested that the proportion of the French electorate for whom the hypothetical left-right scale had no meaning was even larger. This meant that the proportion of the electorate for whom a sense of left-right location might be their main linkage with the party system was hardly greater than the proportion of French voters who professed a partisan identification.

Other attributes of left-right positioning also operated to dampen whatever enthusiasm observers might have had about the possibility that the left-right dimension would prove to be the touchstone for mass political behavior in France. Perhaps the most important of these was the determination that while the terms *left* and *right* were clearly replete with ideological meaning for French political elites (in this instance parliamentary candidates), they were much less so even for the thin stratum of the most politically involved members of the electorate (Converse and Pierce 1986). Descending the scale of political involvement from the great mass of medium involved people to those least involved, the meaning of the left-right distinction shaded off sharply to a simple expression of group conflict or to nothing at all. This finding was fully consistent with related analyses made by Klingemann (1979) of the degree of ideological content of the left-right terminology for the electorates of several other countries. As a consequence of this relative failure of left-right positioning to serve as an organizing framework for mass political attitudes, the linkage of left-right locations with positions on issues was much weaker across the French electorate as a whole than among the political elites, and its clarity moved, as one could now expect, with the degree of political involvement of the voters (Converse and Pierce 1986). Inglehart and Klingemann (1976) reached much the same conclusion for the mass publics of a broad range of European electorates.

Finally, left-right locations turned out to be a less reliable predictor of electoral choices than party identifications. Partisan attachments in France were, as we have seen, comparatively underdeveloped during the late 1960s, and they have always been unstable, but party identifications remained more stable from 1967 to 1968, for people who had them at both dates, than did self-perceptions of left-right location. Moreover, in 1967, party identification proved to be a better forward predictor of electoral choices in 1968 than 1967 left-right locations did (Converse and Pierce 1986).

The Utility of the Left-Right Dimension

The limitations of the left-right dimension as a compass for orienting ordinary French citizens to their political system do not translate into a recommendation that we simply abandon it to some dictionary of obsolete words and phrases. Left-right imagery is so deeply ingrained into modes of thinking about French politics that it is nearly impossible to mount a sustained exposition of French political life without resorting to it.[2] As a kind of super ideology, the left-right dimension operates most clearly and directly among the political elites, for whom it has rich substantive content. Indeed, left-right perceptions play a considerable role as a sort of transmission belt in the representative process in France. Converse and Pierce (1986, 718) found that the left-right composition of French electoral districts was a better predictor of how deputies from those districts voted on specific policy issues than was district opinion on those very issue domains. Nevertheless, once we descend the scale of political involvement below the comparatively small slice of the mass electorate that is highly involved in politics, for whom left-right location still serves as an ideological shorthand, although less predictably than it does for the political elites, we enter a zone where the left-right vocabulary is without any clear metaphorical role.

There are two ways, however, in which the left-right dimension unquestionably clarifies and helps us to understand French mass political behavior. The first way, somewhat paradoxically, is by focusing on those people for whom left-right locations have no meaning—the marais. The second way is to employ mass perceptions of the left-right locations of political objects as a scoring device for analyzing the relative weights of the various components of electoral choice. One of the analytical problems involved in dealing with multiparty systems such as the French one is to establish a system of measurement above the nominal level for expressing party identifications, electoral choices, and attitudes toward candidates and parties more generally. The electorate's perceptions of the left-right locations of parties and candidates provide an excellent means of doing so. Our earlier work with mass perceptions of the left-right positioning of the parties (Converse and Pierce 1986) showed that while there is considerable dispersion of those perceptions for any given party, there are also prominent modes that suggest a significant degree of mass consensus. Moreover, the mean left-right locations of the parties displayed considerable stability, at least across a three-year period. In that earlier study, which dealt with parliamentary representation, we worked principally with the perceived locations of the political parties. Here, we will concentrate on the perceived locations of the presidential candidates. An analogous form of the analysis, however, will be employed.

Examining the marais is the simpler of the two ways of exploiting the left-right dimension, so we will deal with that first. Then, in the next section, we will turn to the use of the left-right scale as a scoring mechanism.

The marais, which consists of people who have little or no interest in politics, includes a disproportionately large number of people who do not participate in elections, but to the extent that the marais does vote it represents an unpredictable but potentially decisive force. The marais is unpredictable in that it is the least clearly anchored group of people in the French electorate. It is potentially decisive in that at close elections, where leftist and rightist forces approach equality, the votes of the marais can tip the scales one way or the other.

Deutsch, Lindon, and Weill (1966) pointed out carefully how important the marais was in determining the outcome of the presidential election of 1965. Almost half of the voters from the marais voted for candidates other than Charles de Gaulle at the first ballot, thereby contributing greatly to his failure to win a widely expected first-ballot victory. At the decisive second ballot, however, almost three-fourths of the marais voters opted for de Gaulle, this time contributing to, if not ensuring, his election. On the other side of the political spectrum, François Mitterrand's long, gradual ascent to the presidency was in no small measure the result of increasing support from the marais. According to SOFRES estimates, 28 percent of the marais voted for Mitterrand at the second ballot in 1965, 34 percent in 1974, and 42 percent in 1981. Our own independent estimate is that 51 percent of the marais contributed to Mitterrand's decisive reelection in 1988. The transfer of the presidency from right to left was to some considerable extent the result of a shift in the political mood of people who were neither one nor the other.

The Left-Right Scoring of Voters and Candidates

Self-Perceptions of Left-Right Locations

The distribution of the self-locations of our 1988 sample of the French electorate along a seven-point left-right scale is set out in figure 4.1. In gross terms, that array strongly resembles the left-right profiles to which students of the phenomenon in France have become accustomed. There are, however, two noteworthy differences between this 1988 distribution and those reported almost three decades earlier by Deutsch, Lindon, and Weill (1966), whose scale was the same as ours, and by Converse and Pierce (1986), who employed a metric scale.

The first difference is a marked decline in the size of the marais. Deutsch, Lindon, and Weill (1966, 22) estimated it to embrace almost one-third of the total electorate; while Converse and Pierce (1986, 129) found it to be even larger. Our estimate is closer to one-fifth of the electorate. It is difficult to know

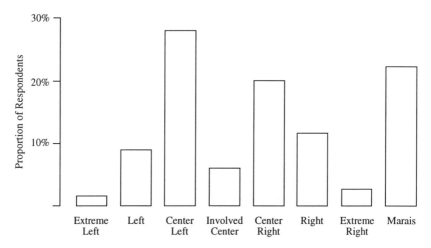

Fig. 4.1. Self-locations on left-right scale, French national electorate, 1988

what to make of this large difference in the absence of any intervening trend lines. Some of the difference may reflect the increase in political interest since the late 1960s, to which we already referred in our discussion in the previous chapter of the increase in the incidence of party identification.

It is clear, as well, that the more recent left-right frequencies reflect the changed political conjuncture, relative to the middle and late 1960s. For the second notable difference from that earlier period is that the "raw" center—the people who spontaneously locate themselves at the center of the scale whether or not they are interested in politics—is not the modal left-right group, which it was in those earlier measures. If we placed the marais column of figure 4.1 on top of the involved center column, the combined height would be the same as that of the center-left column. Inasmuch as the marais as represented in figure 4.1 includes people who did not even assign themselves a left-right location, more people considered themselves to be in the center-left than assigned themselves to the center. In the earlier era, the raw centrists were the distinctly modal category.

The new prominence of the center-left is of a piece with the ascendancy of the Socialist party that we charted in the previous chapter. At the same time, a secondary shift in the frequencies is also notable: a decline among leftists and extreme leftists and an increase in rightists and extreme rightists. This, of course, reflects the eclipse of the Communist party and the rise of Jean-Marie Le Pen's National Front. These changes in the distribution of self-perceived left-right locations, which run parallel to accompanying changes in party for-

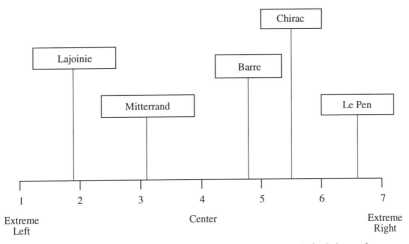

Fig. 4.2. Average perceptions of candidate locations on left-right scale, French national electorate, 1988

tunes, are suggestive of the extent to which we may find it difficult to distinguish left-right locations from partisan identifications.

Mass Perceptions of Candidate Locations

Our respondents were asked to locate the main candidates at the French presidential election of 1988, as well as the major political parties, on the same seven-point left-right scale on which we had already asked them to place themselves. These perceptions display the same kind of dispersion and anomalies that our earlier work (Converse and Pierce 1986) had led us to anticipate, but the mean scores reported by those respondents who had assigned themselves a left-right location, which are displayed in figure 4.2, are wholly consistent with what one might expect from conventional descriptions of those same candidates and parties in elite political discourse. The range of candidates, in perceived left-right terms, offered to the French electorate at the first ballot of the presidential election could hardly have been improved upon. Almost every segment of the seven-point left-right scale is occupied, with André Lajoinie, the Communist candidate, anchoring the left at 1.9, and Jean-Marie Le Pen almost touching the extreme right at 6.6. The perceived left-right locations of the major parties are so similar to those of their respective candidates that they do not warrant separate presentation. The ordering is exactly the same as it is for the candidates, and the largest absolute discrepancy is a mere .18, representing the small margin by which the electorate placed the Communist party to the left of its presidential candidate.

We will assign these mean perceived left-right scores to the respective candidates and parties for measurement purposes.[3] That will permit us to express our respondents' orientations toward the multiple French parties and candidates in pseudo-interval form (Converse and Pierce 1986, 117–27). In that fashion, we will construct variables representing left-right party identification, the left-right presidential vote at the first ballot, and the voters' preferred candidates as registered on the typical thermometer scale or on the basis of perceived issue positions.

The Liberal-Conservative Dimension

The prominence of left-right discourse in France, and the uneven but—in some circumstances—evident role that it plays as an organizing concept, has sometimes led observers of U.S. politics to wonder whether a liberal-conservative dimension might be operative in the United States in ways at least roughly analogous to those associated with the left-right dimension in France. As a result, the U.S. National Election Studies (NES) have been measuring respondents' self-locations on a liberal-conservative scale since the 1970s.[4]

The basic problem with this consideration is that reported liberal-conservative positions in the United States suffer rather more than less from the same deficiencies we recounted earlier in connection with the left-right dimension for France. The NES surveys allow respondents an escape clause in the form of "or haven't you thought much about it?" when asking questions about their positions on the liberal-conservative and other, more specific, issue dimensions. The proportion of voters who opt for that alternative, plus those who do not but then go on to reply that they do not really know where they are located, regularly assume proportions matching those recorded for the marais in France back in the 1960s. Among the remaining respondents, those who do select a location on the scale, there is the same dearth of concrete issue content we have already encountered for left-right positioning at the mass level in France (Converse and Pierce 1986).

We will occasionally employ the liberal-conservative dimension in discussing elections in the United States, for comparative purposes, but it is proper to indicate in advance that we believe that its operational importance at the mass level is quite limited. Indeed, there is good reason to believe that liberal-conservative terminology is even more confined to elite circles in the United States than left-right imagery is in France. Neither liberalism nor conservatism is nominally linked with a major political force or political group historically, in the way that the left is associated in France with the revolutionary tradition. Apart from the Liberal and Conservative parties in New York, no party has adopted either liberal or conservative as all or part of its label, while in France it is a badge of honor for one side of the spectrum, at least, to brandish the banner of the left.[5] Prior to 1988, when George Bush employed the words *liberal* and *liberalism* as terms of opprobrium, presidential campaigns were not fought with slogans in which liberal-conservative vocabulary played any prominent role. Historians may write the political history of the United States in those terms, but such abstractions serve as an orienting framework for a comparatively small proportion of the citizen body.

To the extent that those concepts seep into the public mind, there is a fuzziness around their edges that contrasts with the more sharply etched distinction that the French electorate senses between left and right (whatever the difficulties it may encounter in trying to specify the differences). The U.S. voters' perceptions of the locations of the presidential candidates on a hypothetical liberal-conservative dimension in 1984 and 1988 were, on the average, not much different from the 1988 French voters' mean perceptions of the positions of the main French presidential candidates on the left-right scale. These were 5.1 for Ronald Reagan and 3.3 for Walter Mondale in 1984, and 5.2 for George Bush and 3.1 for Michael Dukakis in 1988 as compared with 5.5 for Chirac and 3.1 for Mitterrand in France in 1988.[6] There was, however, considerably more dispersion around those U.S. means than there was around the French ones, indicating less consensus within the U.S. electorate than the French one over each candidate's location on the relevant scale.

The greater uncertainty on the part of the U.S. electorate, as compared with the French one, about the ideological orientations of the candidates as expressed in scalar shorthand is illustrated in figure 4.3 and figure 4.4, which present the distributions of perceived locations on the relevant scale of all the 1984 and 1988 U.S. candidates and all the 1988 French candidates for whom we have the appropriate measures, respectively. It is clear at a glance that there was much less agreement among U.S. voters than among French ones over where each of the main presidential candidates stood ideologically. While figure 4.3 shows an identifiable bimodal distribution of perceptions as between the Democratic and Republican candidates, that distribution is much flatter than the equivalent one that appears in figure 4.4 relating to François Mitterrand and Jacques Chirac, the two French front-runners in 1988. Barely 40 percent of the U.S. respondents placed Reagan or Bush at the modal location, while less than 30 percent situated Mondale or Dukakis at their modes. In France, by way of contrast, fully 60 percent of the voters for whom the left-right dimension had some resonance agreed that Mitterrand belonged somewhat left of center, while more than 50 percent believed that Chirac occupied the right. That same sharpness of mass definition applies to the other candidates for whom we have appropriate measures as well. André Lajoinie, the candidate of the Communist party, Raymond Barre, and—especially—Jean-Marie Le Pen, the anti-immigrant demagogue, were all seen by large proportions of the electorate as occupying a distinct scalar location. In the United States, however, even Jesse Jackson, who staked his

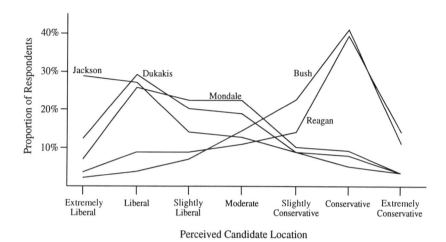

Fig. 4.3. Dispersion of perceived candidate locations, United States, 1984 and 1988

unsuccessful efforts to secure the Democratic party presidential nomination in 1988 on what elite observers understood to be liberal ground (and who is the only person other than the major party candidates themselves for whom we have the necessary measures), was far from clearly perceived in ideological terms by the voters.

We can put a finer touch on the impressions that emerge simply from glancing at figures 4.3 and 4.4 by computing, for each candidate, the coefficient of variation (V), which is simply the standard deviation of the distribution divided by the mean. The larger the coefficient, the greater the dispersion of scores, signifying absence of consensus. In order of increasing dispersion of perceptions, the V for each candidate's distribution was as follows:

Chirac	.140
Barre	.166
Le Pen	.172
Mitterrand	.262
Bush	.263
Reagan	.317
Mondale	.447
Dukakis	.495
Lajoinie	.540
Jackson	.619

Among the French candidates for whom we have measures, only André Lajoinie posed much of a positional problem for the voters who assigned a left-

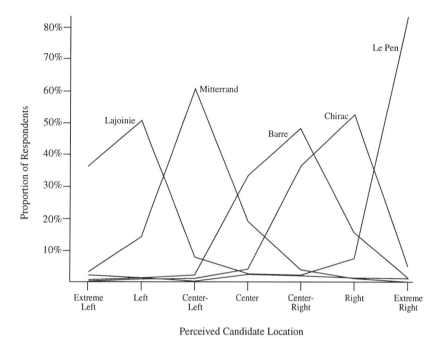

Fig. 4.4. Dispersion of perceived candidate locations, France, 1988

right location to both him and themselves. Lajoinie was the president of the Communist party's parliamentary group in the National Assembly, but he represented a rural district and was virtually unknown to the public prior to the presidential election campaign. On the U.S. side, only George Bush approached the French levels of consensus over the ideological location of the presidential candidates. As figure 4.3 and figure 4.4 show, the general rule was for the mass perceptions of the candidates to be more steeply peaked in France than in the United States.

There is an additional characteristic of the perceptual distribution reported in figures 4.3 and 4.4 that demonstrates the greater clarity of those perceptions in France than in the United States. This relates to the more general property of dispersion, but in a special way. If the ideological shorthand represented by terms such as left and right, or liberal and conservative, has any meaning at all, one elementary component of its meaning should be the notion that the two contrasting poles are mutually exclusive, that left is not right and that liberal is not conservative. In assessing the dispersion of mass perceptions of the ideological locations of the candidates, therefore, we should be attentive not only to overall measures of dispersion but also to the extent that there is ambiguity within the electorate concerning which side of the ideological dichotomy the candidates occupy.[7]

In 1984, about 70 percent of the respondents who claimed to have some location on the liberal-conservative dimension placed Ronald Reagan on its conservative side, and an even larger proportion placed Walter Mondale on the liberal side. But Reagan was also placed among the liberals by some 20 percent of the respondents, and Mondale was assigned to conservative categories by the same proportion of respondents. Mass perceptions were only slightly less ambiguous in 1988. More than 60 percent of the presumably ideologically aware electorate considered Michael Dukakis to be liberal, but more than 20 percent classified him as conservative. Some 70 percent of the voters placed Jesse Jackson among the liberals, but 17 percent thought he was a conservative. Even George Bush, who sought to distinguish himself by vilifying Dukakis for his liberalism, was located by almost 14 percent of the voters on the liberal side of the liberal-conservative scale.[8]

There was far less perceptual crossing of ideological lines in France. Mitterrand was placed on the right by less than 5 percent of the voters; Chirac was placed on the left by less than 2 percent of them. Even Lajoinie, the perceptions of whom showed the widest dispersion relative to the mean, was regarded as a leftist by more than 95 percent of the voters. Similarly large proportions perceived Le Pen to be on the right. For all five French candidates for whom we have measures, the average proportion of deviations from the consensus placement (left or right) was less than 5 percent; for the five U.S. candidates, the average proportion of deviations from the basic liberal or conservative assignment was closer to 20 percent. In France, left is left and right is right, and the twain seldom meet. In the United States, the ideological geography is a lot less distinct.

In fact, the proportions of deviations from the consensus placements of the candidates, on left or right, or as liberal or conservative, may well be even larger than the figures we have so far cited. Butler and Stokes (1969, 206–8) found, in an analogous analysis of the British electorate's perceptions of the left-right location of the Labor party, that some 11 percent of the respondents in their survey placed Labor on the right. Inasmuch as the overwhelming consensus among the more politically involved voters was that the Labor party was on the left, Butler and Stokes reasoned that those 11 percent of the sample electorate must have simply been guessing.

But, they argued further, if one assumes that a voter who guesses the left-right location of a party is as likely to err in one direction as in the other, 11 percent of the respondents who placed the Labor party on the left must also have been guessing, bringing the total number of guessers to more than 20 percent of the electorate. Following that line of reasoning, we would find that an average of about 40 percent of the U.S. voters who claimed to have some liberal-conservative position of their own were simply guessing at the ideological stance of the major presidential candidates in 1984 and 1988, as opposed to some 10 percent of the French electorate that was in the same situation.

Without attributing excessive importance to those absolute numbers, we may safely proceed to the central conclusion that emerges from this part of our analysis. The ideological positions of the candidates are more clearly delineated in the voters' minds in France than in the United States. Moreover, the greater degree of consensus within the French electorate over where the candidates stand ideologically rests on a broader mass base than does the lesser degree of consensus over the same matters in the United States. Ideological orientations, therefore, are more likely to be a factor in electoral choice for the French electorate than for the U.S. one. It remains, however, for us to determine (in chap. 7) just how powerful a factor they may be in either country.

Ideological Positioning versus Party Identification

We will compare the orienting capacity of ideological positions against that of party identifications in more than one context in this book. At this point, we will make such a comparison in simplified form by reporting, for both France and the United States, the relationship between the decisive, two-candidate vote in 1988 and party identification, on the one hand, and the relevant form of ideological location, on the other hand.

The measures are among the simplest we will use in this study. Only respondents who cast valid ballots for one candidate or the other, in each country, will be included. Spontaneous reports of self-location on the liberal-conservative dimension will serve as ideological positioning for the U.S. respondents, while self-assigned locations on the left-right scale (including those of uninvolved centrists) will constitute ideological location for the French sample.[9] Party identification for the U.S. respondents is registered in the form of the familiar seven-point scale combining direction and strength of party identification (excluding the few cases of apoliticals). To match this standard U.S. measure, we have created an analogous variable for France. This variable was formed, first, by sorting our record of nominal party identifications into two categories, the leftist parties and the others. A three-level measure of strength of party identification was then applied to distinguish strong identifiers, weak identifiers, and leaners. Respondents without any party identification were classified as independents. Respondents who replied to the question about party identification by referring to a left-right location or a political leader were excluded from the analysis.

This measure of two-party party identification for France has two main advantages. First, its structure is similar to that of the standard summary party identification measure for the United States, in that it runs from strong attach-

TABLE 4.1. Association between Candidate Choice and Summary Party Identification and Ideological Position, France (Second Ballot) and the United States, 1988 (τc)

	France	United States
Summary party identification	.90 (89%)	.80 (100%)
Ideological position	.86 (97%)	.55 (79%)

Note: Numbers in parentheses indicate proportion of actual voters included in analysis.

ment to a left-wing party, across no partisan identification at all, to strong iden-tification with a rightist party, in the same number of steps (seven) that the U.S. measure includes.[10] Secondly, this summary party identification measure is, for practical purposes, totally independent of the measure of left-right self-location with which it is being compared. The only way in which mass left-right per-ceptions intrude into the measure of summary party identification is in our basic distinction between left-wing and right-wing parties. This does not, of course, mean that partisanship and left-right positioning are not related in the public mind. They clearly are: the correlation (r) between our French summary party identification variable and their own left-right variable (including uninvolved centrists) is a healthy .77 (as compared with the lesser correlation of .41 between liberal-conservative locations and party identification in the United States). What it does mean is that left-right scores are not built into the measure in advance, which is a problem that we will face later in trying to put a finer edge on French partisan attachments.

Table 4.1 sets out the degree of association, for France and the United States, between the decisive, two-candidate vote and, separately, ideological location and party identification. The measures are both staggeringly high for France, with party identification having a marginal and probably insignificant edge. For the United States, there is more variation, in the direction that our ear-lier discussion of the liberal-conservative dimension foreshadowed. Party iden-tification correlates highly with the presidential vote; liberal-conservative posi-tioning correlates with the vote less closely, and the comparatively low incidence of persons who locate themselves spontaneously in those terms also reduces the proportion of the actual voters included in the analysis.

Our provisional conclusion, therefore, is that to the extent that the compet-ing roles of ideological positioning and partisan attachments can be couched in racetrack terms, the two basic attitudes run neck and neck in France. The small field is more spread out in the United States. There, party identification has a comfortable lead (as decades of careful scholarship should lead one to expect), while liberal-conservative sentiments run a distant, if honorable, second.

CHAPTER 5

Issues and Candidates

One of the basic tenets of democratic theory is that popular election is the best means so far devised to ensure that there is some correspondence between government policy and the wishes of the electorate. The stakes in terms of public policy alternatives are almost always high at a democratic election, and they are nowhere higher than in connection with the popular election of the constitutionally powerful chief executives of France and the United States.

Of course, the extent to which presidential candidates articulate their positions on issues, particularly but not exclusively in the United States, is highly variable. Moreover, the candidates' views of what the important issues are can be very elastic, with the result that issues are emphasized that have little relationship to probable public policy. It is recognition of the importance of elections as a device for giving the electorate some minimal say in the direction of public policy, in the face of the sometimes notorious efforts of candidates to avoid committing themselves to little beyond benign generalities, that regularly produces the litany in the elite press of both the United States and France calling for more attention by the candidates to the issues.

The possibility for issue considerations to play a major, independent role in the electoral process is, however, unevenly distributed throughout the electorate. Before issues can have an effect, several conditions must be satisfied. The two most elementary (and familiar) conditions are that the voter must have a position on the issue and must be aware of the positions on that same issue of at least those candidates among whom, for whatever reason, the voter believes that he or she must choose. We will investigate the extent to which these conditions were satisfied by the French and U.S. electorates of 1988, but it should come as no surprise that the proportion of voters who do satisfy them varies directly with the level of political involvement (Converse and Pierce 1986, chap. 9).

Those voters who are in a position to choose between candidates on the basis of issues still require some selection mechanism to help them decide which candidate has a position on any given issue that is most similar to their own. There are two competing theories concerning what may be going on in the voters' minds in this regard. One theory holds that the voters make an estimate of how close the competing candidates' issue positions are to their own, and then select the candidate whose position they perceive to be closest. The other theory assumes that what the voters are most interested in is whether the candidates are on the same side of an issue as they are themselves. After determining which candidates are on their side, the voters then select the one they perceive to be most strongly committed to that side of the issue. We will examine those two theories with a view to showing their implications for the selection of a preferred candidate in both France and the United States. The results will parallel those of the analysis earlier in the chapter in that they too point to the conclusion that issue considerations are not likely to play any major independent role for more than a limited sector of the voting population.

U.S. and French Issue Batteries

Since the 1970s, the series of U.S. NES surveys have posed questions, in polarized seven-point form, designed to elicit the positions of the respondents on various issues of public policy as well as their perceptions of where the main candidates and parties stand on the same issue scales.[1] Some issues are included regularly, with the result that we have an invaluable historic record of mass opinion on those issues, as well as the public's views of the candidates and parties in those issue terms. Other issues are included only for particular elections because they are expected to play a considerable role in the circumstances, and then are dropped when those circumstances change. For the United States, therefore, we have a large database on which to draw in trying to sort out the role of issues at any given presidential election. The only problem, somewhat paradoxically, is that the lode is so rich that it may contain more than is relevant for any given electoral moment. Candidates and parties may not always emphasize the issues about which we have survey data, with the result that there is sometimes little or no actual communication between the political elites and the mass electorate over issues that are recorded in our remarkable U.S. inventory.[2]

When we were constructing the questionnaire for our 1988 French survey, it was clear from the start that given the time and cost constraints imposed by the multiplicity of French parties and presidential candidates, it would not be possible to match the U.S. issue battery in size. In the event, however, while our budgetary constraints surely set limits to what we could achieve, we suffered no undue deprivation in the domain of issue positions. Early on, we made a decision that we would include a question relating to government subsidies for church schools and then set our sights on adding questions concerning three other issues. Our assumption was that the hoary issue of religious schools would provide a baseline against which we could compare mass opinion and mass perceptions of the candidates' and parties' opinions on other issues.[3] At the same time, we thought it was essential that the other issues be issues over which at least some of the candidates were actively engaged during the election campaign, so that we could reasonably expect attentive members of the electorate to have some idea of where the candidates stood on those issues. This proved to be a harder prescription to fill than we had thought it would be. The immigration issue, insisted on by Jean-Marie Le Pen, clearly fitted the bill, and so did the issue of public ownership of industry, which had been a political football since 1981.[4] But that is where the list ended. We followed the election campaign closely, but beyond those two issues, no aspect of public policy was dwelt on at sufficient length or with sufficient clarity to warrant us including it in our issue battery. We had four slots available, but we filled only three of them.

Mass Issue Positions

In the NES surveys in the United States, when respondents are asked to locate themselves on any given issue scale (including the liberal-conservative scale), they are offered an easy way out of answering the question with the phrase "or haven't you thought much about this?" No such escape clause was included in the questions eliciting issue positions in France, so we will not insist on the comparatively small differences we find in the incidence of valid responses in the two countries. Taking "haven't thought much about it" and "don't know" together, a mean of 14 percent of the U.S. respondents were without any position on the battery of eight issue-scale questions posed in 1988 *prior to* the election, as compared with slightly less than 8 percent "don't know" across the three issue questions asked immediately *after* the French presidential election of the same year. In fact, there is probably less difference here than meets the eye. There was considerable variation in the incidence of nonresponse to the three French issue questions. Only some 6 percent of respondents had no opinion on the inflammable question of whether immigrants should be sent back home or helped to become integrated into French society. Even fewer French respondents professed not to have an opinion on government subsidies to church schools, but that issue has been around for more than a century. But more than 12 percent of respondents had no opinion on whether the public sector in France should be enlarged or reduced, a figure that is close to the U.S. mean. If we had included more prosaic issues of this sort, the mean proportion of don't knows in France might well have matched that for the United States.

Polarization of Mass Opinion

Whatever the case with regard to the incidence of mass opinion on specific issues in the two countries, there is greater polarization in France among the people who do profess to have opinions than there is in the United States. We have measured mass polarization over issues in two ways. The first is by examining the ratio of respondents taking extreme positions (e.g., selecting points 1 or 7 on the seven-point scale) to those taking a neutral position (e.g., point 4), which we formed simply by dividing the proportion of extreme positions on each issue by the proportion of neutral positions. The second is by examining the size of the standard deviation of each distribution relative to the size of the mean. Dividing the former by the latter produces a coefficient of variation (V) that enables us to compare the variability of each measure. The two methods produce index scores that are highly correlated with each other ($r = .83$), but they represent two facets of the same phenomenon. Table 5.1 reports the two measures for each issue considered for France and the United States.

More French voters than U.S. ones, on the average, took extreme positions on our batteries of issues. The mean proportion for France was slightly more than 34 percent; for the United States it was less than 28 percent, and would have been some three points lower still if it were not for the highly one-sided (favorable) views of the U.S. electorate toward equal rights for women.[5] Even including that issue, however, the mean ratio for the eight U.S. issues is 1.29, compared with 1.66 for the three French issues. Excluding women's rights, the only U.S. issue that lies within the range of scores for the three French issues is that relating to government versus private health insurance.

Our second indicator of polarization, the coefficient of variation (V), tells much the same story. The coefficient for the issue of women's rights in the United States is again off the map, but even including it in the package, the U.S. mean is .437 compared with a mean of .489 for France.

TABLE 5.1.   Polarization of Mass Opinion, France and the United States, 1988

Issue	Ratio of Extreme Positions to Neutral Positions	Coefficient of Variation
France		
Subsidies for church schools	1.74	.420
Size of the public sector	1.65	.511
Policy toward immigrants	1.58	.536
United States		
Spending on services	0.52	.416
Defense spending	0.47	.279
Health insurance	1.74	.381
Government provide jobs	1.22	.420
Policy toward Russia	0.92	.474
Women's rights	2.99	.708
Government help blacks	1.26	.391
Government help minorities	1.20	.431

An analysis of this sort is, of course, highly sensitive to issue selection. With a little effort, one could no doubt come up with a few more issues on which opinion in the United States is as one-sided as it is with respect to women's rights, or issues for which French opinion would be distributed in a much more rectangular manner than it is on the three issues we have included. Moreover, the issue battery for France is regrettably small. Yet there is also a sense in which the eight U.S. issues and the three French issues are typical. They were not selected with a view toward showing that one system appears to be more polarized on the mass level than the other. On the contrary, the issues were chosen on common principles (that they be relevant to current political debate and be expressible in polar form) that lend themselves to cross-national comparison.

On this assumption, it is provisionally clear that mass opinion on political issues tends to be more sharply divided in France than in the United States. Nothing ordained in advance that this would be the result. On the contrary, given the U.S. two-party system, as compared with the French multiparty system, it would have been reasonable to hypothesize that opinion would be more evenly distributed in France than in the United States.

Organizing Frameworks for Mass Issue Opinions

In the preceding chapter, which discussed ideological orientations in the guise of positioning on a hypothetical left-right dimension for France, and a liberal-conservative dimension for the United States, we considered three aspects of the subject. We recalled, first, that previous relevant research shows that the degree to which self-professed locations on one scale or the other reflect well-developed conceptions of broad policy alternatives is severely limited throughout the mass public. Secondly, to the extent that there is such a correspondence between left-right (or liberal-conservative) positioning and substantive policy choices, it parallels gradations in political involvement, with only the comparatively narrow stratum of most involved citizens displaying the minimal degree of coherence in general ideological and specific policy outlooks that professional observers tend to expect when they conceptualize a relationship between ideology and issue positions. Finally, we underscored the now familiar issue of the respective importance of ideological positioning, on the one hand, and party identification, on the other hand, in affecting the behavior of the mass electorate, by comparing the degree of association between each of those two variables and the decisive 1988 presidential vote in France and the United States. Here we will pursue the comparison between ideological positioning and party identification, this time in their roles as organizing forces for mass attitudes on the specific political issues that are central to this chapter.

The basic form of the analysis is similar to but not identical with the one employed in Converse and Pierce (1986, 233–40), where the magnitudes of the associations between self-locations on the left-right dimension and positions on specific issues were compared among three strata of the sample French electorate, reflecting degrees of political involvement, and a sample of parliamentary elites. The main objective of that particular display was to demonstrate that the extent to which ideological positioning operates as a constraint on specific issue positions was much greater among the political elites than it was even among the top quarter of the mass electorate in terms of political involvement. We have no elite data for 1988 that can be compared with our findings for the mass electorate. Moreover, the earlier analysis rested on a rich inventory of specific issue positions while, as we have already indicated, we are comparatively issue-poor for the 1988 French presidential election. But we will build on the earlier work in two ways. First, we will cast our comparison of the operational effects of left-right positioning with those of party identification in identical terms. Converse and Pierce (1986, 252–54) compared partisanship with left-right locations as a cue to mass issue positions, and found the former to be somewhat more reliable than the latter among respondents having both attributes; but that analysis was not framed in the same manner as the comparison of the linkage between left-right positions and specific policy issues for the mass (stratified by political involvement). We will adopt that latter format for our own comparison of the two potential organizing forces. Secondly, we have repeated the same basic analysis for the United States, in order to generate a full cross-national comparison. As a result, we should be able to generalize reliably about the comparative importance of ideology on the one hand, and partisanship, on the other hand, in structuring the electorate's positions on specific political issues.

The results of the analysis for France are set forth in figure 5.1, which reports the associations between positions on our three specific issues, and both left-right locations and party identifications (for respondents who professed both attributes), for each of three strata of the French electorate in terms of political interest.[6] Figure 5.1 warrants examination in some detail. The main question at issue is the relative importance of left-right positioning and partisanship as an organizing framework for issue positions, but there are variations by issue and by stratum that merit separate attention.

First, it is apparent that the capacity of both left-right positioning and party identification to structure people's attitudes on specific issues was as sensitive to differentiation by degree of political interest in the circumstances of 1988 as it had been during the late 1960s. The matching associations between both potentially constraining and orienting forces and particular issue positions regularly become closer as we mount the simple three-step ladder of political interest, just as they did for the left-right measure alone in the earlier Converse and Pierce (1986) study.

Secondly, the issue that is most sensitive both to left-right positioning and to partisanship, at all levels of political interest, is the size of the public sector.

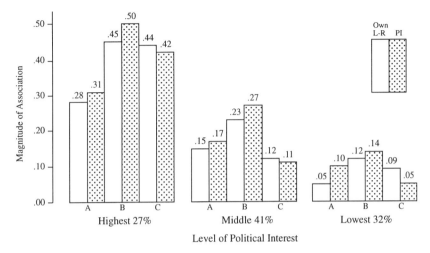

Fig. 5.1. Own left-right positions (L-R) and party identification (PI) as organizing frameworks for mass issue positions, by level of political interest, France, 1988: *A*, subsidies for church schools; *B*, size of the public sector; *C*, policy toward immigrants

The traditionally divisive issue of government subsidies for religious schools runs a distant second. In the basic Converse and Pierce (1986) study, the religious issue was more closely associated with left-right locations than was any other issue tested. That study did not include any questions about the size of the public sector, although it did include questions about attitudes toward the distribution of income and toward unions. Almost surely, the greater salience of attitudes toward the public sector in 1988 reflects the extent to which it had divided both the contending political parties and the probable (and actual) presidential candidates since 1981, and particularly after 1986, when the Chirac government proceeded to reprivatize industries that had been nationalized by the Socialist majority after 1981. The political pendulum that the French refer to as *l'alternance*, which began to swing only in 1981, sharpened mass perceptions of where parties and leaders stood on the issue of the size of the public sector and where those positions fitted within the left-right framework. The framework and substance of political action after 1981 gave an economically relevant meaning to left-right imagery that it had lacked even in the highly charged period of the late 1960s.

Thirdly, attitudes concerning policy toward immigrants behave quite differently from positions on government subsidies for religious schools and the size of the public sector. The latter two issues are linked to both left-right locations and party identifications in parallel fashion, at successively lower levels of magnitude as one descends the ladder of political interest. The immigration issue is more independent of left-right and partisan locations throughout the electorate as a whole. Among the quarter of our sample electorate that is most interested in politics, the magnitude of the association between positions on immigration policy and both left-right locations and partisanship is larger than it is for the religious issue and virtually as great as it is for the issue of the size of the public sector. For the two remaining strata of the electorate in terms of political interest, however, neither left-right positioning nor partisanship supply the voters with much in the way of cues about where they stand on the question of policy toward immigrants.

The religious schools question and the issue of the size of the public sector are classic issues that have historically been both associated with left-right ideology and ingrained in party programs, and they project themselves in those forms in our figure. Immigration is a new issue without any long-established niche in the architecture of French ideology and partisan policy. The most interested French citizens had little difficulty fitting this new issue into either the left-right dimension or the partisan spectrum, but the remaining three-fourths of the active electorate were all at sea. For them, immigration policy was a free-floating, autonomous issue domain, outside the parameters that normally structure, however weakly, their positions on broad policy issues.

Finally, we can return to the question with which we began this section: which organizing framework—left-right positioning or partisanship—does more to structure the issue positions of the French voters? For the most interested fourth of the electorate, there is little difference between the two. This is not particularly surprising. Among this segment of voters, the correlation between left-right positioning and left-right party identification is very strong in the first place ($r = .87$). At lower levels of political interest, however, the answer to the question depends on whether we refer to the classic issues of government subsidies for religious schools and the size of the public sector, or the newer issue of policy toward immigrants. As we have already noted, mass positions on the latter issue among the medium and least involved portions of the electorate are almost wholly independent of left-right considerations. For the two classic issues, however, the pattern is quite intelligible, if not exactly striking. The power of both left-right locations and partisanship is greater among the medium involved than among the least involved voters. And among each segment of the electorate, partisanship is a marginally stronger organizing force than left-right positioning.[7]

Given the small size of our issue battery for France, we do not want to generalize broadly about the relative potency of ideology and partisanship in giving coherence to the positions of the mass electorate on issues of public policy in that country. At the same time, our findings are consistent enough with earlier research for us to repeat the admonition that claims about the superiority of ideology in this domain should be regarded with considerable skepticism.

Ideology and Partisanship in the United States

We have performed the same kind of analysis for the United States that we did for France, employing self-ascribed liberal-conservative positions to represent ideology and the standard summary party identification scale as the potential organizing forces. Given the larger number of issues in the U.S. battery than in the French one, the U.S. results are somewhat more complicated than the French ones, but they can be easily summarized.

First, we find the familiar pattern of generally decreasing association between specific issue positions and either ideology or partisanship as we descend the scale of political interest. This, of course, is not simply a French-U.S. similarity but a well-established political phenomenon generally.

Secondly, there is a sharp distinction in the behavior of two groups of issues. One group, consisting of attitudes toward government services, defense, health insurance, and the role of government in promoting jobs, is almost uniformly more closely related to partisanship than to ideology at each of three levels of political interest.[8] The other group, which includes positions on the government helping blacks, the government helping minorities generally, attitudes toward Russia, and attitudes toward women's rights, reveals the opposite pattern: they are more sensitive to ideology than to partisanship among each of our three strata.

Thirdly, regardless of which group of specific issues we take into account, regardless of whether we consider liberal-conservative positioning or party identification, and regardless of the level of interest of the voters we include, the degree of association between those general orienting factors and the specific issue positions is considerably less than it is for the corresponding category of French voters. Prior research has, or at least should have, prepared us for learning that the liberal-conservative dimension plays a smaller role in structuring mass issue positions in the United States than the left-right dimension does in shaping them in France. We may have been less prepared to learn that partisanship also plays a greater role in that domain in France than it does in the United States. Even among the most interested U.S. citizens, relatively speaking, the distribution of attitudes on matters of public policy is more dis-associated from the relevant ideological underpinnings and organized partisan structure than it is in France.

Mass Perceptions of Candidate Issue Positions

The degree to which policy issues can play a role in electoral choices not only depends on the extent to which the electorate holds opinions on those policy issues but also on the capacity of the electorate to identify the competing candidates with particular issue positions. We have measures of the extent and nature of such candidate-issue linkages among the 1988 French and U.S. electorates, cast in comparable terms. In both the U.S. NES sample survey and our own French sample survey, after the respondents were asked to locate themselves on each seven-point issue scale, they were asked where they would place the principal presidential candidates on the same scale. It is, therefore, possible for us to compare the main aspects of candidate-issue linkage in the two countries. For the United States, we have 14 observations: seven issues for each of two candidates.[9] For France, we have 12 observations: three issues for each of four candidates.[10]

The Incidence of Candidate-Issue Linkages

The mean proportion of the U.S. electorate that failed to link George Bush with the seven issues in the U.S. battery for 1988 was 30 percent; for Michael Dukakis it was slightly larger, some 33 percent. The corresponding figures for our four French candidates and three issues were somewhat smaller, a mean of about 24 percent across the set. We do not, however, want to emphasize that cross-national differential any more than we wanted to emphasize the difference in the incidence of personal opinions on the issues, referred to earlier in this chapter. The data collection process differed in the two countries. In the U.S. NES survey, respondents were given the chance to exit gracefully from each question eliciting their own position on an issue scale, and if they availed themselves of the opportunity, they were not asked where they would locate the candidates and parties on the same scale. We have, of course, excluded from the French linkage analysis the respondents who did not express an opinion on any given issue but, as we pointed out earlier, our questionnaire did not contain the "or haven't you thought much about this" escape clause. If it had done so, we might well have registered more "don't know" category replies.

More interesting than the perhaps spurious cross-national difference in the incidence of candidate-issue linkages is the basic similarity between the two countries in the relationship between the incidence of candidate-issue linkages and the level of political interest. Table 5.2 reports the proportions of voters that linked candidates with issues, in each country, by the number of linkages made and by level of political interest. The association between political interest and the capacity to link candidates with policy issues emerges clearly for both France and the United States.[11] There is only one departure from linearity in table 5.2, in the last column, relating to the least politically interested tier of U.S. citizens, among whom the distribution of candidate-issue linkages may approach randomness.

TABLE 5.2. Proportions of Voters Linking Issues with Main Presidential
Candidates, by Level of Political Interest, France and the United States,
1988, in Percentage

	Level of Political Interest		
Number of Linkages	High	Medium	Low
France			
10–12	87	68	52
4–9	11	29	33
0–3	2	3	15
	100	100	100
N	(226)	(388)	(397)
United States			
11–14	74	55	36
4–10	20	33	28
0–3	6	12	36
	100	100	100
N	(567)	(960)	(509)

There is considerable variation in the French linkage data, both by issue
and by candidate. We have already seen that there was not a large difference in
the mean proportion of voters who linked Bush and Dukakis with the various
U.S. issues. There was, of course, some variation by issue, but the only notable
case concerned the issue of government policy toward Russia. Some 70 percent
of the sample electorate linked Bush with that issue compared with only 61 percent who linked it with Dukakis. The gap in the proportions of linkages of the
two candidates with the same issue was much smaller in all the other cases.

The French situation was rather more complex. Table 5.3 sets out the proportions of our sample French electorate who linked each of the four main presidential candidates with each of the three issues tested, as well as the mean proportions for each candidate and each issue. Two aspects of this table are of
particular interest. First, the variations in the mean proportions of linkages by
candidate express what one would intuitively expect, given the gross levels of
visibility of the candidates. The largest proportions are attached to the two candidates who competed with each other at the runoff ballot: François Mitterrand,
the incumbent president since 1981, and Jacques Chirac, the incumbent prime
minister since 1986. Former prime minister Raymond Barre follows Chirac.
Jean-Marie Le Pen, who made opposition to immigrants virtually his only
theme, brings up the rear in overall issue-familiarity. The differences along this
scale are not large, and their neatness may be purely accidental, but they are
certainly intelligible.

At the same time, table 5.3 demonstrates how successful Le Pen was in making the immigration issue salient to the public and identifying himself with it. More people linked a candidate with the immigration issue, on the average, than with either of the other two issues tested. And while some 90 percent of the sample electorate linked the immigration issue with Le Pen, less than 60 percent linked either of the other two issues with him. Our issue battery for France is too small to permit broad generalization, but within the obvious limits we have a clear demonstration of the extent to which Le Pen was a single-issue candidate in the minds of the French public (Mitra 1988).

Polarization of Perceived Candidate Issue Positions

In chapter 4, in which we discussed broad ideological orientations in the form of left-right locations in France and liberal-conservative positioning in the United States, we briefly touched on the issue of how polarized the mass electorate of each country perceived its main presidential candidates to be. We noted that the French electorate's mean perceptions of the left-right locations of Jacques Chirac and François Mitterrand in 1988 were very similar to the U.S. electorate's mean perceptions of the liberal-conservative positioning of George Bush and Michael Dukakis in the same year, and of Ronald Reagan and Walter Mondale in 1984. At the same time, we pointed out that there was more fuzziness to the perceptions of the U.S. electorate than to those of the French one, in that there was less consensus among U.S. voters over the ideological locations of the candidates.

Here we raise the question of the extent to which the electorates of the two countries perceived the main presidential candidates to be polarized in their positions on specific issues. Our database will be eight issues for the United

TABLE 5.3. Proportions of French Electorate Linking Issues with Major Presidential Candidates, France 1988, in Percentage

	Candidates				
Issue	Jacques Chirac	François Mitterrand	Raymond Barre	Jean-Marie Le Pen	Mean
Subsidies for church schools	74	78	72	59	71
Size of the public sector	79	81	75	56	73
Policy toward immigrants	84	89	79	90	86
Mean	79	83	75	68	

States and the three familiar issues for France.[12] For the United States we will, of course, be concerned with mass perceptions of where George Bush and Michael Dukakis stood on each issue. For France, we will be concerned with perceptions relating to François Mitterrand and Jacques Chirac, the two candidates who survived into the runoff ballot.

Our measure of polarization is simply the difference in the mean locations on the various issue scales assigned to the competing candidates in each country by those members of the electorate who themselves had a position on the same issue and rendered an opinion about where *both* of the contending candidates stood on the same issue. Taking a mean difference of 1.70 as the cutoff point, the ordering of polarization in perceptions of candidate positions, by issue, is as follows:

Size of the public sector (France)	2.95
Policy toward immigrants (France)	2.15
National health insurance (United States)	2.02
Defense spending (United States)	1.98
Subsidies for religious schools (France)	1.79
Government job guarantees (United States)	1.73

The issue of the size of the public sector in France, which we have already indicated was the central pivot around which political conflict turned between 1981 and 1988, heads the list by a wide margin. Where policy conflict is clear and recent, it registers with the mass public. French policy toward immigrants, the issue of how to provide health insurance in the United States, and defense spending in the United States all cluster next within a narrow range, although the conflict over immigration in France is marginally sharper than that over the U.S. issues. The greatest surprise, given the historic importance of the religious schools issue in France, is the relatively low level of polarization around that issue. It is on a par with the basic economic issue of the responsibility of the government to provide jobs and help maintain a decent standard of living in the United States.

On their face, these measures suggest that by and large there is not a great deal of difference in the degree of perceived candidate polarization on major issues in France and the United States. That would, however, be an erroneous conclusion, for the simple reason that the figures cited rest on rather different proportions of the electorate in the two countries. The French scores for the immigration, public sector, and religious schools issues are based on 84 percent, 79 percent, and 71 percent of our sample French electorate respectively. The only U.S. score that rests on a similarly large proportion of the sample U.S. electorate is the one that relates to the defense issue, which is based on 70 percent of the respondents. The score for the jobs issue reflects the views of less than 65 percent of the sample, while the score for the health insurance issue, which is the highest of all the U.S. measures, rests on only 57 percent of the U.S. sample. Some of these cross-national differences may be due to the difference in questionnaire design to which we have already referred, but it remains possible that more French than U.S. voters see the competing presidential candidates as standing for sharply opposing positions on major issues.

Issue-Based Candidate Preferences

To this point in this chapter, we have examined the positions of the French and U.S. electorates on various policy issues as well as the perceptions of those electorates of the positions of the main presidential candidates on the same issues. It remains for us to consider how the voters in each country may employ those two separate pieces of information—their own positions on an issue and their perceptions of where the candidates stand on the same issue—in deciding which candidates to support. It is clear enough that if issues play any role in the voters' choice of a candidate, the mental process that the voters employ must involve comparing the positions of the candidates and then determining which candidate holds the position that is most similar to their own. There is a problem, however, in that there is more than one way in which a candidate's position can be similar to that of a voter. Before we can comfortably leave the subject matter of this chapter, therefore, we must make at least a provisional determination of how the voters assess the candidates in terms of issues, and that requires an examination of alternate models of how the voters decide, on the basis of issues, who their preferred candidates are.

Alternative Analytical Models: Proximity vs. Direction

There are two ways of approaching the role of issues in candidate preference. The standard method has been based on the *proximity* of voter and candidate issue positions. When the issues are scaled (as are those considered here), it is assumed that a voter's preferred candidate will be the one the voter locates closest to the position on the issue scale that the voter selects as his or her own. This method is sometimes referred to as the least-distance technique: the issue position of the preferred candidate is less distant than that of any other candidate from the voter's own issue position.

More recently, it has been argued (Rabinowitz and MacDonald 1989; MacDonald, Listhaug, and Rabinowitz 1991) that the crucial factor in issue-based political preference is not the proximity of the voter to the object of political choice on any given issue scale, but rather the commonality of issue direction and intensity as between the voter and the object of choice. According to this notion, "when voters choose, they do not ask, 'How close are your positions to mine?' but rather, 'Are you on my side?'" (MacDonald, Listhaug, and Rabinowitz 1991, 1126). In this formulation, the voters select a preferred candidate on issue grounds by first determining which candidates are on the same side of a given issue as they are, and then selecting the one who appears to be most firmly wedded to that position.

We have applied both models of issue-based candidate selection, the proximity model and the directional model, to our 1988 data for France and the United States. The basic data for both models are the voters' self-placements on the various seven-point issue scales plus their locations of the candidates on the same scales. Each model, however, requires us to extract a particular set of scores to express the process the model represents.

The proximity model is the simpler of the two. To apply that model, we simply compare each respondent's self-ascribed location on a given issue scale with that respondent's perceptions of the locations of all the candidates on the same scale, and designate as the preferred candidate the candidate whose perceived location is least distant from the voter's own. Of course, ties can complicate the results, and we will return to that aspect of the situation. Here we need only to sketch the basic process, pointing out that for the proximity model the issue scales, which range from 1 to 7, are employed literally, and the resultant distance scores can vary from 0 to 6. A distance of 0 means that the voter and the candidate occupy the same location on the issue scale; a score of 6 means that the two could not be further apart on the issue; and intermediate scores represent intermediate degrees of closeness between voter and candidate in terms of the issue.

For the directional model, the scores from the same seven-point scale must be transformed into clearly opposing values, with the result that they become: $-3, -2, -1, 0, +1, +2, +3$. And while for the proximity model, one simply takes the difference between a respondent's own location on the untransformed issue scale and that respondent's perception of the issue position of a candidate on the same scale, for the directional model one multiplies those two transformed values, creating what the models' inventors refer to as a scalar product. These products can, of course, range from $+9$ to -9, signifying the magnitude of the impact of the issue on the attraction (or repugnance) of the candidate to the voter. A scalar product of $+9$ means that the voter sees eye to eye with the candidate on a given issue, to the maximum measurable extent, with regard both to direction and intensity. A product of -9 signifies that the voter is completely at odds with the candidate over a particular issue. Intermediate scores reflect lesser degrees either of agreement (positive scores) or discord (negative scores) between voter and candidate.

Before proceeding to apply the two models to the 1988 French and U.S. presidential elections, we should pause long enough to make two preliminary statements to prepare the reader for what follows.

First, the logic of the directional model, and the scoring conventions that are required to express the model empirically, will produce far fewer voters who can be counted as likely to be moved in their selection of a preferred candidate by issue considerations than the proximity model (and its empirical expression) will do. If all that counts is "which side are you on?" then the comparatively large numbers of voters who place themselves, or locate candidates, at the midpoint of an issue scale do not count as "issue voters." The elimination of those voters is carried out by means of assigning them (or the matching candidates) a score of 0 which, of course, must produce a result of 0 when multiplied by any other integer. The result is that for voters who place themselves at the 0 midpoint, the preference rankings of all candidates are tied at 0.

The proximity model, in contrast, assumes that closeness counts wherever it can, including between voters who locate either themselves or candidates (or both) at the scalar midpoint of 4 for any given issue. Indeed, pairs of voters and candidates who are both placed at the midpoint (by the voter) are counted as being maximally close to one another on the particular issue just as they would be if they were both placed (by the voter) at the more extreme scores of 1 or 7. We can, therefore, expect a larger proportion of issue voters to show up in our applications of the proximity model than in our representations of the directional model. Many observations that the proximity model treats as determining are discarded by the directional model as being irrelevant.

The second preliminary comment refers to the possibility of ties for the designation of preferred candidates on any particular issue. It is perfectly possible for voters to see no difference between the candidates on any given issue. Indeed, it is a recurrent complaint among elite observers in the United States that there is no difference to be seen between the competing candidates on one issue or another. When voters assign the same issue position to more than one candidate, as well as any score to themselves, there will be ties, whether one is applying the proximity model or the directional model.

The number of ties, other things being equal, can be expected to increase as the number of candidates increases. In the United States, where there were only two presidential candidates in 1988, there could be ties only between those two candidates. In France, however, there were nine candidates, of which we have measurements for the four most important. The number of possible combinations of ties among four candidates is 11. We can, therefore, expect a much more complicated pattern of issue-based candidate preferences in France than in the United States.

The Models Compared

In applying the proximity and directional models to our data relating to the 1988 French and U.S. presidential elections, we first generated the preferred candidate (or candidates) for each respondent, for each issue, according to the assumptions of each model. For the proximity model, we determined for each voter which candidate's perceived location on an issue scale was the closest to the position of that voter. For applying the directional model, we identified the candidate whose scalar product was the largest among the candidates for whom the voter assigned a location on the same issue. Then, we computed the proportions of voters who preferred each candidate or combination of candidates (or none at all) for each separate issue. The results for France are summarized in table 5.4. Those for the United States appear in table 5.5. We will discuss the French situation first, and then compare it with the U.S. case.

Three aspects of table 5.4 stand out, each of which we should be prepared for on the basis of findings reported earlier in this chapter. One is the great fragmentation of issue-based candidate preferences. The second is the larger proportion of four-way ties produced by the directional model compared with the proximity model. The third is the relatively great extent to which Jean-Marie Le Pen's emphasis on immigration as an issue resonated with the French electorate.

The multiple patterns of candidate preferences, which result from ties between candidates, are characteristic of both the proximity model and the directional model. Neither model generated a single candidate who was the preference of more than 31 percent of the sample electorate for any of the three issues. The fragmentation would have been even more marked if we had been able to include the five minor candidates who were excluded from the analysis.

A substantial proportion of the ties that contribute to the variegated pattern of issue-based candidate preferences are illogical ties between Mitterrand, on the one hand, and one or more right-wing candidates, on the other hand. Between 13 percent and 17 percent of the voters, depending on the issue, are in that category for the proximity model. Those ties, as well as others among purely rightist candidates, result to a considerable extent because the proximity model registers people who placed themselves as well as at least two other candidates at the midpoint of the seven-point issue scales. It is highly unlikely that issues actually played any real role in those voters' selection of a preferred candidate. The greater probability is that the scoring conventions have simply counted marks of uncertainty as expressions of preferences.

As we would expect, many more four-way ties between Mitterrand and rightist candidates emerge from the directional model. That is, as we have seen, because voters who score themselves at midpoint automatically generate such ties because the scalar product for each candidate must be 0. The second main feature of table 5.4, therefore, is that the directional model produces a large proportion of what amount to missing data equivalents as compared with the proximity model.

TABLE 5.4. Issue-Based Preferred Candidate Combinations, by Analytic Model and Issue, France, 1988, in Percentage

Preferred Candidate(s)	Proximity Model			Directional Model		
	Church Schools	Public Sector	Immigration	Church Schools	Public Sector	Immigration
Mitterrand	25.9	30.6	26.8	18.5	25.4	29.1
Mitterrand and Barre	4.6	4.0	4.9	1.9	0.8	2.9
Mitterrand and Chirac	2.2	1.4	2.2	0.7	0.7	1.0
Mitterrand and Le Pen	1.2	1.2	0.3	2.0	1.8	0.2
Mitterrand, Barre, and Chirac	4.4	2.4	7.4	1.7	0.8	3.8
Mitterrand, Barre, and Le Pen	0.5	0.4	0.3	1.2	0.3	0.1
Mitterrand, Chirac, and Le Pen	0.0	0.4	0.2	0.1	0.1	0.0
Mitterrand, Barre, Chirac, and Le Pen	3.8	3.6	1.6	19.9	17.9	20.4
Barre	6.7	7.8	7.7	3.6	2.0	0.5
Barre and Chirac	8.8	6.8	11.8	5.4	5.2	1.3
Barre and Le Pen	0.9	0.9	0.6	1.5	0.5	0.5
Barre, Chirac, and Le Pen	4.6	4.7	2.0	4.4	4.8	0.8
Chirac	10.9	9.7	9.9	8.3	9.8	2.2
Chirac and Le Pen	2.9	3.7	2.4	3.6	4.5	1.8
Le Pen	4.7	4.5	14.1	9.3	7.5	27.6
Missing data	17.9	17.9	7.8	17.9	17.9	7.8
	100.0	100.0	100.0	100.0	100.0	100.0

N = 1,013

For the proximity model, when we add the small proportions of meaning-less four-way ties to the missing data, the total does not rise much above 20 per-cent for the church schools and public sector issues, and is considerably less for the more salient immigration issue. In contrast, the proportion of missing data (plus four-way ties) for the directional model ranges from almost 30 percent for the immigration issue to between 32 and 40 percent for the other two issues. This dramatically illustrates the extent to which the directional model reduces the proportion of people who may be considered to be voting on the basis of the issue positions of the candidates, as compared with the proximity model. The reduction here is from 15 to 20 percentage points.

The third main feature of table 5.4 is the comparatively large proportion of voters who preferred Le Pen's version of how to deal with immigration in France in 1988. We have already seen, earlier in this chapter, how clearly the French public associated Le Pen with the immigration issue. Here we see that substantial proportions of the French electorate supported his anti-immigrant position. The directional model, in particular, demonstrates that the issue-aware electorate was divided almost equally between Mitterrand and Le Pen over the question of immigration. The proliferation of rightist candidates in 1988 dis-persed sympathetic voters' candidate preferences when it came to subsidies for religious schools or reducing the size of the public sector. On the issue of immi-gration, however, the right-wing field was dominated by Le Pen.

Table 5.5 presents the same information for the United States in 1988 as table 5.4 contains relating to France in the same year. Table 5.5 is cast in the same form as table 5.4, although at first glance the former appears to differ from the latter. That impression, however, is an optical illusion occasioned by the fact that while table 5.4 reports the issue-based preferred candidates for a situation in which there were four candidates but only three issues, table 5.5 presents the same information for the U.S. case, for which we have seven issues but only two candidates.

The main point that emerges from table 5.5 is that even though the sums of two-candidate ties and missing data are impressively large for each issue sub-jected to the proximity model, the combined ties and missing data assume astonishing proportions for the directional model. More than half of the voters, and in some cases more than 60 percent of them, drop out of the picture. Whichever model one applies to the United States, the message must be disap-pointing for observers who believe that voters ought to select candidates on the basis of the issues (at least if the issues in mind are of the kind we have employed here). The voters who can be thought to seek out candidates who are "on their side" constitute less than half of the potential electorate. Those who might be looking instead for candidates whose issue positions are closest to their own are more numerous, but they still amount, on the average, to barely more than half of the eligible voters.

TABLE 5.5. Issue-Based Preferred Candidates, by Analytic Model and Issue, United States, 1988, in Percentage

Preferred Candidate	Spending on Services	Defense Spending	Health Insurance	Guarantee Jobs	Russian Policy	Women's Rights	Help Minorities
				Proximity Model			
George Bush	31.7	30.9	25.9	29.3	29.5	19.0	27.1
Michael Dukakis	24.8	30.6	24.3	23.7	21.1	26.4	24.1
Both	14.2	14.5	13.4	17.2	20.1	25.1	19.4
None	29.3	24.0	36.4	29.8	29.3	29.5	29.4
	100.0	100.0	100.0	100.0	100.0	100.0	100.0
				Directional Model			
George Bush	22.0	21.1	20.7	27.4	20.8	13.1	22.1
Michael Dukakis	22.4	23.6	22.4	19.0	18.3	25.9	20.1
Both or none	55.6	55.3	56.9	53.6	60.9	61.0	57.8
	100.0	100.0	100.0	100.0	100.0	100.0	100.0

With regard to the valid data reported in table 5.5, it is apparent that the extent to which either of the two competing candidates might have drawn popular support on the basis of issue positions varied according to both the issues themselves and the model of candidate selection employed. Three issues failed to distinguish between the candidates in the public's eye under either model: defense spending, health insurance, and government help for minorities. Among the remaining issues, Bush had a modest advantage over Dukakis on the issues of spending on services and policy toward Russia in proximity terms but not according to the directional model. Dukakis, however, was more favorably viewed than Bush with regard to the issues of guaranteeing jobs and women's rights under both models, and his advantage over Bush concerning women's rights in terms of "which side are you on?" was particularly notable.

It makes a substantive difference, therefore, whether one employs the proximity model or the directional model to generate issue-based candidate preferences. Is that difference substantial as well? If the difference were small, we might conclude that in the final analysis it would not matter very much which model we employed. If the difference were substantial, however, we would surely want to probe the issue more fully before deciding which alternative to incorporate into a fuller blown model of electoral choice.

To try to get at the answer to that question, we ran out intercorrelation matrices of the candidate preferences generated by each formulation, for each issue, for both France and the United States. The mean Pearsonian correlation for the three French issues is .76 (with the lowest *r* of the three separate issues being .69), while the mean correlation for the seven U.S. issues is .75 (with the lowest *r* of the individual issues being .70).[13] These results are inconclusive. The correlations are quite respectable, suggesting that there may not be much difference between the two sets of measures. Nevertheless, the coefficients indicate that only about half of the variance in each measure is shared by the other one. This suggests that there could be a considerable difference between the two issue models in their effects on the selection of a preferred candidate.

We must, therefore, pursue this issue further before we formulate the overall model that we will ultimately use to investigate the influence of the various forces we have been examining—partisanship, ideology, and issue positions—on the voters' choice of a presidential candidate in France and the United States. We will turn our attention to that task in chapter 7, the second chapter that will appear in the next part of this book.

Part 3
Choosing a President

The stage is now set for an examination of how the French and U.S. electorates make their choices for the presidential office. In Part 2, we discussed the main long-term and short-term forces that underlie electoral choice, and in chapter 7 of Part 3, we will apply a model resting on those notions to French and U.S. electoral behavior.

We will, however, do much more than that in Part 3. Before analyzing electoral choice at all, we will pause, in chapter 6, to investigate just what proportions of the eligible electorates actually cast ballots in France and the United States and who, in broad terms, those voters are. Our discussion of this topic should demonstrate how difficult it is to make such estimates, at the same time as it may also shatter some myths about the comparative ease of voter registration in France as compared with the United States.

Chapter 7 applies our model of candidate choice to the two countries. We start by analyzing the complex first 1988 French ballot, with its multiple candidates. Then we consider the 1988 French runoff ballot between the two front-runners, comparing it with the nicely matching U.S. two-party contest of 1984. There are some differences between the behavior of the two electorates, notably the lesser role of ideology among U.S. voters, but the single linear model accounts remarkably well, and in largely parallel terms, for the voters' behavior in both countries.

We are not, however, content only with this. The model applied in chapter 7 rests on what may be called basic attitudes; we are interested also in the social group basis of electoral behavior in France and the United States. In chapter 8, therefore, we investigate the social bases of the electoral coalitions that supported François Mitterrand and Jacques Chirac at the French runoff ballot of 1988, and compare them with the social groups that supported Michael Dukakis and George Bush at the U.S. presidential election of the same year. This permits us to make two sets of comparisons, one internal to each country, the other cross-national. The within-country comparisons point up the differences in the nature, intensity, and polarity of social group mobilization in France in support of the left and the right, and the patterns of group support for the Democrats and the Republicans in the United States. The cross-national comparisons highlight the limited extent to which the French leftist electoral coalition resembled the U.S. Democratic one, as well as how much more closely the French rightist electoral bloc at the community level matched the U.S. Republican voting bloc.

In this fashion, we are able to link the attitudinal forces highlighted in chapter 7 to long-standing social cleavages. These are more often different than similar in the two countries, but they reflect the capacity of deep-seated, historically generated lines of social cleavage to affect how French and U.S. voters cast their presidential ballots in 1988. Moreover, the alternate French leftist and U.S. Democratic party mobilizational strategies that emerge clearly from our analysis have a degree of political immediacy that is matched only by their historical longevity.

CHAPTER 6

Electoral Participation

Electoral participation is a function of three main forces: general predispositions to vote, the opportunity to vote, and incentives for voting.

Among predispositions, the critical factor is political involvement, which reduces ultimately to interest in politics but which is more fully expressed as a sense that politics and elections are important in that the outcome can make a difference in one's personal situation, the affairs of the community, or the life of the nation. Predispositions toward electoral participation are normally accompanied by identification with political parties and some degree of familiarity with political information. These, obviously, are closely associated with levels of education, but they may result as well from the mobilizational efforts of political parties or other politically relevant groups.

Opportunity consists of the extent to which there are barriers beyond the immediate control of individual citizens that affect the probability that they will vote, even if they are predisposed to do so. These include such purely random events as accidents and illness that may prevent people from going to the polls. On a systemic basis, however, opportunity is affected most strongly by the bureaucratic formalities surrounding electoral participation, notably registration requirements.

The incentives for electoral participation have a family resemblance to the predispositions, but they differ from them in that while predispositions are general, the incentives (or disincentives) are specific to the characteristics of each particular election. There are four main incentives for participation. The first is the perceived importance of the forthcoming election to the potential voters. In countries, such as France and the United States, where there are both presidential and national legislative elections, along with several tiers of lesser legislative elections (and, in the United States, gubernatorial and mayoral elections as well), it is inevitable that the voters will locate them within some hierarchy of perceived importance. To the extent that common rankings emerge across the electorate as a whole, participation rates will tend to vary according to the level and type of offices being contested. A second incentive of considerable importance is whether the configuration of competing candidates is such that a voter may select candidates of the same party with which he or she identifies. There is obviously less incentive for voters to cast ballots if the party to which they feel attached has not fielded any candidates than there would be if such candidates were available. The third incentive for voting relates to the attractiveness of the candidates apart from their partisan affiliation. This is particularly true for candidates for executive offices, but it applies to legislative elections as well, at least if they take place within the framework of single-member districts, which allow for the play of individual candidate appeal more than the larger, multimember districts normally associated with the list system do. The fourth and final incentive for electoral participation is the salience to the voters of one or more of the issues raised during the election campaign. Sometimes issues become salient because of the surrounding context of the election; if the country is at war, or in a depression, for example, related issues achieve a high degree of saliency. But people may be moved by one issue or another, even if it is not necessarily linked to a current critical situation; religion, for example, may be an extremely important issue to many people regardless of the immediate social context.

It should be clear that these various incentives, singly or multiply, can interact in different ways with the citizens' predispositions toward voting and even, in certain cases, with their opportunity actually to cast a ballot. People weakly predisposed to vote might nevertheless do so if a candidate was running whom they found particularly appealing, or if they were agitated by some particular issue they felt to be at stake. Conversely, persons only marginally predisposed to vote might sit out some election because they disliked the available candidates or because they believed that the election was meaningless in terms of whatever was important to them. Elections that are perceived to be very important for one reason or another may even incite some people to tackle registration formalities that they might otherwise consider too inconvenient or intimidating, just as they might impel some people to make more of an effort to get to the polls than they normally would.

We will discuss electoral participation, as it relates to each of those three factors, at several places throughout this book. This chapter will provide the fullest treatment. Here, after clearing away some critically important issues of measurement, we will discuss voter turnout mainly in relation to the structure of opportunity as it is reflected in registration procedures. Later, in chapter 9, on thwarted voters, we will consider incentives for electoral participation on the part of registered voters who are prevented by the nomination or electoral process from casting a ballot for their preferred candidate. Finally, in chapter 10, which deals with the linkage between presidential and legislative elections, we will return to the role of incentives in producing differential turnout rates for different kinds of elections.

Turnout in France and the United States

In the wake of each U.S. presidential election, there is a spate of newspaper edi-
torials and feature stories lamenting the low popular turnout and, frequently,
comparing the turnout in the United States with that reported for other countries, including France, which invariably display higher rates of electoral participation. In that fashion, the widely reported turnout rate of 50.1 percent for
the 1988 U.S. presidential election might be contrasted with the 81.4 percent
turnout rate for the first ballot of the 1988 French presidential election (or, even
more sharply, with the 84.1 percent turnout for the second ballot).

Of course, from time to time there are also articles suggesting that the low
reported rates for the United States are to some considerable extent statistical
artifacts and can be misleading if taken to mean that one-half of the U.S. electorate are indifferent to presidential elections (such as Mitofsky and Plissner
1988). It is rarer to find a report in the popular press suggesting that the kind of
comparison mentioned in the previous paragraph is misleading on the French
side as well. Yet that is the case. The widespread notion that turnout rates are
uniformly higher in most European democracies (including France) than in the
United States for equivalent elections cannot, in the present state of our knowledge, be unequivocally demonstrated. At the same time, it *can* be demonstrated
that the large differences in turnout rates that are routinely reported for France
and the United States are at best exaggerated and at worst illusory.

The principal (but not the only) reason why the gap between turnout rates
in the United States and France is not as wide as many horror stories recount is
that the turnout rate in the United States is normally reported as a proportion
based on the population estimated to be eligible to vote at the election by virtue
of age, while the French rate is routinely reported as a proportion based on the
number of registered voters. Inasmuch as the number of age-eligible persons in
any country must be larger than the number of registered voters (because *all*
age-eligible voters cannot reasonably be expected to register), any proportion
based on the age-eligible population will be smaller than the proportion representing the same number of voters when it is based on the number of registered
voters. Employing the different methods of computing turnout that are regularly used in the two countries, the turnout would register as higher in France
than in the United States even if both countries had identical numbers of age-
eligible persons and identical numbers of people casting ballots. When turnout
in France is compared with turnout in the United States, at least in most popular accounts, people are doing the equivalent of comparing apples with oranges.

In these circumstances, the normal procedure is to standardize the measure of turnout, so that it is defined in the same way for each country being compared. This operation can, in principle, be carried out in either of two ways. One

can either compute the turnout rate for France as it is normally done for the United States, as a proportion of the age-eligible population, or one can compute the U.S. rate as it is routinely done in France, as a proportion of the registered voters. We will pursue both paths of standardization, but it will quickly become apparent that it is a good deal easier to describe in principle what ought to be done than it is to do it in actual practice. Neither mode of standardization will produce the kind of unequivocal results that will satisfy the demand for certainty. The French census authorities do not regularly publish estimates of the age-eligible population coincident with national election dates. It is impossible to ascertain the total number of registered voters in the United States at any given electoral moment. Indeed, what normally passes for the total vote in the United States is an equivocal figure, subject to dispute. In point of fact, it is literally impossible to determine in standardized form the exact turnout rates for France and the United States at presidential elections. But if we cannot achieve perfection, we can go a long way toward calculating reasonable approximations. Enough research on electoral participation has been done in both France and the United States to enable us to estimate how much of the large differences in turnout that are routinely reported for the two countries are the product of statistical idiosyncrasies, as opposed to representing real differences in national rates of electoral participation.

The Incidence of Voter Registration in France

The Ministry of the Interior routinely reports the number of registered voters by the appropriate constituency for all French elections. Although presidential elections are, of course, national elections, the number of registered voters is published by department and other subnational units as well as overall.

It is clear that all of the eligible population in France is not registered to vote (Levy 1978; Morin 1983, 1987; Percheron 1986; Mayer and Percheron 1990). The most careful estimate of the proportion of eligible voters registered is probably that of Morin (1983), who reported that more than 11 percent of the potential electorate of metropolitan France was not registered to vote on March 1, 1982. This estimate was made by searching the large "permanent demographic sample" that the French census bureau has maintained (and updated) since the census of 1968, eliminating from it the names of those people who were not eligible to vote on March 1, 1982, because of age, nationality, or conviction for crimes carrying loss of civic rights as a penalty, and then matching the more than 76,000 remaining names with the names on the national list of registered voters (fichier général des électeurs et électrices) that is maintained by the Institut National de la Statistique et des Etudes Economiques (INSEE).

A later study by Morin (1987), on a slightly difference basis, reported a somewhat smaller gap between eligibles and registered voters as of March

1986. This study included only potential voters who had been born in metropolitan France, while the 1982 study also included potential voters who had been born outside of France. On the 1986 basis, the registration shortfall in 1982 would have been only 10.1 percent (as opposed to the 11.3 percent gap recorded on the broader basis). There is, of course, no way of knowing what the 1986 shortfall would have been if the broader 1982 population basis had been used for the analysis.

Morin (1983) scrupulously points out that these estimates are subject to several sources of potential error, including the census data on the basis of which the large demographic sample was drawn, the character of that sample itself, naturalizations and emigration since the census data were collected, and the accuracy of the registration lists transmitted by the local authorities (who compile them) to the fichier général maintained by INSEE. In addition, Morin (1983) reports that "the field covered by the electoral lists and the fichier of INSEE does not coincide perfectly." This suggests that there is some discrepancy between the number of registered voters reported at election time by the Ministry of the Interior and the number recorded by the INSEE fichier for the same period.

We cannot estimate the effects of these several potential sources of error except in a general, directional sense. Census errors and sampling errors more often than not involve undercounting people who are hard to find, particularly young males who tend to be disproportionately mobile. As young people are those least likely to register for voting in any case, undercounting errors would operate to widen the gap between the eligible population and the registered voters. Naturalization and emigration would tend to operate in opposing directions, as new citizens might be registered (but not counted) while emigrants who had been registered would continue to be counted. Errors in the actual registration lists invariably include the listing of people who have died or moved away, thereby inflating the numbers of registered voters for those localities, but that kind of discrepancy should not affect Morin's estimate, as he starts with the names in a sample and matches them with the registration lists, and not the other way around. On balance, Morin's estimate that some 11 percent of the eligible French citizens are not registered to vote may be too small.

That the true estimate is larger is suggested by the results of other sample surveys that have been carried out in France in order to try to determine the proportion of the potential electorate that is not registered. The leading effort of this kind was reported by Mayer and Percheron (1990), who analyzed the data from large sample surveys conducted in 17 of the 22 French regions, supplemented by a smaller national sample survey of more conventional size. These surveys yielded a nonregistration estimate of some 9 percent. There is little reason, however, to accept that estimate at face value. Survey-based estimates of registration rates in the United States tend to run about 10 percentage points higher than the actual, validated rates. There is no reason why the margin of error should be smaller in France.

While there is nothing magic about the 10 percent margin of error referred to above, it happens also to be the average margin by which the respondents in sample surveys in the United States overreport having voted at the most recent election. Similarly, in one of the more reliable French sample surveys, conducted in 1988, the vote over-report was also 10 percent (Mayer and Percheron 1990). There is no obvious reason why the overreporting of voting should be substantially different from the overreporting of registration, so we are left with the conclusion that the 9 percent gap between reported and actual registration rates recorded by Mayer and Percheron (1990) is probably some 10 points too small.

It appears, therefore, that on the basis of Morin's analysis (1983), and duly taking into account the direction of the potential errors to which that analysis is subject, somewhat more than 11.3 percent of the eligible French population is not registered to vote. On the basis of Mayer's and Percheron's analysis (1990), and taking into account the probable error it reflects, as many as 19 percent of the age-eligible French population is not registered to vote. We cannot make a more precise estimate. Wherever the true rate of nonregistration lies, however, it is clear that it contributes toward closing the participation gap between France and the United States that appears when one relies only on the conventionally computed participation rates. If, say, the mean of our limiting estimates, or 15 percent of the eligibles, are not registered in France, the first-ballot turnout at the 1988 presidential election would have been 69 percent in terms comparable to U.S. reporting habits, as opposed to the officially reported turnout of more than 81 percent. That is still considerably higher than the 50.1 percent participation rate "officially" recorded in the United States for 1988, but the difference is less horrendous than the wide chasm that opens when one employs two different bases of measurement.

Turnout in the United States

Turnout Based on Aggregate Data. In the last sentence of the previous paragraph, we placed quotation marks around the word "officially," when using it in connection with the most commonly reported turnout rate for the U.S. presidential election of 1988. Actually, there is no such thing as an official turnout rate for the United States. The collection and compilation of electoral data are the responsibility of the 50 states and the District of Columbia, and there are no nationally prescribed, uniform standards for their presentation and publication. The closest equivalent to the services of the French Ministry of the Interior charged with tabulating the vote (and, in the case of the presidential elections, forwarding the data to the Constitutional Council, which formally announces the results), is the Clerk of the House of Representatives, who reports the electoral results to the House, on the basis of data derived from the state (and D.C.) reports, under the title *Statistics of the Presidential and Congressional Election of* [whatever the date might be; for 1988 it was] *November 8, 1988.* It is the vote totals compiled by the Clerk of the House that people usually have in mind when they refer to the "official" count (Jennings 1990), but there are other reliable sources of electoral statistics for the United States as well.[1] Whatever the source, the total number of votes cast constitutes the numerator for the proportion that is conventionally taken to represent turnout in the United States.

The denominator for that proportion is an estimate of the U.S. population of voting age (i.e., 18 years of age and older) made by the Bureau of the Census.[2] The "official" turnout rate for the presidential election of 1988, to which we referred in the last paragraph of the preceding section, was obtained by dividing the number of votes cast for president, as determined by the Clerk of the House, into the postcensal estimate of the voting age population produced by the Bureau of the Census.

It should immediately be apparent that the reality of the turnout rate of 50.1 percent that results from that simple computation depends upon the appropriateness and the accuracy of both the numerator and the denominator on the basis of which the rate was computed. Neither datum is beyond criticism.

Let us first consider the numerator. Assuming that there are no errors in the vote totals compiled by the Clerk of the House stemming from the lack of uniformity in the base data prepared by the separate states, the main weakness of the official vote totals is that they make no provision for voters who went to the polls but whose votes for president were not counted because of irregularities. French election statistics regularly report the number of invalid ballots, but U.S. election statistics do not do so. In France, at the two presidential elections during the 1980s, the mean proportion of invalid ballots at the first round of voting was about 1.5 percent of the registered voters and almost 2 percent of the people who actually went to the polls. At the second and decisive round of voting, the corresponding proportions were more than 2.5 percent, and more than 3 percent, respectively.

Virtually all of the invalid ballots at the first round of French voting represent involuntary voting irregularities. The difference between the means for the first round and the higher means for the runoff vote represent ballots that were deliberately spoiled by voters dissatisfied with the limited alternatives presented to them (see chap. 9). U.S. voters who involuntarily commit irregularities, or who choose to vent their spleen at the kind of electoral choice they face, do not count in the U.S. scheme of electoral things. Yet there must be many of them, particularly among those who involuntarily cast invalid ballots. The U.S. long ballot, with its multiple candidates for a wide range of offices, to say nothing about local or statewide referendum issues, is far more complicated than a

French ballot, which is limited to the candidates for a single office. At a French presidential election, the only office at stake is the presidency; in a U.S. presidential year, voters may be asked to vote not only for a presidential candidate, but also for a whole host of candidates running for the Senate, the House of Representatives, the governorship, the state legislature, and county and local offices. Most of the candidates will be partisan, but some may be endorsed by both of the major parties and, perhaps, even by a third party. Some of the local offices, such as judgeships, may be nonpartisan. Voters may also be asked for their views on a new version of the local dog-leash law, or on a nearly incomprehensible financial provision. The opportunities for error based on confusion, haste, or inattention are rife (see fig. 6.1). More U.S. voters than French ones must involuntarily cast ballots that are classified as invalid.

Deliberately spoiled ballots represent unexplored territory for the United States, although they are a common feature of the French electoral scene (see chap. 9). Some 2 percent of French first-round voters deliberately cast invalid ballots at the decisive round because their preferred candidate has been forced to drop out of the race. Such active expressions of alienation may not be part of the U.S. electoral culture, but we do not know that for a fact. It is often argued that comparatively low turnout rates in the United States reflect, to some extent, the deliberate abstention of potential voters who are discontented with the limited range of choice among candidates (Schonfeld and Toinet 1975). Such dissatisfaction, combined with high political involvement, might well lead to deliberate ballot spoiling.

There is no way of knowing exactly what the incidence of invalid ballots is in the United States, but an estimate of from 3 to 5 percent of the votes actually counted would not be unreasonable. Those are votes that should be added to the conventional numerator for purposes of computing turnout in the United States.

With regard to the denominator, the main problem with the census estimates is that they refer only to the population that is eligible to vote by virtue of age. There are other requirements for voting eligibility, the most critical of which for our purposes is citizenship. The census estimates include both legal and illegal aliens who are not eligible to vote, but whose incorporation in the denominator of the turnout proportion necessarily reduces it. For 1984, the census estimated that as many as eight million legal and illegal aliens (plus perhaps as many as half a million other ineligibles, including felons and the mentally ill) were included within the estimated population of age eligibles (Kimberling 1992). Those groups amounted to some 5 percent of the age-eligible population. Just as votes that are cast but not counted should be added to the numerator when estimating turnout rates, persons who are not eligible to vote must be subtracted from the denominator. If we make such adjustments to the official numerator and denominator for 1988, by increasing the vote total by 4 percent (to take account of invalid ballots) and by decreasing the age-eligible population by 5 percent (to take account of noncitizens and persons not permitted to vote because of criminality or mental illness), the reported official turnout rate of 50.1 percent rises to 54.9 percent. The increase is not enormous, but it demonstrates the necessity for careful scrutiny of the rough-and-ready methods normally employed for computing turnout in the United States.

Turnout Based on Survey Data. Turnout in the United States is regularly estimated on the basis of sample survey data, as well as on the basis of aggregate statistics of the kind just discussed. Indeed, if—as we intend to do—one tries to estimate turnout as a proportion of the registered voters (as opposed to the age-eligible electorate) it is almost essential to base the analysis on survey data. There is no U.S. equivalent to the French fichier général that purports to be a national list of all the registered voters. Accordingly, most estimates of the size of the population of registered voters, and of the proportions of registered voters who have actually cast ballots at any given election, rest on sample surveys. The U.S. Bureau of the Census conducts a Current Population Survey (CPS) in election years in order to make estimates of the rates of registration and voting. The estimates of turnout as a proportion of the age-eligible population that emerge from this procedure are consistently higher than those arrived at on the basis of aggregate data. For example, we have indicated that when that measure of turnout is based on the conventional aggregate data, the 1988 rate was 50.1 percent. When based on CPS survey data, the 1988 rate was 57.4 percent (Jennings 1990, 21).

The consortium of U.S. political scientists that conducts biennial surveys in the series of U.S. NES also makes estimates of registration and voting rates. For the NES studies, however, the self-reports of the respondents are followed up by a validation procedure that involves checking the registration and voting lists in the respondents' electoral districts (and local polling places) to determine whether their responses relating to registration and voting can be confirmed. This careful procedure should yield estimates that are more reliable than those produced by the CPS. For 1988, the same year for which we already have reported two different estimates of turnout, the valid turnout as a proportion of all the survey respondents was 61.6 percent. This figure is larger than the comparable rate reported by the CPS, but it gains in credibility not only because it rests on validated vote reports, but also because it is 10.1 percentage points lower than the proportion of respondents in the survey who actually claimed to have voted. The overreporting norm of some 10 percent, to which we referred earlier in this chapter, in connection with trying to establish the incidence of voter registration in France, fully applies with regard to the NES survey for 1988, but even after validation procedures, the turnout was 60 percent. Virtually the same results occurred in the NES surveys for 1980 and 1984. Throughout the 1980s, the mean reported vote was slightly over 70 percent, while the mean validated vote was slightly more than 60 percent.

CHARTER TOWNSHIP OF VAN BUREN

INSTRUCTION BALLOT FOR VOTERS

WAYNE COUNTY, MICHIGAN

F-638

WAYNE COUNTY GENERAL ELECTION —TUESDAY, NOVEMBER 3, 1992

TO VOTE YOU MUST—

1. Turn SWITCH LEVER to the RIGHT and LEAVE IT THERE. This Closes curtains and Unlocks the Machine.

2. To vote the PARTISAN BALLOT (WHITE SECTION), you must follow STEP A, B, or C.

NOTE: Candidates for President and Vice President must be voted for as a unit and the vote cannot be split.

A. To vote a STRAIGHT PARTY TICKET: TURN DOWN the PARTY LEVER of your choice. Your Party Ticket has now been registered.

B. To vote a SPLIT PARTY TICKET: TURN DOWN your PARTY LEVER. TURN UP the Lever at the Right of the candidate's name you wish to eliminate and TURN DOWN the Lever at the Right of the name of the candidate for whom you desire to vote.

C. To vote a MIXED PARTY TICKET: DO NOT turn any PARTY LEVER but TURN DOWN the Lever at the Right of the name of each candidate for whom you desire to vote.

NOTE: The Non-Partisan Offices must be voted separately. The Straight Party Lever does not include voting levers for Non-Partisan offices.

3. To vote the NON-PARTISAN BALLOT (BLUE SECTION), TURN DOWN the Lever at the RIGHT of the NAMES of the Candidates of your choice. Vote for not more than the number of Candidates as indicated under the Office Titles. LEAVE VOTING LEVERS DOWN.

4. To vote for a person whose name is not printed on the machine: Push the Reference Trigger and at the same time push back the Metal Slide to the Left of the office for which that person is a candidate and write or place the name of that person on the paper exposed.

5. To vote the PROPOSALS (RED SECTION), TURN DOWN the "YES" or "NO" Lever at the LEFT of each proposal in the last column at the extreme right of the machine. LEAVE VOTING LEVERS DOWN.

WARNING: DON'T PUSH THEM BACK

TO CORRECT A MISTAKE
Turn back the Lever voted in error and turn down another in its place.

6. LEAVE VOTING LEVERS DOWN and THEN SWITCH LEVER to the left. This RECORDS YOUR VOTE and opens curtains.

—indicates PROPOSALS
—indicates PARTISAN Candidates
—indicates NON-PARTISAN Candidates

NOTE!
This Ballot is printed in 3 colors to assist you in voting.

RED   WHITE   BLUE

VOTE the RED, WHITE and BLUE Sections of the Ballot

DON'T FORGET TO VOTE THE QUESTION BALLOT

How to Operate a Voting Machine

OFFICE TO BE VOTED FOR

Office	Column 1 DEMOCRATIC	Column 2 REPUBLICAN	Column 3	Column 4 LIBERTARIAN	Column 5 WORKERS WORLD	Column 6	Column 7 NATURAL LAW PARTY	Column 8 NO PARTY AFFILIATION	Column 10
ELECTORS OF PRESIDENT AND VICE PRESIDENT OF THE UNITED STATES									
REPRESENTATIVE IN CONGRESS									
STATE LEGISLATURE									
REPRESENTATIVE IN STATE LEGISLATURE									
MEMBERS OF THE STATE BOARD OF EDUCATION									
MEMBERS OF THE BOARD OF REGENTS OF THE UNIVERSITY OF MICHIGAN									
MEMBERS OF THE BOARD OF TRUSTEES OF MICHIGAN STATE UNIVERSITY									
MEMBERS OF THE BOARD OF GOVERNORS OF WAYNE STATE UNIVERSITY									
PROSECUTING ATTORNEY									
SHERIFF									
COUNTY CLERK									
COUNTY TREASURER									
REGISTER OF DEEDS									
COUNTY COMMISSIONER									

STATE PROPOSALS

YES   NO
YES   NO
YES
YES

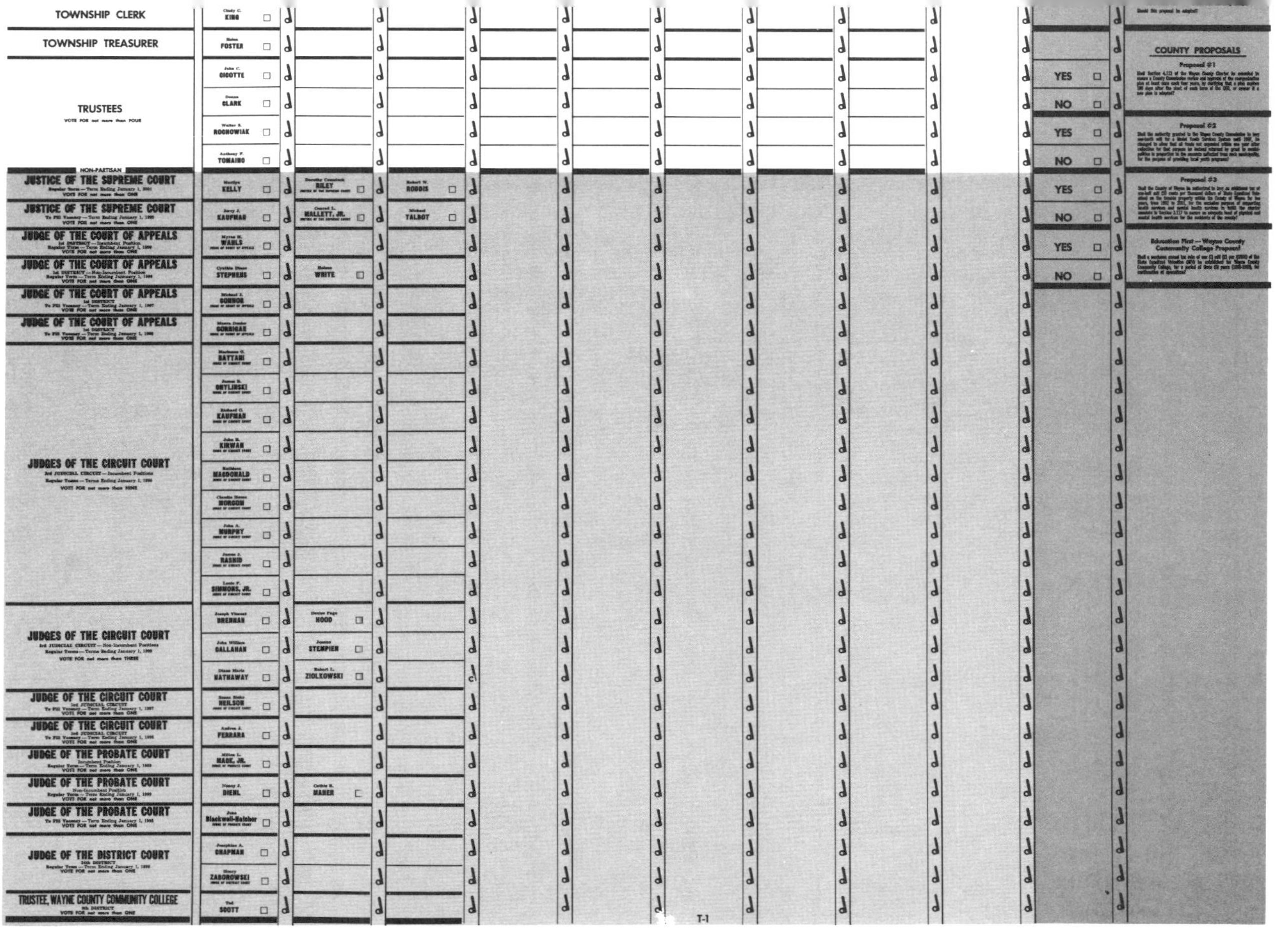

Fig. 6.1. Ballot for voters, Wayne County, Michigan, November 3, 1992

What is of particular interest here, is that the 60 percent rate of turnout among eligible voters for the 1980s also represents an average turnout of about *85 percent of the registered voters*, after validation not only of the vote reports but also of the registration reports furnished by the respondents. That proportion of registered voters fully matches the figures for French presidential elections in the same decade. There remains, however, a substantial difference between turnout in the two countries on the basis of the age-eligible population, which we estimated earlier to be on the order of 70 percent in France (see table 6.1 for the standardized estimates for both countries, averaging across all presidential elections during the 1980s and averaging across the two ballots for the French elections). How can we account for the discrepancy?

The answer lies in the difference in the proportions of the eligible populations that are registered to vote in the two countries. Earlier, we estimated that some 85 percent of the eligible French population is registered to vote. According to validated NES estimates, some 70 percent of the eligible U.S. population was registered during the 1980s, and the same proportion emerged from the actual registration statistics from those states with both registration records and estimates of the voting age population (*Statistical Abstract* 1991, table 451). Roughly the same proportion of registered voters cast ballots in the two countries, but that percentage applies to a larger base in France, proportionately, than in the United States. The main difference between France and the United States is that the proportion of actual voters among the eligible U.S. population is some 10 to 15 percentage points smaller than it is in France. Given that the turnout among registered voters is virtually the same in the two countries, that differential must reflect a difference in registration rates between France and the United States.[3]

TABLE 6.1.   **Mean Estimated Turnout at Presidential Elections, France and the United States, 1980–88, in Percentage**

	France[a]	United States		United States minus France
As proportion of registered voters	83.1	85.1[b]		+2.0
As proportion of eligible voters		58.8[d]		
	70.6[c]		60.2[f]	−10.4
		61.6[e]		

[a]Averaged across both ballots at each election
[b]National Election Studies validated registration and vote
[c]Correction of 15%
[d]U.S. Bureau of the Census survey
[e]National Election Studies validated vote
[f]Mean of d and e

Registration Procedures in France and the United States

Discussions of electoral participation in the United States tend to focus more often on issues bearing on procedures for voter registration than on turnout among the registered. The main reason for this is that systematic exclusion of black people from the franchise was for long carried out in the southern states. This was often achieved by outright intimidation and violence, but it also took the form of legal obstacles to registration that operated overwhelmingly to the disadvantage of black citizens. Legal roadblocks of a blatantly discriminatory kind virtually disappeared during the 1960s and 1970s, but registration procedures continue to be a central issue. The emphasis, however, has shifted away from concern over outright discrimination toward consideration of the convenience and permanence of voter registration. Many students of electoral participation, as well as (mainly Democratic) politicians, argue that the way to augment electoral participation in the United States is to facilitate voter registration.[4]

Advocates of registration reform in the United States, who can easily become frustrated at the large variety of registration requirements that the highly decentralized political system permits, often look with admiration and even envy toward other countries, including France, where voting turnout is normally high and voter registration procedures seem, at least outwardly, to be not only uniform but also simple and convenient. In point of fact, while French registration procedures are certainly uniform, registering to vote is not particularly simple in France, and in some respects the French system of voter registration is more restrictive than the system employed in many populous U.S. states.[5]

The variety of procedures employed in the United States makes it difficult to generalize about voter registration in the United States as a whole.[6] An overall comparison between France and the United States in this domain, however, might well conclude that it is more difficult to become a registered voter in France than in the United States, but that once one is on the electoral roll, a French citizen is less likely than a U.S. citizen to be removed from it and to face the need to reregister.

Registration is formally compulsory in France, but there is no penalty for failure to register, and while official French notices naturally inform the citizens that if they want to vote they must be registered, they mention but do not emphasize the obscure general requirement of registration (see fig. 6.2). French citizens who want to register must take the initiative themselves, just as U.S. citizens must do. There is no "automatic" registration in France, as has sometimes been suggested.[7] The French have considered giving mayors the authority to automatically register persons turning eighteen years of age, but have failed to do so out of fear that some mayors might be politically selective in

MAIRIE DE PARIS

RÉVISION DES LISTES ÉLECTORALES POLITIQUES
L'inscription sur les listes électorales politique est obligatoire

POUR POUVOIR VOTER IL FAUT ETRE INSCRIT SUR LES LISTES ELECTORALES :

CONDITIONS D'INSCRIPTION SUR LES LISTES ELECTORALES :
- Posséder la nationalité française,
- Etre âgé(e) de 18 ans,
- Ne pas être déchu(e) de vos droits civils et politiques.
- Pour vous faire inscrire, munissez-vous :
a) d'une pièce d'identité (de préférence la carte nationale d'identité
ou le livret de famille ou le livret militaire),
b) d'une pièce attestant que vous avez une attache avec l'arrondissement et qui peut être notamment :
- une pièce justifiant d'un domicile ou d'une résidence effective depuis au moins 6 mois
dans l'arrondissement (par exemple une quittance de loyer, d'eau, de gaz, d'électricité),
- un certificat d'inscription au rôle des contributions directes locales faisant apparaître
votre qualité de contribuable communal.

VOUS qui atteindrez l'âge de 18 ans avant le 1er mars de l'an prochain,

VOUS qui êtes venu(e) récemment habiter à Paris

FAITES-VOUS INSCRIRE sur la liste électorale politique de
L'ARRONDISSEMENT dans lequel vous êtes domicilié(e).

VOUS qui avez changé de domicile à l'intérieur de la
ville de Paris ou même au sein de votre arrondissement,

FAITES régulariser votre situation électorale
à la MAIRIE de votre domicile.

LES DEMANDES SONT REÇUES DANS LES MAIRIES DU 1er JANVIER AU 31 DECEMBRE INCLUS.

Votre inscription prendra effet au 1er mars de l'année prochaine

B.E.T. - Hôtel de Ville - 13385

Fig. 6.2. Announcement of voter registration requirements, Paris, 1988

wielding their authority in the matter. Far from being automatic, registration in France is not even particularly convenient. One cannot normally register by mail, for example, as one can in more than half the U.S. states. In France, one must turn up at the town hall (*mairie*) or, in the larger cities, the town hall for the city's main subdivision—the *arrondissement*—where one resides.

On the face of things, the larger cities would seem to be less well served in this regard than the rural areas and small towns. While France's largest cities are not particularly large by U.S. standards, neither are they subdivided into many arrondissements. Paris is divided into 20 arrondissements, Marseille into 16, Lyon into 13. There are, therefore, relatively few sites where one can register in those large cities: one for every 100,000 inhabitants in Paris, on the average; one for every 60,000 in Marseille; and one for every 30,000 in Lyon.

In Miami, Florida, by way of contrast, where for the most part one must register in person, and which has about the same population as Lyon, there are 528 sites where one can register to vote, including not only government offices, such as social service centers, but also private offices, such as banks and real estate agencies. At the same time, in France, there are more than 36,000 towns, each of which has its mairie and, consequently, a central and well-known location where one can register to vote. In these circumstances, it would seem that the comparatively large French cities that are not subdivided into arrondissements are the least well served places with regard to the number of sites where a citizen can register.[8]

In addition to the facts that registration requires as much personal initiative in France as it does in the United States, and that registration in large French cities is not particularly convenient, French registration requirements operate to the disadvantage of people who are mobile, or who decide to register for the first time only when a given election campaign gets under way.

The residence requirement for voter registration in France is very restrictive: one must have lived in the town (or arrondissement) for at least six months (or have been a local taxpayer for five years). That provision works to the disadvantage of people who move any significant distance from where they were previously registered. Geographic mobility is probably the most important nontechnical obstacle to voter registration, apart from motivation, and internal migration in France, as in any modern society, is substantial. Ile-de-France alone, the region that includes the city of Paris along with both its residential and industrial suburbs, attracted some 100,000 new residents annually from 1970 to the early 1990s, while some 170,000 persons per year, most of them 55 years of age or older, left this largely urban area for the provinces (*Le Monde*, June 12, 1992). Depending on the juxtaposition of their moving dates and the occurrence of elections, some fraction of those people could have been prevented from registering regardless of their degree of motivation.

The French registration system is not indulgent toward people who procrastinate about registering for the first time. A French citizen may register at any time between January 1 and December 31 of the same year, but the registration becomes effective only on March 1 *of the following year*. The only sizable numbers of people who may register in order to vote in an election that is to be held in the same year are citizens who attained the age of 18 after the end of February of that year and former aliens who became naturalized citizens after December 31 of the previous year. Those two categories of people were not eligible to register the previous year. However, anyone who *was* eligible to register the previous year (or earlier), but neglected to do so, is out of luck. Those people may not register for an election to be held during the current year and, of course, they cannot vote at that election.

It would be difficult to argue that the French registration system facilitates voter registration in any way that is markedly superior to the range of methods employed in the United States. In comparison with France, residence requirements are negligible in the United States. The modal (and maximum) residence requirement in the United States is 30 days. Even before enactment of the "motor-voter" bill into law in 1993 (see n. 4), registration by mail was possible in more than half the states, and almost half the states permitted citizens to register or obtain registration application forms when they acquired or renewed drivers' licenses. Some cities facilitate voter registration at well-traveled commercial areas, such as shopping malls, as well as at government agencies such as post offices, public libraries, and high schools. In the large, rural states, one can register at the county seat as well as at the city halls in the smaller towns, which do not match but approach the density of the extraordinary French rural administrative structure.

The only possible advantage the French system of voter registration might have over most of the systems employed in the United States is precisely its uniformity and stability, as compared with the variety and impermanence of the techniques and sites that play a role in the various jurisdictions in the United States. There may not be many places where one can register in Paris or Marseille or Lyon, but they are *familiar* places, to which the citizen goes for a whole variety of administrative purposes, from securing an identity card to registering a marriage. Even if one moves from one area of the country to another, the system remains the same. The mairie will be a different building from the last one the citizen entered, but the signs, offices, hard wooden benches, and bureaucratic atmosphere will be the same. In the United States, when citizens move from one registration jurisdiction to another, they may be moving from an ordered system, somewhat similar to the French one, to what approximates a traveling circus. In the final analysis, however, it is doubtful that the predictability of the French registration system outweighs its rigidities to the extent that it facilitates voter registration more than the diverse and sometimes confusing systems that are employed in the United States.

Where the French system of voter registration does seem to be more accommodating to the ordinary citizen than any system employed in the United States is in the *permanence* of registration. Once a French citizen is registered, that person remains registered as long as he or she continues to be legally eligible to vote and continues to reside in the same registration jurisdiction. It is, of course, necessary in France as anywhere else for the electoral authorities to keep the registration lists up to date, not only by adding the names of the people who are newly registered, but also by purging the lists of the names of people who have moved away from the community or died. What is most important in comparing French and American practices in this regard is that in France the authorities may not legally purge people from the registration polls simply because they have not voted in one or more previous elections. In the United States, to the contrary, there are 38 states that purge the registration lists because of failure to vote within a specified time period. This period ranges from two to eight years, with the modal period being four years (Hancock 1992). In France, the authorities may take into account information to the effect that a person failed to vote at "several consecutive elections" (*Code électoral* 1989, 297) when trying to determine whether someone should be purged from the list, but they must in principle have independent reason to believe that such purging is justified. The usual procedure in this regard centers around the practice of periodically sending a voter card (*carte d'électeur*) to each person on the electoral roll. When these cards are returned as undeliverable, an investigation is opened, and it is at that stage that the person's voting record may be taken into consideration. Persons who are purged from the lists must be notified in France, just as they are in all but a handful of states in the United States, although arrangements for appeal in France are less liberal than in the United States, and possibly more intimidating.[9]

This difference in the permanence of registration in France and the United States means that people whose electoral participation is intermittent are much more likely to have to reregister in the United States than in France, where in principle they should not have to do so at all. That difference, by itself, could conceivably account for some of the difference in the overall registration rates for the two countries that we estimated earlier, although we have no way of determining how much. At the same time, we have shown that French citizens must normally register in the year prior to an election to be eligible to vote at that election, and that the six-month residence requirement may temporarily disenfranchise people who have moved any distance from their previous place of residence. Again, we have no way of estimating the numbers of would-be voters who might be affected by these restrictive practices, but they surely operate contrary to the principle of permanent registration.

In summary of this section, while we cannot place precise values on the operational effects of one registration practice or another, we can say that the French registration system does not appear to be so much more conducive to voter registration than those employed in the United States as to account for the some 10 to 15 percent difference in overall national registration rates that we estimated earlier. Whatever accounts for that difference, it is not the differential effects of voter registration practices.

The Nonvoters

Studies of political participation in the United States have shown that, in sociological terms, nonvoters are disproportionately undereducated, young, poor, and of ethnic minority status (see, in particular, Wolfinger and Rosenstone 1980). In psychological terms, political participation in the United States is conditioned primarily by a sense of political involvement, which reflects, although it is not exhausted by, interest in politics (Verba and Nie 1972, chap. 5).

We would, at the outset, expect that nonvoters in France are essentially the same kind of people they are in the United States, with the exception of ethnic minority status, which does not yet apply to enough French citizens to have a significant effect on overall turnout.[10] On a bivariate basis, that is indeed what related French longitudinal data indicate. Since the late 1970s, SOFRES has intermittently recorded the abstention rates reported in their sample surveys by categories of registered voters similar to those who tend disproportionately to abstain in the United States. Table 6.2 presents these findings in the form of indexes for the elections included in the series, and summarizes them by displaying the mean index score for each category across the entire series. The higher the score, the higher the abstention rate.

The SOFRES estimates clearly indicate that political interest has been a potent factor in electoral participation in France, both as measured directly by the question "How much interest do you have in politics?" and indirectly in the form of expressed left-right self-locations. The marais, who are the respondents who either cannot or will not locate themselves on the hypothetical left-right scale, or who assign themselves a location at the midpoint but have very little or no interest at all in politics, have a much higher abstention rate than do the respondents who assign themselves a politically meaningful left-right position. Age also shows up as related to electoral participation across the decade surveyed by SOFRES. Variations in turnout are less pronounced among respondents classified according to the occupation of the head of household, but some traces of a class differential appear: respondents from middle-management and white-collar households, along with those from worker households, show higher rates of abstention than respondents who come from households where the main breadwinner is a top manager, professional, or business proprietor.

The bivariate distributions reported in table 6.2 suggest that both French and U.S. voters respond to similar or identical stimuli with regard to turnout. At the same time, those factors might interact with one another differently in

TABLE 6.2. Sample Survey-Based Indexes of Abstentions by Selected Categories of Citizens, France, 1978–93

	Type of Election and Year							
Category	Legis. 1978[a]	Europ. 1979	Pres. 1981[a]	Legis. 1981[a]	Legis. 1988[a]	Europ. 1989	Legis. 1993[a]	Mean
Political Interest								
Much	0.67	0.56	0.73	0.44	0.61	0.60	0.62	0.60
Some	0.89	0.87	0.91	1.06	0.94	0.89	0.83	0.91
Very little	1.33	1.04	1.36	1.22	1.19	1.08	1.12	1.19
None at all	1.33	1.48	1.09	1.22	1.58	1.55	1.83	1.44
Left-Right Location								
Extreme Left					0.61	0.83	0.79	0.74
Left					1.00	0.96	0.96	0.97
Involved Center					1.13	0.96	1.00	1.03
Right					0.81	0.81	0.83	0.82
Extreme Right					0.64	0.79	0.67	0.70
Marais					1.71	1.49	1.67	1.62
Age								
18 to 24	2.22	1.57	1.73	1.61	1.26	1.15	1.33	1.55
25 to 34	1.33	1.22	1.18	1.44	1.29	1.21	1.25	1.27
35 to 49	0.78	1.00	0.73	0.83	0.90	0.94	0.79	0.85
50 to 64	0.67	0.78	0.82	0.72	0.90	0.85	0.79	0.79
Over 64	0.67	0.65	0.82	0.82	0.74	0.85	0.96	0.79
Sex								
Male	0.89	0.96	0.91	0.83	0.94	0.94	0.96	0.92
Female	1.11	1.09	1.09	1.11	1.06	1.04	1.00	1.07

(continued)

TABLE 6.2—Continued

				Type of Election and Year				
Category	Legis. 1978[a]	Europ. 1979	Pres. 1981[a]	Legis. 1981[a]	Legis. 1988[a]	Europ. 1989	Legis. 1993[a]	Mean
Occupation of Head of Household								
Farmer, farm worker	0.67	0.74	0.91	0.67	0.81	0.91	0.33	0.72
Small business, shopkeeper	0.67	1.00	0.82	1.39	1.16	0.96	0.92	0.99
Big business, top management and professional	0.89	1.04	0.91	1.00	0.94	0.83	1.00	0.94
Middle management and white collar	1.44	1.09	1.27	1.22	1.23	0.96	1.00	1.17
Worker	1.11	1.30	1.09	1.17	1.00	1.23	1.17	1.15
Retired, inactive	0.78	0.74	0.73	0.61	0.84	0.89	0.96	0.79
Actual Abstention Rate	16.8%	38.8%	18.9%	29.1%	34.3%	48.8%	30.7%	

Source: Derived from SOFRES, various years.

Note: The index figure is the abstention rate reported by category divided by rate reported by entire sample.

[a]First ballot

the two countries, so that a single model of turnout would not be appropriate. To ascertain which is the case, we ran parallel logistic regressions, with voting or abstaining at the 1988 presidential election (at the first ballot for France) as the dependent variable. The independent variables included age (coded continuously); a measure of political interest; and an index of socioeconomic status. For the United States, political interest was measured simply by responses to a question about degree of interest in the campaign; for France by an index combining replies to a question about degree of interest in the campaign and a question inquiring about degree of interest in politics generally. The index of socioeconomic status consists of the mean quartile scores of the respondents (in each country) across three variables (measuring educational level, occupational status, and overall family income) grouped into a 10-point scale.

The model fits the U.S. data for 1988 very well. Each of the three independent variables is highly significant statistically (see table 6.3). The same model, however, fits the French data much less well, and only political interest has a statistically significant, independent effect in the expected direction on turnout. Age has a small effect in the expected direction, in that younger people are more inclined than older people to abstain, but the effect is not statistically significant. The most surprising result is that our index of socioeconomic status produces a statistically significant effect on turnout contrary to what we find for the United States and to what table 6.2 suggests: higher-status people were more likely than lower-status people to abstain in France at the presidential election of 1988.

This is a highly interesting phenomenon, not only because of what it suggests about the difference between the factors affecting turnout in France and the United States, but also because it reflects a comparatively rare statistical phenomenon known as "suppression." In the United States, political interest,

TABLE 6.3. **Summaries of Logistic Models of Electoral Participation, France and the United States, 1988**

Independent Variables	United States			France		
	Unstandardized (B)	(B/SE)	Partial %	Unstandardized (B)	(B/SE)	Partial %
Political interest	.39	9.48	3.4	.35	6.10	3.3
Socioeconomic status	.23	10.60	4.2	−.07	2.12	0.4
Age	.03	8.10	2.5	.01	1.29	0.2
	$\chi^2 = 347.08$ $(d.f. = 3)$			$\chi^2 = 36.23$ $(d.f. = 3)$		
	R^2 analogue $= .115$			R^2 analogue $= .038$		
	$N = 1,675$			$N = 981$		

socioeconomic status, and voting or abstaining are all intercorrelated positively and at roughly the same level. In France, however, even though political interest is related both to voting (or abstaining) and socioeconomic status, socioeconomic status is *not* related to voting. At the same time, when one includes both political interest and socioeconomic status in a regression, the presence of the latter *increases* the independent effect of the former on voting by "suppressing" the portion of variance in political interest that is bound up with socioeconomic status.

While suppression has been described as "hard to realize in practice" (McNemar 1969, 211) and as among life's "quasiparadoxical curiosities" (Cohen and Cohen 1975, 91), we are more concerned with what the particular form it takes in France means for practical politics than we are with its rarity. In order to understand the role of socioeconomic status in voting more precisely, we decomposed our composite index into its three constituent elements and reran the regression. This showed that all of the unexpected relationship between socioeconomic status and voting derived from the measure of occupational status. Income and education, independently, had positive but very weak effects on turnout in France, although not at statistically significant levels, while occupational status alone had a significant negative effect. The main difference between France and the United States with regard to turnout is that while people associated with higher-status occupational groups tend to vote more frequently in the United States than people from lower-status occupational groups do, the exact opposite prevails in France, or at least did so in the conditions of the presidential election of 1988.

The explanation for this phenomenon is almost surely that some French parties and candidates make a greater effort than do those in the United States to attract lower socioeconomic citizens to the polls. The French Communist party, in particular, has always directed its recruitment efforts and its electoral appeals to working-class and lower-status voters. Its traditional emphasis on the workplace as the locus of organization facilitated the political mobilization of factory workers and miners. The density of its organizational network made it possible for the party to remain in contact with internal migrants as they moved from the poor rural areas, which the Communists never neglected, to the burgeoning industrial towns, where the party could receive them, much as early immigrant families and communities take in later arrivals from the same towns in the old country. The Communist party was splintering by 1988, and its official candidate was badly battered at the presidential election that year, but almost 80 percent of the votes he received came from people in the lower half of the 10 gradations of our scale of socioeconomic status.

The mobilization efforts of the Communist party, and probably to a lesser extent also of the Socialist party, have almost surely contributed to the higher rate of voter registration in France than in the United States. On the whole, the people who are not registered to vote tend to resemble demographically the registered voters who do not vote. It is hard to imagine that Communist party efforts to integrate poor farmers and workers into their organizational network did not include trying to persuade them to register, as well as to vote Communist once they were registered.

If this analysis is correct, the continuing erosion and probable disappearance of the Communist party raise questions about the long-term prospects for electoral participation by the kinds of people whom the party tried particularly to attract but who are indifferent to electoral politics in the United States. Will registration and voting remain within the inventory of those persons' habitual behavior patterns that are transmitted from generation to generation through family socialization? If so (and assuming no change in the United States), the U.S.-French differential in registration and turnout practices will endure. Or will the poor and downtrodden withdraw in the absence of any pole of attraction that seems particularly attentive to their needs? If that occurs (again assuming no significant change in the United States) the prospect is a convergence of French and U.S. participatory patterns on the U.S. model.

CHAPTER 7

Attitudinal Bases of Electoral Choice

We are now in a position to examine the effects of fundamental political attitudes on the voters' choices of presidential candidates in France and the United States. The basic model of electoral choice that we will apply is both comparatively simple and well established within the domain of the analysis of electoral behavior at U.S. presidential elections (Asher 1992, pt. 1). It distinguishes between long-term forces and short-term forces, thereby including factors that help to account for both stability and change in mass electoral behavior.

The long-term forces are, of course, party identification and ideological positioning. The short-term forces include the impact of issues and candidate evaluations. Virtually all of the necessary groundwork relating to the long-term forces, and to the role of issues, was laid in Part 2. Candidate evaluations, as well as further specifications relating to the other elements of the model, will be discussed below as they apply.

The analysis will proceed in two main stages. First, we will apply our model, in the form of ordinary least squares (OLS) regression, to the first ballot of the French presidential election of 1988. The multiplicity of choices available to the French electorate at the first ballot makes OLS an appropriate analytical procedure. The analysis will enable us to estimate the respective weights of the presumed causal variables in determining the voters' candidate choices within the French context. For a comparison between France and the United States, we will move on to the second stage of the analysis. Here we will apply our model, in as close to matching terms as we can, to the choice of a candidate in the United States and to the choice of a candidate at the French second ballot. In both cases, only two candidates contended, literally in France and in terms of viability in the United States, where there are always what the French refer to as *candidats fantaisistes* in addition to major party candidates or occasional serious third-party candidates. Given that the vote choice was dichotomous in both countries, logistic regression will be employed, although we will also use OLS for special purposes, including trying to distinguish short-term from long-term effects. This analysis will not only enable us to estimate the relative impact of each factor on the choice of a candidate in each country but, of course, also allow us to compare those estimates cross-nationally.

France: The First-Ballot Vote

The dependent variable for the OLS model of French second-ballot candidate choice is a vote for one of the four major candidates (Mitterrand, Chirac, Barre, and Le Pen) expressed in left-right terms. That is, we have assigned to each of those candidates the mean left-right score attributed to them by the French electorate. The set was reduced to include only voters for one of those four candidates in order to permit us to include issue considerations as independent variables. Readers will recall from chapter 5 that we have mass perceptions of issue positions only for those four major candidates.[1]

The long-term forces included as independent variables in the regression are party identification and ideology. Party identification is, like the vote variables, based on the left-right locations assigned by the French electorate to the various major parties. For respondents who claimed to identify with parties for which we had no such mass assignments of left-right location, we attributed left-right locations to their parties on as reasonable bases as possible (see app. B for details). We experimented at some length with measures of ideology, and will report our results later in this section, but at first ideology was scored directly from the locations that the respondents assigned to themselves on the seven-point left-right scale. Uninvolved centrists, whom we have included among the marais for other purposes, are included here among the respondents having an ideological location.

The variables representing the short-term forces of overall candidate evaluations and issue-based candidate preferences were constructed according to the same scoring method that was employed in chapter 5, where mass perceptions of candidate issue positions were introduced. For overall candidate evaluations, we identified, for each respondent, the candidate (or candidates, in the case of ties) to whom they assigned the highest score on the conventional affect (thermometer) scale running from 0 to 100, and then assigned to the respondent the mean left-right score of that candidate or, in the case of a tie, the mean left-right score of the tied candidates.

In computing issue proximity measures, we identified the candidate(s) perceived by the respondent to have the closest position to his or her own on each issue scale, and then assigned the appropriate left-right score for that candidate (or those candidates). We followed the same basic procedure in computing issue direction measures, except that for those measures, the preferred candidates were based on maximal scalar products (as described in chap. 5) and not on least distances.

It will be recalled that we concluded our analysis of the respective properties of proximity measures and directional measures, in chapter 5, by indicating that it still remained for us to ascertain which of the two measures is a better predictor of candidate choice. That question is of direct relevance to us here because the answer determines which measure we should include in our model to represent the causal impact of issues. If the two types of measure were approximately equal in their predictive power, it would matter little or not at all which of them we employed in a fully specified model. If, on the other hand, one measure was clearly superior to the other, we would want to use that one, in order to give issues their maximal expression.[2]

We performed two sets of tests in order to estimate the relative predictive power of the proximity and directional measures. First, we ran a series of OLS regressions in which the dependent variable was the four-candidate presidential vote (scaled in left-right terms as described earlier in this chapter) and, in three separate runs, the only independent variables were paired expressions— in proximity form and directional form—of the same issue. Thus, for one run the independent variables were the two different measures of the church schools issue, for another the two measures of the public sector issue, and for the third the two expressions of the immigration issue. For each pair, we included only respondents who registered a valid response on both variables. Second, we ran two additional regressions, both of which retained the same dependent variable, but each of which included one type of issue measure for all three issues. One run, therefore, employed the three issue proximity measures as independent variables, while the other employed the three issue direction measures. For both sets of runs, missing data and four-candidate ties on the independent variables were set at the mean left-right score of the top candidate(s) selected by the respondents who provided valid responses on each relevant variable.

The results of these operations are set forth in table 7.1. It is evident that by both tests, the proximity measures are more powerful than the directional measures for the issues of the size of the public sector and policy toward immigrants, while the directional measure is modestly superior to the proximity measure for the issue of subsidies for religious schools. Accordingly, in the regression we have used the proximity measures for the public sector and immigration issues and the directional measure for the religious schools issue.

The outcome of the basic regression itself appears in table 7.2. The model is powerful, accounting for more than 70 percent of the variance in the four-candidate first-ballot vote. Party identification registers as the most potent of the individual independent variables, followed by candidate evaluations as expressed by the thermometer scale. Among the issue variables, only policy toward immigrants has a significant effect. The impact of the directional measure relating to subsidies for religious schools has a modest effect contrary to the expected one. That is something of a surprise, given the historic importance of the religious factor in distinguishing between left and right in France. This almost surely reflects the degree to which President Mitterrand soft-pedaled the school question after 1984, when massive demonstrations forced his government to withdraw proposals for increasing state control over private schools.

TABLE 7.1. Comparative Impact of Issue Direction and Issue Proximity on the Presidential Vote, First Ballot, France, 1988; Four Major Candidates Only

	Paired Comparisons, by Issue			
	Unstandardized *B*	Beta	*T*-Ratio	(*N*)
Church schools, direction	.262	.240	3.639	(449)
Church schools, proximity	.232	.200	3.028	
Public sector, direction	.210	.207	2.799	(461)
Public sector, proximity	.428	.388	5.248	
Immigration, direction	.145	.168	2.692	(512)
Immigration, proximity	.419	.402	6.443	

	Grouped Comparisons, by Sets of Issues (*N* = 709)			
	Unstandardized *B*	Beta	*T*-Ratio	Multiple R^2
Church schools, direction	.157	.119	3.467	.577
Public sector, direction	.403	.327	9.580	
Immigration, direction	.328	.339	10.633	
Church schools, proximity	.140	.105	3.098	.606
Public sector, proximity	.410	.325	9.634	
Immigration, proximity	.412	.363	11.398	

More striking, however, and no doubt for some even more surprising, is the comparatively modest independent contribution of ideological positioning to the choice of a presidential candidate, at least when ideology is expressed in the form of self-locations on a left-right scale. Chapter 5 prepared us, to a considerable extent, for the comparatively weak impact of issue positions as a factor in the vote. The numerous ties that we uncovered, many of them against nature in France and all of them against it in the United States, presaged a certain looseness in the match between perceived candidate issue positions and actual electoral choices. Chapter 4, however, in which we discussed the general question of the relative electoral weights of party identification and ideological positioning ended on a note that was likely to prepare us for a more potent showing by ideology in the overall regression than it actually displays.

Ideology vs. Party Identification

Chapter 4 concluded, it may be recalled, by reporting that a simple examination of the relationship between the two-party presidential vote in the United

TABLE 7.2.   **Basic Regression Model of the Presidential Vote, France, 1988, First Ballot; Four Major Candidates Only**

Indicator	Unstandardized B	Beta	T-Ratio	(Probability)
Left-right party identification	.423	.393	7.085	(0.000)
Candidate evaluation	.335	.297	5.846	(0.000)
Own left-right location	.114	.114	2.639	(0.008)
Proximity concerning immigration	.158	.138	5.335	(0.000)
Proximity concerning the public sector	.024	.020	0.706	(0.488)
Direction concerning religious schools	−.018	−.013	0.540	(0.596)
Constant	−.00106			
F-ratio for the regression	249.038	Probability	0.00	
Multiple correlation coefficient	.8535			

Note: $N = 574$

States and the second-ballot presidential vote in France, on the one hand, and party identification and ideological location, separately, on the other hand, showed that the degree of association was virtually identical, in France, for partisanship and ideology. Here, in this chapter, we find that party identification greatly outstrips ideology. How can we account for such a discrepancy?

The most obvious place to start the search for an explanation is with the difference between the two kinds of tests we have applied, first in chapter 4, and now here. The earlier test involved only simple bivariate association, while here we are dealing with multivariate regression. Earlier we were concerned with the French two-candidate second ballot; here we consider the first ballot with four candidates. In chapter 4 we employed a two-party summary measure of party identification that included strength of party identification and collapsed discrete partisan attachments into only two categories, the left and the right; here we use a pseudo-interval scale of party identification that expresses the left-right positions of multiple parties. Finally, the earlier measures were designed as much to maximize the tightness of the comparison between France and the United States as to illuminate considerations wholly internal to the French context. Those differences suggest the avenues to follow in seeking an explanation for the discrepancy.

The difference between bivariate association and multivariate regression is, of course, on the order of the difference between long division and differential calculus. The effects of the one can wash out completely as the other rises to higher levels of computation. So it is when we associate two variables with a third interactively. Nevertheless, the difference between the result of our test in chapter 5 and the current one is stark, and we pursued the problem further.

One main avenue we explored hinged on the difference between employing a pseudo-two-party partisan identification variable and a two-candidate vote variable, in the first test, and using a multiple-party partisan identification variable and a multiple-candidate vote variable, in the multiple regression. It seemed to us that inasmuch as the party identification and vote variables were couched in the same coinage in the regression—mean left-right scores—while the ideological variable took the form simply of locations on a scale of integers from 1 to 7, the party identification variable might have an intrinsically greater probability of literally matching candidate scores on the dependent variable, thereby inflating its coefficient relative to that for left-right location. We tested for that possibility by rerunning the same regression, except that we altered the left-right scores for the candidates on the dependent variable by transforming them from their literal means (which are recorded to the second decimal) to the closest whole digit (thus a vote for François Mitterrand, normally scored at 3.11, was converted to a score of 3, while a vote for Jean-Marie Le Pen, which is regularly scored at 6.62, was altered to a score of 7, and so forth for the other two main candidates included on the dependent variable). We thought that that simple change would shift any artificial advantage the base scoring system might have for the party identification variable (which was left in its original form) to the variable expressing left-right locations in whole digits. In fact, it did not do so. The unstandardized coefficient for left-right location did increase (from .114 to .141), but so did the coefficient for party identification (from .423 to .495). (Another change produced by that tinkering with the scoring system was to increase the weight of candidate evaluations from .335 to .402.)[3]

Left-Right Proximity vs. Left-Right Direction. We have already reported in this chapter that among our three issue-related variables, only that concerned with state subsidies for religious schools registered more strongly when cast in directional form than in proximity form. We have, accordingly, applied it in directional form in our regressions. We also need to ask why that particular issue should act differently in that regard from the other two issues we have used and examined.

The religious schools issue differs from the other two in more than one way, but the most important differences are surely in their age, duration, and social institutionalization. Religion is the basis of the oldest social and political cleavage in France. Compared to the hoary status of the religious issue, the immigration issue is a mewling babe and even the issue of the size of the public sector is a mere adolescent. In that sense, the religious schools issue is not an issue like the others. It is conceptually closer to the left-right distinction itself, which is similarly venerable, and which is universally treated as the expression of enduring ideological outlooks.

That line of thought suggested to us that left-right positioning might well register more forcefully if cast in directional form than in the simple fashion in which it appears in table 7.2 and in the subsequent regressions to which we have referred. That form, it will be recalled, was the respondent's own self-ascribed left-right location, in integers, without regard to the respondent's perceptions of the left-right locations of any of the candidates. Pursuing that idea, we reran the basic regression twice, once with the left-right variable in proximity form and again with it in directional form.[4] That operation is informative on two fronts. First, it relates directly to the broad issue of whether ideology, as expressed in left-right terms, or party identification is a more potent factor in determining the vote in France. This new test is of a piece with our earlier consideration that left-right positioning might register less strongly than party identification in contributing to the first-ballot vote when the left-right variable is measured in simple integers while both the party identification variable and the vote variable itself are expressed in mean scores recorded to the second decimal. That possibility was ruled out when we altered the dependent variable to match the integer scoring system of the original left-right location variable, but that particular test might not have been conclusive. Altering the construction of the left-right variable to match the construction of the dependent, vote choice variable might produce a different result.

Our recasting of the left-right locations variable, into both proximity form and directional form, followed the same procedure we described in chapter 5 concerning the more conventional issues. We identified the candidate(s) closest to the respondent for the proximity measure, and the candidate(s) for whom the scalar product was greatest for the directional measure, and then assigned the appropriate left-right score to those preferred candidates. That scale of scores is identical in form with the scale used for the dependent variable (the actual vote). Regardless of whether the proximity mode or the directional mode is more potent, the new measures might register more forcefully in comparison with party identification than the original, simple left-right variable reported in table 7.2.

At the same time, the test also permits us to determine which new form of the left-right variable—proximity or directional—accounts for more variance in the electorate's candidate choices, in interaction with the other variables included in the basic model. We kill two birds with one stone. We perform yet another test of the ideology versus party identification variety, and we also conduct a test of the proximity versus directional kind.

The results are summarized in table 7.3, where we report the same results that already appear in table 7.2, except that here we include only those independent variables that were statistically significant, as well as the results for the two new regressions, including in one case a left-right directional variable and in the other a left-right proximity variable, along with the same three other basic

TABLE 7.3. Comparative Impact of Alternate Measures of Left-Right Location as a Factor in Presidential Candidate Choice, France, 1988, First Ballot; Four Major Candidates Only

Indicator	Unstandardized B	Beta	T-Ratio	(Probability)
Original Set (*N* = 570)				
Own left-right location	.114	.114	2.639	(0.008)
Left-right party identification	.423	.393	7.085	(0.000)
Candidate evaluation	.335	.297	5.846	(0.000)
Proximity on immigration issue	.158	.138	5.335	(0.000)
R^2 = .854				
Proximity Alternative (*N* = 570)				
Proximity on left-right location	.070	.064	1.467	(0.139)
Left-right party identification	.452	.421	7.746	(0.000)
Candidate evaluation	.348	.309	6.007	(0.000)
Proximity on immigration issue	.165	.144	5.636	(0.000)
R^2 = .853				
Directional Alternative (*N* = 569)				
Scalar product for left-right location	.103	.115	2.932	(0.004)
Left-right party identification	.432	.402	7.677	(0.000)
Candidate evaluation	.325	.289	5.643	(0.000)
Proximity on immigration issue	.166	.145	5.739	(0.000)
R^2 = .855				

independent variables. All three regressions also included the two other insignificant issue proximity variables.

These results are uncommonly clear. Neither change in the structure of the left-right variable affects the overall power of the model, but our intuition about the similar properties of the religious schools issue and broad left-right-locations proved to be well founded. The directional left-right variable is more potent than the left-right proximity variable as a factor in the choice of a presidential candidate. In fact, the left-right proximity variable is not even statistically significant.

At the same time, the role of party identification continues to be predominant. The changes we made in the structure of the left-right variable both result in marginal increases in the impact and statistical significance of party identification as a factor in candidate choice. Just as our experiment in matching the scoring techniques for ideology and candidate choice failed to boost the role of ideology (relative to party identification) when we altered the scoring of the vote variable to match that of the ideology variable, so does our alteration of the structure of the ideology variable to match that of the vote variable fail to change the basic balance of forces in any significant way.

Controlling Mutually for Left-Right and Party Identification. Still trying to disentangle the effects of left-right locations and of party identification on the first-ballot vote, we resorted to a statistical effort to control for the mutual impact of the two presumed causal variables in a way that is not supplied by the standard regressions reported above. This procedure involved three steps. First, we regressed the vote on left-right locations and on party identification, separately. This first operation showed that while left-right positioning accounted for 54 percent of the variance in the vote, party identification accounted for 71 percent of it. In step two, we then regressed left-right locations on party identification and party identification on left-right locations. Finally, in a further pair of regressions, we regressed the variance in the vote not explained by one of the two causal variables being tested (left-right and party identification) on the variance in the *other* variable that was not accounted for by the first variable. That series of operations showed that while the variance in left-right positioning that was not accounted for by party identification explained less than half of one percent of the variance in the vote not explained by party identification, the variance in party identification not accounted for by left-right locations explained more than a third of the (larger proportion of) variance in the vote that was not accounted for by left-right locations.

That is as far as we can take the issue of ideology versus party identification at this time. The results of all of our tests are consistent in that they show that party identification predominates over left-right positioning as a factor in the first-ballot vote, although the margin by which the former distances the latter varies with the nature of the test. We will return to the issue again in the context of the French second-ballot, runoff election. Before proceeding to that stage, however, we must conclude the analysis of the attitudinal bases of the French first-ballot vote.

Separating Long-Term from Short-Term Forces

The findings that appear in table 7.2 come from a single regression, which implicitly reflects a model of the attitudinal bases of electoral choice that treats all the attitudes included as though they shared a common conceptual status.

The model that we have sketched verbally, however, does not consider all the potential electoral forces in the same way. As we have indicated several times, ideological positioning and party identifications are considered to be long-term forces that, while not being immutable, are highly stable over time, while candidate preferences and issue positions are short-term in character, even though they may be powerful enough at any given election to cause some people to defect from their ostensibly longer-standing political commitments.

Whether long-term or short-term in constitution, those attitudes can reasonably be expected to operate simultaneously on any given voter while he or she is in the voting booth, and in that sense there is absolutely nothing wrong with including all of those attitudes in a single regression equation to measure their individual and collective contributions to the overall voting decision of any collectivity. At the same time, there would seem to be more than mere esthetic value in separating analytically the long-term forces from the short-term ones, if only to try to learn how much explanatory power is added to the long-term variables by the short-term ones.[5]

Accordingly, we employed the same three-step method that we outlined in connection with trying to distinguish between the effects on the vote of left-right positioning and party identification. We first regressed the first-ballot vote on our two long-term variables, party identification and left-right locations; then we regressed each of the short-term variables on the same two long-term variables. Finally, we regressed the variance in the vote that was not explained by the long-term forces, on the variance in the short-term forces that was similarly not accounted for by the long-term forces.

This sequence of steps indicated that the short-term forces added little to the long-term ones in accounting for the first-ballot vote. The two long-term forces accounted for 69 percent of the variance in the vote, while the short-term ones accounted only for four additional percentage points. The second step in the operation, however, provides important information concerning the relationship between the short-term and long-term forces, at least when they are measured simultaneously. The main point in this regard is that issue-based candidate preferences are much more independent of party identification and left-right positioning than more general candidate evaluations are. Party and ideology together account for less than a fifth of the variance in candidate preference linked to the religious schools issue, a fourth of the variance in candidate preference resting on the immigration issue, and less than a third of the variance in candidate preference related to the issue of the size of the public sector. When it comes to overall candidate evaluation, however, the situation is very different. Party identification and left-right locations together account for some 80 percent of the variance in that summary measure of candidate preference. This means that the independent status of overall candidate evaluations is much more limited than that of issue-based candidate preferences when they are included simultaneously with partisanship and ideology in a single regression such as that reported in table 7.2. By the same token, however, when every effort has been made to separate overall candidate evaluations from the two presumably more basic attitudes, as we have done here, any residual potency of candidate evaluations should be all the more respected.

Such respect is due here. We have indicated that our four short-term variables add little to the overall explanatory power of the two long-term variables with regard to the first-ballot vote in France. Most of that added value comes from candidate evaluations which, along with candidate preferences based on the immigration issue, is statistically significant as a factor in the vote. The two other issues—the size of the public sector and subsidies for religious schools—had no independent, statistically significant effect on the vote.

Overall Predictive Accuracy

Before leaving our consideration of the factors in the first-ballot vote at the French presidential election of 1988, it may be useful to return for a moment to assess the overall accuracy of the simultaneous model whose results are reported in table 7.2. Two summary measures are available: (1) the correlation between the predicted vote and the actual vote for the four major candidates, and (2) the proportion of cases whose votes were correctly predicted.

The Pearsonian correlation between the predicted and the actual vote was a healthy .85.[6]

The model correctly predicted the vote of 61 percent of the cases, broken down by candidate as follows: Mitterrand (94 percent); Barre (64 percent), Chirac (81 percent) and Le Pen (41 percent).[7] The results are, of course, impressive for the first three of those four candidates, but poor for the fourth, Le Pen, the right-wing extremist. It is, of course, not particularly surprising that so many of Le Pen's voters should fail to register within the range of left-right scores that we assigned to them. We have seen, in chapter 5, both that Le Pen was clearly identified in the public mind with the immigration issue and that that issue was itself only weakly associated with left-right ideology among the three-fourths of the electorate that was not much interested in politics. Our linear model is driven principally by partisanship, candidate attractiveness, and ideology, all of which are expressed in left-right currency, which also provides the organizing framework for the candidate choices that the model predicts. Although Le Pen's virtually exclusive issue, immigration, registers significantly in the model, it is largely independent of the left-right ideological axis that underlies the model.

Le Pen drew support in comparatively large proportions across the entire range of predicted values produced by our regression. In addition to the some 40 percent of his votes that came from our predicted rightists, another third came from voters whom we assigned to Chirac, and the remaining fourth came from voters whose predicted scores indicated that they would vote for Barre or even Mitterrand. Le Pen drew votes from the entire spectrum of voters, as their positioning on our set of long-term and short-term variables arrayed them. Le Pen is indeed the right-wing extremist he is conventionally portrayed as being, but fewer than half of his electoral supporters in 1988 matched that same description, at least as expressed by the measures at our disposal.[8]

France and the United States: The Decisive Ballot

We are now in a position to compare the application of our basic model of electoral choice to the French runoff ballot at the presidential election of 1988 with its application to a two-candidate presidential election in the United States. Before doing so, it is important to specify our measures in ways that maximize the validity of the comparison.

The most serious potential problem is that while all our measures for France in 1988 were obtained at a postelectoral survey, for most U.S. presidential elections, including that of 1988, the critical measures were obtained at preelectoral surveys.

Fortunately, however, the U.S. NES survey for 1984 asked the questions that yield the necessary measures at both preelectoral and postelectoral interviews. This happenstance produces a double bonus. First, it permits us to estimate the differences between employing preelectoral and postelectoral independent variables to account for the same electoral outcome in the United States. And second, by requiring us to concentrate our attention on the 1984 U.S. election, it directs us toward making a comparison with France in 1988 that is in one major respect more appropriate than a comparison between the two presidential elections of 1988 would be. Comparing the two elections that were held in the same year would permit us to control for the temporal environment. But the attri-butes of the competing U.S. candidates were more similar in 1984 than they were in 1988 to the attributes of the 1988 French candidates. The 1984 U.S. election pitted an incumbent against a well-known challenger, just as the 1988 French election did. In that respect, the 1984 U.S. election is a close counterpart of the 1988 French election. Moreover, in 1984 (as in 1988), there were only two serious U.S. presidential candidates. Our basic comparison, therefore, will match postelectoral measures for the United States in 1984 with postelectoral measures for France in 1988.

The independent variables include, for each country, measures of party identification, ideology, candidate evaluation, and three issue variables. The party identification variable for the U.S. is the standard 7-point summary party identification scale with which researchers are highly familiar; for France, it is the pseudo-two-party 7-point summary variable that we described in chapter 4 and that is the closest counterpart we can create for the standard U.S. summary party identification variable, which combines both direction and strength of partisanship. Ideology is expressed for France in terms of left-right self-location, and for the United States as liberal-conservative self-positioning, in both cases on 7-point scales. Candidate evaluations are represented in scales running from 0 to 6 for both countries. In each case, the conventional 100-point thermometer scale was converted to a 7-point scale, and then, for the United States, we subtracted the score for Mondale from the score for Reagan, while for France we subtracted the score for Mitterrand from the score for Chirac.

Three issue positions were included for each country. For France, we used the three familiar issues: the size of the public sector and policy toward immigrants in proximity form, and subsidies for religious schools in directional form. The left-right scores of the preferred candidates were generated, including those of the two candidates for whom we had the relevant data and who ran at the first ballot but not the second. The French issue position scores, therefore, ranged from 3.11 to 6.62.

For the United States, we were limited to only three issues, rather than being able to employ the more numerous issue positions that are normally obtained in U.S. NES surveys, because only three appropriate issue-scale questions were asked both in the 1984 preelectoral and postelectoral surveys. These issues related to government providing fewer services and reducing spending versus government providing more services and increasing spending; the government seeing to it that every person has a job and a good standard of living versus the government letting each person get ahead on his own; and the United States becoming more (versus less) involved in internal affairs of Central America. Voter positions on those three issues were cast in proximity form, with a score of 1 assigned to closer proximity to Mondale and a score of 10 assigned to closer proximity to Reagan.

The dependent variable for each country was the candidate choice, scored as 0 for François Mitterrand or Walter Mondale and 1 for Jacques Chirac or Ronald Reagan.

Three logistic regressions were run: one for France in 1988 based on our postelectoral measures; another for the United States in 1984, also based on postelectoral measures; and the third for the United States in 1984, but based on preelectoral measures of the same variables included in the second regression. We can, therefore, compare France and the United States directly, as well as observe the differences that result from using postelectoral, as opposed to preelectoral measures, for the United States. Table 7.4 reports the principal results of the three regressions.

Before exploring the cross-national comparison between France and the United States, it may be of some interest to compare the results of the logistic regression relating to the French second ballot with those of the OLS regres-

TABLE 7.4. Logistic Regression Models of the Presidential Vote, France, 1988, Decisive Ballot; United States, 1984

	A. France (Postelectoral Measures)		Indicator	B. U.S. (Postelectoral Measures)		C. U.S. (Preelectoral Measures)	
Indicator	Unstandardized B	B/SE		Unstandardized B	B/SE	Unstandardized B	B/SE
Own left-right location	.735	3.01	Own liberal-conservative location	.070	.93	.228	1.89
Party identification	.560	3.49	Party identification	.684	8.79	.385	4.91
Candidate evaluation	1.435	7.90	Candidate Evaluation	1.362	12.00	1.053	9.90
Proximity public sector issue	.304	1.36	Proximity services and spending	.062	1.67	.089	3.10
Proximity immigration issue	−.168	−0.87	Proximity jobs and standard of living	.017	0.45	.029	1.02
Direction religious schools issue	.420	1.66	Proximity Central America	.037	0.99	.036	1.28

A. France: $\chi^2 = 840.04$ (d.f. = 6), R^2 analogue = .782, $N = 761$

B. U.S.: $\chi^2 = 1186.01$ (d.f. = 6), R^2 analogue = .688, $N = 1,163$

C. U.S.: $\chi^2 = 948.78$ (d.f. = 6), R^2 analogue = .635, $N = 993$

sion that we applied to the French first-ballot vote for the four major contestants (see table 7.2). Those two analyses are of very different types, and we would not expect them to produce identical results. They do not: the ordering of the independent variables is quite different in the two models. In the model for the first-ballot vote choice, party identification carries more weight than candidate evaluations, and the latter, in turn, registers more forcefully than left-right positioning. In the model for the decisive French ballot, candidate evaluations emerge as the predominant factor, and left-right self-locations place ahead of party identification. It is not particularly surprising that candidate evaluations should gain in importance at the second ballot, when the previously wider field of candidates narrows down to only two. Indeed, there is a sense in which electoral choice in a two-candidate contest ultimately rests exclusively on candidate evaluations, with other factors—including party identification—operating only when the voter evaluates the candidates similarly (Markus 1982, 556). The change in the relative potency of party identification and left-right ideology as presumed electoral forces, from one ballot to the next, is more noteworthy, as it furnishes new data to be considered in trying to determine which of those two attitudes has the larger bearing on candidate choice in France.

The logistic model for the French second ballot surely suggests that while party identification is a stronger force than left-right locations in candidate selection at the first ballot, the reverse is true for the second ballot. Before accepting that proposition as final, however, it is worth considering the extent to which the reordering is less a reflection of actual French political behavior than an artifact of differences in measurement techniques. There are three main differences between our analyses of the French first-ballot vote and the second-ballot vote. The dependent variables are different, in that at the first ballot there were multiple candidates, scored in left-right terms, while at the second ballot there were only two candidates, scored nominally. Party identification was also measured differently for the two analyses. For the first ballot, it was couched in terms of the mean left-right locations of the parties identified with. For the second-ballot analysis, party identification was scored in terms of identification with either a leftist party or a rightist party, scaled according to three degrees of strength of partisan attachment, in order to sharpen the comparison with the United States. Finally, the regression model for the first-ballot vote was based on OLS, while the second ballot analysis rested on logistic regression. We can not do anything about the differences in the dependent variables; they are rooted in the structure of candidate choice at each ballot. We can, however, examine our renditions of party identification more closely, as well as consider the difference between the two forms of multiple regression employed, to see what kinds of special effects they may have produced.

The extent to which the results of the models are sensitive to the particular measure of party identification employed can be demonstrated very simply.

When, in the model of the first-ballot vote that is reported in table 7.2, we replace the left-right party identification scale originally used with the pseudo-two-party party identification measure, the order of the coefficients for left-right location and party identification changes to what it is in table 7.4 for the second-ballot model, except that the difference in the magnitudes of the coefficients is small. The coefficient for party identification falls from .423 to .120, while that for left-right location rises from .114 to .145. (At the same time, the significance level of party identification remains higher than it is for left-right positioning, although only marginally so.)

Similarly, when we replace the pseudo-two-party measure of party identification originally used for the model of the second-ballot choice, recorded in table 7.4, with the left-right party identification scale, there is a shift in the coefficients that enhances the relative importance of party identification. There is, however, no change in the order of the variables; left-right ideology still registers more forcefully than party identification, but the gap between the two coefficients narrows (.783 vs. .684, as compared with the original .735 vs. .560). Moreover, in the revised, test-case model, the significance levels of the two variables are equal.

With regard to the differences between the properties of a linear OLS model and those of a logistic model, it is not unusual for the two models to produce different estimates of the relative contributions of the same independent variables to changes in the level of the dependent variable. Denk and Finkel (1992, 797) indicate that "there is no simple explanation for these differences," but they note that a partial explanation would include the fact that the differences between the two types of model will increase as the predicted probabilities generated on the dependent variable by the logistic model depart from linearity. The predicted probabilities produced by our logistic regression relative to the French second-ballot vote are far from linear. Figure 7.1 plots those predicted probabilities against the dependent scores generated by the OLS model. It is evident at a glance that while the OLS predictions are a long rectangular band, the logit predictions are clumped into barbell shape. Almost 75 percent of the logit predictions are clustered within three points of either the probability of 0 or that of 100. The linear model records the independent effects of such strong and intercorrelated variables as party identification, left-right location, and candidate evaluations. Candidate evaluations, however, are so powerful in the logistic regression that the inclusion of party identification or of left-right locations adds little to the prediction. How much is added by either of them really becomes a secondary issue, immune to precise estimation.

The principal conclusion that emerges from this analysis is that the more finely we record party identification for measurement purposes, the more strongly and sharply it registers as a factor in candidate choice, whether that choice be among several or only two candidates, although it is more suited to

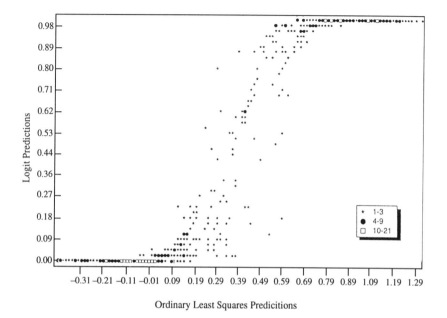

Ordinary Least Squares Predicitions

Fig. 7.1. Scatterplot of ordinary least squares predictions by logit pre-dictions of the presidential vote, France, decisive ballot, 1988

the multiple candidate case. Left-right self-locations emerge all the more strongly as the measure of partisanship loses the capacity to produce direct and exact matches between the party identified with and the party chosen, because either the party identification variable or the candidate choice variable is blurred by measurement conventions, or both are.

At the same time, there is no escaping the fact that when party identification is scaled in left-right terms, it becomes enmeshed with ideological imagery in a virtually inseparable way. The bulk of the evidence suggests that on the individual level, partisanship has a more direct impact on electoral choice than ideology, but that cannot be unequivocally demonstrated with the available data (although Converse and Pierce [1986], who worked with panel data, could make a more convincing case for the primacy of partisanship).[9] We have taken the issue of partisanship vs. ideology, within the French context, as far as we can, and we will return to it only incidentally in the remainder of this volume.

One other point should be made about the difference between the outcomes of the models for the first and second French ballots, before we move on to the French-U.S. comparison. There is a change in the direction of the effects of two of the three issue-based variables. Although attitudes toward immigration were a statistically significant factor in the first-ballot vote, in that hostility toward immigrants was associated with support for rightist candidates, anti-immigrant attitudes were slightly (but not significantly) associated with a vote for Mitterrand at the second ballot. This suggests that while Le Pen and possibly other dropout candidates drew the support of many voters who were hostile toward immigrants, enough of those voters shifted to Mitterrand at the second ballot to reverse the relationship between attitudes toward immigration and support for a leftist candidate. Conversely, while support for state subsidies for religious schools was minimally associated with voting for leftist candidates at the first ballot, the same position was linked with support for Chirac, the rightist candidate, at the decisive ballot, although the relationship was not statistically significant in either case.

France vs. the United States

In comparing the results of our model of candidate choice for France at the second ballot, with those for the United States, we will rely on columns A and B of table 7.4, which both rest on data obtained at postelectoral surveys. In this regard, the first point to be made is the general one that the model produces an excellent fit for both countries. The levels of statistical significance are off the map, and while the R^2 analogue for France is rather larger than it is for the United States, that summary measure for logistic regressions is only indicative.

With regard to the relative importance of the various independent variables that we assume to be motivating factors in the vote, the results show considerable convergence of the two countries, and where there is divergence, it is wholly intelligible.

Candidate evaluations emerge as the main factor in candidate choice in both countries, with party identification ranking second in importance in the United States, but third in France, following ideological outlooks as expressed in left-right self-positioning. In the United States, liberal-conservative self-identifications play only a modest (and statistically insignificant) role. Issue positions have generally weak effects in both countries, although the hoary religious schools issue in France and the issue of government services and expenditures in the United States approach statistical significance.

The prominence of candidate evaluations indicates that candidate appeal is a major consideration for the electorate at the decisive ballot in both France and the United States, and the roughly equal levels of importance of party identification in the two countries (as expressed by the unstandardized B coefficients), testifies to the concomitant role of partisanship. The main difference in the results of the models, the minimal importance of ideology in the United States compared with its relative importance in France, is something that we should have been prepared for by chapter 4, where we highlighted the modest role of ideology in U.S. electoral behavior. The liberal-conservative dimension has just not worked its way into the mass consciousness in the United States to the extent that left-right imagery has done in France (where, nonetheless, its importance at the mass level can easily be exaggerated).

Having said all that, it is nevertheless important to keep in mind that our presumed causal variables are highly intercorrelated and were measured simultaneously, which means that we must be extremely cautious in estimating their independent effects. When we push the analysis further in an effort to determine how much of the variance in our short-term measures, which include the ostensibly powerful candidate evaluations and the weaker issued-based attitudes, was accounted for in each country by the long-term factors of party identification and ideology jointly, we obtain some highly interesting results (see table 7.5). These may be summarized as follows:

1. Candidate evaluations were more independent of party identification and ideology in the United States in 1984 than they were in France in 1988.
2. Party identification registered as a more potent factor than ideology in accounting for candidate evaluations in both countries.
3. Issue-based attitudes were more independent of party identification and ideology in the United States in 1984 than they were in France in 1988.
4. Ideology was more important than party identification in accounting for issue-based attitudes in France, while the reverse was the case in the United States.

Our interpretation of table 7.4 needs to be tempered by these background findings. Candidate evaluations are probably more important independent factors in candidate choice in the United States than in France. Partisanship is probably also more important in the United States than in France, but that is far from certain. Ideology is weak in the United States, as we have had reason to point out repeatedly, but it probably is less strong in France than a literal reading of table 7.4 would suggest. Ideology contributes less than partisanship to the powerful factor of candidate evaluations, while the issue-based attitudes, to which ideology contributes more than partisanship does, are only weak factors in explaining the second-ballot vote.

Postelectoral vs. Preelectoral Measures

Our comparison of the forces shaping presidential candidate choice in France and the United States rests on measures that were obtained at postelectoral surveys, of necessity for France and by choice for the United States. The more customary way of analyzing candidate choice in the United States is to employ

TABLE 7.5. Decomposition of Long-Term and Short-Term Effects on the Presidential Vote, by OLS, France, 1988, Decisive Ballot; United States, 1984

Independent Variable	Unstandardized B	T-Ratio	Dependent Variable	Multiple R^2
		FRANCE		
I. Own left-right location	.095	8.2581	Candidate choice	.85
Party identification	.155	20.2598		
II. Own left-right location	.582	8.1072	Candidate evaluation	.82
Party identification	.851	17.8217		
Own left-right location	.237	6.1530	Proximity public sector	.60
Party identification	.191	7.4434		
Own left-right location	.361	7.8219	Proximity immigration issue	.47
Party identification	.044	1.4458 n.s.		
Own left-right location	.166	3.9911	Direction religious schools issue	.44
Party identification	.134	4.8646		
III. Residual variance on candidate evaluation	.065	12.2188	Residual variance on candidate choice	.44
Residual variance on proximity public sector issue	.030	2.9572		
Residual variance on proximity immigration issue	−.015	−1.8135 n.s.		
Residual variance on direction religious schools issue	.014	1.5243 n.s.		
		UNITED STATES		
I. Own liberal-conservative location	.035	6.4206	Candidate choice	.74
Party identification	.144	30.0822		
II. Own liberal-conservative location	.276	9.8146	Candidate evaluation	.66
Party identification	.695	27.5638		
Own liberal-conservative location	.261	4.3264	Proximity services/ spending issue	.24
Party identification	.371	6.8821		

(*continued*)

TABLE 7.5—*Continued*

Independent Variable	Unstandardized B	T-Ratio	Dependent Variable	Multiple R^2
Own liberal-conservative location	.240	3.8682	Proximity jobs/standard of living issue	.24
Party identification	.384	6.9248		
Own liberal-conservative location	.184	3.2069	Proximity Central America issue	.15
Party identification	.200	3.8911		
III. Residual variance on candidate evaluation	.090	23.0007	Residual variance on candidate choice	.57
Residual variance on proximity services/ spending issue	.006	2.0037		
Residual variance on proximity jobs/standard of living issue	.001	.4615 n.s.		
Residual variance on proximity Central America issue	.873E-03	.3602 n.s.		

measures derived from preelectoral surveys. Column C of table 7.4 shows the results of the logistic regression of the 1984 presidential vote on the same variables included in column B, except that they rest on preelectoral measures. A comparison of columns B and C gives us some idea of the differences in the results that relate to using one set of measures or the other.

The overall pattern of the two sets of results is very similar. The significance levels are high in both cases, and there is little difference between the R^2 analogues. Moreover, the ordering of the coefficients by independent variable is the same for both models. Two nonnegligible differences, however, are that the issue of government services and expenditures achieves statistical significance in the preelectoral model, while it does not in the postelectoral one. Similarly, liberal-conservative positioning approaches statistical significance in the "before" model but is far from it in the "after" model.

Whether it is better to employ preelectoral or postelectoral measures is a question that cannot be answered in the abstract, as the answer depends on how long the pre- and postelectoral interviewing periods last, and how many and what kinds of potentially opinion-altering events occur during those periods. For the United States in 1984, the postelectoral survey is probably at least as satisfactory for our purposes as the preelectoral one, as the preelection interviews were spread out over a two-month period and subject to the vagaries of the campaign, while the postelection interviews were virtually completed in little more than a month.[10] Our postelectoral French survey was completed within only a few days. We need have no regrets, therefore, that we have only a postelectoral French survey with which to work. Instead, our impulse is to thank the NES scholars who designed the 1984 U.S. study that made a postelectoral analysis possible.

It should be added that we can draw no inferences from the comparison of the before-and-after results for the United States in 1984 for what a preelectoral model for the second ballot of the 1988 French presidential election might look like. The period prior to the French decisive ballot is even more potentially destabilizing (in the attitudinal sense) than the U.S. campaign period is. The campaign prior to the French first ballot has many similarities to a U.S. campaign. Partisan attitudes unfold, candidate perceptions form, and issue positions may come into play. Four successive surveys (*Sondages*, 1965) conducted prior to the first ballot of the French presidential election of 1965 record the stages of mobilization of support between late October and early December, among leftist and centrist partisans, in favor of Jean Lecanuet and away from Charles de Gaulle. Cayrol (1988) shows how a series of six surveys conducted between August 1980, and the middle of April 1981, prior to the first ballot of the 1981 presidential election, captured a decline (from 65 percent to 54 percent) in the proportion of voters who claimed to be relying mainly on the personality and competence of the candidate in casting their votes and the corresponding increase in the percentage (from 29 to 43) who reported instead a primary reliance on the candidate's party and program. But such a crystallization of opinion is crucial, across the entire electorate, only for the first ballot. The preelection campaign ends abruptly with a vote that produces a new situation for the many people whose preferred candidate is eliminated from the race.[11] During the hectic two-week period between the first and decisive ballots, a new campaign unfolds. Fresh endorsements are made (or with held); new strategies are improvised; a debate between the two front-runners is televised; and the circumstances invite a flow of new or refitted information.[12] It is questionable whether a survey conducted during such a period would capture the distribution and intensity of mass opinion any better than a promptly administered postelectoral survey such as our own for 1988.

Implications

This chapter has covered a good deal of ground. We have analyzed the attitudinal factors affecting the French first-ballot presidential vote, involving multiple candidates, and we have compared the impact of those same factors on the French two-party decisive presidential ballot and on the two-party presidential vote in the United States. Along the way, we have paid close attention to issues of measurement, and in doing so we have experimented with alternate ways of pursuing the electoral effects of the attitudinal forces involved. All of those refinements have their proper places, and we have tried dutifully to report what they signify for the understanding of electoral behavior in France and the United States. But there is always a risk that in exploring byways one will lose track of the main route, so it is appropriate to return in conclusion to the main message that emerges from the analyses reported in this chapter.

That message is simply that the attitudinally-based theory of electoral choice, centering on but far from exhausted by the concept of party identification, is as useful in understanding mass electoral behavior in France as it has been in the United States, the country of its origin. A common model of mass electoral choice, employing the same set of variables, accounts very well for the selections made by the French electorate among multiple presidential candidates, and for those made by both French and U.S. voters at decisive two-candidate contests. The three elections, two French and one American, become intelligible in terms of a single set of perceptual categories, including partisanship, ideology, candidate evaluations, and issue positions.

The carefully controlled comparison between France and the United States shows, further, that when the frameworks within which electoral choices must be made are structurally similar, the reach of the model is basically the same, and the relative weight of each factor in accounting for the presidential vote is remarkably similar. Candidate evaluations and partisanship affect the probabilities of voting for one candidate or the other similarly (and considerably) in both France and the United States, while issue positions affect those same probabilities much less. Only the role of ideology, which we have cast in terms of left-right locations for France and liberal-conservative positioning for the United States, shows signs of operating differently in the two countries. But even in this connection, the magnitude of the difference is uncertain as it varies with the measurement conventions by which we express ideology as it applies to the French voter.

What we find, therefore, is that two different electorates—French and American—which have been socialized within different cultures and incorporated into different sets of institutional frameworks base their presidential electoral choices on essentially the same set of politically relevant stimuli. There is little room here for the notion of "exceptionalism," whether of a French or American cast.

CHAPTER 8

Group Bases of Electoral Choice

The kinds of attitudes that we related in the preceding chapter to the voters' choices of presidential candidates in France and the United States are not distributed randomly throughout the electorates of the two countries. In both countries, the proportions of people identifying with any given political party, favoring any particular candidate, or sharing some ideological outlook or issue position may vary widely from one social group to another. This means, of course, that to the extent that those attitudes shape electoral choices (and we have seen with considerable precision just how much they actually do affect candidate choice), the contributions made by various social groups to the electoral outcome at any given election also may vary greatly.

Differential group support for one political party or another is an old phenomenon. Politicians have always had an intuitive and practical (if not always accurate) understanding of the importance of voting blocs, and political historians have long directed their attention to the social sources of electoral gains and losses. In recent decades, appreciation for the group basis of mass electoral behavior has become increasingly widespread, and the care with which it is examined has become highly refined. In both France and the United States, there is a lively journalistic interest in the ways in which various social groups cast their votes and close scholarly examination is given to the contributions made by various groups to one or another electoral coalition.

After each French election, SOFRES and other public opinion survey organizations report their sample estimates of the distribution of the vote for the various parties and candidates by standard demographic categories, usually on a univariate basis, but occasionally also in simple multivariate form. Similarly, in the United States, the results of postelectoral surveys are tabulated and presented in leading journals and newspapers, again usually in univariate but sometimes also in multivariate terms (see, for example, the *New York Times*, November 10, 1988, 18 and November 5, 1992, B9). These surveys are not exclusively directed toward obtaining information about the age, sex, occupation, religion, and other attributes of the voters that contribute to determining the group bases of each party's or candidate's electoral support. They normally include additional information of an attitudinal kind, similar to the items we discussed in the previous chapter, sometimes in combination with demographic characteristics.[1] But in both France and the United States, the attentive public is familiar with the notion that particular parties or candidates may be supported by quite distinctive and usually enduring social groups.

On the academic level, the main efforts have been aimed at estimating the independent contributions made by various social groups to one or another of the major U.S. parties over time. In this regard, the pioneering work was done by Axelrod (1972, 1974, 1978, 1982, 1986), who made estimates of the group support for the two U.S. parties at presidential elections from 1952 to 1984. Stanley, Bianco, and Niemi (1986) attacked a similar problem, in this case the evolution of the group bases of identification with the Democratic party from 1952 to 1984, employing different and newer techniques. Stanley and Niemi (1991) extended this work to include identification with the Republican party through 1988, and incorporating new group categories not employed in the earlier study. Between those two contributions, Erikson, Lancaster, and Romero (1989) employed similar techniques, not to analyze the group bases of party identification, but rather to estimate the group components of the major-party presidential vote from 1952 to 1984.

We have profited greatly from these analyses, although our purposes are rather different from those attendant on the earlier studies. Our main objective is to compare the group bases of the electoral support for the presidential candidates at the decisive ballot in France and the United States in 1988, with a view toward determining how much the group support for the "leftist" candidate (or "rightist" candidate) at the decisive presidential ballot in one of the countries in 1988 resembled that for the corresponding candidate in the other country. We know that there is a great deal of similarity in the structure of popular presidential choice in the United States, with its predominantly two-party system, and in France, where the presidential selection process narrows down to a choice between only two candidates at the decisive ballot. Most of the time, therefore, the choice before the voters in both countries is between two candidates, one of whom is perceived to be more leftist (or more liberal) than the other, however vague those summarizing labels may turn out to be as they circulate further and further away from elite circles. In those terms, we have no difficulty aligning Michael Dukakis (and the Democratic party) with François Mitterrand (and his supporting party elites), and pairing George Bush (and the Republican party) with Jacques Chirac (and his partisan support). The question that interests us here is whether, and if so to what extent, that structural parallelism is accompanied by similarities in mass electoral support, defined in terms of conventional social groups, for the same side in each country.

In order to answer that question, we first inventoried the groups in each country that previous research has identified as being likely disproportionately to support one party or coalition over the other. Our list naturally included the groups considered in the works, cited above, relating to electoral coalitions in the United States, as well as those—relating in particular to religion and social class—that have figured prominently in France (Michelat and Simon 1977; Converse and Pierce 1986; Pierce and Rochon 1988). It should be emphasized that our aim was a comparative analysis and, accordingly, we did not intend to segregate categories on a national basis. On the contrary, our intention was to search for the electoral effects of the same group in both countries, whenever such a test seemed reasonable, regardless of whether the group in question had been conventionally associated with a particular partisan coloration in one country but not the other. One main objective of the analysis was precisely to see whether there were any social groups, familiar as an electoral force to the students of politics in one of the countries but generally overlooked by students of electoral behavior in the other country, that might actually have significant effects there.

Armed with our collection of potentially important social groups, we then proceeded to build models of the group-based support for each of the four leading presidential candidates in France and the United States in 1988. Employing logistic regression, we eventually ended up with four models, each of which includes those groups whose members had a greater probability of voting for the candidate in question than nonmembers of the group, and for which (in most cases) that difference in probabilities was statistically significant. In each of our four models, the dependent variable was dichotomized between casting a vote for the candidate in question and either voting for the other candidate *or abstaining*. This, of course, implies that our notion of group contribution to an electoral coalition includes the proportion of the group that turns out to vote as well as the proportion of the voters from the group that casts a ballot for the coalition's candidate.[2]

The core groups included in the two leftist coalitions are presented in figure 8.1; those constituting the nuclei of the two rightist coalitions appear in figure 8.2. In both figure 8.1 and figure 8.2, the degree of statistical significance (*B*/SE) is indicated for each group. Additional supporting data appear in table 8.1 and table 8.2. Tables 8.1 and 8.2 indicate, for the leftist and rightist coalitions respectively, the average difference for members in each group between their probability of voting for the designated candidate and what that probability would have been if they were not members of the group, along with the size of each group as a proportion of the total sample for the country involved.

Our discussion will center on figure 8.1 and figure 8.2. These have been constructed so as to facilitate cross-national comparison. Taken together, however, the two figures provide a great deal of information relevant to each country separately, and we will proceed by first comparing the overall patterns of group-based electoral conflict in the two countries before moving on to considering how similar (or different) the group components of the leftist and rightist electoral coalitions were in France and the United States in 1988.

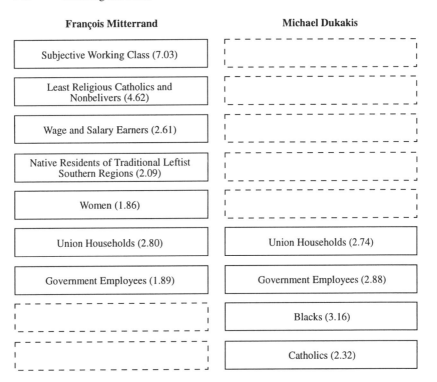

Fig. 8.1. Core group coalitions of French and U.S. leftist presidential candidates, 1988. Group members with a markedly greater probability than nonmembers of the group of voting for the candidate in question, assuming "average" positioning in the other groups listed for the candidate. Statistical significance appears in parentheses.

Coalitional Polarization in France

The main point to be made at the outset is that, in group terms, the French electorate in 1988 was much more polarized along a small number of central social dimensions than the U.S. electorate was. The French electorate was sharply divided simultaneously on the bases of social class and religion, and perhaps also on the basis of gender.

Class and Religion

Several measures of social class testify to its importance in shaping French electoral coalitions. The one that stands out most clearly is simply the voters' sub-

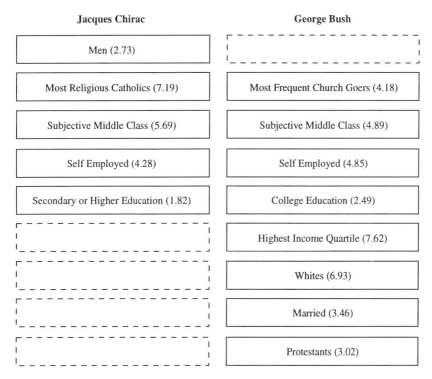

Fig. 8.2. Core group coalitions of French and U.S. rightist presidential candidates, 1988. Group members with a markedly greater probability than nonmembers of the group of voting for the candidate in question, assuming "average" positioning in the other groups listed for the candidate. Statistical significance appears in parentheses.

jective sense of whether they belong to the working class or the middle class. Subjective class is, strictly speaking, an attitudinal variable and not a sociological one, but we need not be concerned here with that distinction because, both for France and the United States, it is supplemented by several related variables that are sociological in nature and operate consistently with the subjective class variable whenever that appears: status as a wage or salary earner versus self-employment, presence of a union member in the household, and levels of income and education.

Our indicator of religion for France is a combined sociological and behavioral measure that expresses the respondents' degree of attachment to the Catholic Church. It stratifies respondents who declared themselves to be Catholics according to five categories of frequency of church attendance: at least once a week, often during the year, sometimes, rarely, and never. To these,

TABLE 8.1. Incremental Probabilities of Voting for Leftist Candidates, by Group, in France and the United States, 1988

François Mitterrand			Michael Dukakis		
Subjective working class	.273	(39%)			
Least religious Catholics and nonbelievers	.205	(59%)			
Wage and salary earners	.201	(74%)			
Government employees	.130	(28%)	Government employees	.113	(23%)
Union households	.125	(20%)	Union households	.111	(22%)
Native residents of traditional leftist southern regions	.115	(9%)			
Women	.049	(52%)			
			Blacks	.118	(13%)
			Catholics	.068	(26%)
N = 951			N = 1,193		

Note: Average difference between predicted probability of group members supporting the candidate and what the probability would have been without the effect of membership in the group. Size of the group as a proportion of the total sample is given in parentheses.

TABLE 8.2. Incremental Probabilities of Voting for Rightist Candidates, by Group, in France and the United States, 1988

Jacques Chirac			George Bush		
Most religious Catholics	.242	(37%)	Most frequent churchgoers	.131	(39%)
Self-employed	.219	(22%)	Self-employed	.208	(15%)
Subjective middle class	.211	(50%)	Subjective middle class	.211	(45%)
Secondary or higher education	.091	(40%)	College education	.206	(22%)
Men	.068	(48%)			
			Whites	.350	(84%)
			Highest quartile income	.204	(28%)
			Married	.139	(57%)
			Protestants	.082	(38%)
N = 967			N = 1,251		

Note: Average difference between predicted probability of group members supporting the candidate and what the probability would have been without the effect of membership in the group. Size of the group as a proportion of the total sample is given in parentheses.

a sixth category was added to represent the respondents who claimed to be without a religion. The comparatively few cases of respondents who professed a religion other than Catholic were removed from the analysis.

Those indicators of social class and attachment to the Catholic church form the social underpinnings of two sets of social groups that were starkly opposed to each other politically. On the left, supporting François Mitterrand, we find voters who perceived themselves as members of the working class, who were or had been wage or salary earners, who came from households containing at least one member of a union, and who may also have been an employee of the government or a state-owned industry. At the same time, Mitterrand was disproportionately supported by Catholics who rarely or never went to church, and by people who were without any religion.

The group composition of Jacques Chirac's electorate, by way of contrast, included self-perceived members of the middle class; people who were or had been self-employed; and Catholics who attended church sometimes, often, or at least once a week. In terms of class status and church attachment, the Mitterrand and Chirac decisive-ballot electorates were polar opposites. Moreover, the politically opposing group coalitions virtually exhausted the adult population. The number of people who did not locate themselves in the terms we have employed was negligible. What we have here is powerful testimony to the durability of social cleavages, whose modern manifestations date back over a century, and whose political potency has been widely believed to be waning under the impact of modernity and the generation of new issues. France is as modern a nation as any in Western Europe, and the currents of political conflict there are amply expressive of new issues. France fielded an ecology candidate at the first ballot of the 1988 election, as well as the standard-bearer of a party centering on the new issue of policy toward immigrants. But when they can no longer express their preference for one candidate among many and must make a decisive choice between only two, French voters regroup according to ancestral norms reflecting class and religion. The most-religious and middle-class voters turn rightward; the least-religious and working-class citizens cast their lot with the political left.

This group polarization at the electoral level in France is wholly consistent with the distributions of mass issue positions and mass perceptions of the candidates' issue positions that we noted in chapter 4. There was a stronger tendency among French voters than among those in the United States to take extreme positions on issues. Among the issues tested, it will be recalled, were the class-related issue of the size of the public sector and the religion-related issue of government subsidies for religious schools. The high degree of polarization in the voters' positions on those issues parallels the electorate's sharp division, in terms of group membership, over the choice of a presidential candidate.

At the same time that the French electorate was highly polarized in its own positions on issues, it perceived the positions of the two main candidates on those same issues to be sharply polarized as well. This was particularly true of the issue of the size of the public sector. The degree of perceived candidate polarization over that issue was greater than for any other tested, in both France and the United States. French perceptions of the positions of the candidates on the issue of state subsidies for religious schools revealed less polarization, but still more than the U.S. electorate perceived for most issues tested. We have already suggested that this dampening of mass perceptions was due to the comparatively moderate image projected by François Mitterrand with regard to that issue, after the failure of the rabid anticlericals within the Socialist party to alter the legislation governing private schools shortly after the legislative elections of 1981. But Mitterrand's moderation did not obscure the French electorate's views of which sides he and Chirac would be on if it came to a showdown on the issue. Voters who were strongly attached to the Catholic church voted for Chirac; Catholics less attached to the church, as well as nonbelievers, voted for Mitterrand.

A French Gender Gap?

There are indications that, in addition to being polarized around class status and religion, the French electorate was also divided politically by gender. As figure 8.2 shows, men constituted one of the core groups of Chirac's electoral coalition. It is less clear that the opposite was the case—that women were part of the Mitterrand coalition. As figure 8.1 indicates, the greater probability that women would support Mitterrand than men would skirts just below statistical significance.[3] But the possibility that French electoral conflict in 1988 was polarized around gender as well as around class and religion is too important to be ignored.

During the 1980s, a considerable literature appeared in the United States on the issue of whether there was a political gender gap in the country. The subject was stimulated by the fact that in 1980, some 10 percent fewer women than men voted for Ronald Reagan, the Republican candidate for president, even though he won the election. That gap narrowed to some 7 percent in 1984, enough to cast some doubts on the permanency of any such gap, but not enough to close the debate. This turned on such points as whether there might be differences in issue positions and priorities between men and women that would lead them differentially to support the candidate of one U.S. party over the other. Questions of this kind, so fully discussed in the United States, naturally led us to consider whether there was some sort of gender gap operating in France in 1988.

At the outset, it should be emphasized that the gender gap is normally measured in terms of differential support for one party or another *among voters* of different gender. That is not the same currency that we employ in our models of group coalitions, which refer to probabilities of voting for one candidate (or the other) or not voting for that candidate, including abstaining. We will depart from the assumptions of the models for the moment, and return to them later. Here and now, we will accept the voters-only assumption that is normally employed in the United States.

On that basis, there probably was a gender gap in France equivalent to the one that appeared in the United States at the same time. We estimate that about 7 percent more women than men voted for Mitterrand than for Chirac, as compared with the sample estimates of a 6-point differential in favor of Dukakis in the United States in the same year. But while the modest gender gap in the United States in 1988 was consistent with the results for 1984 and 1980, referred to above, it was a wholly new phenomenon in France.

The largest gender gap at a French presidential election almost surely occurred in 1965, when a survey (*Sondages*, 1965) conducted between the first and the decisive ballots indicated that 12 percent more women than men planned to vote for de Gaulle over Mitterrand. SOFRES estimates for the presidential elections of 1974 and 1981 indicated that the gap had narrowed considerably; still, some 7 percent more women than men favored the rightist candidate. If our own estimate for 1988—that Mitterrand won 7 percent more votes from women than from men—is accurate, that was a turnaround of considerable proportions, made all the more impressive by the fact that women are more attached to the Catholic church than men are.

The reasons why women do not show up more strikingly as an element of the Mitterrand coalition displayed in figure 8.1, while men figure prominently in the Chirac coalition sketched in figure 8.2, lie partly in the properties of a logistic model and partly in an important politically relevant attribute of French women in 1988. A logistic model downplays the importance of group membership for an individual who is otherwise either highly likely or highly unlikely to engage in the behavior of interest (Stanley, Bianco, and Niemi 1986). Some of the female support for Mitterrand in 1988 probably washes out of our model in the wake of the more powerful class-based factors. But probably even more important, women were more likely than men not to vote at all, a major consideration in the application of our models, which distinguish between support and nonsupport for each candidate, with nonsupport including abstention.

In chapter 6, we presented estimates of French electoral participation by gender across six elections recorded between 1978 and 1993 (see table 6.2). Abstention rates were uniformly higher among women than among men. The same phenomenon prevailed in 1988, when there was about a 10 percentage point differential in turnout between men and women. Part of the reason why men show up in our estimates as an element of the Chirac coalition while women figure only marginally in the Mitterrand coalition is that women were more likely than men not to cast their ballots for anyone.[4]

Asymmetric Coalitions in the United States

The competing core group coalitions that formed for the 1988 U.S. presidential election had a different structure from those that shaped the French presidential election of the same year. As in France, class and religion were the main electoral group foundations in the United States, but in France the characteristic pattern was polarization while in the United States it was fragmentation. Among the groups tested in the United States, the races were the only ones to produce a configuration similar to the French one.

In the domain of class, only the union households supporting Dukakis as opposed to the self-employed of the Bush coalition approach the kind of stark confrontation typical of French group conflict. For the rest, while one candidate enjoyed the support of a given group, more likely than not the opposing candidate could not count on the support of an opposing group. The middle class went for Bush, but the working class did not support Dukakis. The richest fourth of the country supported Bush, but Dukakis did not win notable support from the poorest fourth. College graduates liked Bush, but the less educated did not, as a group, significantly support Dukakis. Furthermore, except for the self-perceived middle class, none of these groups approached 50 percent of the population. Most of the class categories represented about a fourth of the potential voters. The group basis of French politics resembles big battalions facing each other across a well-marked frontier. The U.S. pattern is more like a mosaic of guerrilla groups.

Religion follows class in importance in defining the group components of the opposing U.S. electoral coalitions. Catholics were more likely than non-Catholics to support Dukakis; Protestants were more likely to support Bush.[5] In addition, people who professed to attend church frequently (not limited to the Protestants separately included in the Bush coalition) were differentially likely to support Bush. The Bush coalition dominated in numbers with regard to religion, as frequent churchgoers and Protestants each amounted to almost 40 percent of the electorate, as compared with the Catholic fourth that was more likely to support Dukakis. Nevertheless, the pattern remains more checkered than the starkly polarized French design.

Just as French group polarization is echoed in the tendency toward mass polarization over issues and the propensity to perceive the candidates as being polarized themselves over the same issues, so do the U.S. coalition mosaics reflect the more rectangular distributions of opinion typical of the U.S. electorate. Mass opinion on issues and the group substructure of electoral politics appear to be less coherent in the United States than in France.

Cross-National Comparisons

The briefest of glances at figure 8.1 and figure 8.2 indicate that while there is little overlap in the models of group electoral support for the two leftist candidates in 1981, there was a considerable amount of commonality attaching to the rightist coalitions. We will now consider both of these phenomena, starting with the more similar right-wing group coalitions.

Parallelism on the Right

To a remarkable extent, the tents that housed the Chirac and Bush group coalitions in 1988 were cut from the same cloth. The basic fabrics were class and religious piety. Frequent church attendance, middle-class self-perceptions, self-employment, and educational privilege virtually exhaust the definition of the core conservative group coalitions in both France and the United States in 1988.

Of course, there are some national differences. Protestants veered toward Bush, but they have no significant counterpart in France, and may be ignored here. The other differences are more interesting. Bush was able to mobilize the rich in a way that Chirac could not. The class conflict that governs so much of the political competition at the group level in France is dissociated from income differentials, while the less pervasive, but still real expressions of class in the United States, particularly on the conservative side, are clearly associated with income.

We have already discussed the possibility that there is a gender gap in France. Chirac did have an advantage among males, while Mitterrand may have had an edge with females. There was a gender gap in the United States, among voters, of some 6 percent, but that was not large enough to register in our models, either among women for Dukakis or among men in favor of Bush. There was, however, one eccentric group factor that may have played very heavily in favor of Bush, but that has no counterpart, in any form, for the Chirac or Dukakis group coalitions. Married people, constituting a healthy majority of the U.S. electorate, inclined toward Bush. This is almost surely a reflection of the drawing power of the social issues, including abortion, school prayer, drugs, and crime, that helped Ronald Reagan win the presidency in 1980 and 1984, and that Bush similarly exploited in 1988. It is possible, also, that we have here the germs of the exaggerated emphasis on "family values" that Bush and his party were to invoke at the Republican party's nominating convention in 1992, with negative consequences.

Divergence on the Left

If the rightist group coalitions in France and the United States were strikingly similar, it must be immediately added that the two core leftist group coalitions were very different. Only two groups were components of both the Mitterrand and Dukakis coalitions: respondents from households with at least one union member and government employees, and the statistical significance of the latter group in France is not assured. These two items are, of course, related. The old industrial unions have been losing members in both countries, while the unions representing the growing numbers of government employees have prospered by comparison.

Apart from these two comparatively small groups, there was no overlap between the Mitterrand and Dukakis coalitions. Mitterrand enjoyed the favor of the phalanxes of self-perceived working-class respondents and wage earners, but these were absent from the Dukakis coalition. Mitterrand mobilized the people least attached to the Catholic church, who amounted to some 60 percent of the respondents included in the sample, while Dukakis, ironically in view of the dearth of Catholic support for the French left, was favored by U.S. Catholics. Mitterrand may have had a significant margin of support from women; Dukakis definitely did not.

The remaining group within the Dukakis coalition recorded in figure 8.1 consisted of black voters. This group was a relatively small fraction of the overall U.S. electorate, but the electoral behavior of America's black citizens is highly distinctive, in that they vote overwhelmingly for Democratic presidential candidates. Even though an unusually large proportion of blacks abstained from voting at the 1988 presidential election,[6] blacks still registered as the most statistically significant group component of the 1988 Dukakis coalition.

Race and Religion

There is no direct counterpart in France to America's black population. It is possible that one day, France's Muslim inhabitants, consisting mainly of immigrants from North Africa, will constitute a significant electoral force, but for the moment Muslim voters exercise little electoral influence. At the same time, there are analogies between the political impact of race in the United States and the political role of religion in France that may be distant but are far from fanciful. Both of course are powerful electoral forces. But the similarities between race and religion in the two countries run deeper than their obvious electoral influence: they extend to the very origins of that influence itself.

Race and religion became political forces because they were central factors in the formation of the modern political systems of the United States and France respectively. The forces themselves are of distant origin. The contemporary political influence of race in the United States has its roots in the Atlantic slave trade; that of religion in France in the Enlightenment. But because both were institutionalized, albeit in very different ways, they endured, sometimes in the background, sometimes at center stage, but always as part of the political environment. Race and religion were inextricably linked, respectively, to the greatest domestic explosions France and the United States have experienced, the great Revolution of 1789 in France and the Civil War in the United States. Those two traumatizing events occurred almost a century apart, but racial considerations had clearly been present at the U.S. Constitutional Convention of 1787,[7] and became increasingly salient as the nineteenth century progressed, just as the legacy of the French Revolution lost little of its divisive power as France experimented with a variety of political regimes between the end of the revolutionary era and the establishment of the French Third Republic in 1875, not long after the end of the U.S. Civil War. Then, during the last third of the nineteenth century, the impact of the two distinct forces developed concurrently in ways that were to make them enduring influences on electoral behavior in France and the United States.

In one of the most frequently cited works of post–World War II political science, Lipset and Rokkan (1967) argued that the nineteenth- and early-twentieth-century party systems of the liberal states of western and central Europe reflected, in part, the conflict between a centralizing nation-building culture and the resistance to it of dissenting groups, whether isolated or allied with an established church whose privileges were threatened by the newly forming regime. Indeed, they went on to say that those (and other) early societal cleavages continued to shape European party systems in the current era much as they had done almost a century earlier.

French political experience fits those propositions uncommonly well. During the Old Regime, church and state were so intertwined that an attack on one was inescapably an attack on the other, with the result that even revolutionaries whose main grievances were against the state and not the church were perceived as a threat by the ecclesiastical establishment and its defenders. The result was that throughout the nineteenth century, those liberal groups that regarded themselves as the heirs of the revolutionary tradition were opposed by church authorities and, among the common folk, by those most attached to the church. The people who gave higher priority to political reform, and whatever social reforms were perceived as accompanying it, inevitably became anticlerical if they were not already.

This long experience of political conflict along a clerical-anticlerical dimension in no way abated when parliamentary democracy was introduced into France with the founding of the Third Republic in 1875. On the contrary, the conflict at first was exacerbated, as devout Catholics opposed the regime and the victorious republicans sought both to inoculate the population against clerical influence and to take their revenge on the ecclesiastical authorities who had tried so hard and for so long to frustrate their ambitions. Their most enduring action was in the domain of public education. When the Third Republic was founded, primary education was almost everywhere in France controlled by the

Catholic church. The new political masters quickly turned their attention to establishing a public school system that would be compulsory, free, and secular. The teaching corps that earlier had been heavily populated by priests and nuns was transformed into an army of dedicated supporters of the separation of church and state. Teachers unions were formed under the banner of secularism, and a tradition was established that endured well into post–World War II France that the minister of education must be an anticlerical. What was at stake, from the viewpoints of both the church and the new state, was nothing short of the moral development and political socialization of France's children. The symbols of political and social conflict at the local level were the *curé* (the parish priest) and the *instituteur* (the primary school teacher).

Catholics were dismayed at and angered by these steps, but their claims were weakened by the poor prior state of instruction. Their position was weakened further when Pope Leo XIII, who had even earlier decided that to oppose the Third Republic was a losing proposition, issued an encyclical in 1892 that legitimized it. This *ralliement* was only grudgingly accepted by many French Catholics; others became even more extreme in their antagonism to the Republic, as the regime's anticlerical leaders became more aggressive and even vindictive in their attitude toward religious institutions. In that fashion, religion became the most salient dimension of political and electoral conflict in France, with Catholicism being associated with political reaction and social conservatism, and anticlericalism being associated with parliamentary democracy and the expression of progressive values.

Although the Lipset-Rokkan framework has more or less become the canon for analyzing the modern origins of European party systems, it has not to our knowledge been applied to the United States. We have no interest in making excessive claims for an already well-respected conceptual framework, but it is worth pointing out that it is as useful for understanding the origins of race as a source of political cleavage in the United States as it is for understanding the importance of religion as a source of dissension in France.

The United States was a nation in the making for well over a century. This development bore no direct resemblance to the French experience, with its anticlerical, republican movement eventually gaining political domination over an already territorially united nation containing large sectors of clerical and antirepublican resistance. The American experience was very different. This "first new nation" (Lipset 1963) absorbed immigrants at a staggering rate and discharged hordes of them westward into undeveloped lands armed with plows, branding irons, pickaxes, and rifles. The westward flow seemed unending, as one new territory after another was opened for settlement: the early Northwest, Louisiana, Kansas, Missouri, Texas, California. This population movement was not directed by some central culture whose crusading zeal was sharply opposed by contending sectors of national opinion. The victims of this imperial course were the native tribes who were murdered and displaced from their lands, but they represented an alien civilization. There were skeptics, but there was no U.S. counterculture opposed to manifest destiny.

There was, however, a searing conflict among the nation-builders themselves over what kind of culture would be imported into the newly populating territories. The issue was slavery. Would the new territories (and, eventually, states) be slave or free? And for those that would be free, what kind of policies would they be permitted to follow with respect to slaves who had escaped from slave territories or slave states? Slavery was kept out of the Northwest Territory, but following the Louisiana Purchase compromise after compromise had to be worked out in Washington to satisfy the interests of the free North and the slave-holding South. Compromise ended with southern secession and the Civil War. The victory of the North preserved the union, but it was a union built with blood and iron. The modern United States was created on the field of battle.

The European developmental analogue for the United States is not France, but Germany or Italy, for whose unification military power was decisive (if less destructive of lives and property than it was in the United States). The Civil War, however, forged an approximation of the Lipset and Rokkan (1967, 14) "central nation-building culture," which left the defeated white South resentful for a century and made the condition of the newly freed black slaves a central factor in U.S. partisan development.

The former slaves should normally have given their political allegiance to the party of Abraham Lincoln, who had freed them, but southern whites adopted two parallel strategies to counter whatever political influence the new citizens might have. They developed a one-party system that endured as the solid (Democratic) South until the 1960s, and they prevented blacks from exercising their right to vote by ruse, intimidation, and violence. Until the Great Depression, black citizens would have supported the Republican party if they had been permitted to vote, but that potential reinforcement for the Republican party was effectively neutralized.

With the coming of the depression, black people switched their allegiance to the Democratic party, at least at the presidential level, and the various obstacles to voting that had been imposed on them were progressively eliminated after World War II. During the 1960s, the Republican party began to appeal successfully to southern white voters, and the Democratic monopoly in the South was broken. Between the 1930s and 1960s, therefore, both southern whites and blacks everywhere were faithful elements of the Democratic party coalition, but by the time of our study, only black voters continued to display such partisan fidelity.

In a distant sense, therefore, race is to U.S. politics what religion is to French politics: an electoral fault line of historic dimensions. There are, of course, important differences between the two lines of cleavage. There have been no major shifts in the political allegiances of the French voters located near one pole or the other of the clerical-anticlerical dimension, while we have seen that there have been such transfers of partisan loyalty both on the part of black people (during the 1930s) and white southerners (during the 1960s). The political differences between clericals and anticlericals have been more firmly institutionalized than those between black and white Americans, with the result that they have been more consistent. In the United States, conflicts between the races occur mainly at the individual and community levels. In France, the clerical-anticlerical conflict is amplified by enduring institutional structures: mainly the church and the resolutely secular teachers unions, each side being seconded by large and vocal nationally organized citizens associations. Since the demise of governmentally enacted and enforced discrimination against black people, mainly by the southern states, there has been no comparable array of institutional forces in the United States.[8]

There is one other feature in common between the electoral effects of religion in France and race in the United States that characterized electoral politics in the two countries for a long time, and to a lesser extent still does. This is regional variation in the electoral strength of the main parties. Successive studies of electoral geography, which has been the dominant form of electoral analysis in France, regularly recorded for decades that the conservative political parties were strongest in the heavily Catholic eastern and western regions, while the leftist groups predominated in traditionally anticlerical areas of southern and south-central France. Similarly, the Republican party of the post–Civil War era was anchored in abolitionist New England and diffused across the north-central agricultural regions, while the Democratic party took refuge in the solid South.

This pattern, established in the nineteenth century, endured well into the twentieth, and even into the post–World War II era, but it inevitably became blurred with changes in the economic structure and massive internal migrations. As early as 1980, Goguel (1983, chap. 7) pointed out that the geographical distribution of the partisan vote in France was becoming more uniform, and we have already noted that the once solid Democratic South became competitive during the 1960s. Indeed, since then, the Democratic party has not been able to carry the southern states at a presidential election unless their candidate is a native southerner.

Because this shift in partisan support in the South may have been the result of internal migration as well as of changes in ancestral political orientations, researchers interested in tracing the evolution of the group bases of the New Deal Democratic party coalition have been interested in the electoral behavior not simply of white southerners generally but of native white southerners in particular (Stanley, Bianco, and Niemi 1986; Stanley and Niemi 1991).[9] We found that the latter group did not contribute significantly to the Dukakis coalition in

1988, according to our measures. Following the same logic for France, however, we uncovered a hitherto unknown, migratory effect in that country.

As we indicated above briefly, France too has had a solid South. Since the middle of the nineteenth century, French leftist parties have dominated electorally within a belt of 20 departments along the Mediterranean coast and the neighboring hinterland that extends into the southwest and northward toward west-central France. That pattern of left-wing predominance has been eroding, almost surely because of internal migration. Since the 1950s, the entire area—and particularly its most southern regions (the *Midi*)—has been the destination of large numbers of prosperous northerners seeking sunny sites for second homes and comfortable places for retirement. French citizens from Algeria, Morocco, and Tunisia emigrated to the area after those countries gained their independence, and (mainly nonvoting) North African Muslims have flocked to the region in pursuit of a livelihood. The Midi is France's sunbelt; the Côte d'Azur is a French Florida; Marseille is a French Miami.

The impact on electoral patterns has been dramatic. As figure 8.1 indicates, natives of these departments[10] supported Mitterrand significantly more strongly than did the residents of the rest of France within the overall Mitterrand coalition. When we test for the electoral effects of all the current residents of those departments, and not of the natives only, the margin of incremental support for Mitterrand drops well below the significance level. The old-timers retain the leftward electoral reflex; the newcomers bring along whatever orientations they acquired elsewhere.

Symbolic vs. Substantive Class Conflict

The most striking aspect of our findings in this chapter is surely the extent to which class-related groups furnished the underpinnings of both French and U.S. presidential electoral politics in 1988. Despite the electoral importance of some groups ostensibly definable in other terms, class influences were pervasive in shaping the group coalitions that supported each of the major presidential candidates in the two countries.

The main force that rivals the electoral pull of class is, of course, religion, particularly in France, but even with respect to religion there are qualifying considerations that serve to place class in bold relief. The clerical-anticlerical dimension was alive and well electorally in France in 1988, but there is evidence that the political potency of religion, relative to that of class, had declined since the late 1960s, while the electoral importance of class had actually increased.[11] At the same time, those religious groups in the United States that displayed notable candidate preferences are closely associated with ancestral class distinctions. Catholics, who were more prone to support Dukakis than were non-Catholics, were projecting the old propensity of working class immigrants to vote for the Democratic party, especially in the northern cities. Conversely, the Protestant support for Bush reflects the higher social status regularly claimed and often enjoyed by those denominations since the nation's infancy. And the racial divide in the United States, particularly in the form of the overwhelming support by black citizens for Dukakis, is also associated with class, in that blacks are disproportionately poor, unemployed, and undereducated.

Class factors so dominated the group composition of the opposing electoral coalitions in France and the United States in 1988 that they eclipsed other presumably critical groups whose roles have been enthusiastically hailed in recent years. Middle-class radicalism failed to make any significant dent in the conservative coalition in either country. There was no gender gap in the United States, and possibly none in France either. And the much heralded generational change had no marked political impact, at least as we have measured it, in either country. There was no significant trace of the U.S. baby boomers (Light 1988) or of *la génération Mitterrand*, claims to which were plastered all over France by the Socialist party during the 1988 presidential election campaign. The opposing group coalitions of 1988 were saturated with class distinctions, in the light of which those other forces faded into insignificance.

We have already noted that the structure of group conflict was more sharply polarized in France than in the United States, where it displayed considerable asymmetry. The two French electoral coalitions consisted mainly of complementary and opposing social groups, while there was much less complementarity in the U.S. group coalitions. The Bush coalition resembled Chirac's pattern of group support, but the Dukakis coalition was only a diluted version of Mitterrand's. Class conflict was more complete in France than in the United States.

Those different patterns conform to certain conventional expectations. France is a comparatively small country with a revolutionary tradition that has been popularly cast in terms of a progressive left being constantly frustrated by a conservative and even reactionary right.[12] This historic imagery, as well as current political conflict, were given enduring class content by Marxist domination of the French working-class movement and the leftist political parties. From this point of view, the opposing French group coalitions of 1988 were simply the contemporary expression of an old political schism rooted in opposing social classes.

U.S. political mythology is quite different. The United States eventually became a country of continental dimensions whose main political conflicts were long rooted in sectionalism, rather than class. And when industrialization and urbanization made class considerations inevitable, these somehow lost their collective importance through dissolution into particular groups. If Marx was the prophet of French electoral politics, Madison was the godfather of the interpretation of U.S. political conflict. Viewed in the light of these two contrasting traditions, the Marxian and the Madisonian, the differences we find in the group composition of the French and U.S. electorates are familiar and untroubling.

There is, however, another way of interpreting the data we have displayed in this chapter that is less familiar and more than a little disturbing. This is that, at least in 1988, the class conflict in France shows signs of having become an empty shell, more rhetorical, routinized, and reflexive than real, while in the United States, the uneven, fragmented mosaic of class-related, group-based political conflict reflected harsher social realities than anything represented by the opposing class coalitions in France.

The group polarization in France, apart from its traditional clerical-anticlerical aspect, rested essentially on occupational distinctions, along with their associated subjective class perceptions. The old Marxist interpretation of class as the reflection of relationships to the means of production gains clear expression in the unpropitious environment of 1988. But the opposing groups are all defined purely formally; there is virtually nothing in the French columns of figures 8.1 and 8.2 to suggest the *condition* of the opposing groups. Educational privilege peeps through on the right, but perhaps not significantly. The distribution of income is strangely absent. French politics involve real transfers of resources, but these do not register in our analysis, quite likely because the campaign focused on such a formal and almost ritualistic issue as the size of the public sector, an issue that symbolizes the distribution of power but has little to do with the course of people's everyday lives.

For indications of real class distinctions affecting electoral behavior, one must turn to the U.S. columns of figures 8.1 and 8.2. There we find unambiguous political expression of an uneven distribution of wealth, opportunity, and social status. The French rightist candidate could not mobilize the wealthy in 1988, but the U.S. Republican candidate did. George Bush gained the support of the educationally advantaged; Jacques Chirac won no significantly extra margin of support from university graduates. We have already commented on the implications for social status of the U.S. patterns of electoral support among Catholic and certain Protestant religious groups in 1988. The religious divide in France no longer reflects equivalent disparities of social standing, although its historic stature serves to reinforce the symbolic aspects of French political conflict by giving it an almost churchly gloss, on both sides of the spectrum.

What emerged in the United States in 1988 was almost, but not quite, the "politics of rich and poor" (Phillips 1991). We have no trouble locating the rich in the group electoral coalitions, but the poor—as occurs so often—are invisible. So are the subjective working-class, the blue-collar workers, and the people with less than a college education.[13] The rich seemed to have no difficulty identifying their champion; the poor as a group evidently did not recognize anyone as their own.

The asymmetric group basis of politics in the United States in 1988 has important implications for a debate that has been going on intermittently within the Democratic party for a long time, but which acquired a new sense of urgency after the Democrats lost the fifth of the six presidential elections since that of 1968. The debate, of course, was over why they had lost so often, and what kind of strategy they should follow in order to win the next time. Two broad strategic alternatives emerged, each of which relates to the group patterns we have discerned. The two strategies had multiple sources, but we will label one an aggressive version of the French alternative, and the other, the Clinton alternative, after the next and successful Democratic presidential candidate, who adopted it.

The aggressive French alternative, of which Jesse Jackson was the leading exponent, was to try to mobilize the same kind of working-class coalition in the United States that had carried Mitterrand to victory in France, although Jackson would also have aimed specifically at the poor (absent from the Mitterrand coalition) and racial and other minorities (still not available as electors in France). This would have been a strategy of class conflict, adapted to the conditions of the racially diverse United States population.

The Clinton strategy, which of course prevailed, was not to try to capture a working class that was absent from the Democratic group coalition in 1988 but rather to try to capture middle-class voters who had actually been part of the Republican group coalition. The rationale for that strategy has been presented by Edsall and Edsall (1992), who argue, in effect, that working-class solidarity is electorally impossible in the United States (see also Huckfeldt and Kohfeld 1989). This results, according to their analysis, because the Democratic party is widely perceived by lower- and middle-class white voters as excessively dedicated to trying to improve the economic and social conditions of black people and other minorities by measures of which they—the lower- and middle-class white people—pay most of the cost. That perception, which was both encouraged and exploited by the Republican party, and not adequately refuted by the Democratic party, contributed to splitting blue-collar and white-collar workers along racial lines to the electoral advantage of the Republicans and the economic advantage of their traditional upper-status supporters.

It is beyond our brief to try to arbitrate between the arguments underlying those two competing strategies. In practical terms, the middle-class Clinton strategy carried the day in 1992. The continuing dynamics of the political process will determine whether the French leftist strategy will again acquire powerful support within the U.S. Democratic party.

Part 4
Electoral Solidarity
and Consistency

In Part 4 we pursue the comparison of French and U.S. electoral behavior into domains that have seldom if ever been subjected to comparative analysis.

The first of these relates to a class of voters, variable but ultimately unmeasurable in size, that we have baptized "thwarted voters." These are the voters in France and the United States who do not have the opportunity to cast a vote for their preferred candidate at the decisive ballot. In France, the bulk of these voters are those who preferred a candidate at the first ballot who was eliminated from the runoff. What do these voters do? Switch to another candidate of the same left-right tendency? Switch to the candidate of the opposing tendency? Abstain? Or even deliberately spoil their ballots, in gestures of electoral frustration that the French electoral authorities duly register and report even if the vote-counters in the 50 U.S. states simply throw them in the wastebasket?

In the United States, the source of electoral frustration lies mainly in the selection of candidates for major-party nomination. Primary elections give the voters of some states, although not necessarily for both parties, some kind of a choice of candidates, but that choice is not likely to be uniform across all the states that have primaries. Even in states where there is a fairly large electoral field available to the voters of each party, there will still be some choosy and discontented voters who would have preferred still another candidate to carry their party's banner. What do these voters do? Swallow their pride and vote for their party's duly authorized candidate? Abstain? Or vote for another candidate?

These questions are matters of more than idle curiosity, for they go to the core of an important issue: is there greater partisan solidarity in the United States than there is left-right coalitional solidarity in France? The answer has important implications for the issue of the permeability of party boundaries in two-party as opposed to multiparty systems. Chapter 9 holds the answer.

Chapter 10 raises the issue of partisan or coalitional consistency in other forms. What is the relationship between voting for presidential candidates and voting for legislative or even regional or local elected offices? This broad question leads us into the special domains, long familiar to students of U.S. politics and of growing interest to students of French politics as well, of split-ticket voting, presidential coattails, and the midterm slump. The results of the analyses in chapter 10 are consistent with those in chapter 9, which we will now reveal. Among thwarted voters, coalitional solidarity in France is stronger than partisan solidarity in the United States, and with respect to linkages between presidential and legislative elections, coalitional consistency in France is more pronounced than partisan consistency in the United States.

CHAPTER 9

Thwarted Voters

In both France and the United States, a substantial proportion of the electorate
is not able to cast a vote at the decisive presidential ballot for the candidate
whom they prefer the most. This class of voter, whom we describe as thwarted
voters,[1] results in France from the two-ballot electoral system, and in the United
States from the widespread use of primary elections for the nomination of the
major parties' presidential candidates.

Under the French presidential election system, with its two ballots, only
the two front-runners at the first round of voting may compete at the second,
decisive round. This inevitably divides the first-ballot voters into two groups:
those who voted for the front-runners and can accordingly vote for the same candidate at the second ballot, and those who voted for candidates who were eliminated from the race. The latter group consists of the thwarted voters in France.

The United States has only a single-ballot electoral system for the presidency, but the nomination process for U.S. presidential candidates relies heavily on primary elections, and those primary voters whose preferred choices are
not nominated are—at the election itself—in the same situation as French first-
ballot voters whose preferred candidates did not survive into the runoff. Indeed,
the first ballot of a French presidential election functions to some extent in the
same fashion as U.S. primary elections: it determines who the ultimately competing presidential candidates will be. The first ballot of French presidential
elections (and of legislative elections as well) is often referred to in France as
"the primaries." To the extent that the French first ballot amounts to a primary
election, it is a national primary that takes place on a single day, in contrast to
the primary election system that prevails in the United States, where primaries
may be (and are) held in different states at different times. But U.S. primaries,
like the French first ballot, produce thwarted voters who will not have the satisfaction of being able to vote for their preferred candidate at the decisive presidential poll.

The Incidence of Thwarted Voters

It is a simple matter to calculate the number of thwarted voters in France at any
given presidential election. All one has to do is to add up the votes cast for first-

ballot candidates who were eliminated from the race, and then report the sum as a proportion of the total number of valid ballots cast, or of the overall number of registered voters, or both. The results of this simple computation, for all French presidential elections, appear in table 9.1.

It is apparent that thwarted voters in France are numerous. For the five elections between 1965 and 1988, thwarted voters amounted, on the average, to more than a third of the actual voters and more than a fourth of the entire electorate. At the two presidential elections held during the 1980s, more than 45 percent of the first-ballot voters were unable to repeat their choice of a candidate at the decisive, runoff ballot.

There is considerable variation in the proportion of thwarted voters in France from one election to another. This is not a function of the number of candidates who compete. It is true that the smallest number of candidates (6) ran in 1965, when there were fewer thwarted voters than at any other French presidential election, but the proportion of thwarted voters was virtually the same in 1974 as it had been in 1965, and in 1974 there were more presidential candidates (12) than at any other election. Naturally, the more candidates there are, other things being equal, the larger the number of thwarted voters is likely to be. But most of the candidates who enlarge the field beyond 5 or 6 are marginal in their electoral appeal and do not add greatly to the ranks of the thwarted.

What counts most is the number of major-party leaders who compete. In the context of the French party system of the period under consideration, the number of major-party candidates reflects the extent to which the two main electoral blocs, on the left and on the right, combine their efforts on behalf of a single candidate. Sometimes the rightist parties have been more successful in uniting their electoral forces for the first-ballot, sometimes it is the leftist

TABLE 9.1.   The Incidence of Thwarted Voters in France, Presidential Elections, First Ballot, 1965–88

Year	Number of Candidates	Number of Thwarted Voters (in thousands)	Proportion of Registered Voters	Proportion of Valid Ballots Cast
1965[a]	6	5,732	19.8%	23.6%
1969[b]	7	7,284	24.7	32.2
1974[a]	12	6,167	20.2	24.1
1981[c]	10	13,310	36.6	45.8
1988[c]	9	13,975	36.6	46.0

[a]Rightist coalition divided
[b]Leftist coalition divided
[c]Leftist and rightist coalitions divided

parties. When only one bloc is divided at the first-ballot, the number of thwarted voters is comparatively low, as in 1965 and 1974, when the left was united but the right was divided, and in 1969, when the right was united but the left entered the election in disarray. When both left and right are divided, the number of thwarted voters approaches the maximum. This was the situation in 1981 and 1988, when both Socialists and Communists on the left, and both Gaullists and non-Gaullist conservatives on the right, fielded candidates at the first-ballot. In 1988, this double division, on the left and right, was aggravated by the relative success at the first ballot of Jean-Marie Le Pen, the candidate of an extreme right-wing party that had not contested any previous presidential election.

There are large numbers of thwarted voters in the United States, as well as in France, but we cannot determine how many there are as exactly as we can calculate their numbers in France. The origin of the thwarted voters is essentially the same in France and the United States, in that they represent the disappointed voters in the two countries' primaries, but the French primary in question is very different from the U.S. primary system. To the extent that the French first-ballot functions as a primary election, it is a national primary that normally attracts a large turnout and in which all the presidential candidates compete simultaneously. Once the results are announced, a modest effort at simple addition is all that is required to determine precisely how many thwarted voters there are.

The U.S. primary system rules out any such simple calculation. In the United States, primary elections are held at different times in the separate states, turnout is typically low, the configuration of candidates is not uniform from one state primary election to another, and the elections are spread out over a period of several months. This kind of a system does not permit any computation that would be directly analogous to the French one. One could, of course, produce a total number of "confirmed" thwarted voters by adding up the total vote cast in all the primaries for candidates who did not eventually receive their parties' nominations. That sum, however, would inevitably fall short of the real number of potential voters whose preferred candidate did not run at the actual presidential election. People in states where there are no primaries differ over their preferences for their party's nomination, and some of those must be counted as among the thwarted. Similarly, even in states where there are primary elections, all the potential candidates may not compete, with the result that some voters in those states must also be frustrated about their eventual choice of presidential candidates.

In the absence of any more exact measure, we estimated the proportion of thwarted voters in the United States on the basis of the preelection sample surveys conducted for the series of NES surveys across the five presidential elections from 1972 to 1988. At each of those surveys, the respondents were asked to rate various political leaders on a thermometer scale ranging from 0 to 100, with 0 being the lowest rating and 100 being the highest. Confining the analysis for each presidential year to party leaders who were contenders for their party's presidential nomination, we computed the proportion of persons, among those identifying with either the Democratic party or the Republican party, who assigned a higher thermometer rating to an unsuccessful contender for their party's nomination than they gave to the person who actually became their party's standard-bearer at the election.[2] In determining party identification, we counted only those respondents who spontaneously declared themselves to be Democrats or Republicans and omitted the leaners who acknowledged that they were closer to one party or the other only after having indicated that they were independents.[3] To be included in the analysis, an identifier had to supply a thermometer rating for the candidate of his or her party and for at least another contender for the nomination of that same party. All ties were excluded.

On this basis, we estimate that from 1972 to 1988, some 15 percent of the total U.S. electorate, on the average, were thwarted voters. If one takes into account only those people who actually cast ballots at the various presidential elections, almost one-fourth, on the average, were similarly frustrated.

Throughout that series of presidential elections, there was some variation in the overall proportion of thwarted voters in the United States, but those fluctuations were overshadowed by (and largely caused by) the variations by party. Just as the leftist bloc or the rightist bloc in France has been more or less united around a single presidential candidate at the first-ballot, so the identifiers with one party or the other in the United States have been more or less united in their support for the person who became their party's presidential candidate. From 1972 to 1988, the Democrats were much more divided over who should be their standard-bearer than the Republicans. The mean proportion of thwarted Democratic party identifiers across the five presidential elections of the period was 45 percent, while the proportion of thwarted Republican identifiers (across only four elections, as Richard Nixon was not contested for the nomination in 1972) was less than 30 percent. To some extent, this difference reflects the imbalance in incumbencies between the two parties. Incumbents are less likely than challengers to be contested for their party's nomination. Still, incumbency is not the whole story. In 1980, when Jimmy Carter was the incumbent, he was less popular among Democratic party identifiers, relative to his party rivals, than he had been in 1976, when he was the challenger. Gerald Ford, the unelected incumbent in 1976, was not relatively stronger among Republican identifiers than Carter was to be among Democratic identifiers four years later.

The incidence of thwarted voters reflects above all the sharpness and depth of the divisions, reflected in rival candidates for the presidential nomination, over what the political thrust of the national party should be. The high-water marks for such divisiveness, during the period considered here, were 1972 and 1984 for the Democrats and 1980 for the Republicans.[4] Already in 1968, the

New Deal Democratic coalition of union members, black people, white southerners, and Catholics was becoming badly frayed under the pressure of George
Wallace's defection and the burgeoning politics of protest sparked by the
Vietnam War. In 1972, the Democratic party hopefuls who expressed various
strands of the old New Deal tradition were unable to stem the protesting tide,
with the result that the Democratic presidential party was captured by the anti-
war protesters who had been rebuffed at the Democratic nomination convention of 1968. George McGovern became the Democratic party's standard-
bearer, but while McGovern carried the convention, he did not come close to
carrying his party; more than two-thirds of Democratic identifiers preferred
another Democrat to George McGovern in 1972.

Jimmy Carter succeeded in reuniting the Democrats in 1976, mainly by
bringing back into the fold southern whites who had strayed off in the direction
of George Wallace or the Republicans in the late 1960s and early 1970s. Carter
managed to rally Democrats to his support at a rate that more or less approximated the level of popularity achieved by Republican candidates during the
period. Carter's relative appeal among Democratic identifiers dropped by 1980,
as we have noted, but he still retained a large margin of support over his challengers that year. In 1984, the Democratic candidate—Walter Mondale—had
to overcome several rivals for the nomination, but the most important one was
Gary Hart. Mondale was, perhaps, the last of the consummate New Dealers,
who instinctively thought in terms of making alliances with organized groups
and using government power to try to achieve socially desirable ends. Hart (and
John Glenn) believed that these formulas were obsolete, that what the
Democrats needed was not so much group support as a broad appealing message, and that that message should be far more market oriented than Mondale's
traditional approach. The cumulative effect of Hart's and Mondale's other
rivals' appeal was to make him almost as unpopular, relative to his rivals for the
nomination, as McGovern had been more than a decade earlier. Some 60 percent of Democrats preferred some other Democrat to Mondale in 1984.

While 1972 and 1984 were highly divisive years for Democrats, 1980 was
a notable year for dissension among Republicans. We referred, in chapter 2, to
the rancorous dispute within the Republican party between supporters of the
old eastern business and financial establishment, symbolized by Nelson
Rockefeller, and the western and southern based purveyors of rugged individualism, who nominated Barry Goldwater in 1964. Richard Nixon bridged that
divide and prevented it from dominating Republican party preoccupations in
Washington, but Goldwater's conservative message remained alive and well in
the hinterland. The same program that brought almost humiliating defeat to
Goldwater at the presidential election of 1964 catapulted Reagan to the governorship of California for two four-year terms, beginning in 1966, and neither
he nor a dedicated core of right-wing true believers abandoned it during the

years Nixon and Ford occupied the White House. Reagan challenged Ford for the Republican presidential nomination in 1976, when Ford was the unelected incumbent, and Ford, in turn, along with several other aspirants, competed with Reagan for the nomination in 1980. Reagan carried the day, of course, but he was not the preferred choice of a majority of Republican party identifiers. More than half of Republican identifiers preferred another Republican to Ronald Reagan in 1980.

We have had to define the thwarted voters in the United States differently from the way we can identify them in France, so we cannot easily make direct comparisons about their numbers in the two countries. It is apparent, however, that in both countries, a very substantial proportion of the electorate cannot vote at the decisive presidential ballot for the candidate whom they prefer.[5] These voters are faced with the necessity of making what amounts to a forced choice. They may vote for the official candidate of their party (who was not their first choice), they may abstain from voting at all, or they may vote for the candidate of an opposing party.[6] How the thwarted voters behave at the decisive ballot can have a powerful effect on the actual electoral outcome.

Promoting Electoral Solidarity

The main priority of the two major-party candidates in the United States and the two runoff candidates in France is to gain the electoral support, at the decisive ballot, of the thwarted voters. In the United States, this means simply that the Democratic party's candidate will seek the votes of Democratic party identifiers who voted for other candidates in the primaries and, by extension, of all Democrats who preferred that some other candidate had received the Democratic party nomination. The Republican party's candidate will, of course, similarly pursue the votes of the normally Republican party supporters whose preferred candidate did not win the Republican presidential nomination.

In France, the situation is essentially the same as it is in the United States, except that it differs somewhat in the details. France does not have a two-party system, but at four of the five presidential elections between 1965 and 1988 the runoff ballot pitted a leftist candidate against a rightist. We saw in chapter 1 that while France has a multiparty system, for much of the Fifth Republic the system consisted predominantly of two competing electoral coalitions, one oriented toward the left, the other toward the right. At the runoff ballot, therefore, the French leftist candidate will try to gain the support of voters who cast their votes in favor of other left-wing candidates at the first round of voting, while the right-wing candidate will try to win over rightist voters who preferred other rightist candidates at the first-ballot. Each major-party candidate in the United States tries to establish some semblance of party unity, while each finalist in France tries to create coalition solidarity.

The candidates have more time to try to accomplish this result in the United States than they do in France. They have at least the period between the nominating conventions, which are held in August, and election day, which is always the first Tuesday following the first Monday in November. In some cases, they may have even more time. The primary election season ends before July, and if all potential challengers have conceded victory to a front-runner by or before that date, the prospective nominee has additional time for trying to patch up old quarrels and restoring party unity. In France, by way of contrast, the runoff candidates have a mere two weeks during which they can rally their troops.[7] That is not much time for trying to create harmony among forces that may have been bitterly opposing one another for months and even years prior to the first-ballot of the presidential election.

In the attempt to gain the support of the thwarted voters, the finalists in both countries depend heavily on endorsements by their formal rivals. In the United States, party solidarity is usually made visible for the press and television media by a joining of the upraised hands of all the contenders, who stand together on a raised convention platform after the party has nominated its presidential candidate. Statements to the press by the unsuccessful aspirants reflect the various degrees of their enthusiasm for the actual nominee. Defeated candidates for the nomination may then go on to lend their services in an active way by campaigning for their party's nominee. Of course, there are times when the differences among contenders are so great that they cannot be overcome, even symbolically. Nelson Rockefeller could not bring himself to support Barry Goldwater in 1964. Sometimes a loser's support is given conditionally, as seems to have been the case with Jesse Jackson's on-again, off-again efforts on behalf of Michael Dukakis in 1988. Disappointed rivals may make minimal formal gestures but, for the most part, sit on their hands, particularly if they hold secure electoral offices themselves.

In France, this entire range of activity must be compressed into a two-week period. Defeated candidates must decide what kinds of endorsements, if any, they will make very soon after the first-ballot results are in, at a time when their own sense of disappointment is acute. Most French endorsements of candidates for the second ballot are given grudgingly. Jacques Chirac was less than stirring in his 1981 recommendation to his first-ballot supporters that they vote for Valéry Giscard d'Estaing at the runoff, and Raymond Barre was unenthusiastic in his endorsement of Jacques Chirac in 1988. In the latter year, Jean-Marie Le Pen refused to endorse either Chirac or Mitterrand. While most unsuccessful first-ballot contenders endorse a runoff candidate as the lesser of two evils, Le Pen in effect said "a plague on both your houses."[8]

On the whole, U.S. political elites succeed in patching up their differences prior to presidential elections more successfully than French political leaders do. This can be attributed, at least in part, to the existence of the U.S. two-party system. Although some third-party presidential candidates occasionally make respectable electoral showings, the avenue toward presidential election passes through nomination by a major party. If aspirants for the nomination expect the support of others in the future, they must be prepared to offer that support to others in the present. Claims to loyalty must be earned by demonstrating loyalty.

The French situation is more complex. While the logic of reciprocity is similar in both countries, mutual support is practiced less consistently in France than in the United States, particularly along the center and rightist segments of the political spectrum. This is largely due to the multiparty system, which requires presidential candidates to build electoral coalitions out of two or more separate and usually competing parties. The requirements of party loyalty and the advantages of maintaining long-term allegiances are clearly and widely understood within the arena of a major party, which has regular procedures, norms of behavior, and avenues of advancement. Coalitions of two or more parties, which necessarily have rival leaderships, do not lend themselves to such predictability and do not furnish similar incentives for their members to display the equivalent of institutional loyalty. The result is that for some French presidential aspirants, parties are not so much channels of promotion as instruments for manipulation. French parties are more numerous, they meet more frequently, and they have more authority over candidacies and programs than U.S. parties, but they are also more fragile and have a shorter life expectancy. They are vulnerable to leadership crises and subject to splits that can have deleterious consequences for their electoral success. These crises and splits are often directly connected with presidential election politics, as aspirants maneuver for strategic locations on the political chessboard.

Partisan vs. Coalitional Electoral Solidarity

The two-bloc system that characterized French electoral politics across four of the five presidential elections between 1965 and 1988 (the election of 1969 being an exception) is sometimes likened to a pseudo-two-party system, at least in its application at the second and decisive ballot of the elections. It is, therefore, of more than casual interest whether that two-bloc system rests on more or less solidarity at the level of the individual voters than does the older and institutionalized two-party system in the United States. The extent to which the thwarted voters in the two countries return to their respective folds at the decisive ballot provides a powerful indicator of the relative cohesion of partisanship at the mass level in the United States, as compared with coalitional solidarity in France. Do U.S. partisans support their party's standard-bearer, despite their preferences for another candidate, at a higher or lower rate than French voters support the remaining candidate at the decisive ballot who represents their left-right tendency despite the fact that they voted for a different candidate (of a different party) at the first-ballot?

Before turning to the answer to this question, we should indicate that there are two logically plausible, but contradictory, hypotheses that we might construct in advance. On the one hand, we might hold that because partisan identifications are more stable across time in the United States than evaluations of political leaders are (Converse and Markus 1979), the intensity of partisan attachment ought also to prevail in the short term over frustrations regarding the party's leadership. Moreover, one might extend that reasoning comparatively by arguing, further, that interparty movements are less likely in a two-party system than in a multiparty system, because movement from one party to another involves a greater psychological distance in a two-party system than in a multiparty one. In a two-party system, the other party necessarily is the enemy; in a multiparty system, passage from one party to another may appear less menacing, even if it involves crossing some perceived left-right divide, at least if the movement is between neighboring parties.

On the other hand, the countervailing hypothesis is that the ideological distance between left and right in France is much greater than it is between major parties in the United States. In this view, while it might be easier for French voters to exchange allegiances between parties on one side or the other of the left-right ideological divide than it would be for U.S. voters to switch support from one party to the other, it is much more difficult psychologically for French voters to cross the left-right barrier than it is for a U.S. party identifier to vote for the candidate of the opposing party.

In point of fact, the degree of coalitional solidarity displayed by thwarted French voters is considerably greater than the degree of partisan discipline exercised by thwarted voters in the United States. In France, at the three presidential elections that unambiguously pitted a leftist candidate against a rightist at the decisive ballot, we estimate that more than 85 percent of the thwarted voters who cast a valid ballot at the runoff voted for the candidate of the left-right tendency of their unsuccessful first-ballot choice (see table 9.2). Thwarted voters in the United States, defined as partisans who preferred an unsuccessful contender for their party's nomination to the actual candidate, are considerably less likely than their French counterparts to support their party's choice. At the three U.S. presidential elections between 1980 and 1988, an average only of some 73 percent of thwarted voters, among those who cast presidential ballots, returned to their partisan folds.[9]

There is, of course, some variation in these figures from election to election, from coalition to coalition, and from one party to another within a given coalition. In the United States, thwarted Republican voters tend to be more loyal partisans than Democratic ones, although that may simply reflect the more frequent Republican incumbents during the 1980s. George McGovern was a par-

TABLE 9.2. Estimates of French Thwarted Voters' Second-Ballot Behavior, Presidential Elections, 1969–88

Year	Voted for		Abstained or Spoiled Ballot[a]
	Same Tendency	Opposing Tendency	
1969[b]	74%	26%	56%
1974[c]	88%	12%	6%[d]
1981[e]	88%	12%	10%[f]
1988[g]	85%	15%	9%

Sources: Data for 1969, the Converse-Pierce study; for 1974 and 1981, SOFRES; for 1988, the Pierce 1988 study (an independent SOFRES study for 1988 produces virtually identical results).

[a]As proportion of registered voters
[b]Considering Poher left, Pompidou right
[c]Chaban-Delmas voters only
[d]"Ne se prononcent pas"
[e]Considering Lalonde left
[f]Abstained and no response
[g]Considering Waechter left

ticularly weak candidate in terms of rallying partisan support; less than 40 percent of Democrats who opposed his candidacy voted for him. In France, in 1988, supporters of Raymond Barre rallied to the candidacy of Jacques Chirac in larger proportions than did Jean-Marie Le Pen's first-ballot voters. Despite such variations, left-right coalitional solidarity is greater in France than partisan discipline is in the United States. Substantial minorities of Democratic and Republican identifiers cross party lines when they are unhappy with their own party's nominee, as compared with much smaller proportions of French leftists or rightists who jump the left-right divide in analogous situations.[10]

Thwarted voters are not, of course, limited only to deciding between remaining loyal to their party or tendency, on the one hand, and defecting to the candidate of the opposing party or tendency, on the other. There is a third alternative available to them: they can simply sit out the election. U.S. voters who do not like their party's candidate can stay at home on election day, just as French voters whose first-ballot choices do not survive into the runoff ballot can abstain from that decisive round of voting. Indeed, as we have already pointed out, the most disgruntled of French thwarted voters have a stronger way to register their dissatisfaction with the forced choice imposed upon them: they can deliberately spoil their ballots. In France, the proportion of invalid ballots (and abstention rates) are always much higher among first-ballot voters who cannot repeat their choice of candidate at the second ballot than among those who can do so. At the 1988 French presidential election, abstentions plus invalid ballots were more than three times more numerous among the thwarted voters than among those who could repeat their first-ballot candidate choice.

In estimating French abstention rates on the basis of survey data, we are without the advantage of voter validation information of the kind obtained since 1980 by the U.S. NES. For France, therefore, we will limit ourselves to indicating that reported abstention rates (including invalid ballots) among thwarted voters in 1974, 1981, and 1988 averaged about 10 percent, and never rose as high as the proportion of thwarted voters who cast a decisive ballot for the candidate of the opposite left-right tendency.[11]

Abstention is not a preferred strategy among thwarted voters in the United States. There were, however, two occasions on which significant numbers of thwarted voters in the United States abstained in large numbers. The first was among Republican identifiers in 1980 when, as we have indicated, Ronald Reagan was not the preferred candidate of Republican party identifiers. At that election, the difference between the abstention rate among Republicans who preferred Reagan and those who preferred someone else was some 8 percent.

The second instance was among Democratic identifiers in 1988, and it was even more strikingly different from the usual pattern of behavior among thwarted voters. In that year, the abstention rate among Democrats who preferred Jesse Jackson to Michael Dukakis was almost 12 percentage points higher than it was among Democrats who preferred Dukakis to Jackson. At the same time, those thwarted Democrats who did not abstain voted for their party's candidate at the same rate as the Democrats who preferred Dukakis did. Whereas prior to 1988, the characteristic pattern was for a substantial proportion of thwarted voters to defect to the opposing party, but not to abstain, in 1988 almost no thwarted Democrats defected, but almost half of them chose to sit out the election.

This historically atypical phenomenon was produced largely by black voters. The reason for it is almost surely that 1988 was the first year when the contest for the Democratic presidential nomination was exclusively between a black contender, Jesse Jackson, and a white contender, Michael Dukakis. Jackson had been a candidate for the Democratic nomination in 1984, but in that year the field was crowded, and the media focused on the contest between Walter Mondale and Gary Hart. By 1988, Jackson had gained experience and national visibility, and throughout virtually the entire season running from the presidential primaries to the Democratic presidential nominating convention, the most salient issue for Democrats was to find grounds for accommodation between Jackson and Dukakis, who differed not only in color but also in style, electoral strategy, and programmatic priorities.

Against this background, black voters in 1988 broke the U.S. pattern of thwarted voter behavior. While more Democrats who preferred Jackson to

Dukakis remained loyal than is usually the case for thwarted voters, more of them also chose to abstain. Unlike frustrated Democrats in earlier years, who preferred voting Republican to abstaining, black Democrats who could not bring themselves to support their party's presidential candidate in 1988 preferred abstention to defection.

A Model of Constrained Electoral Choice

We have seen that in both France and the United States, there is a variable but substantial fraction of the citizenry that cannot vote for their preferred presidential candidates at the decisive ballot. The characteristic behavior of these thwarted voters differs in the two countries. More French voters remain loyal to their left-right political tendency, proportionately, than U.S. party identifiers remain loyal to their party. Conversely, more frustrated voters in the United States, proportionately, cross over the psychological barrier that separates the two major U.S. parties, than thwarted French voters bridge the time-hallowed categories of left and right. In addition, more French citizens than U.S. ones take refuge from the constraints facing them in forced-choice situations by abstaining (or deliberately spoiling their ballots), at least in comparison with the behavior of their national counterparts who *are* in a position to vote for their preferred candidates at the decisive ballot.

Two groups of citizens, one French and the other American, find themselves in analogous situations, albeit for different reasons, having to do with the particular characteristics of the electoral and party systems in their countries. In these circumstances, it is reasonable to assume that the two groups of voters are subject to similar forces impelling them toward one political choice or another. Yet the distribution of choices varies across the two groups. This suggests that if the voters in both countries are indeed subject to similar forces, those forces must operate differentially in each national context. It remains for us, therefore, to try to identify the main factors that influence thwarted voters and to assess how much each of those factors may actually do so.

Drawing on elements of an enlarged theory of partisanship that Converse and Pierce (1985, 1992) have been elaborating, as well as on the theory of elections that underlies earlier chapters of this book, we can identify three factors that are likely to affect the choices of thwarted voters. The first is the extent to which they prefer the absent candidate over their party's or tendency's actual candidate; we will label this *impedance*. The second is the extent to which they prefer one of the actual candidates over the other; we will call this *candidate preference*. The third is the strength of their attachment to one of the two parties or left-right tendencies; this is simply *strength of tendency*. We will examine these three factors in greater detail.

Impedance

Impedance refers to the relative strength with which a voter prefers an absent candidate over the surviving candidate of the same party or tendency. We assume that other things being equal, the more a voter prefers an absent candidate over the active one, the smaller the probability that the voter will cast a ballot for the surviving candidate. We employ the term *impedance* to designate the phenomenon because attachment to a given candidate for whom the voter is prevented from casting a ballot is an impediment against the voter supporting another candidate. We borrow the term from Converse and Pierce (1992, 251), who employ it to designate the operation of partisanship in a similar context. Strength of partisanship is an impediment to switching parties. Strength of attachment to a candidate, by analogy, is an impediment to supporting a different candidate.[12]

We have measured impedance by subtracting the voter's affect for the actual party (tendency) nominee, as registered on the conventional thermometer scale, from the voter's affect for his or her preferred candidate. For the United States in 1988, we can perform that operation as it relates to all the major party contenders, Dole and Robertson as opposed to Bush, the actual Republican party nominee, and Jackson as opposed to Dukakis, the Democratic party candidate. For France in 1988, we cannot include all the relevant contenders, as cost considerations prevented us from obtaining thermometer scores for every one of the nine first-ballot candidates. We did, however, obtain those measures for the three most important candidates who did not survive into the decisive ballot: André Lajoinie, the candidate of the "official" Communist party; Raymond Barre, the neo-Giscardian candidate; and Jean-Marie Le Pen, the extreme right-wing candidate. We also obtained, of course, thermometer ratings for the major runoff candidates, François Mitterrand and Jacques Chirac.[13]

For the U.S. measures, we have used the preelectoral thermometer scores for the various candidates. Our French survey was exclusively postelectoral, so we necessarily employed postelectoral thermometer scores in computing the impedance factor for our French respondents. Preelectoral measures would have been preferable, but there is a high correlation between the pre- and postelectoral thermometer scores obtained in the United States in 1988, and we assume that the same would have been true for France.

Candidate Preference

This is simply how much the individual voters preferred one of the two surviving candidates over the other. The assumption relating to this measure is that, other things being equal, the more a voter prefers one of the two remaining candidates, the greater the probability that the voter will opt for that candidate at the decisive ballot. The measure is also hypothetically important in accounting for abstentions. We would assume, further, that the less the affect differential, the greater the probability that the voter will abstain from making a choice. As in the case of the impedance measure, the candidate preference measure rests on differences in affect as registered in the thermometer scores, except that we standardized the French and U.S. measures by employing the postelectoral U.S. thermometer scores.

Strength of Tendency

This factor is the degree to which voters feel attached to their party (in the case of the United States) or to their left-right tendency (in the case of France). The assumption is that the more strongly attached U.S. voters are to the party with which they identify, the more likely they will be to vote for the official candidate of their party, other things being equal. Similarly, the more leftist or rightist French voters regard themselves as being, the more likely they will be to vote at the decisive ballot for the surviving candidate of their left-right tendency.

For the United States, the strength of tendency measure is simply the strength of the respondent's partisan identification (recall that all U.S. thwarted voters are party identifiers by definition). In the French case, strength of party identification does not apply, as thwarted voters in France may or may not identify with a given party, and even when they do, neither runoff candidate may be a representative of that same party. For France, therefore, we take strength of tendency to mean the respondent's own assessment of his or her location on the seven-point left-right dimension. The logic, of course, is that the more leftist (or rightist) the voters are subjectively, the more likely they will be to vote for the surviving leftist (or rightist) presidential candidate.

Results of the Model

The elements are now in place for the construction of a model of constrained electoral choice, with impedance, candidate preference, and strength of tendency as the independent variables, and the thwarted voter's actual electoral behavior as the dependent variable. This variable is trichotomous, consisting of remaining loyal to one's party (or left-right tendency), abstaining, or defecting to the opposing party (or left-right tendency).

We have, in fact, applied two versions of our model to the data for the French and U.S. presidential elections of 1988. One is an ordinary least squares regression. The other is an ordered multinomial logistic regression which is, in certain respects, more appropriate given the nature of the dependent variable.[14] The results of the two sets of models are presented in table 9.3. Four aspects of these models are of particular interest: their overall power; their relative applicability to France and the United States; the relative weight of identical or analogous variables in the two countries; and their predictiveness.

The models are powerful. In conventional regression terms they account for from a fourth to more than a third of the variance in constrained electoral choices. In addition, the goodness of fit represented by the χ^2 measures for the ordered logits are highly significant. The logic of what is a very simple model is sound, as the model explains a great deal.

In the terms just employed, the model applies better to France than to the United States. The multiple R^2 and the χ^2 for France are larger than they are for

TABLE 9.3.   Models of Thwarted Voter Electoral Behavior, Presidential Elections of 1988, France and the United States

	OLS					
	Unstandardized B	Partial R	T-Ratio	(Prob)	Multiple R^2	Variance Explained
France (N = 299)						
Impedance	−.14359E-03	−.006	0.1108	(0.908)	.593	.351
Candidate preference	−.01220	−.572	11.9954	(0.000)		
Strength of tendency	.01486	.078	1.3469	(0.176)		
United States (N = 215)						
Impedance	.00392	.104	.1529	(0.124)	.493	.243
Candidate preference	−.00754	−.358	5.5830	(0.000)		
Strength of tendency	.08017	.250	3.7550	(0.000)		

	Multinomial Ordered Logit				
	Unstandardized B	T-Ratio	(Prob)	χ^2	Significance
France (N = 299)					
Impedance	−.970872E-040	−0.016	(0.987)	139.86 (3)	.32173E-13
Candidate preference	−.687146E-010	−10.238	(0.000)		
Strength of tendency	.109746	1.684	(0.0922)		
United States (N = 215)					
Impedance	.147211E-010	1.835	(0.0665)	57.759 (3)	.32173E-13
Candidate preference	−.260361E-010	−5.715	(0.0000)		
Strength of tendency	.281602	3.691	(0.0002)		

Note: Dependent variable: Loyal = 0/Abstain = 1/Defect = 2

the United States. At the same time, there are aspects of the model that fit the United States better than France. The main element of this sort is the behavior of the impedance variable. This variable reflects the distance between the voters' preferred candidate and the actual candidate on the thermometer scale, and given the scoring of our dependent variable (loyalty, abstention, defection) its effect on the dependent variable should be positive. In fact, it is literally negative in both versions of the regression for France, although it is close to zero in its independent effect. For the United States, impedance is not only correctly signed but also, in the logistic regression, approaches statistical significance.

For both countries, the candidate preference variable carries most of the model's weight, and is highly significant statistically. Strength of tendency, however, contributes significantly to the outcome in the United States but not in France. This is of modest interest in the context of the debate to which we referred in chapters 4 and 7 about the extent to which subjective left-right locations, as opposed to direct partisan attachments, are the main electoral anchor for the French voter. Our model does not compare the relative importance of left-right locations and partisan identification within France, but it does indicate that, at least among thwarted voters, strength of party identification plays a larger role in the United States than left-right locations do in France.[15]

As we would expect, given the greater overall power of the model for France, as compared with the United States, the model predicts individual outcomes more accurately for France than for the United States. Between 80 and 90 percent of the French cases, but barely more than 55 percent of the U.S. cases, are predicted correctly. The model is most successful, for both countries, in predicting loyalty to the voter's basic party or tendency. The model is least successful differentially. For France, the model does least well in predicting abstentions; for the United States it does least well in predicting defections. There is a mild irony here in that, historically, thwarted French voters have been more likely than U.S. ones to take refuge in abstention, while thwarted U.S. voters have been more likely than French ones to defect to the opposing party or coalition. Our model, while logically sound and empirically acceptable, still does not account for all the mysteries of French and U.S. electoral behavior.

CHAPTER 10

Linkage between Presidential
and Legislative Elections

The previous chapter, which discussed the class of people we labeled thwarted voters, may be regarded as an investigation into the links at the mass level between two successive elections. In France that is literally the case, in that there are two ballots for a presidential election, with the second ballot being the decisive runoff between the two leading contenders at the first one.[1] The situation in the United States is, of course, different. There is no succession of nationally organized elections, but voters in states that hold presidential primary elections have an opportunity to participate in the selection of a partisan candidate as well as to participate later, at the election itself, in the choice of one or another of the actual candidates. Even in states where there are no primaries, and voters do not have any role in the selection of the partisan candidates, there is a constant flow of information about the primary competition elsewhere, and there is often considerable uncertainty about the probable outcome as well. In this atmosphere, attentive partisans are likely to develop candidate preferences whether they can vote in a primary election or not, with the result that there may be a kind of vicarious two-stage election process. The first stage is purely judgmental, while the final choice is, of course, decisive.

Those two-step processes in France and the United States may also be thought of as vertical linkages between two moments of a single, overall electoral mechanism, in much the same way as industrial planners once organized (and perhaps still do organize) a series of stages in the production process. In this chapter, we will shift our attention away from those vertical linkages to what, by contrast, may be considered horizontal linkages, between elections for different offices, notably between presidential elections and legislative elections. As in the preceding chapter on thwarted voters, we will be especially interested in comparing partisan fidelity at the mass level in the United States with coalitional solidarity in France. Within that broad perspective, we will consider comparatively three classes of phenomena. The first of these, increasingly remarked upon in analyses of U.S. voting behavior and beginning to make an appearance in France, is split-ticket voting. The other two are presidential coattails and the midterm slump, two phenomena that are associated empirically and linked conceptually under the notion of "surge and decline" (A. Campbell 1960; J. E. Campbell 1987, 1993; Brown 1991).

Split-Ticket Voting

Split-ticket voting refers to differences in partisan choices made by the same voter at simultaneous elections for more than one office. More often than not, the paired elections that U.S. commentators think of in that context are for the presidency and Congress, and those are the elections we will consider here. It is clear from the start, therefore, that we cannot produce any direct match between U.S. and French electoral behavior because there has never been a French presidential election at the same time as a legislative election. France and the United States operate on different electoral calendars for those national offices.

From World War II until 1986, French voters had never been called on to vote for candidates for more than one office of any kind on the same day. In 1986, the terms of the National Assembly and the regional councils expired at the same time, and elections for their renewal were held on the same day. At the end of 1990, the electoral schedule was altered so that elections to the regional councils and to one-half of the departmental councils would regularly take place on the same day, which occurred for the first time in 1992.[2]

The establishment of simultaneous elections for two offices made the notion of split-ticket voting applicable to France for the first time, although it is not clear that a term to describe the situation has been generally accepted. Lehingue (1987, 155 n.) prefers *bulletin éclaté* as the translation specifically of "split ticket," while a collective volume on the 1992 experience (Habert, Perrineau, and Ysmal 1992) is entitled *Le vote éclaté*, but treats the noun *éclatement* in the more general sense of splintering, including but not being limited to a simple two-way split.[3]

The reason it is often more appropriate to think of French electoral choices in terms of splintering rather than mere division (with the implication, for the United States, that the division will be into two) is that the partisan alternatives offered to the voters may be very different at two elections, even if these are held simultaneously. If what French political analysts call the "electoral supply" differs widely from one election to the other, the very possibility of repeating one's partisan vote will be reduced.[4] That was the situation in 1992, when the simultaneous elections for regional and departmental councilors were conducted under different electoral laws and offered the voters a bewildering variety of choices that were far from uniform across the nearly 2,000 electoral districts. Only the Communist party and Jean-Marie Le Pen's National Front ran candidates in virtually every district, for both the departmental and regional councils (Garraud 1992). Voters with identical partisan preference orderings, but in different *cantons*, could find themselves in situations that required them to make different pairs of selections, including the option of abstention. That sort of confusion rarely occurs in the United States, even though a U.S. voter may be called upon to vote simultaneously for a dozen or more candidates, because of the basic two-party system. U.S. voters vote simultaneously for numerous offices, but the partisan choices are few. French voters have only recently begun to vote for two offices at the same time, but their range of partisan choice, while enormous in national aggregate terms, may still be less than optimal for some voters at the relevant constituency level.

Still, it is important not to exaggerate. The elections we are interested in here, presidential and legislative, are normally conducted in more coherent terms than the dual elections of 1992. The choice of presidential candidates ultimately reduces only to two, and the second-ballot French legislative elections, at which most of the seats are allocated, also reduce almost everywhere to a straight fight between a leftist candidate and a rightist one. And even if we consider the first ballot of legislative elections, where multiple candidates compete, there is rarely much of a problem assigning them to the right or to the left.[5] What Parodi (1992) calls the "accordéon électoral" does not open as wide at presidential and legislative elections as it has done at regional and local elections, and the existence of the two-bloc party system during the years under consideration here simplifies the structure of electoral choices considerably.

The greatest obstacle to an exact comparison of split-ticket voting in France and the United States, at the national level, is that French presidential and legislative elections are not simultaneous and, for the most part, they are not held on dates fixed well in advance. There are limits to a presidential or a legislative term that set outer temporal boundaries, but within those limits, presidential or legislative elections may take place as the result of several different sets of circumstances. If, as is usually the case in the United States, one thinks of the impact of a presidential election on a simultaneous legislative election (and not the other way around), the only two pairs of French presidential and legislative elections that approximated simultaneity were those of 1981 and 1988. In 1981, the first ballot of the legislative election was held 35 days after the second ballot of the presidential election, while in 1988 only 28 days separated the decisive presidential ballot from the first round of legislative voting. The 1965 presidential election was not followed by a legislative election for well over a year, and the presidential elections of 1969 and 1974 were not followed by legislative elections for almost four years.[6] For purposes of comparison with the United States, we will rely on the French paired elections of 1981 and 1988, taking due account of the fact that they were not literally simultaneous and did not rest, in each year, on an identical pool of registered voters.

Aggregate Indicators of Split Tickets

One simple gauge of split-ticket voting that is widely used in the United States is the proportion of House electoral districts that are won by congressional candidates of one major party but carried by the presidential candidate of the opposing party. On that basis, the incidence of split districts trended upward from 1944 to 1988 (Jacobson 1990, fig. 2.5). Split district-level results were somewhat more likely to occur when Republican candidates won the presidency than when Democratic candidates won, but even in the latter case the mean approached 30 percent of the districts. In 1980 and 1988, about one-third of the house districts divided, while almost half of them did in 1984.

At the two pairs of French elections that most closely approximated the simultaneity of U.S. presidential election years, those of 1981 and 1988, there was a large difference in the incidence of split districts. In 1981, François Mitterrand's election to the presidency was followed by a landslide legislative election victory for the Socialist party and its leftist allies. Only 11 percent of the metropolitan districts divided, and more than two-thirds of those that did so were districts that Giscard d'Estaing carried at the presidential election but which went leftist at the ensuing legislative election.[7] To match that low level of split districts in the United States one must go back to the wartime election of 1944.

In 1988, the proportion of French split districts rose to some 25 percent, or about the same level characteristic of the United States in 1960, 1968, and 1976. Mitterrand was reelected to the presidency by a larger margin than he had enjoyed in 1981, but his partisan allies did not do as well at the legislative elections of 1988 as they had done in the wake of his earlier victory. The great majority of split districts in 1988 were districts that Mitterrand had carried at the presidential election but which right-wing or centrist candidates captured at the legislative election that followed.

The increase in the proportion of split districts in France from 1981 to 1988 is consistent with postwar U.S. experience. Just as split districts multiplied in association with Mitterrand's comfortable reelection, so did they increase markedly all three times an incumbent U.S. president was reelected. In all three cases (as in France), the incumbent was reelected by a wider popular vote margin than he had enjoyed initially, and the proportion of split districts jumped markedly: by almost 50 percent when Ronald Reagan was reelected in 1984 and by almost 100 percent when Dwight Eisenhower and Richard Nixon were reelected in 1956 and 1972 respectively.

We can hardly generalize broadly on the basis of so few cases, but these results suggest that in both France and the United States, a comparatively popular presidential incumbent becomes dissociated in the public mind, and probably also in his own, from his fellow partisan legislative candidates. The first time around, partisan presidential and legislative candidates move in electoral tandem more closely than they do at the repeat performance from four to seven years later.

The logic of the situation is similar in the two countries, even if the details may vary. At the initial pair of elections, the presidential candidate emphasizes party (or coalitional) solidarity. The candidate is out of office, struggling to get in, possibly against an incumbent, as Mitterrand was in 1981 and Reagan in 1980. Indeed, in the United States at least, the nominating process virtually requires aspiring presidential candidates to cultivate their fellow partisans and, once nominated, to cooperate with them during their legislative election campaigns. Incumbent presidents have fewer constraints upon their freedom of action.

They also acquire the trappings of high office that distance them from all but their most intimate partisan colleagues. In 1981, François Mitterrand was a party leader, identified closely with building an electoral and even a governing coalition of leftist parties. He was the personal symbol of something called "the left," and the meaning of his individual candidacy was inextricably bound up with the success of his supporters in their bids for legislative seats. By 1988, that unity of purpose evaporated, and so did much of the cooperative effort that it implied. French presidents do not campaign at legislative elections in any case. At most they issue declarations from the Olympian heights of the presidential palace that are minutely dissected by the political and journalistic elites for their every nuance, but whether they have any impact on mass opinion has never been confirmed. These statements, however, do express the presidential state of mind even if they may not move voters. In this regard, it is telling that on the eve of the second ballot of the 1988 legislative elections, President Mitterrand appealed on television for a "clear" majority but not an "excessive" one.

U.S. presidents are not constrained by tradition from campaigning directly for legislative candidates, but by no means all of them have done so. Ronald Reagan actually made more than the customary presidential effort to further the legislative fortunes of other Republican candidates in 1984, although he directed most of his attention toward Senate candidates and was criticized by some Republicans for having selected too few House candidates for the presidential gloss (Ornstein 1985). Both Eisenhower in 1956 and Nixon in 1972 ran campaigns that were independent of and separate from those conducted by their parties on behalf of House and Senate candidates (Ornstein 1985). The specific details naturally vary with circumstances, but it seems clear that once the presidency has been attained, whether in France or the United States, the impulse toward partisan electoral solidarity across the presidential-legislative divide loses its force. The president is less likely to encourage his own electoral supporters to cast their votes for his party's legislative candidates than he was at the earlier election that lifted him to such a lofty position in the first place. The more or less coordinated electoral efforts at the elite level that contributed to the initial victory give way to a policy of every man for himself.

In these circumstances, it is not particularly surprising that there is less joint electoral support at the district level for presidential and legislative candidates when one of the presidential candidates is the incumbent than when neither is. The president is the most visible political personality in the country, and if he fails to convey enthusiasm for his party's legislative candidates, some falloff in their electoral support can reasonably be expected.

Individual-Level Indicators of Split Tickets

So far we have discussed split tickets in terms of the proportions of electoral districts carried by presidential and legislative candidates of the same party. Those aggregate measures are perfectly acceptable indicators of the phenomenon under discussion, and of course the actual partisan distribution of legislative seats is of great practical importance for the president who is elected. But there is a rigidity to the measures we have thus far employed in that they involve majority thresholds that must be crossed before any given district can be assigned to one category or another. There is, moreover, a certain crudeness to the measure in that we have been indifferent to whether any single district passed from one category to another because of a shift in a mere handful of votes or because of a massive change of electoral allegiance on the part of the district's voters. To the extent that we are interested not only in changes in the distribution of legislative seats but also the behavioral habits of the voters, we need to move from the aggregate to the individual level.

In this regard, we are faced with a sharply asymmetrical database between the United States and France. For the United States, we can rely on the long series of NES surveys that contain both the presidential and congressional vote reports of the respondents. There are no comparable survey data for France,[8] although we will hazard one estimate for that country in 1988.

The U.S. data have been collated by Jacobson (1990, fig. 2.4), who reports that between 1952 and 1972 there was a steep rise in the proportion of respondents who indicated in the NES surveys that they had voted for a presidential candidate of one party and a congressional (House) candidate of the opposing party. He shows, further, that the curve flattened out somewhat after 1972, with split-vote reports ranging from about 25 percent to 35 percent between 1972 and 1988. For 1988, we estimate from the NES data that split-ticket voters represented about 25 percent of the voting public, or the lower reach of the recent range reported by Jacobson. About a third of the voters who supported George Bush voted for a Democratic House candidate, while some 15 percent of Michael Dukakis' voters cast a ballot for Republican House candidates.

The only French survey data that provide some basis for comparison is a SOFRES survey conducted after the legislative elections of 1988 at which the respondents were asked not only to report their legislative vote but also to recall their votes at each ballot of the preceding presidential election. More than 90 percent of the respondents who claimed to have voted at both elections reported that they had voted for the same left-right tendency at the first ballot of the legislative election and the second ballot of the presidential poll. Some 14 percent of the reported Mitterrand voters supported a centrist or rightist legislative candidate, while only about 4 percent of Chirac's supporters cast a ballot for the legislative left. Vote recall data are, of course, unreliable, and we would not want to emphasize those exact numbers. We can say, however, that the direction of the reported switches is consistent with the overall aggregate results of the two successive elections, while the smaller proportion of switchers in France relative to the United States is also consistent with the greater degree of coalitional solidarity among thwarted voters in France in comparison with the United States that we reported in the last chapter.

Correlational Indicators of Split Tickets

Still another way of estimating how consistent U.S. and French voters are in their partisan (coalitional) choices for president and legislative representative is to examine the correlations between the proportion of votes cast for the presidential candidate of a given party (or coalition) and the proportion of votes cast for the legislative candidate of the same party (or coalition), in each legislative electoral district, across the entire set of legislative districts in each country.[9]

Even during the 1950s, the district-level correlations between the partisan vote for presidential and congressional candidates in the United States were below .70, which means that less than half of the variance in the vote for one candidate was explained by the vote for the other. The correlation dropped to a mere .45 in 1976 and then rose slightly to .53 for the presidential election years of 1980 and 1984. That generally downward trend is consistent with the other evidence, already reported, of diminishing party solidarity in the United States and increased ticket splitting.

The French experience has been quite different. We are not dealing with simultaneous presidential and legislative elections in France, as we are in the United States, but the 1981 presidential vote correlates with the legislative vote of about one month later at .82, and the corresponding correlation for the paired 1988 French elections is .80. Indeed, the degree of coalitional solidarity at the district level in France between the presidential vote and later legislative votes is most impressive. The correlation for the 1965 presidential election and the 1967 legislative election is .78; that across the four years separating the 1974 presidential election and the legislative election of 1978 is .84; the seven-year span between 1974 and 1981 registers at .82; while the eight-year gap between 1965 and 1973 is bridged by a correlation of .79. On the average, therefore, about two-thirds of the variance of the legislative vote in France, at the district level, is accounted for by the district's vote for president.

It should be emphasized that this greater partisan electoral consistency at the district level in France, relative to the United States, applies only to the linkage between votes for presidential and legislative candidates. The cross-time partisan solidarity of the French and U.S. electorates on the district level is much the same with regard to voting for presidential candidates and legislative candidates separately. For example, the correlation between the district-level U.S. presidential vote for 1952 and 1956, when the same major-party candidates contended, is .90. The parallel French correlation for 1974 and 1981, which also witnessed the same two second-ballot contestants, is .92. There is some raggedness in the corresponding continuity correlations linking district-level votes for legislative candidates in the United States, as compared with a spectacular French demonstration of how the passage of time can erode partisan continuity,[10] but even here there is nothing like the large cross-national difference that we find in mass electoral linkages between presidential and legislative candidates in France and the United States. The evidence indicates that French and U.S. voters do not differ widely in the degree to which they are constant in the partisan basis of their choices for president or for legislative representative. However, French voters' preferences for presidential and legislative candidates are much more tightly bound by coalitional solidarity (on a left-right basis) than the equivalent choices in the United States are constrained by partisanship.

Presidential Coattails

Pundits, politicians, and political scientists in the United States have for long been interested in tracking the phenomenon of presidential coattails. This refers to the presumed capacity of a popular presidential candidate to contribute to the electoral success of congressional candidates from the same party who, in the absence of the accompanying presidential election, would not have fared so well. Such candidates, as the terminology suggests, would be swept into office on a victorious president's coattails.

Recent investigations of presidential coattails in the United States have focused on such central issues as whether there really is any such phenomenon and, if there is, how it works and what its effects have been historically. It should be apparent that, within limits, the same questions can be asked within the French context. Twice during the decade of the 1980s, a French presidential election was promptly followed by a legislative election. Did the earlier presidential elections have any impact on the later legislative elections? And if so, just what was the impact and what were its operational characteristics? The French have no conventional term for coattails, although the political press quickly recognized that something like them might exist by using such terminology as *l'effet Mitterrand* (the Mitterrand effect) and *la dynamique présidentielle* (presidential momentum) to describe the possible effects of Mitterrand's presidential victories of 1981 and 1988 on the legislative elections that followed. We will pursue here the question of whether presidential coattails have come to France, and whether the French might do well to coin a word for them.

Investigations into coattails in the United States have taken various forms and rest on different kinds of data. Calvert and Ferejohn (1983) employed individual-level data to try to uncover the motivational bases of coattail outcomes. Ferejohn and Calvert (1984) used national aggregate data to chart the impact of coattails historically. Campbell (1986, 1991, 1993) also relied on national aggregate data to establish and trace the effects of presidential coattails across time. Edwards (1979) used district-level aggregate data to chart coattails in the United States for the 20 years from 1952 to 1972. Brown (1991) analyzed the "congressional mobilizational cycle" on the basis of U.S. county-level electoral totals from 1950 through 1984.

For France, there is neither a relevant individual-level database nor a historic record analogous to that for the United States. We do, however, have comparatively rich district-level aggregate data, for both France and the United States, of the kind we exploited in the final portion of the preceding section of this chapter, dealing with split-ticket voting. District-level data are well suited to analyzing coattails, because coattails effects, when they occur, do so within the boundaries of individual constituencies. Moreover, because we have data in identical form for both France and the United States, we can make direct comparisons between the two countries.

The skein of logic that underlies coattails analysis with district-level data holds that the larger the vote for the winning presidential candidate in the district, the greater the probability of the legislative candidate of the same party winning that district's seat, controlling for the expected level of electoral support for that candidate in the absence of the stimulus supplied by the presidential candidate (Edwards 1979). There are alternate ways of expressing the variables in that statement. The legislative outcome to be explained can be measured by changes in the proportion of the vote received by the candidate of the presidential winner's party, by whether or not the candidate wins the seat, or by whether or not the candidate *gains* the seat. The expected vote can also be expressed in more than one way. One can resort to more or less complicated ways of establishing some mean level of expected district-level partisan support, or one can make a simple estimate. Inasmuch as redistricting (in both France and the United States) makes it difficult to compute district means across several successive elections, we have chosen simply to consider the legislative vote at the previous election to be the expected vote at the following one (for identical districts). For our outcome variable, however, we have employed all three alternatives described above: changes in the proportion of the legislative vote, whether the candidate wins the seat, and whether the candidate gains the seat.

Employing logistic regression, we have applied that simple model to France in 1981 and 1988, and to the United States in 1976 and 1984, with respect both to seat victories (win/lose) and (except for France in 1988) seat gains (gain/no gain).[11] Both analyses indicate the presence of strong coattails effects in France in 1981 (but not in 1988) and in the United States in 1984 (but not in 1976).[12] These findings are consistent with what the casual counter of votes and seats might have predicted. The Democrats gained only one seat in the House of Representatives when Jimmy Carter was elected president in 1976, but the Republicans picked up 17 seats when Reagan was reelected in 1984. In France, the leftist coalition won 69 percent of the seats for metropolitan France in 1981 compared with 42 percent at the previous election in 1978, while in 1988 the coalition's legislative gains were much more modest, to 51 percent from 44 percent in 1986.

Coattails may have been at work in both France and the United States as recently as the 1980s, but a moment's thought indicates that the forces producing that common effect cannot have been identical in the two countries. The main reason for this is that whenever coattails phenomena occur in the United States they are associated with an increase in voter turnout while the coattails effect in France in 1981 was associated with a *decrease* in turnout.

In presidential election years in the United States, turnout for congressional elections typically increases more than 10 percentage points over the turnout for congressional races during off-years. Indeed, this increase in turnout is the "surge" phase of the theory of surge and decline, first put forward by A. Campbell (1960) and later stated in revised form by J. E. Campbell (1987, 1993). The surge part of the argument is that when congressional elections are held at the same time as a presidential election, the party of the winning presidential candidate benefits at the House election by the increased turnout, which disproportionately includes voters who are attracted to that party by the long-term pull of party identification or whatever short-term forces are operating to the advantage of the presidential victor.

Presidential elections can have such a stimulating effect on turnout for congressional elections in the United States because of the simultaneity of the two levels of election. In France, however, presidential and legislative elections have never been held simultaneously; in 1981 (and 1988) the presidential election preceded the legislative election by about one month. This sequencing had the effect of depressing turnout at the legislative election well below the level of turnout at the prior presidential election. In France, turnout at presidential elections has regularly exceeded 80 percent, except for the 1969 election, which was distinguished by the absence of a stark left-right confrontation. During the same period, turnout at the first ballot of legislative elections also reached or exceeded 80 percent when there was no presidential election during the previous year. In 1981, however, turnout at the legislative election was more than 10 percentage points lower than it had been at the presidential election only one month before, while in 1988 the equivalent drop in turnout was more than 15 percentage points. It appears that in each year, the legislative elections struck the electorate as anticlimactic, unexciting sequels to the main bout of a month before.[13]

In order to estimate the role of turnout differentials in the operation of the coattails phenomenon, we have factored them into matching OLS regressions for France and the United States, for which the dependent variable is the increase in the proportion of votes for the legislative candidates of the presidential winner's party or coalition. The independent variables include the same two that we employed in assessing the role of coattails in affecting the distribution of seats—the share of the vote won by the presidential victor's party (or coalition) at the previous legislative election and the proportion of the vote won by the successful presidential candidate—plus the differential in turnout, upward in the case of the United States, and downward in the case of France.

The results appear in Table 10.1. The structure of the two equations is very similar.[14] All the independent variables are highly significant. The earlier electoral strength of the party (coalition) in question is inversely related to its later gains, the difference in turnout registers clearly, and the coefficients for the presidential vote strongly suggest some coattails effect. We cannot make any affirmations of causality, of course, but the nonsimultaneity of the French presidential and legislative votes, with the presidential vote preceding the later legislative outcome, gives added credibility to claims of causal power for the U.S. presidential candidate, whose fit in the U.S. equation is so similar to that of the French presidential candidate in the other one.

There is, therefore, reason to believe that something like a coattails effect operated in France in 1981 and in the United States in 1984. It cannot, however, have been propelled by identical forces. It may well be the case that in the United States, Ronald Reagan attracted electoral support in 1984 for Republican legislative candidates among Republican party identifiers and independents who would not have turned out to vote if he had not been running as the Republican presidential candidate, although we cannot demonstrate that that was so. We do know, however, that the same mechanism could not have been operating in France in 1981. There, turnout did not increase; on the contrary, it decreased.

TABLE 10.1. Coattails Effects on Increase in Percentage of Vote Won by President's Party (or Coalition) since Previous Legislative Election, by Districts, France, 1981; United States, 1984, by OLS Regression

Indicator	France, 1981 ($N = 474$) Unstandardized B	Beta	T-Ratio	Indicator	United States, 1984 ($N = 365$) Unstandardized B	Beta	T-Ratio
Percentage left vote, 1978	−.608	−.913	13.362	Percentage Republican vote, 1982	−.303	−.564	10.051
Percentage Mitterrand vote, 1981	.772	.802	11.819	Percentage Reagan vote, 1984	.386	.442	7.804
Turnout differential, 1978–81	.504	.316	8.163	Turnout differential, 1982–84	.362	.214	4.680
Constant	−9.102			Constant	−9.344		
Multiple correlation coefficient	.328			Multiple correlation coefficient	.268		

To the extent that François Mitterrand's electoral victory at the presidential election of 1981 helped the cause of leftist legislative candidates a month later, it did so less by attracting leftist-inclined voters to the polls than by discouraging rightist voters from participating. The Mitterrand effect in 1981 did not bring out more leftist voters but rather persuaded rightists to stay at home. Indeed, one astute electoral observer noted soon after the 1981 legislative elections (Goguel 1981, 1982, 1983, chap. 9) that the proportion of votes won by leftist candidates at the decisive ballot in 1981, computed on the base of registered voters (and not simply on the base of those voting), was virtually identical with what it had been in 1978, while the proportion of rightist votes, computed in the same fashion, dropped by almost 10 percentage points. Such a situation was, of course, rich in implications for what might happen to Mitterrand's partisans electorally if, other things being equal, rightist voters returned to the polls at anything like their 1978 participation rate. The balance of partisan strength had shifted sharply to the left, but leftist legislative dominance was hostage to continuing discouragement among right-wing voters. If these were remobilized, the strength of the left would shrink even if it did not lose a single vote from the 1981 electorate. The elections of 1981 produced an unprecedented triumph for François Mitterrand's legislative supporters. It did so in circumstances that left them poised precariously for what in the United States would be called the midterm slump.

The Midterm Slump

After the predictability of U.S. national election dates, perhaps the most impressive regularity in U.S. politics is the midterm slump, the phenomenon of the loss of congressional seats by the party that won the presidency two years earlier. Between 1960 and 1990, the average net loss in seats for the presidential party at midterm elections was more than 20, with a range of from 5 to almost 50. Those figures varied very little by party in absolute terms, although proportionately the losses were greater for the Republican party than the Democratic party because the latter always held the lion's share of the House seats during those years.

The midterm slump is the obverse of the gain in House seats by the presidential party in presidential election years that is frequently attributed to the coattails effect that we have just discussed. We have seen that that effect in the United States is associated with an increase in electoral turnout that is disproportionately favorable to the presidential party. That increase in turnout is the surge phase of the surge and decline cycle. The midterm slump represents the decline part of the process, the properties of which are more or less the opposite of those of the preceding surge. Interest and turnout decline at midterm House elections because there is no presidential candidate to arouse the voters, and whatever electoral premium the president's party enjoyed at the previous election as a result of the uneven play of party identification and short-term forces centering on the presidency evaporates in the mists of popular indifference.

There is no direct French counterpart of the U.S. midterm slump, because of the differences between the electoral calendars of the two countries. Presidential and congressional elections in the United States occur at regular intervals; in France, they are variable. U.S. congressional elections are held every two years; in France, the modal legislative term is five years. Inasmuch as the surge and decline cycle in the United States occurs in two phases of two years duration apiece, it is apparent that there can be no literal French analogue. Nevertheless, French electoral experience, and the French electoral calendar, do present two types of functional equivalence to the U.S. midterm slump. One is the way in which the legislative fortunes of the leftist legislative electoral coalition declined in 1986 after the left's sparkling success of 1981, and again in 1993 after its lesser but still respectable performance in 1988. The other is the extent to which the local or regional elections that French political analysts call *élections intermédiaires* (intervening elections) have been interpreted as pseudo-referenda on presidential performance (Duhamel 1989; Parodi 1983, 1989, 1992). Taken literally, these two developments are rather distant from the U.S. experience. From a more fundamental point of view, however, they represent the same force that is at work in the U.S. surge and decline cycle: the impact of presidential popularity on the outcome of elections for other offices.

In the United States, the opportunities for presidential popularity (or its absence) to affect the outcome of congressional elections are channeled by the fixed electoral calendar, with the result that when coattails operate or the midterm slump occurs they do so according to a set rhythm. In France, those same opportunities are framed differently and more haphazardly. But the regularity of those opportunities, while important, is not the only relevant consideration. The basic phenomenon is how much mass attitudes toward the winning presidential candidate or presidential incumbent contribute to the electoral fortunes of candidates of the president's party when they run for legislative or other offices. In this regard, it is clear that—particularly in recent years—there has been a close linkage between presidential popularity in France and the fate of the president's supporters in other electoral arenas.

Each of the two recent collapses of electoral strength of the French presidential coalition at the legislative level, in 1986 and 1993, occurred five years after the same coalition's electoral success. Such a long interval differs greatly from the two-year lapse during which the midterm slump germinates and comes to fruition in the United States. One would hardly proclaim the existence of a five-year slump in France. At the same time, those sharp losses for the presidential coalition were associated with deep declines in the popularity of the president. Public confidence in President Mitterrand was comparatively high at the time of his supporters' electoral victories in 1981 and 1988, while it was at or near its lowest shortly before the legislative elections of 1986 and 1993 (see fig. 10.1). We have already seen that there is considerable electoral solidarity within French electoral blocs, across different elections and across electoral districts. The linkage between presidential popularity and mass support for the presidential coalition at the legislative level is further testimony to this coherence.

Intervening Elections

There could be no midterm slump at the national level in France, in the literal sense, but the left-wing forces received ample warning that they were in trouble with the electorate well before they actually suffered the defeats of 1986 and 1993. These warnings took the form of adverse effects at a series of elections—municipal, departmental, regional, and European—that had no effect on the distribution of power at the presidential and national legislative levels but which gave the voters opportunities to register their displeasure with the parties in power. Those elections have increasingly been referred to in the French scholarly literature as intervening elections (Parodi 1983, 1989, 1992). The term conveniently locates those elections both temporally and hierarchically. They take place between presidential or legislative elections, but while they may have implications for the current balance of national political opinion, they do not actually affect the allocation of national offices.

The number of intervening elections has multiplied in recent years. Municipal and departmental elections have long been standard features of French democratic practice, but the popular election of members of the European Parliament began in 1979, and the French launched popular regional elections as recently as 1986.

Municipal and departmental elections were almost never accorded national significance prior to the simultaneous introduction constitutionally of the popular election of the president and creation politically of the two-bloc system of competing partisan coalitions, or even during the first decade of the operation of that system (Goguel 1989). Local factors figured prominently at those elections and the configurations of local partisan alliances were not always consistent with those current at the national level. Moreover, the constituency structure for departmental elections was hopelessly biased against the heavily populated urban areas, a bias that still holds today in less extreme form.

That situation, reflecting the comparative autonomy of local political conflict from the national pattern, began changing in the 1970s. Local politics took on the same bipolar character, pitting left versus right, that dominated the national political scene. Accordingly, local elections could be interpreted as

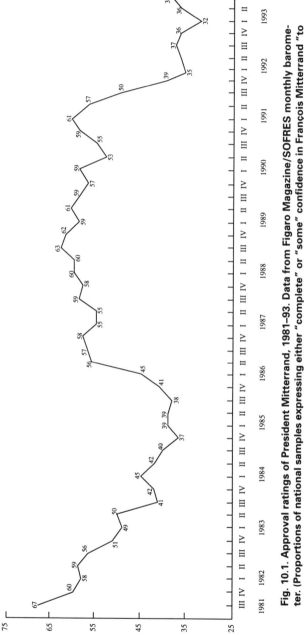

Fig. 10.1. Approval ratings of President Mitterrand, 1981–93. Data from Figaro Magazine/SOFRES monthly barometer. (Proportions of national samples expressing either "complete" or "some" confidence in François Mitterrand "to resolve the problems facing France at this time.")

expressions of current attitudes toward the president and the governing coalition, as well as an indication of how the next national election might turn out. Out of this situation, what Parodi (1983, 1989, 1992) calls the "mini-model" of intervening elections emerged. That model, which represents an attempt to specify the conditions under which intervening elections may be related to the prior national election (and perhaps the forthcoming national election as well), has certain conceptual links with the notion of surge and decline that we discussed earlier in this chapter. Intervening elections are, in a sense, midterm elections, although not for national office. Depending on circumstances, notably consistency in the patterns of partisan electoral conflict, intervening elections can serve as a barometer of changes in public opinion since the last national election. Such changes as do register must be evaluated carefully, because they normally reflect differential participation rates as well as actual partisan switching.

There is no regularity to these intervening elections, relative to the dates of the elections for which they may be offering a corrective or for which they may be premonitory. Some have occurred only a year after a presidential or legislative election (or both); some have taken place only a year before the next major national election. Duhamel (1989) takes the local elections of 1971 as the very "model" of the intervening election: two years after the presidential election of 1969 and two years before the legislative election of 1973. But that circumstance was accidental, produced by de Gaulle's resignation from the presidency, which occasioned the unplanned presidential election of 1969.

French commentators tend to accord all types of intervening elections equal status, although they have different attributes that may affect their reliability as expressions of national political trends. We have already referred to the rural bias of departmental elections. Differences in normal turnout are probably the most important grounds on which they should be distinguished. Turnout at municipal elections tends to be almost as high, on the average, as it is for national legislative elections.[15] Turnout varied widely between the regional elections of 1986 and 1992; it was almost 80 percent in 1986, when the regional elections were held simultaneously with the national legislative elections, but it dropped almost 10 percentage points in 1992, when the regional elections were accompanied by departmental elections. Turnout at European elections, never high to begin with, hovered around 50 percent in 1989 and 1994.

In these circumstances, municipal and regional elections are probably the most trustworthy bellwethers, although it must be said that in recent years, the results of all intervening elections have tended to be consistent with one another. Thus, the departmental elections of 1976, as well as the municipal elections of 1977, pointed toward softening of support on the right, which had elected Giscard d'Estaing to the presidency in 1974. With regard to the more recent Mitterrand era, departmental elections in 1982, municipal elections in

1983, and the European elections of 1984 all pointed toward the left-wing coalition's national legislative defeat of 1986. Similarly, although less sharply in its early stages, the sequence of intervening elections between 1988 and 1993 signaled unmistakably the crushing defeat of the leftist coalition at the legislative elections of 1993 (Habert, Perrineau, and Ysmal 1992). Both stages of that electoral trajectory from 1981 to 1986, and from 1988 to 1993, paralleled the curve of presidential popularity that we have recorded in fig. 10.1.

Concluding Comments

The common theme of this chapter has been the linkage between presidential elections and other elections, notably—but for France not exclusively— national legislative elections. Pursuit of that theme has taken us into the domains of split-ticket voting, cross-temporal and cross-district consistency of partisan (or coalitional) voting, the phenomenon of presidential coattails, and even the hallowed U.S. midterm slump. Pursuing both direct and constructed comparisons, we can say that presidential voting is more closely associated with legislative voting in France than it is in the United States. There are fewer split districts in France than in the United States, and district-level correlational analysis consistently yields higher correlations for the French presidential-legislative linkage than for the U.S. one.

There is evidence of coattails effects in both the United States and France, although not as a regular feature of presidential elections. The U.S. midterm slump has no direct French analogue, but French analysts intuitively know that something like it would occur if it could: they have identified its surrogate as an intervening election of a certain kind, one with the Cassandra-like properties of the municipal elections of 1983 or the regional elections of 1992, which correctly pointed toward defeat for the legislative supporters of François Mitterrand. Those intervening elections, along with the later legislative losses of the leftist coalition, were themselves linked to the failing popularity of the president himself, even though he was not standing for reelection—another sign of the high degree of coalitional electoral consistency at the mass level in France.

Part 5
Assessing the Results

This fifth and final section of the book assesses the results of the two different sets of arrangements by which France and the United States choose their presidents. Any such assessment must draw on multiple indicators, as presidential outcomes may be considered from more than one perspective. There is no single summary criterion against which a process as complex as presidential selection can be evaluated. Nevertheless, the two chapters that follow are inspired by a unifying theme. That theme rests on the notion of representation.

The presidency is not a representative office in the same sense as a legislative body is, but insofar as incumbents spring from or enjoy the support of political parties and owe their positions to votes cast by the mass electorate, they cannot fail to act as representatives of some groups, interests, causes, or sets of aspirations, as opposed to others with lesser claims to presidential sympathy. The forms that this representational activity may take are varied, the gamut across which it may operate is wide, and specific presidential contributions may sometimes be elusive. But whatever missions presidents assign to themselves, they act on behalf of others and seek support or solace in a favoring public opinion.

The two chapters of Part 5 discuss various aspects of the representative quality that presidents can express, in an ascending order of abstraction. Chapter 11 starts by treating the distribution across electorally critical social groups of popular satisfaction with the outcomes of the presidential elections of 1988 in both France and the United States. This will be at the most concrete level of analysis, in a form that does not match but does bear a family resemblance to studies of legislative representation. Chapter 11 then moves on to a discussion of the potentiality of the U.S. presidential electoral system for producing electoral college majorities based on small proportions of the popular vote. This analysis is enriched by a simulation of what French electoral outcomes would have been in certain years if an electoral college system similar to the U.S. one had been employed.

Chapter 12 ratchets the analytic perspective a notch higher. First, we ask which system of presidential recruitment, the French one or the U.S. one, is more open to fresh ideas and new sources of political energy. Secondly, we show that despite the many differences in the methods of presidential selection that we have analyzed throughout this book, there are remarkable similarities, rooted in common situations, between the broad missions that particular French and U.S. presidents have sought to fulfill. Finally, chapter 12 concludes on a note that closes a circle opened by the first lines of chapter 1.

Throughout this book, the explicit time frame used for the comparison between the French and U.S. systems of presidential selection is the period from 1964 (for the United States) or 1965 (for France) to 1988, with only occasional references to earlier or more recent years. Yet the opening lines of chapter 1 recall that France is an old nation with a new political system while the United States is a new nation with an old political system. When a gun is introduced in the first act, it must go off in the last one. We conclude by comparing France between 1959 and 1995 with the United States between 1789 and 1837.

CHAPTER 11

Popular Satisfaction and Electoral Systems

It may appear odd to raise the question of how satisfied the French and U.S. electorates are with any given set of presidential election results. The one inescapable property of a presidential election is that there is a winner, which means that there is also a loser. The people who voted for the winner may be presumed to be at least relatively content, while the loser's supporters have every reason to be dejected. Soon after the French presidential election of 1988, 55 percent of a SOFRES national sample reported that they were "rather satisfied" with the result, while 34 percent were "rather disappointed" and the remainder were indifferent. Similarly, a Gallup survey conducted among reported voters during the two days following the 1988 U.S. election found that 56 percent thought that George Bush would make an excellent or a good president, while 41 percent thought he would be "only a fair one, or a poor one," and the small remainder had no views on the matter (*Gallup Report*, November 1988, 25). Not surprisingly, in both surveys the satisfied voters consisted overwhelmingly of persons who had voted for the winning candidate, while the more pessimistic respondents were largely people who had supported the loser.

Moreover, newly elected or even reelected presidents quickly pass from the context of the election into a fluid world in which all kinds of new forces condition their behavior. Dependence on others, stubborn realities, unforeseen problems, foreign crises all affect presidential behavior, and executive actions normally meet with varying degrees of popular approval as the presidential term proceeds. Presidential popularity curves undulate, with the result that early postelectoral evaluations may quickly become obsolete (Edwards and Gallup 1990; Parodi 1971, 1983; Dupin 1992).

Still, the levels of tension between supporters of the competing candidates, as registered at the time of the elections, may vary from country to country and, indeed, from one electoral period to another within a single country. At an early postelectoral SOFRES survey in 1988, only 42 percent of the respondents thought that the outcome of the presidential election would affect their daily lives in one way or another (whether favorably or unfavorably), while in 1981—at the onset of the Mitterrand era—almost 60 percent had thought that the presidential election of that year would indeed have consequences, whether good or ill, for their everyday lives. The preelectoral NES surveys in the United States also register large variations in perceptions of electoral importance, although not always in the same sequence as in France. In 1980, only 56 percent of the U.S. sample electorate cared "a good deal" about which party would win the election, while in 1984 that proportion rose to almost 65 percent. François Mitterrand initially conveyed more hopes and fears than Ronald Reagan did, but the second time around Mitterrand projected avuncular serenity. The electorate regarded Reagan as a paper tiger in 1980, but by 1984 Reagan had succeeded in raising the political energy level several orders of magnitude.

Satisfaction with the Outcomes

In order to produce comparable measures of the degree of political heat at the French and U.S. presidential elections of 1988, we have constructed a set of variables for each country designed to capture the extent to which each respondent preferred one of the two main candidates over the other with regard to each political issue in our issue batteries. For each issue, this variable takes the following form:

$$[R\text{-}PL \text{ (unsigned)}] - [R\text{-}PR \text{ (unsigned)}]$$

where R is the respondent's own position on a given issue, PL is the respondent's perception of the position of the leftist candidate (Mitterrand or Dukakis) on the same issue, and PR is the respondent's perception of the position of the rightist candidate (Chirac or Bush) on that same issue. In this formulation of issue-based candidate preference, the larger the negative score, the more the respondent favored the leftist candidate on the particular issue, while the larger the positive score, the more the respondent preferred the rightist candidate with regard to the issue.

We then proceeded to analyze the variance on each of these issue-based candidate preference variables within and between politically relevant groups of voters, with a view toward determining how much polarization in preferences there was between those groups. The logic underlying the analysis is simply that the greater the polarization, the greater the societal tension, and—in turn—the less satisfactory the electoral outcome from the point of view of the supporters of the losing candidates.

The measure of polarization employed is a familiar one that we have found useful in other contexts as well (Converse and Pierce 1986, 511–16; Pierce and Converse 1990, 306). This is eta, which expresses the amount of variance *between* groups divided by the sum of that variance plus the amount of variance *within* each of the groups. When there are only two groups included in the analysis, eta is a direct measure of polarization. When there are multiple groups, the notion of polarization does not apply, but eta still represents the relative amount of between-group variance. Eta can range from zero to one, and the higher the score the larger the relative between-group variance.

We have applied this form of analysis to each country, for each issue in our issue batteries, to three categories of groups. The first category is simply the actual voters, divided into two groups depending on which of the two major candidates they supported. The second category includes all those highly important social or economic groups, recorded in table 8.1 and table 8.2, and in figure 8.1 and figure 8.2, that constituted the bases of the leftist (Democratic) and rightist (Republican) voting coalitions at the 1988 elections. The analysis here, as in the case of the first category, is dichotomous, with each critical social or economic group considered in contrast to everyone not in the group. The third category of groups considered is geographically based, including more than half of the states in the United States and 21 of the 22 regions in France (excluding Corsica).[1] The results of the analysis, in the form of etas, appear in table 11.1 and table 11.2. We have included in table 11.1 and table 11.2 only those groups for which there was at least one eta on a given issue that was .200 or larger (rounded). Also, we have completely omitted from table 11.2 the issues of policy toward Russia and equal rights for women, as no groups achieved the minimum eta for those issues (except for the purely political dichotomy between Bush voters vs. Dukakis voters, which registered at .549 and .422 respectively, the lowest values for that pair of groups among all the issues inventoried).

The first point to be made about the data reported in table 11.1 and table 11.2 is that the degree of polarization between groups with respect to issue-based candidate preferences is uniformly highest in both countries for the two

TABLE 11.1.   Group Divisiveness of Issue-Based Candidate Preferences, France, 1988 (eta)

		Church Schools (1)	Public Sector (2)	Immigration (3)	Summary (4)
I.	Vote at 2d Ballot	.634	.643	.515	.744
II.	Most/least Religious	.323	.200	.172	.311
	Middle class/working class	.116	.248	.049	.169
	Wage and salary earner/others	.205	.224	.171	.233
	Government employee/others	.145	.211	.209	.228
III.	21 Regions	.187	.150	.201	.176

Note: The summary in column 4 rests on the sum of the data for columns 1–3.

TABLE 11.2.   Group Divisiveness of Issue-Based Candidate Preferences, United States, 1988 (eta)

		Spending on Services (1)	Guarantee Jobs (2)	Help Minorities (3)	Summary (4)	Defense Spending (5)	Health Insurance (6)
I.	Presidential vote	.647	.579	.553	.670	.622	.563
II.	Whites/others	.300	.290	.292	.350	.233	.232
	Blacks/others	.276	.278	.264	.324	.229	.181
	Richest third/others	.175	.180	.153	.220	.093	.180
	Middle class/ working class	.169	.210	.107	.216	.089	.182
III.	30 States	.208	.202	.200	.249	.178	.187

Note: The summary in column 4 rests on the sum of the data for columns 1–3.

groups of voters who supported opposing candidates. The proportions of total variance represented by the variance between the supporters of different candidates outstrips by a wide margin, and in both countries, the amount of between-group variance for any other pair of groups surveyed.

This testifies to how much political choices are independent of the social and economic group contexts out of which they may emerge, even if those group contexts exercise political magnetism or repulsion in their own right. The large etas associated with simple candidate preferences reflect factors such as partisanship, ideology, and candidate appeal, which we have analyzed in chapters 3, 4, and 7, and those forces—in interaction with the play of group associations that are illustrated in chapter 8—far outstrip the polarizing potential of social group affiliations alone.

Furthermore, while there is some variation in the etas across the sets of issues reported for the opposing groups of voters in the two countries, the main impression is one of rough similarity. Polarization in issue-based candidate preferences reaches its peak in the United States concerning the issue of government spending on services, but it is barely greater than the equivalent degree of polarization in France over the issue of the size of the public sector. The summary value for France, reported in column 4 of table 11.1, is higher than the more or less equivalent summary computed for the United States in column 4 of table 11.2, but the U.S. summary values are sensitive to which separate items are included (if we included the defense issue rather than the jobs issue in the U.S. summary, the eta would rise to .727). Moreover, the means of the etas reported in the first three columns of table 11.1 and table 11.2 are .616 and .597, respectively, which reverses the lead in electoral group polarization of the kind we are investigating here.

With regard to polarization between social or economic groups, the only kinds of group differences that produce etas of .300 or more relate to religious attachments in France and racial category in the United States. This provides confirmation, if any were necessary, of how much racial differences in the United States are akin to religious differences in France in their political expression. At the same time, however, there is a difference in the attitudinal fallout from the two types of group distinction, religious and racial, as reflected in table 11.1 and table 11.2. In France, the people representing the two religious groups involved, those persons most attached to the church and those least attached to it, differ strongly only over which candidate they prefer with regard to providing subsidies for religious schools; they differ only minimally concerning which candidate is better with respect to the size of the public sector or policy toward immigrants. Logically enough, French religious groups differ most politically over religion-related issues.

Racial differences in the United States, by way of contrast, operate across most of the spectrum of issues, and not solely (or even particularly strongly) with regard to government help for minorities. Among the five issues reported in table 11.2, racial differences fail to produce an eta of at least .200 only in the case of health insurance as an issue. Racial issues overlap class issues in the United States in a way that religious issues do not in France. Indeed, racial differences in the United States are associated with different candidate preferences even with regard to defense spending.

The remaining social or economic group differences recorded in table 11.1 and table 11.2 relate to various elements of socioeconomic status. The etas for France contain few surprises, unless one be that the immigration issue, which we know from earlier analyses to be largely distinct from the others investigated here, should divide government employees from others. That would seem to be a largely chance result. For the rest, the class-based group differences are not systematically related to differences in candidate preferences based on the church schools issue, while they are so related to preferences based on the issue of the size of the public sector.

For the United States, the purely class-based groups reported in table 11.2 produce modest etas for the summary variable and with regard to candidate preferences relating to the issue of guaranteeing jobs. Apart from those cases, class divisions register only feebly for the United States when they are considered independently of racial differences.

One final set of comments is in order before we leave the category of social and economic groups. The inventories of such groups reported in table 11.1 and table 11.2 are smaller than the lists of groups in table 8.1 and table 8.2, and in figure 8.1 and figure 8.2, from which those tested were derived. Union membership did not register minimally for either country, nor did government employment for the United States. None of the religious measures that were more or less prominent in defining the Bush and Dukakis core voting coalitions, as discussed in chapter 8, produced etas that reached our .200 threshold. What this means is that the people in those electorally important categories did not really see much difference between the candidates on the issues we have reported, relative to their own positions on those same issues. For example, the most frequent churchgoers, who supported George Bush significantly more strongly than the least frequent churchgoers did, were not much more in favor of Bush with respect to our battery of issues than the latter group was. The religion-related support for Bush and Dukakis in 1988 was more traditional than issue oriented, at least with regard to the particular issues we have been able to explore. It is, of course, possible—indeed probable—that if we could examine certain religion-related issues for the United States, in the same way that we can investigate the issue of subsidies for religious schools in France, the picture would be very different.

The conclusion that suggests itself on the basis of our analysis so far is that in terms of issue-based candidate preferences, the distribution of implied satisfaction and dissatisfaction with the electoral results is very similar in France and the United States. Among each electorate as a whole, there was just about as much difference between French Mitterrand supporters and Chirac supporters, on our particular measures, as there was between U.S. voters who opted for Dukakis and those who voted for Bush. We have found no reason why the supporters of the winning candidate, overall, should have grinned more broadly in one country than in the other, or why the voters on the losing side should have been more dejected in one of the countries than in the other.

Among specific social or economic groups, however, there are differences between the two countries, although these lie more in the distribution of presumed dissatisfactions than in their magnitude. In France, the group that appears to have suffered the most acute sense of deprivation in 1988 consists of the voters who were most attached to the Catholic Church, although mainly with regard to the specifically religious issue of government subsides for religious schools. In the United States, the most distressed were the nonwhites, who suffered disappointment in terms of their issue-based candidate preferences across almost the entire menu of political issues.

Whatever sense of loss may have been experienced by certain socioeconomic groups in France who preferred Chirac over Mitterrand essentially because they preferred to shrink the public sector, or by those in the United States who were oriented toward government help for the underdog, registers in our figures as less acute and less widely shared. Class conflict has not disappeared from France or the United States, but it is secondary to religious distinctions in the former and to racial differences in the latter.

There is one further entry in table 11.1 and table 11.2 that deserves attention. This is the treatment of geographically defined groups, including the states in the United States and the regions in France. Modest levels of interstate differences in issue-based candidate preferences in the United States appear for four of the five issues recorded in table 11.2. A similar degree of interregional differences in France occurs only for the immigration issue, reflecting the geographically localized patterns of immigrant settlement. These variations in the geographical distribution of issue-based candidate preferences reflect other factors, of course, notably the distribution of basic political orientations. These once followed distinct sectional lines in both France and the United States, and even though—as we have pointed out in chapter 8—those regional distinctions have attenuated since World War II, we would not have been surprised to find traces of them in both countries. Instead, we find such vestiges only in the United States, while they appear to have evaporated in France.[2]

Our interest in investigating the amount of relative between-group variance on the geographic level is directly relevant to the main formal difference between the French and U.S. systems of presidential election. The basic decision rule for France is that the candidate who receives a majority of the popular votes wins the office. In the United States, the winning candidate is the one who receives a majority of the electoral votes or, in the absence of such a majority, the one who receives a majority of the votes in the House of Representatives, with each state delegation voting as a bloc. By examining aspects of the interstate variance in the United States, we hoped to shed some light on the question of whether there was enough variation in the United States to warrant such sensitivity to state particularisms. By making a parallel investigation of interregional variation in France, we hoped to make an assessment of whether something like the U.S. electoral college system might be appropriate for France. On the basis of our measures, which of course reflect only a partial test of the appropriateness of an electoral college as opposed to majority rule, the case for the U.S. electoral college is surely not strong, while there is no basis at all for suggesting that the French adopt some variant of the U.S. system.

Electoral Colleges, Real and Imagined

There is not, in any case, the slightest interest among the French political elites in altering the majority rule component of their presidential election system. In the United States, however, there is continuing if not exactly widespread concern about the potentially disturbing consequences of the operation of the electoral college system. Although in recent decades, the typical effect of the electoral college has been to transform narrow victories in the popular vote to larger ones in the electoral college, whenever there is a close election pundits regularly point out that a shift of relatively few votes in certain states would have sharply altered the outcome, either by preventing any candidate from winning a majority of the electoral votes and thereby throwing the election to the House of Representatives for decision (1960, 1968) or by giving a majority of the electoral votes to the candidate who received fewer popular votes than his opponent (1948, 1960, 1976) (Longley and Braun 1972, viii, 1–21; Asher 1992, 317).

It is sometimes argued that the best way for the United States to avoid such outcomes would be to switch to a system of direct popular election of the president, including a runoff ballot to ensure that the winning candidate received a majority of the votes. That is, of course, the French presidential electoral system, although to my knowledge the French experience is never referred to in discussions of the proposal for direct elections in the United States. The most common objection to the proposal (apart from the additional costs it would entail) is that it would encourage the multiplication of candidates at the first ballot and, perhaps, lead to the disintegration of the two-party system.

It is not possible to evaluate that argument in the abstract. Quite apart from the issue of whether the multiplication of candidates and even the breakdown of the two-party system would be developments to be deplored or welcomed, much would depend on details, notably the eligibility requirements for competing at the first ballot. The potential dynamics associated with any such reform also need to be taken into account. It might well be the case that candidacies would multiply furiously at the first experience with the new system, but that greater restraint would quickly become the norm, either because of self-imposed or rule-imposed party discipline.

We can, however, at least broaden our perspectives on the issue by simulating what the French experience would have been if France had been operating under a variant of the U.S. electoral college system. In this regard, the elections of 1974 and 1981 interest us most. There are two main reasons for this. First, these two were the only elections of the five held between 1965 and 1988 at which the front-runner at the first ballot did not also win the runoff. In 1974, François Mitterrand outdistanced Valéry Giscard d'Estaing at the first ballot by 43 percent to 33 percent, but Giscard nosed out Mitterrand at the decisive ballot by a tiny margin. In 1981, Giscard had a slight edge over Mitterrand at the first ballot (28 percent to 26 percent), but Mitterrand won the runoff. The possibility of the first-ballot leader losing at the decisive ballot is at the heart of the two-ballot system. It affects the range of candidate strategies by augmenting the number of objectives at which candidates may aim. Under a single-ballot system, each candidate must aim at winning. There is no substitute for victory. Under the two-ballot system, a candidate may quite reasonably enter the race believing that he or she will not be the front-runner at the first ballot but will be the runner-up with a good chance of emerging on top at the runoff. If Theodore Roosevelt could have known in advance the results of his try for the presidency in 1912, he presumably would not have run. If the French system had been in effect he surely would have tried and might very well have won.[3]

The second reason the elections of 1974 and 1981 are of special interest is that they provide two different configurations of major candidates at the first ballot for our consideration. The 1974 French election was a three-candidate race very similar to the third-party contests that periodically occur in the United States, producing concern about the possibility of a minority winner or no winner at all on the basis of electoral votes. In 1974, the two main leftist parties, the Communists and the Socialists, were united behind the single candidacy of Mitterrand, while each of the two main rightist parties, the Gaullists and the Giscardians, fielded a candidate (Chaban-Delmas and Giscard d'Estaing). This distribution of candidates skewed the first-ballot votes so that Mitterrand won some 43 percent of them while Giscard won 33 percent (and Chaban only 15 percent).[4] The 1981 election was more fragmented. In that year, both the left and the right were divided in their preferences for the presidential nomination, so there were four main candidates at the first ballot: Mitterrand; the Communist leader Georges Marchais; Giscard; and Jacques Chirac. Giscard led that field with only 28 percent of the votes, while Mitterrand garnered 26 percent, before moving on to a narrow victory at the runoff.

Before proceeding further in simulating the U.S. presidential electoral process in France, we have to construct a hypothetical electoral college for that country. There are two alternate possibilities: one based on the departments, the other based on the regions. The department is the main French subnational political unit, but the departments—of which there are 96 in metropolitan France—are too small generally to be authentic counterparts of U.S. states. The other main alternative is the region, of which there are 22. These are of much more recent origin than the departments and they are more analogous to the U.S. states in size. There is a sort of official policy of highlighting the existence of the regions, and they may gain in political and administrative importance, but they do not evoke much of a sense of popular identification and we have seen (in chap. 1) that when restrictions were imposed on multiple-office holding French politicians almost uniformly gave higher priority to mayoralties and the presidencies of departmental councils than to regional office. Fortunately, we do not have to opt between the two possibilities; we will employ them both, in part to see whether and how much the choice of one over the other matters.

We have, therefore, assigned a number of "electors" to each department, and to each region, on the basis of the same formula employed in the United States for allocating electors to the states: the number of deputies plus senators.[5] That operation produced a hypothetical electoral college of 735 members for the election of 1974 and one of 760 members for the election of 1981. These were, of course, allocated differently when we took the department as the basis for the system and when we employed the regions.[6]

What would have happened at the French presidential elections of 1974 and 1981 if, instead of the two-ballot system, one or the other of these hypothetical electoral colleges had been operative? In 1974, when Mitterrand outdistanced Giscard at the first ballot by 10 percentage points but Giscard won narrowly at the runoff ballot, Mitterrand would have won the election with some 80 percent of the electoral votes. The (simulated) U.S. electoral system would have produced an outcome opposite to the actual result. In similarly contrary fashion, in 1981, when Mitterrand defeated Giscard at the runoff but trailed Giscard by a mere 2 percentage points at the first ballot, Giscard would have won 60 percent of the electoral votes and been declared the winner.[7]

There are, of course, severe limits to the extent to which purely hypothetical experience in one country may have implications for analogous, but still different, situations in another country. Our French electoral colleges are contrived; the U.S. electoral college is real. Nevertheless, given the degree of concern about the potential production of perverse results by the U.S. electoral college and the necessarily limited amount of U.S. historical experience, it is worth contributing even purely hypothetical comparative data to the discussion.

In this regard, the main conclusion that emerges from our counterfactual experiment is a confirmation of the powerful leverage that pluralities can exert in a winner-take-all electoral college system. The U.S. experiences of 1912 (when Woodrow Wilson won 82 percent of the electoral votes with 45 percent of the popular votes), 1968 (when Richard Nixon won 56 percent of the electoral votes on the basis of 44 percent of the popular vote), and 1992 (when Bill Clinton converted 43 percent of the popular vote into 69 percent of the electoral votes) are seconded not only by the imaginary "victory" of Mitterrand in 1974, with 43 percent of the popular vote but some 80 percent of the electoral votes, but also by the fanciful "triumph" of Giscard in 1981, on the basis of a mere 28 percent of the popular vote but a resounding 60 percent of the electoral votes.[8] When transported into the U.S. context, the French election of 1981 suggests strongly that the main risk of the U.S. electoral college system when there are multiple candidates is less that no candidate will receive a majority of the electoral votes than that one of the candidates *will* win such a majority, even if that candidate has won the support of only a small proportion of the electorate.

Whether that risk points toward the desirability of the United States adopting some variant of the French runoff system for presidential elections is another matter. There is nothing in our experiment with a hypothetical French electoral college that bears directly on that question. In fact, taking all aspects of the presidential selection process into account, there would be distinct disadvantages to the U.S. employing a runoff system.

Such a system would almost certainly produce multiple candidates, although that in itself would not necessarily be harmful. The potentially more damaging feature of a runoff system in the United States would be the persistence of intraparty disputes from the start of the primary elections season to the first ballot of the election. We have already pointed out, in chapter 9, that U.S. parties have the comparatively long period between the end of the primary season and election day in which to try to heal the wounds created by the acerbities of the contests for major-party nomination. From the perspective of trying to maintain some balance between the necessity for division and debate, on the one hand, and the risk of straining social ties, on the other hand, that must be counted an advantage of the U.S. presidential electoral system. In France, the patching-up process must be accomplished in two weeks, which is almost surely too short a period for what can be a difficult task. A runoff system might well destroy one real advantage of the current U.S. system and import a new disadvantage.

Under a runoff system, candidates who were defeated for their parties' nominations might stay in the race and try their luck at the first ballot, thereby prolonging the rancor of the primary season into the electoral period itself. Then there would be only whatever lapse of time separated the first ballot from the runoff for the front-runners to try to mend fences and create some semblance of parties sufficiently united to govern the country responsibly. That would be a high price to pay to avoid the possibility of presidents being elected by small pluralities. The United States, with its system of primary elections, not only does not need a runoff system but actually might suffer badly from adopting one. France, which does not use primaries, does need such a system. Neither the U.S. system nor the French one is ideal, but each is adapted to the larger political context in ways that argue against fundamental change.

CHAPTER 12

Institutional Arrangements and Political Results

In chapter 11, we considered presidential elections in France and the United States from two different aspects of the representational concept, broadly construed. First, we sought to chart the distribution of implied satisfaction and dissatisfaction with the actual 1988 results in both countries, by examining the issue-based candidate preferences of the social and economic groups that constituted the core elements of the two-party (or two-coalition) electorates in France and the United States in 1988. Then, we reflected on the potentiality for minority victors under the U.S. electoral college system and a simulated French electoral college system operating on the same design as the U.S. one.

In this chapter, we will consider two other vantage points from which the French and U.S. systems can instructively be compared within the broad framework of political representation. First, we will discuss how open the presidential recruitment process in each country is to the representatives of new ideas and social forces. Then, we will pursue the representational analysis still further by exploring the unexpected similarity—underlying all the institutional differences we have been at pains to discuss—in the ways the men who have emerged victorious from the two different forms of competition have melded into the societies that selected them.

Openness of Recruitment

We have already seen, in chapter 2, that at the presidential level both France and the United States recruit from small pools of political elites. For both countries, these include the incumbents above all and for the United States, vice presidents. For France, they include as well senior ministers and long-established party leaders; for the United States, senators and governors. But what can we add about the breadth of choice within those already thinly populated ranks? How much opportunity is there for the maverick, the dissenter, the nonconformist to challenge the inertia of politics as usual or to serve as a credible symbol of broadened political opportunity? Mill wrote in *Representative Government* (1946, 145) that "improvement in human affairs is wholly the work of the uncontented characters." What possibilities do the French and U.S. systems of presidential selection offer for "uncontented characters" to acquire the mass support necessary to express their discontent at the apex of the political system?

Breadth of Choice

In the United States, the two-party system limits the breadth of partisan choice offered to the voters, but the system of presidential primaries confers a large and increasingly decisive role on the electorate in the selection of partisan candidates. In France, the multiparty system, combined with the extremely permissive rules governing eligibility for candidacy, virtually ensures that the first ballot will offer a broad range of partisan choice to French voters, but these play no role at all in the determination of who those candidates will be (Duhamel and Jaffré 1987, 66).

Of course, the French electorate decides which two of the competing first-ballot candidates will move on to the runoff.[1] This is the procedure that French commentators liken to U.S. primaries. If, however, one considers the selection of the runoff candidates within the framework of the two-bloc system that normally prevails at the second ballot, where a leftist confronts a rightist, the electorate's ability to select its standard-bearers has usually been limited to the right wing of the political spectrum. In 1965, the Communist and Socialist parties decided to support François Mitterrand in common at the first ballot precisely in order to deprive the voters of the opportunity to decide which leftist candidate should run at the decisive ballot. Neither party at the time relished the idea of providing a candidate to be beaten by de Gaulle. In 1974, the two main leftist parties again jointly supported Mitterrand at the first ballot, although this time they thought their candidate had a real chance to win.

Sometimes, the distribution of partisan electoral strength going into a presidential election, so far as it can be determined, may be such as to make it hopeless for certain candidates to emerge as front-runners. That means, in practice, that loyal partisans may simply be wasting their votes at the first ballot. That was true most notably of non-Gaullist rightists in 1965 and, more recently, of Communist voters at the election of 1988, which followed a legislative election in 1986 that made it apparent that the diminished and splintering Communist party was no match for the Socialists.

From the standpoint of the evenness of the playing field, on both the right and left segments of the partisan spectrum, the election at which voters could most reasonably believe that they would actually be selecting their respective standard-bearers for the runoff was that of 1981. In the actual event, the first-ballot outcome was lopsided, with Giscard d'Estaing and François Mitterrand winning the right to compete with each other at the decisive ballot by wide margins. Giscard easily defeated Jacques Chirac, while Mitterrand similarly outdistanced Communist Georges Marchais. But that result was not preordained.

The 1978 legislative elections had produced close to identical national vote totals for each major party in each coalition: the Giscardians and Chirac's Rassemblement pour la République (RPR), on the right, and the Socialists and the Communists, on the left. Voters in 1981 could believe they had a real opportunity to select the left-wing and right-wing runoff contenders, and they did indeed make the selection. On other occasions, it was only right-wing voters who had such a choice. In 1974, they chose Giscard over Jacques Chaban-Delmas, even though the latter's Gaullist party had won twice as many votes at the legislative elections of 1973 than did the candidates who could be regarded as Giscardians. In 1988, Chirac barely eked out a narrow plurality over Raymond Barre and Jean-Marie Le Pen.

When circumstances permit it, French voters can select the leftist and rightist finalists. There must be a choice of candidates within each competing coalition, and there must be a realistic chance for either of those candidates to win. The parties cannot determine whether the second condition will be met, but allied parties can eliminate the electorate's "primary" role by agreeing on a candidate in advance. And whatever the conditions surrounding an election, the voters never have a voice in the selection of any party's nominee. That is left to whatever procedures the parties apply. De Gaulle and his supporters adopted the French presidential system that still prevails, and they deliberately made eligibility simple to achieve, in order to break the grip of the parties on the selection of the chief executive. Despite their best efforts, the system remains dominated by the parties. The electorate chooses the president, but the parties choose the candidates.

French politicians have considered the possibility of establishing some variant of primary elections as a means of designating presidential candidates. The initiative in this regard has come from the orthodox right, whose defeats at the presidential elections of 1981 and 1988 have sometimes been attributed, at least in part, to the fact that the RPR and the UDF presented competing candidates at the first ballot. In the summer of 1989, Charles Pasqua, an RPR heavyweight and frequent minister of the interior, convened a committee of politicians and jurists to design a system of primaries "à la française" by which RPR and UDF voters and elected officials could together designate a single, preferred presidential candidate (*Le Monde*, June 8, 1989). A procedure was worked out, and both the RPR and the UDF accepted it in principle the following year, but there was grumbling about it from the start (*Le Monde*, June 28, 1990), and the plan was soon shelved.

In 1994, when potential rightwing presidential candidates were multiplying, Pasqua dusted off the earlier scheme and tried again to persuade his political friends to adopt it so that whatever fratricidal conflict might ensue among rightist candidates could be confined to a period well in advance of the election itself (*L'Express*, July 14, 1994). The novelty, complexity, and uncertainty of a new system, however, combined with the strategic calculations of contenders who believed that they would be favored by the existing state of affairs, made it unlikely that any such experiment would be tried.

Primaries vs. Improvisation

In the United States, both major parties (but particularly the Democratic party) tinker with their formal presidential nominating processes. This is usually done at the behest of groups seeking to enhance the future chances of a particular candidate or type of candidate. In fact, these changes have increasingly been marginal to the outcome of the candidate selection process. This is now the result, for both major parties, of the system of primary elections.

The primary system, combined with the fixed four-year presidential term (even if filled out by a succeeding vice president), structures the nominating process in ways that enhance the chances of would-be candidates who are outside the center of the Washington, D.C.–based political elites. The dates of each primary election are fixed well in advance. Potential candidates can plan their strategies over comparatively long periods, select the most advantageous primaries to enter, and at least seek an unprejudiced hearing among various social and economic groups. Once the primary season begins, the field may narrow quickly, as some aspirants stumble or simply fail to catch on. For those who survive the early days, there is the opportunity to gain in visibility, resources, and perhaps even stature. The main point is that potential candidates with limited elite-level support within the customary halls of Washington power have an opportunity to overcome that handicap by garnering mass support on a carefully selected state-by-state basis.

The French system for the recruitment of presidential candidates operates quite differently from the U.S. one. In the absence of primaries, parties control the selection of candidates, which means that would-be contenders must jockey for position within their party hierarchies. This does not mean that external considerations are totally irrelevant. In the French multiparty system, where partisan coalitions are usually essential, the capacity to build interparty support is an asset, as long as the potential coalition parties are appropriate for one's own party's strategy.[2] And party leaders are not indifferent to signs of mass appeal that self-starting aspirants might display. But in the final analysis, French presidential contenders must win the support of their parties. Given the extent to which these organizations are narrow oligarchies, the eligibles inevitably come from a small circle of party elites, who must survive within organizations that are more hierarchical than elective in character.

This gives a special quality to the behavior of would-be presidential candidates, at least within the major parties. Aspirants almost always have to try to dislodge higher-level elites who are often themselves presidential contenders.

And they must do so within a system in which the elites in place have powerful resources, in which they may be subject to rules of party discipline or ministerial solidarity, where positions of power and high visibility have been limited by the practice of multiple-office holding, and which is without regular institutional procedures for governing the inevitable conflict for advancement to the country's highest office, which itself carries a term of seven years, renewable. In the United States, sitting presidents are challenged in primaries and at nominating conventions. At the French Socialist party congress held at Lille, in April 1987, the presidential election, which could be held no later than May 1988, was not on the agenda because President Mitterrand had not yet indicated whether he would run for a second term. Jacques Chirac was president of his party, mayor of Paris, and the prime minister of a government supported by a coalition of right-wing parties prior to the election of 1988. That is a formidable base, virtually impregnable to attacks from within (and below). He could be opposed on the right only by a peer, former prime minister Raymond Barre, or by a rank outsider, Jean-Marie Le Pen, whose support came directly from the electorate.

In this kind of unstructured situation, presidential aspirants must either be patient and serve a long apprenticeship,[3] improvise to gain advantage and public visibility, or both. The need for improvisation is what gives French political life its appearance of constant fluidity, amidst comparatively little change. There is a ceaseless war of maneuver, as contenders seek to exploit every opportunity, however fleeting, to advance their chances. The sound and the fury are rather more obvious in the center and on the right than on the left, but that is because the center-right segment of the spectrum contains more parties that are in the game than the left does, and not because of major structural differences. The Socialist party is as much a field of maneuver as the neo-Gaullist RPR or the more decentralized, Giscardian-oriented UDF.

Techniques of Self-Promotion

The problem for the challenger who has not already arrived, who is not (yet) a member of the small group consisting of the incumbent president, the prime minister, relatively recent former prime ministers, and major-party leaders, is to acquire a secure electoral base, develop an elite political following of one's own, win a reputation for independence without incurring complaints of disloyalty, sow doubts about the probability that those higher up the ladder can advance the party's fortunes, and achieve a high and enduring level of public visibility. That is not an easy problem to solve. In the course of trying to solve it, presidential aspirants in France have pursued a variety of methods, sometimes successfully, more often unsuccessfully. These methods fall into four main categories: achieving distinctive electoral success; leading a successful party revolt; resigning (or threatening to resign) a high position with éclat; and exploiting one's personality and nonpolitical resources.

Electoral Efforts. These have been of two kinds: the individual level and the national level. The individual-level efforts have been to contest high-profile by-elections, special elections held in single districts to fill seats vacated for various reasons, including the death or resignation of the incumbent.[4] That can be helpful for two reasons. First, if the aspirant wins, he or she has an indispensable parliamentary seat. "If you want to elect me president," veteran politician Edgar Faure told his supporters in 1969, when he ran at a by-election, "you first have to elect me deputy" (*Le Monde*, October 14, 1969). Secondly, because by-elections are not normally held in more than a handful of districts at any one time, and sometimes only in a single district, they enjoy a degree of national attention that no single seat can hope to attract during a general election, when the entire chamber is elected all at once. The publicity is magnified, of course, if the particular by-election is distinguished for one reason or another.[5]

The most spectacular, if futile, effort to exploit the by-election opportunity was made by Jean-Jaques Servan-Schreiber in the fall of 1970. Servan-Schreiber was the editor of the popular French weekly *L'Express* and the author of a widely read and internationally successful book entitled *Le Défi américain* (1967) [*The American Challenge*, 1968]. He became general secretary of the small, middle-of-the-road Radical party late in 1969, and ran successfully for a seat at Nancy, in eastern France, at a by-election in June 1970. Servan-Schreiber then took the high-risk gamble of challenging Jacques Chaban-Delmas, the prime minister and also the longtime and immovable mayor of Bordeaux, for Chaban's parliamentary seat at Bordeaux. Servan-Schreiber would, indeed, have been catapulted to political heights if he had defeated Chaban in the latter's electoral fief. Unfortunately for Servan-Schreiber's future political advancement, Chaban easily won the election at the first ballot.

Michel Rocard's experience with a spotlighted by-election was more successful than Servan-Schreiber's rash attempt. Rocard, fresh from his early experience as a presidential candidate in 1969, when he won less than 4 percent of the votes, ran for a parliamentary seat at a by-election outside Paris against de Gaulle's longtime foreign minister and short-term prime minister, Maurice Couve de Murville. Rocard won the seat (but lost it in 1973), while any hopes that Couve de Murville might one day advance to the presidency were effectively laid to rest.

These efforts to achieve national visibility via candidacy at special elections in individual legislative districts clustered during the early years of direct presidential elections, when they presented virtually the only opportunity to make a distinctive electoral impact. More recently, emerging political figures interested in testing their standing, along with what to stand on, have sought the broader base offered by the French elections to the European Parliament. The

European elections are almost an ideal vehicle for launching trial balloons with presidential implications. Like presidential elections, they are national in scope. The entire country is a single constituency that elects 81 deputies to the European Parliament on the basis of a list system of proportional representation. Access to the ballot is easy to obtain, so an aspiring leader with 80 political friends can enter the fray at the head of a list of candidates.

Moreover, the European elections pose special problems for several of the main parties, the neo-Gaullist RPR and the Giscardian UDF in particular. The European elections tend to focus on issues relating to European integration, but while those two parties are normally allied, they are to varying degrees divided both internally and vis-à-vis each other over the pace, modalities, and even the principle of European integration. These conflicts surface periodically, and did so conspicuously in the fall of 1992 at a referendum over ratification of the Maastricht Treaty providing for eventual monetary union and steps toward political union for the members of the European Community. The country's senior statesmen—President Mitterrand, Jacques Chirac, Giscard d'Estaing—all supported ratification, but other, second-tier figures from the RPR and UDF campaigned actively for a "no" vote. In the end, the electorate approved the treaty, but by such a narrow margin that the vote amounted virtually to a repudiation of the French political establishment.

It is, therefore, especially difficult for the orthodox rightist parties to formulate coherent positions on European integration. When the RPR and UDF try to present a common front they must make special efforts to soft-pedal their differences over Europe. And these differences make each of them vulnerable to dissidents who can stake out a distinctive position on Europe at the same time as they profess party or coalitional loyalty more broadly construed.

This weakness of the rightist parties on European policy was exploited at the European elections of 1994 by Philippe de Villiers, a fiercely nationalistic and protectionist UDF deputy from western France. De Villiers ran his own list of candidates, separate from (and necessarily in opposition to) a coalition list presented by the RPR and UDF. De Villiers, in effect, campaigned against the Maastricht Treaty at the same time as he professed his loyalty to the RPR-UDF coalition whose candidates he opposed. De Villier's list won about half as many votes as the joint RPR-UDF list did, a showing that was impressive enough to make de Villiers a powerbroker, if not an actual contender, at the next presidential election.

Factional Leadership. The best illustration of this relates to the Socialist party, which not only explicitly takes its several factions into account in the allocation of party offices, but is also the only French party that applies genuine electoral procedures in determining party policies. Michel Rocard, like his senior and—so far—more successful rival, François Mitterrand, became the leader of a faction within his party soon after he joined it. This both assured him a voice in all intraparty bargaining and provided him with a network of supporters throughout the country. Other leading Socialists who indicated at one time or another between 1981 and 1988 that they would run for the presidency (always, of course, if President Mitterrand chose not to seek another term) were also leaders of factions or other high governmental or party officials with well-defined factional support.

In parties where factions are frowned upon and not institutionalized, a factional base is harder to establish. In these situations, there are unstructured party revolts, sometimes referred to as *frondes*, in evocation of the rightist religious backlash against the French revolution in western France. In the spring of 1989, such an outbreak occurred within the RPR, and spilled over into the UDF as well, in the form of appeals for new policies (if not, at least explicitly, new leaders) on the part of younger, self-styled *rénovateurs*, whose complaints and proposals naturally earned them more attention than was given to the backers of the parties' current leaders. Such prominence is fleeting, however, unless it can be given institutional support. Where that is lacking, dissidents have little choice but to continue to improvise in what sometimes seems to be an unceasing search for even marginal and short-lived advantage.

Resignation. One way to attract attention to a political position, and its supporter, is to accompany some pronouncement with a grand gesture. The conventional form this takes is for a cabinet minister to resign from a government whose policy he or she cannot support. In fact, resignations on those grounds occur rarely, in France or elsewhere, despite the fact that the principle underlying them is widely regarded as a cardinal rule of parliamentary government. Be that as it may, resignations do occasionally take place, as do threats of resignation which, if made public, may convey a similar message: that the minister feels sufficiently strongly about some matter to give up his or her post in the government. In the spring of 1985, Michel Rocard resigned his position as minister of agriculture in protest against the government's adoption of proportional representation for the forthcoming legislative elections in the place of the two-ballot, runoff system that had been used since the advent of the Fifth Republic. This caused problems for Rocard's factional followers, but it did not seem to damage his reputation with the public.

In June 1987, as thoughts were turning toward the presidential election of 1988, François Léotard, an up-and-coming young party leader associated with the UDF and a minister in the government of Prime Minister Chirac, declared that he had not ruled out becoming a candidate for the presidency. He also attacked the prime minister for allegedly turning over too much political and administrative power to partisans of the RPR. This hardly endeared him to any of the presidential heavyweights at the time, and particularly the prime minister. Threats of resignation were bandied about, and Chirac, whose government rested on a razor-thin parliamentary majority, could not afford to lose any support, so the affair was patched up, but not before it had called the attention of at least the Parisian political elite to Léotard's availability for the presidency.[6]

It is possible, of course, both to resign dramatically *and* to run for office ostentatiously. That was the tactic employed by Michel Noir, the mayor of Lyon (France's second-largest population center). Noir, like Léotard, was a deputy of the successor generation whom Chirac had made a minister in 1986 and who repaid the honor by making life difficult for his chief. Noir was associated with Léotard among the self-styled renovators of the French right during the spring of 1989, and at the end of the following year he struck out on a more independent course by resigning both his membership in Chirac's RPR and his seat in the National Assembly. He (and two other RPR deputies who had resigned with him) then sought to regain their parliamentary seats at by-elections in January 1991. Noir was reelected on a small turnout, one of his two fellow rebels lost her seat, and the whole affair failed to produce the national awakening it was aimed at, partly because it coincided with a larger event, France's participation in the Gulf War with Iraq. Noir quickly lost whatever elite following he might have had in the presidential sweepstakes.[7]

Nonpolitical Resources. Every once in a while, a flamboyant personality, endowed with nonpolitical resources, emerges suddenly at or near the top of the political hierarchy. This phenomenon is actually comparatively rare, in both France and the United States, but the spectacular entry of Ross Perot onto the presidential political scene in the United States in 1992 demonstrates that money and reputation can equal political experience as a factor in getting to the starting gate of the biggest race in the country. To some extent, the odyssey of Jean-Jacques Servan-Schreiber falls into this category. His principal resource was a lively and popular weekly, read by virtually everyone in the French political elite, and Servan-Schreiber had not hesitated to use it in the electoral interests of others.[8] His book, *Le Défi américain* (1967), was an intelligent and well-received analysis of France's economic place in the world that also attracted attention.

A more recent and more characteristic case of this sort was the checkered political career of Bernard Tapie, an energetic and outspoken business buyout specialist and soccer promoter who forcefully and unambiguously opposed Jean-Marie Le Pen and his xenophobic policies right in Marseille, which passed for Le Pen's main electoral stronghold. Tapie's comparative electoral success and unmistakable vitality gained him rapid promotion, and in the spring of 1992 he was appointed minister of urban affairs in the leftist government of Premier Pierre Bérégovoy. Within a month of his appointment, however, he was sued for commercial fraud and resigned from the government. The suit against him was later dropped, Tapie was reinstated in his ministerial post, and he survived the leftist debacle at the legislative elections of March 1993 by winning a seat in the Marseille area. Like Philippe de Villiers, he ran at the head of a separate list of candidates at the European elections of 1994 and received almost as many votes as the official Socialist party list did under the leadership of Michel Rocard. At times, it seemed as though Tapie might become a strong populist contender for the presidency by exploiting popular disillusion with the political professionals, much as Ross Perot tried to do in the United States. But each of Tapie's political successes was diminished by subsequent scandal. The pugnacious ex-minister could not be counted out, but he was repeatedly beset by liabilities from which many of his erstwhile allies preferred to distance themselves.

A Closed Elite. Presidential sorties of the kind we have just described are usually shallow and short-lived, because they rarely rest on sustained policy positions or a stable base of popular support. Even at the very highest levels, the conflicts are based on ambition and not on alternate political visions. Prior to the 1988 French presidential election, former president Giscard d'Estaing said that he would stay out of the race because "there is no longer any ideological difference between the RPR and the UDF" (*L'Année Politique 1988* 1989, 21), but the following month Giscard's long-time prime minister, Raymond Barre, threw his own hat into the ring. If he had not done so, someone else from the UDF surely would have. In that sense, the rivalry among the leaders of the respectable rightist parties is more akin to Senator Edward Kennedy's challenge to presidential incumbent Jimmy Carter in 1980, than to Ronald Reagan's challenge to incumbent Gerald Ford in 1976. The latter rested on different conceptions of national policy, the former did not.[9]

One major exception to the suggestion above that most improvised presidential flyers lack substantive issue content relates to the Socialist party in general and the career of Michel Rocard in particular. Rocard's name has appeared frequently in our brief survey of challenging methods. Rocard's durability and stature, however, rest on more than a plethora of political ploys. Rocard was as inventive and determined to serve his purposes as anyone, but he did have purposes. From the time when François Mitterrand reconstituted the Socialist party at the end of the 1960s, at least until about 1983, there was a real struggle within the French Socialist party over the main lines of economic policy similar to that which characterized the British Labor party for an even longer period. Rocard was the leader of the moderate Socialists. That was what made him a factional leader, and he stuck to his position consistently at a time when he was constantly being overruled in order to maintain an electoral alliance with the French Communist party. With the Communist party weakened, and the leftist alliance a useful but empty formula, Rocard could emerge as a leader who no doubt had had to act with agility now and then to keep his position close to center stage, but who did not waver in his convictions about the kinds of policies that were appropriate for France.

Some twenty years ago, Michel Crozier wrote a book whose title, *La Société bloqué* (1970), became a popular description of France as a society whose vitality and capacity for change were seriously obstructed by outmoded political institutions and excessive conservatism masquerading as progressive egalitarianism. Whatever the validity of that analysis for its time, there is a sense in which the recruitment of presidential contenders in France combines a misleading institutional openness (the ease of eligibility) with bureaucratic rigidities that cannot fail to be conservative in their consequences. It is difficult in any political system to find the means to harness personal ambition to the service of national needs. The French system of presidential recruitment goes a long way to ensuring that the main contenders will be experienced in the affairs of state at the highest levels (Duhamel and Jaffré 1987, 67). It scores less well as a system for injecting fresh perspectives into the higher reaches of the executive branch.[10]

Sources of New Perspectives

The amount of room for variety among the main contenders for the presidency in either France or the United States is limited. In the United States, elections are held only every four years, and a president may serve for eight years. In France, presidential elections are even less frequent (barring accidents), and French presidents can succeed themselves as often as the voters and the life span permit. The electoral opportunities are infrequent and the relevant candidate populations are small, which militates against diversity from the start. Moreover, at a national election, candidates inevitably must try to be consistent with voter expectations that were generated in the past; when they try to expand their range of appeal, they must be careful not to alienate their supporting core. The risks of error are enormous. All of this encourages caution.

In circumstances such as these, the wonder is not why the range of variation among French presidential candidates (controlling for party) is as narrow as it is, but rather why the U.S. system generates such variety among contenders for the top political job. For the roster of presidential contenders in the United States in recent decades is impressive in its diversity. The main sources of this are the country's continental size and consequent regional variety, its characteristic patterns of population mix, and its sometimes exaggerated conception of its role in world affairs.

The political history of the United States is frequently presented in terms of sectionalism, descriptive of the regional variation in interests and outlooks. It is a minor irony that France, the home of electoral geography and where the distribution of virtually every quantifiable attribute inevitably appears somewhere on a map, has been comparatively immune to the play of regional distinctions at the presidential level. Governments and, especially, the legislature are sensitive to regional considerations, and presidential hopefuls have their geographical seats of strength, usually as mayors of cities that dominate a comparatively small region. But presidential nomination and election strategies are not prominently based on regional considerations. In the United States, by way of contrast, Barry Goldwater shifted the core of the Republican party westward and southward, inaugurating the "southern strategy" that Richard Nixon continued to follow. Jimmy Carter, a southerner himself, recaptured the South temporarily in 1976, but Ronald Reagan and George Bush maintained the southern and western emphasis that Goldwater had initiated much earlier. There is nothing in recent French experience to match this deliberate shifting of regional targets in the United States, a strategic turn that brought new kinds of presidential candidates to the fore. French politicians, like U.S. governors and senators, need a local base, but they are not counted on to convert it into broader regional support, as Goldwater did the West, and Carter the South in the United States.

Regional emphases naturally overlap with programmatic themes. Goldwater and Reagan pushed, in particular, for rugged individualism over social responsibility, catering to presumably frontier traits. Their southern strategy was more sinister in implication, as it sought to exploit white resentment against black people, now gaining in confidence and electoral power. In that fashion, presidential politics fused regional identity with the country's racial diversity, as it had done more blatantly in 1948 when J. Strom Thurmond carried four southern states on behalf of racial segregation, and as it was to do again in 1968, when George Wallace won even more electoral votes than Thurmond had.

The system can open opportunities for some elements of its variegated population even as it has been used to exploit the fears of others. John F. Kennedy laid to rest the notion that a Catholic could not be elected president, and the decisive step in the unfolding of that demonstration was a primary election, in Protestant West Virginia, at which Kennedy defeated Hubert H. Humphrey. There is no corresponding barrier against Protestants in France, where Protestants (and Jews) have served as prime minister, and by the same token, the election of a Protestant president in France would not provoke the same sense of expanding citizenship that Kennedy's election did.[11] Jesse Jackson's pursuit of the Democratic party's nomination in 1984 and, especially, in 1988 was a liberating force as well, even though it was accompanied by disappointment, with results that were discussed in chapter 9, for thwarted voters.

Finally, there are the repercussions from errors in U.S. foreign policy, which are necessarily magnified by the enormous resources the country can deploy and by the centrality of the country's role in international affairs. When the United States judges incorrectly, the cost is bound to be great and virtually no other country is likely to be indifferent. The U.S. experience with the Vietnam War was such an event, and its principal reflection in presidential politics was the nomination of George McGovern by the Democratic party in 1972. McGovern was virtually a single-issue candidate, whose overwhelming priority was to end the Vietnam War.[12]

The most nonconforming U.S. presidential candidates, for their times, were Barry Goldwater and George McGovern. Both men were overwhelmingly defeated by candidates who were closer to what passed at the time for the mainstream. Partisans of the French system might say that their own, more closed presidential system is well off without such hapless eccentrics. But we have tried to show, in chapter 2, that Goldwater, for better or for worse, was a premonitory figure who in more ways than one put his stamp on Republican presidents for more than two decades. McGovern's legacy is harder to decipher. Would the Vietnam War have been brought to an end when it was, if a more orthodox contender had won the Democratic party nomination in 1972? No one can know. All we can say is that new policies require new people, and how the recruitment process is structured limits the kinds of people who are likely to ascend the heights. On that basis, the U.S. system of presidential recruitment is more likely to produce a wider range of presidential candidates than the French one.

Presidential Roles

We saw in chapter 2 that the prior political experience of French presidents has, more often than not, been different from that of U.S. presidents during the same period. We have also argued, in this chapter, that the different methods of recruiting presidential candidates in the two countries produces different strategies and even different types of political personalities and presidential policies. Yet, if we raise our sights a bit higher, above the level of political origins, tactics, and particular programmatic orientations, we find that the experiences in office of the two national sets of chief executives display remarkable similarities. Just as the two countries' different constitutional and party systems create different paths of presidential recruitment, the common situation of high executive office in a modern democratic society both creates common problems for the incumbents and limits their range of behavior.

The first three presidents listed in table 2.1, Johnson, de Gaulle, and Nixon, were forced to conclude their presidential tenure prematurely. In the face of widespread opposition to his prosecution of the Vietnam War, Johnson decided not to seek a second nomination for the presidency in 1968. Already weakened by the mass discontent revealed by the upheaval of May 1968, de Gaulle was defeated at a popular referendum in 1969 and promptly resigned the presidency. Nixon resigned in 1974 rather than face impeachment on charges that he had knowingly failed to uphold the laws of the United States.

Nixon's failure was personal, but there are political factors common to the cases of Johnson and de Gaulle. Both had unduly specialized experiences and preoccupations. De Gaulle's "domaine réservé" was foreign and defense policy, Johnson's was domestic policy. Johnson had never had the kind of experience that had made de Gaulle skeptical of professional military claims and sensitive to the domestic costs of foreign adventures; had he done so he might have avoided the debacle of Vietnam. By the same token, de Gaulle might have avoided the 1968 outburst if he had had more understanding of the daily concerns of the ordinary citizen that Johnson had acquired from years on the hustings and familiarity with legislators whose political survival required them to keep their ears to the ground. De Gaulle's penchant for speaking in grandly abstract terms served him well enough in foreign and colonial affairs, but in the end it failed to satisfy the more mundane interests of the electorate.

While both Johnson and de Gaulle were presidents bent on major reforms, de Gaulle in constitutional organization and foreign affairs, Johnson in domestic and, particularly, social policy, de Gaulle and Nixon were given special missions to make peace. Both de Gaulle and Nixon inherited wars that they did not start (but had not opposed), and that they were expected to end. Both came to office with more support from people who wanted them to achieve military victory than from those who advocated negotiation and withdrawal, but both maintained sufficient ambiguity about their intentions to keep the hopes of both groups of supporters alive. In the end, both presidents conceded to the realities that made military victory impossible. In each case, it took four years to accomplish the mission.

De Gaulle's resignation in the face of electoral defeat and diffuse mass discontent, and Nixon's resignation in disgrace, left France and the United States (at different dates) in need of calm and opportunity for at least some political reconciliation. Georges Pompidou in France, Gerald Ford in the United States, were cast in the role of internal pacifiers. Both men reached out as far as they thought safe (Pompidou rather farther than Ford). Pompidou appointed a liberal Gaullist as prime minister (Jacques Chaban-Delmas) whose principal adviser for social affairs was Jacques Delors, a trade unionist from the moderate left who was later to become François Mitterrand's minister of finance and, eventually, the president of the Commission of the European Community. Pompidou also sought reconciliation with advocates of European integration (by supporting British entry into the European Community, which de Gaulle had twice personally vetoed) and of cooperation with the United States. Ford pursued domestic tranquility more through rhetoric than acts, and more within the Republican party than between Republicans and Democrats. His pardon of Richard Nixon for any crimes he might have committed while president was unpopular with most Democrats and even a large minority of Republicans (*Gallup Opinion Index*, October 1974, 24–25), although it probably spared Nixon the pain and the citizenry the spectacle of an epochal criminal trial that would have exacerbated the already intense political conflict that Nixon symbolized. He sought to appease moderate Republicans by naming Nelson Rockefeller as his vice president. Such emphasis on good feelings naturally aroused the suspicions and discontent of Gaullist and Republican hard liners. Pompidou was pressured to drop Chaban-Delmas in favor of the uninspiring but orthodox Pierre Messmer prior to the legislative elections of 1973,[13] and western-based Republican true believers launched Ronald Reagan in the effort, which turned out to be unsuccessful, to deprive Ford of the nomination in 1976.

Valéry Giscard d'Estaing and Jimmy Carter had the misfortune of presiding over their respective countries from weak political bases during the stagflation years of the middle and late 1970s. For the first time during the postwar period, unemployment and inflation grew simultaneously, and conventional macroeconomic stabilization and adjustment policies failed to produce the expected results. Giscard, an experienced minister of finance, was better equipped than Carter to deal with the complexities of such a situation, although there is a sense in which both men approached their roles as "technocrats"—technical experts equipped to solve problems presented in objective, as opposed to, political terms. Carter, coming from an engineering and small-business background, enraged almost everyone in Washington with his interest in zero-base budgeting; Giscard appointed as his (second) prime minister Raymond Barre, whom he described as "France's greatest living economist," and who turned out to be the only top-level French politician with a sense of humor ("I am a square man in a round body").

Sooner or later, even technocrats require political support, but Giscard and Carter had unusually weak partisan bases. Most Gaullist elites detested Giscard: he was European oriented, he was "Atlanticist," he had failed to support de Gaulle at the referendum of 1969, and—worst of all—he had outdistanced Chaban-Delmas at the 1974 presidential election, thereby depriving the Gaullists of the presidency that they had come to believe was their birthright.

The Gaullists had to back Giscard at the second ballot of the election, but they felt little urgency about doing so after he became president, with the result that the Giscard administration was a long battle of maneuver between Giscardians and Gaullists. Carter, too, had been an outsider, in a different fashion. A one-term former governor of Georgia, in aggregate terms he was at best a regional candidate, as he was associated with no broad programmatic current within the Democratic party and was totally without experience in Washington. He was successful in the early primaries, less successful in the later ones, but Carter competed everywhere while his strongest opponents opposed him only locally, with the result that he won the nomination fairly and squarely but aroused little enthusiasm outside his native South. Few members of the Democratic congressional elite had any considerable stake in his success.

In both the United States and France, the electoral cycle that we sketched at the beginning of this chapter reached closure in the early 1980s with the advent of the most ideologically oriented presidents the two countries had known. The messages and policies of Ronald Reagan and François Mitterrand were polar opposites in economic and social affairs, but in each case they reversed the prevailing national currents of the middle 1960s. Reagan's victory in 1980 avenged Goldwater's defeat in 1964, while Mitterrand's 1981 election gave him the presidential prize that had eluded him since 1965. The new leaders of the 1980s marched to power brandishing ideas that had been rejected 15 years earlier.

With a zeal unmatched in the United States since the post–Civil War era of Reconstruction, the Reaganites tried to undo the past. They proceeded to dismantle virtually every program designed to relieve the poor, aid minorities, protect consumers, or preserve the environment. With a comprehensiveness and dedication not seen in France since the early post–World War II years, the Mitterrand forces enlarged the nationalized sectors of industry and finance, extended the social security system, and gave added legal protection to organized labor. Neither Reagan's nor Mitterrand's policy could be sustained indefinitely, but Reagan's—in its more abstract, free market formulations, if not in its meaner applications—had the great advantage of being in harmony with currents of economic thought and practice that were beginning to sweep the capitalist, the mixed, and eventually even the socialist worlds. Mitterrand's policies were in large part obsolete, the last expression in the twentieth century of the socialism of the nineteenth. French socialist policy was swimming against the tide, while the rationale, if not the expression, of U.S. policy *was* the tide. Within two years, Mitterrand called a halt and, without repudiating any of his cherished principles, reversed course in numerous operational (but not structural) ways.

Mitterrand lost control of French government policy (but not his job) in 1986, when legislative elections returned a narrow right-wing parliamentary majority. Jacques Chirac became prime minister, and he proceeded to dismantle many of Mitterrand's socialist initiatives, particularly by denationalizing several major industrial and financial firms that Mitterrand had nationalized. Reagan's efforts to establish a virtually unregulated market economy in the United States did not pass through a series of stages analogous to those that Mitterrand's policies did. They wound down gradually in the face of increasing congressional resistance. By 1988, however, there was a rough parallelism of outcomes in the two countries. Neither Mitterrand nor Reagan had achieved all their goals, but they had accomplished many of them. Moreover, at the elections of 1988, the voters in both countries preferred watered-down versions of what Mitterrand and Reagan had wrought, rather than challengers who might undo (further) the changes that they had brought about. But George Bush was not the counterpart of Ronald Reagan, and the François Mitterrand of 1988 was not the Mitterrand of 1981. The age of dramatic, if contradictory, reforms was temporarily over in the two countries. The visionaries gave way to the brokers.[14]

Dynastic Descents

While the record that we have just reviewed indicates that common situations have tended to promote equivalent executive behavior in France and the United States, there is more than one time frame within which it is appropriate to compare presidential selection in the two countries. The comparison so far is almost literally contemporaneous, implicitly defining the situation in terms of the forces, pressures and urgencies characteristic of the last quarter of a century. Yet that is not the only way in which the situational framework for comparison between the two countries can reasonably be defined. The United States is a young country by comparison with France, but it operates under an old, deep-rooted political system, while France is an old country operating under a young political system that was still in its infancy during the middle 1960s. It is as appropriate and instructive to take the respective formative years of the two political systems as the temporal base for the comparison as it is to concentrate on the contemporary period.[15] One can compare presidential selection in France and the United States between 1964 and 1988; one can also compare France between 1959 and 1995 with the United States between 1789 and 1837.

From the latter perspective, the most salient characteristic that the two systems share in common is the movement away from the founding dynasty, at first gradually, later with a sharp and decisive political rupture (see table 12.1). In considering the equivalence of political developments during the early years of the French Fifth Republic and the one and only United States republic, it is of course important not to be overly literal-minded. Charles de Gaulle was not the

TABLE 12.1. **Founding Presidential Successions, France, 1959–95, and the United States, 1789–1837**

France	United States
Charles de Gaulle, 1959–69	George Washington, 1789–97
Georges Pompidou, 1969–74	John Adams, 1797–1801
(Prime Minister, 1962–68)	(Vice President, 1789–97)
	Thomas Jefferson, 1801–9
	(Vice President, 1797–1801)
	James Madison, 1809–17
	(Secretary of State, 1801–9)
	James Monroe, 1817–25
	(Secretary of State, 1811–17)
Valéry Giscard d'Estaing, 1974–81.	John Quincy Adams, 1825–29
(Minister of Finance, 1962–66, 1969–74)	(Secretary of State, 1817–25)
François Mitterrand, 1981–95	Andrew Jackson, 1829–37

father of his country in quite the same sense that George Washington was the father of his; the French Gaullists did not dominate the early years of the new regime the way the U.S. Federalists did, nor did they disappear completely when their founding mission was accomplished. And so forth. But the parallels are too striking to be ignored and they may well express imperatives that emerge from common situations rather than accidental oddities on the fields of political chance.

De Gaulle and Washington were founders, not mere reformers. Presidential powers were written into the French and U.S. constitutions by people who were secure in the foreknowledge that the first incumbent would be de Gaulle in France, Washington in the United States. Washington was unopposed at each of his two elections; de Gaulle met with only limited opposition at his first election in 1959 (before direct popular election of the president was introduced). Each man established constitutional precedents and tried as well to set the tone of the new republic.

We have already seen how the presidential succession in France passed through high executive office. De Gaulle was succeeded by Pompidou who had been prime minister for seven years; Pompidou was succeeded by Giscard d'Estaing, who had been minister of finance under both previous presidents. The descent was very similar in the early U.S. period. The presidency passed from Washington to John Adams, who had been his vice president, and then to Thomas Jefferson who had been Adams's vice president. The next three presidents, Madison, Monroe, and John Quincy Adams, had each served as secretary of state under the previous president. The supreme executive office circulated within only a small sector of the political elite.

In partisan terms as well, there is a similarity between the two sets of early years, as far apart as they were in real time. We have already shown how Giscard d'Estaing stole the Gaullists' presidential birthright in 1974, in effect ending the Gaullist dynasty a mere 15 years after its foundation. Although Jefferson was an unalloyed member of the Virginia dynasty in the United States, his electoral victory in 1800 effectively terminated the Federalist ascendancy. Jefferson's relationship with the Federalists who preceded him differs in many details from the relationship between Giscard d'Estaing and the Gaullists. But on the core issue, the similarity prevails. Jefferson destroyed the Federalists, and the Gaullists have not to this day recovered from Giscard's victory of 1974.

The Jeffersonian succession to the Federalists lasted a quarter of a century; control of the French presidency by the non-Gaullist right, in the person of Giscard d'Estaing, lasted only one seven-year presidential term. Yet in both countries, from the viewpoint of the founding dynasty, worse was yet to come. By 1824 in the United States, and as early as 1974 in France, the barbarians were at the gates: Andrew Jackson, the candidate of the masses, François Mitterrand, the single candidate of the left.

The gates were smashed in 1981 in France, in 1828 in the United States. But the age of Jackson and the Mitterrand era were already foreshadowed at the previous elections. We know how narrow Giscard's 1974 victory was. The bitterness between Giscardians and Gaullists during Giscard's administration weakened the claim to further presidential office of both groups. Giscard's term was the transitional period between the transfer of power from the Gaullists to the Socialists.

In this sense, Giscard was the French John Quincy Adams. Adams, the son of the second U.S. president, and expressive of Federalist interests, received fewer electoral votes than Jackson in 1824, but Jackson lacked the required majority for election, and it was left to the House of Representatives to decide. Henry Clay, the Speaker of the House, threw his support to Adams, and Jackson (like Mitterrand in 1974) had to wait for the next election, when he triumphed.[16]

Within 40 years of the founding in the United States, within only 22 years in France, the presidency passed into the hands of opposition leaders who had either (as in the case of Mitterrand) actually opposed the constitution under which he was to govern or (as in the case of Jackson) been so out of sympathy with many of the institutional arrangements that the Federalists had erected that he might well have been an anti-Federalist at the time of the adoption of the constitution.[17] Each made his peace with the constitution that had earlier provoked his opposition or skepticism. Each struck fear into the hearts of his opponents. Each pursued his new, distinctive agenda for reform. Both were reelected. We know the history that followed in the United States. The subsequent history in France remains to be made.

Appendixes

The Survey of the French Electorate

The data source for most of the analyses of French electoral behavior in 1988 that appear in this book is a national sample survey of French registered voters conducted by SOFRES between May 11 and May 14, 1988, among 1,013 respondents. The sample design consisted of two elements: the selection of *communes* (municipalities) and the selection of individual respondents.

Selection of Communes

The first stage of the sampling procedure involved the designation of 24 strata by classifying all of France's some 36,000 communes by 4 population categories and 6 geographic regions, exclusive of the Paris region. On the basis of the 1982 census figures, and aiming at a target of 1,000 interviews, each stratum (as well as the Paris region) was assigned a number of interviews proportional to the population of the stratum. Then, individual communes were selected by random sampling within each stratum (and the Paris region) on the assumption that 10 interviews would be conducted in each commune. In all, interviews were conducted in 111 communes within 77 departments (see table A.1).

Selection of Respondents

The selection of the individual respondents was the responsibility of the interviewers, subject to the requirements that they respected the quotas assigned to them and adhered to the various procedures established by SOFRES to ensure appropriate dispersion of the sample and proper conduct of the interviews.

The quotas, again based on the 1982 census data for each commune, related to the sex, age, and occupation of the respondents. Within broad occupational categories, SOFRES interviewers are required to vary the specific kind of work done by the respondents. Communes with more than 20,000 inhabitants are divided into *quartiers* (neighborhoods) among which interviewers must rotate their activity. Interviewers must also alternate interviews between different types of housing units; they may not conduct more than one interview in a single apartment building or more than three interviews along the same street. All interviews were conducted in the respondents' homes, without any

TABLE A.1. Geographic Dispersion of French Sample, 1988

Region	Number of Departments	Number of Communes[a]	Number of Interviews
North	5	11	103
West	14	21	173
Southwest	12	15	132
Southeast	16	21	210
Center	11	14	112
East	11	13	119
Paris area	8	16	164
	77	111	1,013

[a]*Quartiers* for communes of more than 20,000 inhabitants.

third parties present, and each interviewer conducted interviews during at least one evening (as opposed to during the daytime).

Reassigning Missing Data on Vote Reports

Inasmuch as we were working with a sample size of only slightly more than 1,000 cases, and each case was therefore even more than ordinarily precious to us, we examined with great care certain reports on the critical vote variables that, on their face, would have automatically been treated as missing data. For the first-ballot vote report, there were 35 refusals and 11 reports of having cast a blank or otherwise spoiled ballot. For the second ballot, there were 28 refusals and 25 cases of blank or spoiled ballots. We reasoned that some substantial proportions of the refusals simply concealed failure to vote, while some smaller proportion might actually conceal a vote for one candidate or another. The reports of spoiled ballots were considered in the same way, except that such reports for the first ballot are more suspect than those for the second ballot, when (as we have indicated above in chap. 9) they are often intelligible and usually of more than negligible proportions. The respondents reporting having spoiled their ballots might be concealing either abstentions or an actual vote, but we were sensitive to the likelihood that such reports would be more likely to be exact for the second ballot than for the first.

Accordingly, we carefully examined each relevant respondent's position on a number of other variables relating to degree of political interest and political orientation: party identification, own left-right location, and thermometer ratings for the major candidates. This analysis led us to assign 23 of the 35 first-ballot refusals, and 9 of the 11 first-ballot reports of spoiled ballots, to abstentions, while most of the remainder were assigned as votes for particular candidates. Seven of the 25 reports of spoiled second ballots were converted to abstentions, and the remaining 18 were unchanged. Of the 28 second-ballot refusals, 24 were treated as abstentions and 4 were assigned as actual vote reports (see table A.2 for details).

Weighting the Sample

The raw data set produced from the sample obtained is biased in a leftist direction. The actual results of the second ballot of the 1988 French presidential election were (among voters only) 53.8 percent for François Mitterrand and 46.2 percent for Jacques Chirac, while our raw sample contained 60.4 percent votes for Mitterrand and only 39.6 percent for Chirac.

When formulating the survey questionnaire, we included a question (RS.17) asking the respondents how often during the previous week they had been home at the same time as the time they were interviewed. Our intention was to convert the replies to that question into a set of weights that would reflect the probability of response for each person interviewed. Our hope, when we discovered the leftward bias of our sample, was that application of those weights would restore a proper sample estimate of the vote. The weights reflecting probability of response did move the sample estimates in the desired direction, but they had other consequences that led us, in the end, to abandon them.

The main reasons for doing so were that their range was comparatively wide and their distribution excessively located at the extremes. The weights ranged from .5 to 4.0 and the proportion of cases that would have had to be weighted at or close to those limiting values was comparatively large.

Weighting for differences in selection probabilities may reduce biases, but it can also have the effect of increasing variances, which amounts to the same thing as reducing the sample size. Kish (1992, 191) has devised a formula by which this loss can be measured on a standardized basis: $n\Sigma k_j/(\Sigma k_j)^2$, where n is the sample size and k the weights. Our own set of weights produced a value of 1.85 on that accounting, which is equivalent to a reduction in sample size of almost 50 percent, which we regarded as excessive. We experimented with various sets of truncated weights, but those too increased the variances more than we felt to be justified, so we abandoned the notion of weighting for probability of response.

We were, however, unsatisfied with the leftist bias in the original sample and constructed three sets of compensating weights, R1 relating to the first-ballot vote, R2 relating to the second-ballot vote, and R3 to be used for the second-ballot vote among actual voters only. The two weights, R1 and R2, also include factors to restore the inevitable underreporting of abstentions to their actual values. These three weights increase the variances only slightly, and they have virtually no effect on the distribution of the sample along the population parameter dimensions (see table A.3), but they do reduce the leftist bias of the original sample (see table A.4).

TABLE A.2. Bases for Reassignment of Vote Reports

	Reported Votes		Thermometer Ratings					PI	Own L-R[a]	Political Interest[b]	Assigned Votes	
ID	1st Ballot	2d Ballot	Mitterrand	Chirac	Barre	LePen	Lajoinie				1st Ballot	2d Ballot
51	Lajoinie	Spoiled	40	15	15	15	100	PCF	2	1	Same[c]	Same
53	Lajoinie	Refuse	50	50	40	0	0	None	Marais	4	Same	Abstain
92	Spoiled	Spoiled	Refuse	Refuse	Refuse	Refuse	Refuse	None	Marais	4	Abstain	Abstain
137	Refuse	Mitterrand	100	0	50	0	70	PS	3	3	Mitterrand	Same
146	Chirac	Spoiled	50	70	70	0	0	None	Marais	3	Same	Abstain
162	Le Pen	Spoiled	15	40	40	100	0	CNI	7	1	Same	Same
172	Refuse	Refuse	50	50	50	0	40	PS	3	4	Abstain	Abstain
174	Barre	Spoiled	50	50	40	15	0	NA	Marais	3	Same	Same
184	Lajoinie	Spoiled	50	30	40	0	70	PCF	3	2	Same	Same
202	Refuse	Mitterrand	85	50	50	0	50	PS	3	3	Mitterrand	Same
207	Spoiled	Chirac	40	50	40	0	15	RPR	Marais	4	Abstain	Chirac
210	Refuse	Spoiled	70	60	85	0	50	None	3	3	Abstain	Abstain
238	Abstain	Refuse	85	30	50	0	0	PS	3	2	Same	Abstain
246	Refuse	Refuse	0	15	15	0	0	Refuse	DK	4	Abstain	Abstain
296	Refuse	Refuse	0	100	60	40	50	RPR	5	3	Chirac	Chirac
343	Refuse	Refuse	70	40	50	15	50	PS	3	3	Mitterrand	Mitterrand
372	Refuse	Refuse	Refuse	Refuse	Refuse	Refuse	Refuse	Refuse	Refuse	3	Abstain	Abstain
392	Refuse	Refuse	70	60	60	0	0	Refuse	5	4	Abstain	Abstain
413	Refuse	Refuse	50	50	50	50	50	None	Marais	4	Abstain	Abstain
414	Refuse	Refuse	50	50	50	50	50	Center	Marais	4	Abstain	Abstain
420	Refuse	Refuse	50	50	50	0	0	None	Marais	3	Abstain	Abstain
428	Refuse	Chirac	15	100	70	0	0	RPR	5	3	Chirac	Same
429	Abstain	Refuse	Refuse	Refuse	Refuse	Refuse	Refuse	Refuse	6	3	Same	Abstain
430	Mitterrand	Refuse	70	50	70	50	15	PS	Marais	3	Same	Abstain
432	Mitterrand	Refuse	85	60	60	40	50	DK	Marais	4	Same	Abstain

(continued)

TABLE A.2—Continued

ID	Reported Votes		Thermometer Ratings					PI	Own L-R[a]	Political Interest[b]	Assigned Votes	
	1st Ballot	2d Ballot	Mitterrand	Chirac	Barre	LePen	Lajoinie				1st Ballot	2d Ballot
434	Refuse	Mitterrand	85	60	50	85	60	FN	7	2	Le Pen	Same
450	Refuse	Refuse	25	70	90	0	0	RPR	5	2	Barre	Chirac
457	Spoiled	Mitterrand	70	60	0	0	0	PS	3	4	Abstain	Mitterrand
464	Spoiled	Chirac	50	50	50	50	50	RPR	Marais	3	Abstain	Chirac
484	Spoiled	Mitterrand	50	0	40	0	100	PCF	2	4	Lajoinie	Same
494	Refuse	Mitterrand	85	40	60	0	50	PS	3	1	Mitterrand	Same
497	Refuse	Mitterrand	100	50	50	0	50	PS	3	2	Mitterrand	Same
499	Refuse	Refuse	50	50	50	0	40	DK	DK	4	Abstain	Abstain
515	Barre	Spoiled	60	40	60	0	15	PS	Marais	3	Same	Same
553	Barre	Spoiled	0	50	100	15	0	UDF	4	1	Same	Same
579	Le Pen	Spoiled	0	30	0	100	0	FN	7	3	Same	Same
580	Le Pen	Spoiled	40	40	15	100	15	FN	5	3	Same	Same
585	Refuse	Abstain	50	40	50	0	15	None	3	3	Abstain	Same
595	Laguiller	Spoiled	70	40	50	0	30	PS	3	3	Same	Same
648	Refuse	Refuse	70	60	50	0	50	Refuse	5	2	Abstain	Abstain
665	Refuse	Refuse	30	50	50	30	0	Chirac	5	3	Abstain	Abstain
680	Refuse	Refuse	15	50	60	70	15	None	Marais	3	Abstain	Abstain
683	Barre	Spoiled	70	60	85	15	30	CDS	4	2	Same	Same
699	Refuse	Refuse	DK	DK	70	DK	DK	None	Marais	4	Abstain	Abstain
703	Refuse	Chirac	40	85	70	30	0	RPR	5	2	Chirac	Same
712	Laguiller	Spoiled	60	60	60	15	50	None	Marais	3	Same	Same
716	Refuse	Chirac	40	60	50	15	0	DK	Marais	4	Abstain	Same
731	Refuse	Chirac	0	70	85	50	DK	RPR	6	2	Barre	Same
736	Le Pen	Spoiled	50	50	40	40	0	PS	Marais	3	Same	Same
751	Spoiled	Spoiled	0	0	60	0	0	None	DK	3	Same	Same

(continued)

TABLE A.2—Continued

| | Reported Votes | | Thermometer Ratings | | | | | | Own | Political | Assigned Votes | |
ID	1st Ballot	2d Ballot	Mitterrand	Chirac	Barre	LePen	Lajoinie	PI	L-R[a]	Interest[b]	1st Ballot	2d Ballot
764	Spoiled	Chirac	40	60	70	0	30	RPR	5	4	Abstain	Same
767	Refuse	Refuse	DK	DK	DK	DK	DK	Refuse	Marais	3	Abstain	Abstain
772	Barre	Spoiled	70	70	85	0	30	Barre	4	2	Same	Same
774	Barre	Spoiled	60	40	85	0	30	PS	Marais	3	Same	Same
777	Refuse	Spoiled	30	30	50	0	0	UDF	5	3	Abstain	Abstain
823	Lajoinie	Spoiled	60	40	50	0	85	PCF	2	2	Same	Same
901	Spoiled	Spoiled	70	60	60	40	50	PS	Marais	3	Abstain	Abstain
939	Refuse	Refuse	70	30	70	30	50	Refuse	DK	4	Abstain	Abstain
952	Refuse	Refuse	70	30	20	0	40	PS	3	1	Mitterrand	Mitterrand
971	Waechter	Spoiled	30	40	60	0	50	PS	4	2	Same	Same
1076	Refuse	Refuse	Refuse	Refuse	Refuse	Refuse	Refuse	None	Refuse	4	Abstain	Abstain
1085	Spoiled	Spoiled	50	50	50	0	30	None	3	3	Abstain	Abstain
1102	Spoiled	Spoiled	30	15	40	15	50	None	DK	4	Abstain	Abstain
1129	Abstain	Refuse	30	70	60	0	30	None	DK	4	Same	Abstain
1131	Refuse	Refuse	30	60	70	30	15	None	5	3	Abstain	Abstain
1143	Refuse	Refuse	60	60	60	0	0	UDF	5	3	Abstain	Abstain
1149	Refuse	Abstain	30	30	60	0	0	None	DK	4	Abstain	Abstain
1201	Barre	Spoiled	70	40	85	0	0	Center	Marais	4	Same	Same
1205	Spoiled	Chirac	50	50	50	50	50	None	Marais	3	Abstain	Same
2485	Refuse	Refuse	Refuse	Refuse	Refuse	Refuse	Refuse	None	Marais	4	Abstain	Abstain

[a]1 = Extreme left   2 = Left   3 = Center-left   4 = Involved center   5 = Center-right   6 = Right   7 = Extreme right   Marais = Uninvolved center
[b]1 = Much   2 = Quite a lot   3 = A little   4 = None
[c]Same = No change

TABLE A.3. Sample Comparisons with Population Parameters, Unweighted and Weighted, France, 1988

	Proportions Sought	Proportions Obtained			
			Weighted		
		Unweighted	R1	R2	R3
Sex					
Male	47.2	47.3	47.4	47.6	48.1
Female	52.8	52.7	52.6	52.4	51.9
	100%	100%	100%	100%	100%
Age					
18–24	14.7	13.3	13.4	13.5	12.3
25–34	21.1	22.1	21.8	21.8	21.7
35–49	23.5	25.4	25.3	25.2	25.5
50–64	22.3	20.7	21.1	21.0	21.3
65 and older	18.4	18.5	18.4	18.5	19.2
	100%	100%	100%	100%	100%
Occupation of Head of the Household					
Farmer	5.9	5.6	5.8	5.8	6.5
Business proprietor	7.5	7.7	7.9	7.9	8.0
Upper management and professional	8.5	9.6	10.0	10.0	9.4
Middle management and supervisory white collar	13.8	14.2	13.9	14.2	14.2
Sales and clerical white collar	10.5	9.1	9.1	8.9	9.0
Worker	25.8	25.4	24.7	24.5	23.7
Inactive or retired	28.0	28.4	28.6	28.7	29.2
	100%	100%	100%	100%	100%
Urbanization of Place of Residence					
Rural (less than 2,000 inhabitants)	28.0	27.8	27.5	27.4	29.3
2,000–20,000 inhabitants	15.9	14.9	14.9	14.9	14.8
20,000–100,000 inhabitants	13.2	14.3	14.4	14.3	14.0
More than 100,000 inhabitants	27.5	27.7	27.6	28.1	26.6
Parisian urban area	15.4	15.3	15.6	15.3	15.3
	100%	100%	100%	100%	100%
Region					
North	10.3	10.2	10.2	10.1	10.5
West	16.7	17.1	17.0	17.3	16.6
Southwest	13.1	13.0	12.7	12.9	13.2
Southeast	20.8	20.7	20.7	20.6	21.0
Center	11.4	11.1	11.0	11.1	10.8
East	11.4	11.7	12.0	11.9	11.7
Paris region	16.3	16.2	16.4	16.1	16.2
	100%	100%	100%	100%	100%
		(1,013)	(999.47)	(999.42)	(886.30)

Note: Case numbers are given in parentheses.

TABLE A.4. Sample Comparisons with the Actual Vote, Unweighted and Weighted, France, 1988

	Actual Vote	Unweighted Sample Vote		Weights			Weighted Sample Vote		
		Before Reassignment	After Reassignment	R1	R2	R3	R1	R2	R3
First Ballot									
Lajoinie	5.5%	6.6%	6.7%	.82			5.6%	5.9%	
Boussel	0.3	0.6	0.6	.50			0.3	0.5	
Laguiller	1.6	1.9	1.9	.84			1.6	1.7	
Juquin	1.7	2.7	2.7	.63			1.7	2.2	
Mitterrand	27.3	31.1	31.8	.86			27.6	27.3	
Waechter	3.1	3.9	3.9	.79			3.2	3.7	
Barre	13.3	13.8	14.0	.95			13.5	14.9	
Chirac	15.9	14.2	14.5	1.10			16.2	16.1	
Le Pen	11.7	9.6	9.7	1.21			11.9	10.2	
Invalid	1.6	1.1	0.1	1.00			0.1	0.1	
Abstention	18.0	11.2	14.1	1.28			18.3	17.4	
Refusal	—	3.3	—	—			—	—	
	100.0	100.0	100.0				100.0	100.0	
Second Ballot									
Mitterrand	44.0% (54.0%)	52.5%	52.8%		.83	.891	47.6%	44.4%	53.8%
Chirac	37.5 (46.0%)	34.5	34.6		1.09	1.167	37.4	38.3	46.2
Invalid	3.1	2.5	1.8		1.00	0.0	1.7	1.8	—
Abstention	15.4	7.7	10.8		1.42	0.0	13.3	15.5	—
Refusal	—	2.8	—		0.00	0.0	—	—	—
	100.0	100.0	100.0				100.0	100.0	100.0
							1.020[a]	1.025[a]	1.149[a]

[a]Kish (1992) ratio (see app. A)

APPENDIX B

Left-Right Scoring of French Candidates and Parties

The left-right scoring of the political parties and, especially, the presidential candidates has played a major role in several of the principal analyses carried out in this book. Most of the time, these scores have been employed as attributes of the candidates, as in the case of designating the first-ballot vote in terms of the left-right scores of the competing candidates, or for purposes of identifying which candidate was preferred by each respondent along one or another issue dimension. But the left-right scores of the parties have also been treated as attributes of the voters. When, in chapter 7, we included party identification as an independent variable in our model of the first-ballot vote in France, we were attaching left-right party scores to the voters in their capacity as actors, as opposed to defining them in terms of their choices or preferences (even when these latter are also necessary elements of the equation). It is, therefore, of some importance to know where those left-right scores come from.

As described briefly in the text (in chap. 4), we have the perceptions of the left-right locations of the five main presidential candidates and five major parties supplied by the respondents in our survey. For those candidates and parties, we have simply employed the mean left-right location assigned to them by our sample. In computing those means, we included the reports of all respondents who volunteered a location, whether or not they indicated that they had a left-right location of their own. We also generated the mean perceptions of the slightly more restricted set of voters who themselves had left-right positions, but they were virtually identical with the others, so we retained the original set.

There were several presidential candidates, as well as an even larger number of parties or groups with which our respondents professed to identify, for which we had no mass left-right assessments. In those cases, we had to resort to assigning scores on what appeared to us to be reasonable grounds. We will start, first, with those scores that were primarily employed as attributes of the candidates, particularly for the first-ballot vote (see table B.1).

There were nine presidential candidates, for five of whom we were able to employ the mean left-right locations attributed to them by our sample electorate. Those five means appear in boldface in table B.1. The three leftist can-

TABLE B.1.   Left-Right Scoring of Presidential Candidates, France, 1988

Score	Candidate
1.93	**André Lajoinie**
2.00	Pierre Boussel
2.00	Arlette Laguiller
2.00	Pierre Juquin
3.11	**François Mitterrand**
3.87	Antoine Waechter
4.79	**Raymond Barre**
5.55	**Jacques Chirac**
6.62	**Jean-Marie Le Pen**

Note: Boldface type indicates that the candidate's left-right score derives directly from mean sample perceptions.

didates from minor parties, Pierre Boussel and Arlette Laguiller, both Trotskyites, although from different organizations, and Pierre Juquin, the leader of dissidents from the French Communist party called the *rénovateurs* (renovators), were all assigned a score of 2.00, placing them close to the official Communist party candidate, André Lajoinie, but clearly to the left of François Mitterrand. Antoine Waechter, the ecology candidate, was placed at 3.87, which represents the same distance to the right of Mitterrand that, on the basis of mean mass perceptions, Jacques Chirac stood to the right of Raymond Barre.

Analogous considerations presided over the assignment of left-right scores to the longer list of voter attributes in the form of left-right party identifications. The complete list of referents mentioned by our respondents in reporting their party identifications, and the left-right scores we assigned to them, appear in table B.2.

The parties for which we have sample perceptions of left-right positioning are, of course, assigned the sample mean scores, and when respondents indicated that they identified with the party of some candidate for whom we had a perceived left-right mean we assigned that mean score to the respondent's choice. References to left or right were assigned scores reflecting the labeling on the left-right scale that was shown to the respondents when they were making their left-right assessments. Combinations of parties, such as RPR-UDF, were assigned the relevant mean. The two large affiliates of the Union Pour la Démocratie Française (UDF), the Centre des Démocrates Sociaux (CDS) and the Parti Républicain (PR), were assigned the same score that we attached to the UDF on the basis of mean sample perceptions.

TABLE B.2. Left-Right Scoring of Party Identification Referents, France, 1988

Score	Referent
1.00	Extrême-Gauche
1.75	**Parti Communiste Français (PCF)**
1.93	**Parti de Lajoinie**
2.00	Communiste Rénovateur, Lutte Ouvrière (LO), Parti Socialiste Unifié (PSU)
2.50	**Gauche**
3.00	Mouvement des Radicaux de Gauche (MRG), Centre-Gauche
3.06	**Parti Socialiste, Parti de Rocard**
3.11	**Parti de Mitterrand**
3.87	Ecolos
4.00	Parti Radical, Mouvement Républicain Populaire (MRP), Centre
4.75	Gaulliste Centriste
4.79	**Parti de Barre**
4.83	**Union pour la Démocratie Française (UDF), Centre des Démocrates Sociaux (CDS), Parti Républicain (PR), Parti de Giscard**
5.00	Centre-Droite
5.16	Rassemblement pour la République (RPR)—Union pour la Démocratie Française (UDF)
5.48	Rassemblement pour la République (RPR)
5.50	Gaulliste, Centre Nationale des Indépendants (CNI), Droite
5.55	**Parti de Chirac**
6.08	**Entre Chirac et Le Pen**
6.62	**Parti de Le Pen**
6.66	**Front National**

Note: Boldface type indicates that the referent's left-right score derives directly from mean sample perceptions.

APPENDIX C

Sources of Constituency-Level Electoral Data

Legislative Elections

France

République Française, Ministère de l'Intérieur. 1963. *Les Elections législatives de 1962*. Paris: Imprimerie Nationale.
———. 1967. *Les Elections législatives de 1967*. Paris: Imprimerie Nationale.
———. 1969. *Les Elections législatives de 1968*. Paris: Imprimerie Nationale.
———. 1973. *Les Elections législatives de 1973*. Paris: Imprimerie Nationale.
———. 1978. *Les Elections législatives de 1978*. Paris: Imprimerie Nationale.
———. n.d. *Les Elections législatives de 1981*. Paris: Imprimerie Nationale.
Cahiers du Communisme. 1988. *Elections législatives de 1988: Résultats, Commentaires*. Paris: Comité central du Parti communiste français. This volume contains the complete results of the legislative elections of 1986 and 1988 by 1988 legislative constituency.

United States

Congressional Quarterly. 1980. Returns for Governor, Senate and House. November 8, 1980, 3338–45.
———. 1982. Returns for Governor, Senate and House. November 6, 1982, 2817–25.
———. 1984. Returns for Governor, Senate and House. November 10, 1984, 2923–30.

Presidential Elections

France

L'Election présidentielle des 5 et 19 décembre 1965. 1970. Paris: Armand Colin. (Cahiers de la Fondation Nationale des Sciences Politiques, 169). Contains the complete 1965 presidential election results, for both ballots, by legislative constituency.
Le Monde, Dossiers et Documents. March 1978. *Les Elections législatives de mars 1978*. Paris. *Le Monde*. Contains the number of votes received by Valéry Giscard d'Estaing and François Mitterrand at the decisive ballot of the 1974 presidential election by legislative constituency.

246

Bon, Frédéric. 1978. *Les Elections en France: Histoire et Sociologie*. Paris: Editions du Seuil. Contains the proportion of the valid ballots cast for François Mitterrand at the decisive ballot of the 1974 presidential election, by legislative constituency.

Cahiers du Communisme. 1981. *Elections législatives de 1981: Résultats et Commentaires*. Paris: Comité central du Parti communiste français. Contains the complete 1981 presidential election results, for both ballots, by legislative constituency.

Le Monde, Dossiers et Documents. June 1981. *Les Elections législatives de juin 1981*. Paris. *Le Monde*. Contains the proportion of the valid ballots received by Valéry Giscard d'Estaing and François Mitterrand at the decisive ballot of the presidential election of 1981, by legislative constituency.

Cahiers du Communisme. 1988. *Elections législatives 1988: Résultats, Commentaires*. Paris: Comité central du Parti communiste français. Contains the complete 1988 presidential election results, for both ballots, by legislative constituency.

United States

Barone, Michael, Grant Ujifusa, and Douglas Matthews. 1979. *The Almanac of American Politics 1980*. New York: E. P. Dutton. Contains the number of votes and the proportions of the two-party vote won by Richard Nixon and George McGovern at the 1972 presidential election, and the number of votes and the proportions of the two-party vote won by Jimmy Carter and Gerald Ford at the 1976 presidential election, by congressional electoral district.

Barone, Michael, and Grant Ujifusa. 1981. *The Almanac of American Politics 1982*. Washington, D.C.: Barone and Company. Contains the number of votes won by Jimmy Carter and Gerald Ford at the 1976 presidential election and the number of votes won by Ronald Reagan, Jimmy Carter, and John Anderson at the 1980 presidential election, by congressional electoral district.

———. 1985. *The Almanac of American Politics 1986*. Washington, D.C.: National Journal. Contains the number of votes and the proportions of the two-party vote won by Ronald Reagan and Walter Mondale at the 1984 presidential election, by congressional electoral district.

Presidential Election Results, 1964–92

Metropolitan France

Numbers are in thousands.

	Dec. 5, 1965	Dec. 19, 1965	June 1, 1969	June 15, 1969
Registered Voters	28,223	28,233	28,774	28,762
Abstentions	4,231 (15.0%)	4,360 (15.5%)	6,282 (21.8%)	8,907 (31.0%)
Invalid Ballots	244 (1.0%)	665 (2.4%)	287 (1.0%)	1,295 (4.5%)
Charles de Gaulle	10,387 (43.7%)	12,644 (54.5%)		
François Mitterrand	7,659 (32.2%)	10,554 (45.5%)		
Jean Lecanuet	3,767 (15.9%)			
J.-L. Tixier-Vignancour	1,254 (5.3%)			
Pierre Marcilhacy	413 (1.7%)			
Marcel Barbu	278 (1.2%)			
Georges Pompidou			9,761 (43.9%)	10,688 (57.6%)
Alain Poher			5,201 (23.4%)	7,871 (42.4%)
Jacques Duclos			4,780 (21.5%)	
Gaston Defferre			1,128 (5.1%)	
Michel Rocard			814 (3.7%)	
Louis Ducatel			285 (1.3%)	
Alain Krivine			236 (1.1%)	

	May 5, 1974	May 19, 1974	April 26, 1981	May 10, 1981
Registered Voters	29,779	29,774	35,459	35,459
Abstentions	4,493 (15.1%)	3,606 (12.1%)	6,487 (18.3%)	4,810 (13.6%)
Invalid Ballots	228 (0.8%)	349 (1.2%)	467 (1.3%)	888 (2.5%)
V. Giscard d'Estaing	8,254 (32.9%)	13,082 (50.7%)		
François Mitterrand	10,863 (43.3%)	12,738 (49.3%)		
J. Chaban-Delmas	3,646 (14.6%)			

	May 5, 1974	*May 19, 1974*	*April 26, 1981*	*May 10, 1981*
Jean Royer	809 (3.2%)			
Arlette Laguiller	591 (2.4%)			
René Dumont	336 (1.3%)			
Jean-Marie Le Pen	189 (0.8%)			
Emile Muller	175 (0.7%)			
Alain Krivine	93 (0.4%)			
Bertrand Renouvin	43 (0.2%)			
Jean-Claude Sebag	40 (0.1%)			
Guy Héraud	18 (0.1%)			
François Mitterrand			7,437 (26.1%)	15,542 (52.2%)
Valéry Giscard d'Estaing			7,930 (28.0%)	14,219 (47.8%)
Jacques Chirac			5,139 (18.0%)	
Georges Marchais			4,413 (15.5%)	
Brice Lalonde			1,118 (3.9%)	
Arlette Laguiller			661 (2.3%)	
Michel Crépeau			639 (2.2%)	
Michel Debré			469 (1.6%)	
Marie-France Garaud			381 (1.3%)	
Huguette Bouchardeau			318 (1.1%)	

	April 24, 1988	*May 8, 1988*
Registered Voters	37,049	37,039
Abstentions	6,667 (18.0%)	5,690 (15.4%)
Invalid Ballots	602 (1.6%)	1,145 (3.1%)
François Mitterrand	10,094 (34.0%)	16,304 (54.0%)
Jacques Chirac	5,884 (19.8%)	13,900 (46.0%)
Raymond Barre	4,915 (16.5%)	
Jean-Marie Le Pen	4,352 (14.6%)	
André Lajoinie	2,042 (6.9%)	
Antoine Waechter	1,142 (3.8%)	
Pierre Juquin	635 (2.1%)	
Arlette Laguiller	601 (2.0%)	
Pierre Boussel	115 (0.3%)	

Data from *Recueil des Décisions du Conseil Constitutionnel*, 1965, 1969, 1974, 1981, and 1988.
Paris: Imprimerie Nationale.

United States

Year	Candidate	Popular Vote (thousands)	Electoral Vote
1964	Lyndon B. Johnson	42,826	486
	Barry M. Goldwater	27,147	52
1968	Richard M. Nixon	31,910	301
	Hubert H. Humphrey	30,838	191
	George C. Wallace	9,446	46
1972	Richard M. Nixon	46,740	520
	George McGovern	28,902	17
1976	Jimmy Carter	40,826	297
	Gerald R. Ford	39,148	240
	Ronald Reagan	—	1
1980	Ronald Reagan	43,643	489
	Jimmy Carter	35,481	49
1984	Ronald Reagan	54,167	525
	Walter Mondale	37,450	13
1988	George Bush	48,643	426
	Michael Dukakis	41,717	111
	Lloyd Bentsen	—	1
1992	Bill Clinton	44,910	370
	George Bush	39,104	168
	Ross Perot	19,742	0

Data for 1964–88 from *Statistics of the Presidential and Congressional Election* 1965–93. Washington, D.C.: U.S. Government Printing Office.

Data for 1992 from *Federal Elections 92*. Washington, D.C.: Federal Election Commission. June 1993.

French Questionnaire

Bonjour Madame, Monsieur. Je voudrais vous poser des questions.

Q.1 - Par rapport à il y a un an, diriez-vous que votre situation matérielle et celle de votre famille est :

... plutôt meilleure 18

... plutôt moins bonne 19

PASSER A Q.2b

- Ne sait pas 20

- Ne veut pas répondre 21

PASSER A Q.3

A CEUX QUI PENSENT QUE LEUR SITUATION MATERIELLE EST PLUTOT MEILLEURE

Q.2a - Plus précisément, pensez-vous que votre situation matérielle et celle de votre famille est...

... nettement meilleure 22

... ou un peu meilleure 23

- Ne sait pas 24

- Ne veut pas répondre 25

PASSER A Q.3

A CEUX QUI PENSENT QUE LEUR SITUATION MATERIELLE EST MOINS BONNE

Q.2b - Plus précisément, pensez-vous que votre situation matérielle et celle de votre famille est...

... nettement moins bonne 26

... ou un peu moins bonne 27

- Ne sait pas 28

- Ne veut pas répondre 29

A TOUS

Q.3 - Et la situation de l'économie française, estimez-vous que depuis un an...

... elle s'est améliorée 30

... elle est sans changement 31

PASSER A Q.5

... ou elle s'est dégradée 32

PASSER A Q.4b

- Ne sait pas 33

- Ne veut pas répondre 34

PASSER A Q.5

A CEUX QUI PENSENT QUE L'ECONOMIE FRANCAISE S'EST AMELIOREE

Q.4a - Plus précisément, diriez-vous qu'elle s'est...

... beaucoup améliorée 35

... ou un peu améliorée 36

- Ne sait pas 37

- Ne veut pas répondre 38

PASSER A Q.5

A CEUX QUI PENSENT QUE L'ECONOMIE FRANCAISE S'EST DEGRADEE

Q.4b - Plus précisément, diriez-vous qu'elle s'est...

... beaucoup dégradée 39

... ou un peu dégradée 40

- Ne sait pas 41

- Ne veut pas répondre 42

A TOUS

Q.5 - D'une manière générale, êtes-vous satisfait de l'action de M. Mitterrand comme Président de la République :

	Q.5	Q.6
- Très satisfait	43	49
- Assez satisfait	44	50
- Pas très satisfait	45	51
- Pas satisfait du tout	46	52
- Ne sait pas	47	53
- Ne veut pas répondre	48	54

Q.6 - Plus précisément, êtes-vous satisfait de l'action de M. Mitterrand dans le domaine de la politique étrangère ?

Q.7 - D'une manière générale, avez-vous été satisfait de l'action M. Chirac comme premier ministre :

	Q.7	Q.8
- Très satisfait	55	61
- Assez satisfait	56	62
- Pas très satisfait	57	63
- Pas satisfait du tout	58	64
- Ne sait pas	59	65
- Ne veut pas répondre	60	66

Q.8 - Plus précisément, avez-vous été satisfait de l'action de M. Chirac dans le domaine de la politique étrangère ?

Q 9   Je voudrais maintenant connaître votre sentiment personnel sur les partis politiques et les principaux candidats à l'élection présidentielle. A l'aide de cette échelle, voulez-vous mettre une note de 0 à 100 aux personnes ou groupes que je vais vous citer en fonction de la sympathie que vous éprouvez pour eux
> TENDRE L'ECHELLE
- 100 signifie que vous avez beaucoup de sympathie
-    0 signifie que vous ne les aimez pas du tout
- 50 signifie que vous n'avez ni sympathie, ni antipathie ou que vous ne savez pas grand chose d'eux.
Quelle note donneriez-vous à :
ENQUETEUR : CALER A DROITE EX 025

Q.9a) - François MITTERRAND |____|____|____|

- Ne sait pas 200
- Ne veut pas répondre 201

Q.9b) - Le Parti communiste |____|____|____|

- Ne sait pas 300
- Ne veut pas répondre 301

Q.9c) - Jacques CHIRAC |____|____|____|

- Ne sait pas 400
- Ne veut pas répondre 401

Q 9d) - Le Front national |____|____|____|

- Ne sait pas 500
- Ne veut pas répondre 501

Q.9e) - Raymond BARRE |____|____|____|

- Ne sait pas 600
- Ne veut pas répondre 601

Q.9f) - Le R.P.R. |____|____|____|

- Ne sait pas 700
- Ne veut pas répondre 701

Q.9g) - André LAJOINIE |____|____|____|

- Ne sait pas 800
- Ne veut pas répondre 801

Q 9h) - L'U.D.F. |____|____|____|

- Ne sait pas 900
- Ne veut pas répondre 901

Q 9i) - Jean-Marie LE PEN |____|____|____|

- Ne sait pas 202
- Ne veut pas répondre 203

Q 9j) - Le Parti socialiste |____|____|____|

- Ne sait pas 302
- Ne veut pas répondre 303

Q 10   D'une manière générale, estimez-vous que personnellement vous vous intéressez à la politique...

... beaucoup 87

... assez 88

... un peu 89

... ou pas du tout 90

Q 11 - Quel est le parti dont vous vous sentez habituellement le plus proche ?
ENQUETEUR : NE RIEN SUGGERER - NOTER DE FACON TRES PRECISE CE QUE VOUS DIT L'INTERVIEWE MEME SI CE N'EST PAS LE NOM D'UN PARTI

_____

_____

_____

_____

_____

- Aucun .... | 01
- Ne sait pas .... | 02
- Ne veut pas répondre .... | 03
                                    | PASSER A Q.13 |
F.02
Q 12 - Diriez-vous que vous vous sentez très proche de ce parti, assez proche ou pas très proche ?

- Très proche 01

- Assez proche 02

- Pas très proche 03

- Ne sait pas 04

- Ne veut pas répondre 05

A TOUS

Q 13 - D'après leurs opinions, on classe habituellement les Français sur une échelle de ce genre. Comme vous le voyez, il y a deux grands groupes : la gauche et la droite. On peut se classer plus ou moins à gauche ou plus ou moins à droite. Vous personnellement, où vous classeriez-vous sur cette échelle ?
> TENDRE L'ECHELLE

|_1_| |_2_| |_3_| |_4_| |_5_| |_6_| |_7_|
EXTRE-   EXTRE-
ME   GAUCHE   DROITE   ME
GAUCHE   DROITE

- Ne sait pas 8

- Ne veut pas répondre 9

Q 14a) - Et sur cette échelle qui va de l'extrême gauche à
l'extrême-droite, où classeriez-vous les partis
suivants : le Parti socialiste ?

➤ TENDRE L' ECHELLE

| 1 | 2 | 3 | 4 | 5 | 6 | 7 |
EXTRE-   EXTRE-
ME   GAUCHE   DROITE   ME
GAUCHE   DROITE

- Ne sait pas 8
- Ne veut pas répondre 9

Q.14b) - Et le R.P.R. ?

| 1 | 2 | 3 | 4 | 5 | 6 | 7 |
EXTRE-   EXTRE-
ME   GAUCHE   DROITE   ME
GAUCHE   DROITE

- Ne sait pas 8
- Ne veut pas répondre 9

Q.14c) - Et le Front national ?

| 1 | 2 | 3 | 4 | 5 | 6 | 7 |
EXTRE-   EXTRE-
ME   GAUCHE   DROITE   ME
GAUCHE   DROITE

- Ne sait pas 8
- Ne veut pas répondre 9

Q 14d) - Et le Parti communiste ?

| 1 | 2 | 3 | 4 | 5 | 6 | 7 |
EXTRE-   EXTRE-
ME   GAUCHE   DROITE   ME
GAUCHE   DROITE

- Ne sait pas 8
- Ne veut pas répondre 9

Q.14e) - Et l'U.D.F. ?

| 1 | 2 | 3 | 4 | 5 | 6 | 7 |
EXTRE-   EXTRE-
ME   GAUCHE   DROITE   ME
GAUCHE   DROITE

- Ne sait pas 8
- Ne veut pas répondre 9

Q 15a) - Et enfin, où classeriez-vous les principaux candidat
à l'élection présidentielle : Jacques CHIRAC ?

| 1 | 2 | 3 | 4 | 5 | 6 | 7 |
EXTRE-   EXTRE-
ME   GAUCHE   DROITE   ME
GAUCHE   DROITE

- Ne sait pas 8
- Ne veut pas répondre 9

Q.15b) - Et où classeriez-vous Jean-Marie LE PEN ?

| 1 | 2 | 3 | 4 | 5 | 6 | 7 |
EXTRE-   EXTRE-
ME   GAUCHE   DROITE   ME
GAUCHE   DROITE

- Ne sait pas 8
- Ne veut pas répondre 9

Q 15c) - Et François MITTERRAND ?

| 1 | 2 | 3 | 4 | 5 | 6 | 7 |
EXTRE-   EXTRE-
ME   GAUCHE   DROITE   ME
GAUCHE   DROITE

- Ne sait pas 8
- Ne veut pas répondre 9

Q.15d) - Et Raymond BARRE ?

| 1 | 2 | 3 | 4 | 5 | 6 | 7 |
EXTRE-   EXTRE-
ME   GAUCHE   DROITE   ME
GAUCHE   DROITE

- Ne sait pas 8
- Ne veut pas répondre 9

Q 15e) - Et, enfin, André LAJOINIE ?

| 1 | 2 | 3 | 4 | 5 | 6 | 7 |
EXTRE-   EXTRE-
ME   GAUCHE   DROITE   ME
GAUCHE   DROITE

- Ne sait pas 8
- Ne veut pas répondre 9

Q.16 - Personnellement, vous êtes vous intéressé à la campagne pour l'élection présidentielle...

... beaucoup 28

... assez 29

... peu 30

... ou pas du tout 31

- Ne sait pas 32

- Ne veut pas dire 33

Q.17 - Au cours de la semaine précédant le second tour, avez-vous regardé les informations à la télévision...

... tous les jours (sept jours) 34

... six jours sur sept 35

... cinq jours sur sept 36

... quatre jours sur sept 37

... trois jours sur sept 38

... deux jours sur sept 39

... un jour sur sept 40

... jamais 41

- Ne sait pas 42

- Ne veut pas répondre 43

PASSER A Q.19

Q.18 - Au cours de ces émissions, avez-vous porté aux informations sur la campagne électorale une attention :

- Très grande 44

- Assez grande 45

- Assez faible 46

- Très faible 47

- Aucune attention 48

- Ne sait pas 49

- Ne veut pas répondre 50

A TOUS

Q.19 - Avez-vous regardé le débat télévisé du 28 avril entre François Mitterrand et Jacques Chirac ?

- Oui ....
- Non ....
- L'a écouté à la radio ....
- Ne veut pas répondre ....

PASSER A Q.20

Q.19bis - Avez-vous regardé le débat en entier ou seulement en partie ?

- En entier 5

- Seulement en partie 5

- Aurait voulu le regarder en entier mais n'a pas pu 5

- Ne veut pas répondre 5

A TOUS

Q.20 - Entre les deux tours, avez-vous regardé les émissions de la campagne officielle de François Mitterrand ?

	Q.20	Q
- Beaucoup	59	6
- Plusieurs	60	6
- Seulement une ou deux	61	6
- Aucune	62	6
- Ne sait pas	63	6
- Ne veut pas répondre	64	7

Q.21 - Et entre les deux tours, avez-vous regardé les émissions de la campagne officielle de Jacques Chirac ?

Q.22 - Au cours de la semaine précédant le second tour, vous personnellement avez-vous lu un quotidien...

... tous les jours (sept jours) 71

... six jours sur sept 72

... cinq jours sur sept 73

... quatre jours sur sept 74

... trois jours sur sept 75

... deux jours sur sept 76

... un jour sur sept 77

... jamais 78

- Ne sait pas 79

- Ne veut pas répondre 80

PASSER A Q.24a

Q 23 - En lisant ce quotidien, avez vous porté aux informations sur la campagne électorale une attention :

- Très grande 81

- Assez grande 82

- Assez faible 83

- Très faible 84

- Aucune attention 85

- Ne sait pas 86

- Ne veut pas répondre 87

A TOUS

Q.24a - Au cours de la semaine précédant le second tour, vous personnellement avez-vous lu des hebdomadaires d'information générale (l'Express, le Nouvel Observateur, le Point, l'Evénement du Jeudi, etc.) ?

- Oui 88

- Non .... | 89 |

- Ne sait pas .... | 90 |

- Ne veut pas répondre .... | 91 |
    | PASSER A Q.25 |

F.03

Q.24b - En lisant ces hebdomadaires, avez-vous porté aux informations sur la campagne électorale une attention :

- Très grande 01

- Assez grande 02

- Assez faible 03

- Très faible 04

- Aucune attention 05

- Ne sait pas 06

- Ne veut pas répondre 07

A TOUS

Q.25 - Beaucoup d'électeurs n'ont pas voté au premier tour de l'élection présidentielle le 24 avril. Vous-même, avez-vous voté au premier tour de l'élection présidentielle ?

- Oui 08

- Non .... | 09 |

- Ne veut pas répondre .... | 10 |
    | PASSER A Q.27 |

Q 26 - Comment avez-vous voté au premier tour de l'élection présidentielle le 24 avril ?
Pour répondre, il vous suffit de placer dans l'enveloppe le bulletin du candidat pour lequel vous avez voté. Pour que votre vote reste confidentiel, je vous demande de garder les bulletins que vous n'aurez pas utilisés.

ENQUETEUR :

1) Tendre un jeu de bulletins SAUMONS à l'interviewé

2) Lui laisser le temps nécessaire

3) Faire mettre le bulletin dans l'enveloppe.

A TOUS

Q 27 - Beaucoup d'électeurs n'ont pas voté au second tour de l'élection présidentielle le 8 mai. Vous-même, avez-vous voté au second tour de l'élection présidentielle le 8 mai ?

- Oui 11

- Non .... | 12 |

- Ne veut pas répondre .... | 13 |
    | PASSER A Q.29 |

Q 28 - Comment avez-vous voté au second tour ?
Pour répondre, il vous suffit de placer dans cette enveloppe le bulletin du candidat pour lequel vous avez voté. Pour que votre vote reste confidentiel, je vous demande de garder le bulletin que vous n'aurez pas utilisé.

ENQUETEUR :

1) Tendre un jeu de bulletins BLEUS à l'interviewé

2) Lui laisser le temps necessaire

3) Faire mettre le bulletin dans l'enveloppe et l'enveloppe dans l'urne..

Q 26 - VOTE AU 1ER TOUR (SAUMONS)

- André LAJOINIE 01

- Pierre BOUSSEL 02

- Arlette LAGUILLER 03

- Pierre JUQUIN 04

- François MITTERRAND 05

- Antoine WAECHTER 06

- Raymond BARRE 07

- Jacques CHIRAC 08

- Jean-Marie LE PEN 09

    - A voté blanc ou nul 10

    - N' a pas voté 11

    - Ne veut pas voter dans l' urne 12

Q.28 - VOTE AU SECOND TOUR (BLEUS)

- François MITTERRAND 13

- Jacques CHIRAC 14

    - A voté blanc ou nul 15

    - N' a pas voté 16

    - Ne veut pas voter dans l' urne 17

Q 29a) - J'aimerais maintenant que vous m'indiquiez quelle est votre position personnelle sur un certain nombre de grands
problèmes et ce qu'est à votre connaissance, la position des formations politiques et des principaux candidats sur ces
problèmes.
Imaginez que d'après leurs opinions sur les subventions de l'Etat aux écoles libres, on classe les Français sur une
échelle de ce genre. Certains, à l'une des extrémités de cette échelle au point 1 pensent que "l'Etat devrait accorder
davantage de subventions aux écoles libres" D'autres, à l'autre extrémité de l'échelle au point 7 - estiment que
"l'Etat ne devrait accorder aucune subvention aux écoles libres" Enfin, d'autres personnes qui ont des opinions intermédiaires, se situent au point 2, 3, 4, 5 et 6.
Vous personnellement, où vous classeriez-vous sur cette échelle et si vous n'avez pas d'opinion, dites-le nous, cela nous
intéresse aussi.

➤ TENDRE L'ECHELLE

L'Etat devrait accorder | 1 | | 2 | | 3 | | 4 | | 5 | | 6 | | 7 | L'Etat ne devrait accor-
davantage de subven-   der aucune subvention
tions aux écoles libres   aux écoles libres

- Ne sait pas 8
- Ne veut pas répondre 9

Q 29b) - Et où situez-vous Jacques CHIRAC ?

L'Etat devrait accorder | 1 | | 2 | | 3 | | 4 | | 5 | | 6 | | 7 | L'Etat ne devrait accor-
davantage de subven-   der aucune subvention
tions aux écoles libres   aux écoles libres

- Ne sait pas 8
- Ne veut pas répondre 9

Q.29c) - Et François MITTERRAND ?

L'Etat devrait accorder | 1 | | 2 | | 3 | | 4 | | 5 | | 6 | | 7 | L'Etat ne devrait accor
davantage de subven-   der aucune subvention
tions aux écoles libres   aux écoles libres

- Ne sait pas 8
- Ne veut pas répondre 9

Q.29d) - Et Raymond BARRE ?

L'Etat devrait accorder | 1 | | 2 | | 3 | | 4 | | 5 | | 6 | | 7 | L'Etat ne devrait accor
davantage de subven-   der aucune subvention
tions aux écoles libres   aux écoles libres

- Ne sait pas 8
- Ne veut pas répondre 9

Q.29e) - Et le R.P.R. ?

L'Etat devrait accorder | 1 | | 2 | | 3 | | 4 | | 5 | | 6 | | 7 | L'Etat ne devrait accor
davantage de subven-   der aucune subvention
tions aux écoles libres   aux écoles libres

- Ne sait pas 8
- Ne veut pas répondre 9

Q 29f) - Et où situez-vous l'U.D.F ?

L'Etat devrait accorder |__1__| |__2__| |__3__| |__4__| |__5__| |__6__| |__7__| L'Etat ne devrait accor
davantage de subven-   der aucune subvention
tions aux écoles libres   aux écoles libres

    - Ne sait pas 8
    - Ne veut pas répondre 9

Q.29g) - Et le Front national ?

L'Etat devrait accorder |__1__| |__2__| |__3__| |__4__| |__5__| |__6__| |__7__| L'Etat ne devrait accor
davantage de subven-   der aucune subvention
tions aux écoles libres   aux écoles libres

    - Ne sait pas 8
    - Ne veut pas répondre 9

Q 29h) - Et le Parti socialiste ?

L'Etat devrait accorder |__1__| |__2__| |__3__| |__4__| |__5__| |__6__| |__7__| L'Etat ne devrait accor
davantage de subven-   der aucune subvention
tions aux écoles libres   aux écoles libres

    - Ne sait pas 8
    - Ne veut pas répondre 9

Q.29i) - Et le Parti communiste ?

L'Etat devrait accorder |__1__| |__2__| |__3__| |__4__| |__5__| |__6__| |__7__| L'Etat ne devrait accor
davantage de subven-   der aucune subvention
tions aux écoles libres   aux écoles libres

    - Ne sait pas 8
    - Ne veut pas répondre 9

Q.29j) - Et, enfin, Jean-Marie LE PEN ?

L'Etat devrait accorder |__1__| |__2__| |__3__| |__4__| |__5__| |__6__| |__7__| L'Etat ne devrait accor
davantage de subven-   der aucune subvention
tions aux écoles libres   aux écoles libres

    Ne sait pas 8
    - Ne veut pas répondre 9

Q.30a) - Imaginez maintenant, que d'après leurs opinions sur le rôle de l'Etat dans l'économie, on classe les Français sur échelle de ce genre.
Certains, à l'une des extrémités de cette échelle - au point 1 - pensent que . "il faut réduire le rôle de l'Etat dans l'économie en continuant à privatiser des entreprises publiques". D'autres, à l'autre extrémité de l'é le au point 7 - estiment que "il faut que l'Etat conserve un large secteur public". Enfin, d'autres personnes qui on opinions intermédiaires, se situent au point 2, 3, 4, 5 et 6.
Vous personnellement, où vous classeriez vous sur cette échelle et si vous n'avez pas d'opinion, dites-le nous, cela intéresse aussi.

▶ TENDRE L'ECHELLE

Il faut réduire le rôle de l'Etat dans l'écono- | 1 | | 2 | | 3 | | 4 | | 5 | | 6 | | 7 | Il faut que l'Etat cons mie en continuant à privatiser des entreprises   ve un large secteur pub publiques

- Ne sait pas 8
- Ne veut pas répondre 9

Q.30b) - Et où situez-vous Jacques CHIRAC ?

Il faut réduire le rôle de l'Etat dans l'écono- | 1 | | 2 | | 3 | | 4 | | 5 | | 6 | | 7 | Il faut que l'Etat cons mie en continuant à privatiser des entreprises   ve un large secteur pub publiques

- Ne sait pas 8
- Ne veut pas répondre 9

Q 30c) - Et François MITTERRAND ?

Il faut réduire le rôle de l'Etat dans l'écono- | 1 | | 2 | | 3 | | 4 | | 5 | | 6 | | 7 | Il faut que l'Etat cons mie en continuant à privatiser des entreprises   ve un large secteur pub publiques

- Ne sait pas 8
- Ne veut pas répondre 9

Q.30d) - Et Raymond BARRE ?

Il faut réduire le rôle de l'Etat dans l'écono- | 1 | | 2 | | 3 | | 4 | | 5 | | 6 | | 7 | Il faut que l'Etat cons mie en continuant à privatiser des entreprises   ve un large secteur pub publiques

- Ne sait pas 8
- Ne veut pas répondre 9

Q.30e) - Et le R.P.R. ?

Il faut réduire le rôle de l'Etat dans l'écono- | 1 | | 2 | | 3 | | 4 | | 5 | | 6 | | 7 | Il faut que l'Etat cons mie en continuant à privatiser des entreprises   ve un large secteur pub publiques

- Ne sait pas 8
- Ne veut pas répondre 9

Q 30f) - Et où situez-vous l'U.D.F. ?

Il faut réduire le rôle de l'Etat dans l'écono- |_1_| |_2_| |_3_| |_4_| |_5_| |_6_| |_7_| Il faut que l'Etat conser-
mie en continuant à privatiser des entreprises   ve un large secteur public
publiques

    - Ne sait pas 8
    - Ne veut pas répondre 9

Q 30g) - Et le Front national ?

Il faut réduire le rôle de l'Etat dans l'écono- |_1_| |_2_| |_3_| |_4_| |_5_| |_6_| |_7_| Il faut que l'Etat conser-
mie en continuant à privatiser des entreprises   ve un large secteur public
publiques

    - Ne sait pas 8
    - Ne veut pas répondre 9

Q.30h) - Et le Parti socialiste ?

Il faut réduire le rôle de l'Etat dans l'écono- |_1_| |_2_| |_3_| |_4_| |_5_| |_6_| |_7_| Il faut que l'Etat conser-
mie en continuant à privatiser des entreprises   ve un large secteur public
publiques

    - Ne sait pas 8
    - Ne veut pas répondre 9

Q.30i) - Et le Parti communiste ?

Il faut réduire le rôle de l'Etat dans l'écono- |_1_| |_2_| |_3_| |_4_| |_5_| |_6_| |_7_| Il faut que l'Etat conser-
mie en continuant à privatiser des entreprises   ve un large secteur public
publiques

    - Ne sait pas 8
    - Ne veut pas répondre 9

Q 30j) - Et, enfin, Jean-Marie LE PEN ?

Il faut réduire le rôle de l'Etat dans l'écono- |_1_| |_2_| |_3_| |_4_| |_5_| |_6_| |_7_| Il faut que l'Etat conser-
mie en continuant à privatiser des entreprises   ve un large secteur public
publiques

    - Ne sait pas 8
    - Ne veut pas répondre 9

Q. 31a) - Et enfin, comment vous situez-vous par rapport à ces deux opinions :
- "Il faut que les immigrés retournent dans leur pays d'origine"
- "Il faut intégrer les immigrés qui vivent actuellement en France dans la société française".
Si vous n'avez pas d'opinion, dites-le nous, cela nous intéresse aussi.
▶ TENDRE L'ECHELLE

Il faut que les immigrés retournent dans | 1 | | 2 | | 3 | | 4 | | 5 | | 6 | | 7 | Il faut intégrer les immigrés
leur pays d'origine   qui vivent actuellement en
                                                                                                   France dans la société française

- Ne sait pas 8
- Ne veut pas répondre 9

Q. 31b) - Et où situez-vous Jacques CHIRAC ?

Il faut que les immigrés retournent dans | 1 | | 2 | | 3 | | 4 | | 5 | | 6 | | 7 | Il faut intégrer les immigrés
leur pays d'origine   qui vivent actuellement en
                                                                                                   France dans la société française

- Ne sait pas 8
- Ne veut pas répondre 9

Q. 31c) - Et François MITTERRAND ?

Il faut que les immigrés retournent dans | 1 | | 2 | | 3 | | 4 | | 5 | | 6 | | 7 | Il faut intégrer les immigrés
leur pays d'origine   qui vivent actuellement en
                                                                                                   France dans la société française

- Ne sait pas 8
- Ne veut pas répondre 9

Q. 31d) - Et Raymond BARRE ?

Il faut que les immigrés retournent dans | 1 | | 2 | | 3 | | 4 | | 5 | | 6 | | 7 | Il faut intégrer les immigrés
leur pays d'origine   qui vivent actuellement en
                                                                                                   France dans la société française

- Ne sait pas 8
- Ne veut pas répondre 9

Q. 31e) - Et le R.P.R. ?

Il faut que les immigrés retournent dans | 1 | | 2 | | 3 | | 4 | | 5 | | 6 | | 7 | Il faut intégrer les immigrés
leur pays d'origine   qui vivent actuellement en
                                                                                                   France dans la société française

- Ne sait pas 8
- Ne veut pas répondre 9

Q.31f) - Et où situez-vous l'U.D.F. ?

Il faut que les immigrés retournent dans |_1_|_|_2_|_|_3_|_|_4_|_|_5_|_|_6_|_|_7_| Il faut intégrer les immigrés
leur pays d'origine qui vivent actuellement en
France dans la société français

- Ne sait pas 8
- Ne veut pas répondre 9

Q.31g) - Et le Front national ?

Il faut que les immigrés retournent dans |_1_|_|_2_|_|_3_|_|_4_|_|_5_|_|_6_|_|_7_| Il faut intégrer les immigrés
leur pays d'origine qui vivent actuellement en
France dans la société française

- Ne sait pas 8
- Ne veut pas répondre 9

Q.31h) - Et le Parti socialiste ?

Il faut que les immigrés retournent dans |_1_|_|_2_|_|_3_|_|_4_|_|_5_|_|_6_|_|_7_| Il faut intégrer les immigrés
leur pays d'origine qui vivent actuellement en
France dans la société française

- Ne sait pas 8
- Ne veut pas répondre 9

Q.31i) - Et le Parti communiste ?

Il faut que les immigrés retournent dans |_1_|_|_2_|_|_3_|_|_4_|_|_5_|_|_6_|_|_7_| Il faut intégrer les immigrés
leur pays d'origine qui vivent actuellement en
France dans la société française

- Ne sait pas 8
- Ne veut pas répondre 9

Q.31j) - Et, enfin, Jean-Marie LE PEN ?

Il faut que les immigrés retournent dans |_1_|_|_2_|_|_3_|_|_4_|_|_5_|_|_6_|_|_7_| Il faut intégrer les immigrés
leur pays d'origine qui vivent actuellement en
France dans la société française

- Ne sait pas 8
- Ne veut pas répondre 9

Q.32 - Selon vous, qui de François Mitterrand ou de Jacques Chirac, a joué le plus grand rôle dans le domaine économique et
social depuis un an ?
UNE SEULE REPONSE

- François MITTERRAND 74

- Jacques CHIRAC 75

- Les deux également 76

  - Les deux, mais François MITTERRAND dans le domaine social et
    Jacques CHIRAC dans le domaine économique 77

  - Les deux, mais François MITTERRAND dans le domaine économique et
    Jacques CHIRAC dans le domaine social 78

  - Ni l'un, ni l'autre 79

  - Ne sait pas 80

  - Ne veut pas répondre 81

RS.1 - Sexe

- Homme 01
- Femme 02

RS.2 - Quel est votre âge ? |____|____| ans

RS.3 - Actuellement, quelle est votre situation professionnelle ?

   - J'ai un travail .... | 03 |

   - Je suis au chômage ou ayant déjà travaillé,
    je suis à la recherche d'un emploi .... | 04 |
                      | PASSER A RS.4 |

   - Je suis à la retraite 05

   - Je suis femme au foyer .... | 06 |

   - Je suis à la recherche d'un premier emploi .. | 07 |

   - Je suis étudiant ou lycéen .... | 08 |

   - Autre sans profession .... | 09 |
                  | PASSER A RS.6 |

RS.3bis - Avez-vous exercé une profession avant d'être à la
retraite ?

   - Oui 10

   - Non .... | 11 |
                 | PASSER A RS.6 |

RS.4 - Quelle est votre profession actuelle (ou quelle était
votre ancienne profession) ?
(Si chômeur : demander la dernière profession
exercée)
NOTER EN CLAIR EN FAISANT PRECISER LE
PLUS POSSIBLE (fonction, grade...)
(ex : employé à la comptabilité, cadre technique
dans une entreprise d'informatique, professeur certifié de collège, receveur des P.T.T. 4ème classe...)

_____

_____

_____

_____

- Agriculteur exploitant 1 5 1
- Artisan 2 5 3
- Commerçant 2 5 4
- Industriel 2 5 5
- Profession libérale 3 5 6
- Cadre, profession intellectuelle supérieure 3 5 7
- Profession intermédiaire 4 5 8
- Contremaître 4 6 0
- Employé 5 5 9
- Personnel de service 5 6 3
- Ouvrier qualifié (OQ, OP, P1, P2, P3, P4
compagnon) 6 6 1
- Ouvrier spécialisé 6 6 2
- Ouvrier agricole 6 5 2

RS 5 - Etes-vous (ou étiez vous) :

... travailleur indépendant, à votre compte 12

... salarié de l'Etat ou d'une collectivité locale   13

... salarié d'une entreprise publique ou
nationalisée 14

... salarié d'une entreprise privée 15

A TOUS

RS.6 - Etes-vous le chef de ménage ?

   - Oui .... | 16 |
              | PASSER A RS.10 |

   - Non 17

RS.7 - Actuellement, quelle est la situation professionnelle
du chef de ménage ?

   - Le chef de ménage a un travail .... | 18 |

   - Le chef de ménage est au chômage ou ayant
    déjà travaillé, est à la recherche d'un emploi | 19 |
               | PASSER A RS.8 |

   - Le chef de ménage est à la retraite 20

   - Le chef de ménage est femme au foyer ...... | 21 |

   - Le chef de ménage est à la recherche d'un
    premier emploi .... | 22 |

   - Le chef de ménage est étudiant ou lycéen .... | 23 |

   - Le chef de ménage est "autre sans profession" | 24 |
              | PASSER A RS.10 |

RS.7bis - Le chef de ménage a-t-il exercé une profession
avant d'être à la retraite ?

   - Oui 25

   - Non .... | 26 |
              | PASSER A RS.10 |

RS.8 - Quelle est la profession actuelle du chef de ménage (ou quelle était son ancienne profession) ?
(Si chômeur : demander la dernière profession exercée)
NOTER EN CLAIR EN FAISANT PRECISER LE PLUS POSSIBLE (fonction, grade...)
(ex : employé à la comptabilité, cadre technique dans une entreprise d'informatique, professeur certifié de collège, receveur des P.T.T. 4ème classe...)

_____

_____

_____

_____

- Agriculteur exploitant 1 5 1
- Artisan 2 5 3
- Commerçant 2 5 4
- Industriel 2 5 5
- Profession libérale 3 5 6
- Cadre, profession intellectuelle supérieure 3 5 7
- Profession intermédiaire 4 5 8
- Contremaitre 4 6 0
- Employé 5 5 9
- Personnel de service 5 6 3
- Ouvrier qualifié (OQ, OP, P1, P2, P3, P4 compagnon) 6 6 1
- Ouvrier spécialisé 6 6 2
- Ouvrier agricole 6 5 2

RS.9 - Le chef de ménage est-il (ou était-il)...

... travailleur à son compte 27

... salarié de l'Etat ou d'une collectivité locale 28

... salarié d'une entreprise publique ou nationalisée 29

... salarié d'une entreprise privée 30

A TOUS

RS.10 - Vous-même ou une autre personne de votre foyer est-elle syndiquée ?
PLUSIEURS REPONSES POSSIBLES

- Oui, moi-même 31

- Oui, une autre personne 32

- Non, personne 33

- Ne sait pas 34

- Ne veut pas répondre 35

RS.11 - On parle souvent des différentes classes sociale. La plupart des gens disent qu'ils appartiennen soit à la classe moyenne, soit à la classe ouvrièr Vous-même, avez-vous le sentiment d'apparte à l'une ou à l'autre de ces classes ?

- Oui ....

- Non, ni à l'une, ni à l'autre ....

- Ne sait pas ....

- Ne veut pas répondre ....
| PASSER A RS.11 TER |

RS.11bis - Laquelle ?

- Classe moyenne ....

- Classe ouvrière ....
| PASSER A RS.12 |

A CEUX QUI ONT REPONDU NON OU QUI N'ON
PAS REPONDU A RS.11.

RS.11ter - Si vous aviez à choisir, diriez-vous que vous appartenez à la classe moyenne ou à la classe ouvrière ?

- Classe moyenne ....
- Classe ouvrière ....
- Ni à l'une, ni à l'autre ....
- Ne sait pas ....
- Ne veut pas répondre ....

A TOUS
RS.12 - Quel est le dernier établissement d'enseigneme que vous avez fréquenté comme élève ou comme étudiant ?
Est-ce un établissement ...

... primaire ....

... primaire supérieur ....

... secondaire ....

... technique ou commercial ....

... supérieur ....
- N'est jamais allé à l'école ....
- Ne veut pas répondre ....

RS.13 - Quelle est votre situation de famille actuelle ? Etes-vous...

... marié ....

... vivant maritalement ....

... vivant sans conjoint, étant célibataire ....

... vivant sans conjoint, après un divorce ....

... vivant sans conjoint, étant veuf ....

RS 14   Quand vous aviez entre 10 et 18 ans, dans quel
département viviez-vous ou si vous viviez hors de
France, dans quel pays ?
ENQUETEUR : NOTER EN CLAIR - SI L'IN-
TERVIEWE A VECU DANS PLUSIEURS
ENDROITS DIFFERENTS - NOTER CELUI
OU IL A VECU LE PLUS LONGTEMPS

_____

_____

_____

_____

N° de département : |_____|_____|

- DOM - TOM 96

- Afrique du Nord 97

- Afrique noire 98

- Autres pays 99

RS.15 - Pouvez-vous me dire quelle est votre religion ?

- Catholique 59

- Protestante 60

- Juive 61

- Musulmane 62

- Autre religion 63

- Sans religion 64

- Ne veut pas répondre 65

[PASSER A RS.16]

RS.15bis - D'habitude, allez-vous à l'Eglise (au temple, à
la synagogue, à la mosquée)...

... au moins une fois par semaine 66

... souvent dans l'année 67

... quelquefois 68

... rarement 69

... jamais 70

- Ne veut pas répondre 71

A TOUS

RS.16   Pour pouvoir analyser les résultats de cette enquête
en fonction des revenus familiaux des personnes que
nous avons interrogées, je vais vous demander de
faire un rapide calcul pour classer votre foyer dans
une des tranches de revenus figurant sur cette liste.
▷ TENDRE LISTE REPONSE
N'oubliez pas de tenir compte de toutes les rentrées
d'argent et en particulier des salaires et traite-
ments de tous les membres du foyer (mois double,
primes, allocations familiales, rentes, revenus du
capital, etc.)
Pour répondre, il vous suffit de me citer la lettre qui
correspond à votre tranche de revenus.

C - Moins de 1 500 francs par mois .... 7.

E - 1 501 à 2 000 francs par mois 7

H - 2 001 à 2 500 francs par mois 7

A - 2 501 à 3 000 francs par mois 7

J - 3 001 à 4 000 francs par mois 7

L - 4 001 à 5 000 francs par mois 7

K - 5 001 à 7 500 francs par mois 7

I - 7 501 à 10 000 francs par mois 7

G - 10 001 à 15 000 francs par mois 8

D - 15 001 à 20 000 francs par mois 8

F - 20 001 à 30 000 francs par mois 8

B - Plus de 30 000 francs par mois 8

- Ne veut pas répondre 8

RS.17 - Pour compléter notre analyse, pouvez-vous
me dire au cours de la dernière semaine - sans
compter aujourd'hui - combien de fois vous avez
été chez vous à la même heure qu'aujourd'hui ?

- Aucune 2

- Une fois 2

- Deux fois 2

- Trois fois 2

- Quatre fois 8

- Cinq fois 9

- Six fois 9

- Sept fois 9

RS.18   ENQUETEUR : A CODER IMPERATIVEMENT

L'interviewé habite :

- Un quartier populaire 9

- Un autre quartier 9

Notes

Chapter 1

1. A brief and comprehensive description of the French presidency, in French, is Massot (1986). A detailed description of the structure and operation of the French constitutional system into the 1970s, in English, is Andrews (1982).

2. The French second chamber, called the Senate, is not popularly elected but, rather, is chosen mainly by France's municipal councilors. Although once a powerful body, the Senate was stripped of much of its power after World War II, and, if the government wishes, it can be overridden by the National Assembly.

3. At least since the adoption in 1804 of the Twelfth Amendment, which prevented the possibility of the election of a president from one party and a vice president from another party.

4. Paris has a special status, in that it is both a municipality and a department, with a single council.

5. Large majorities of the public repeatedly express a preference for a five-year term over a seven-year term. A SOFRES survey conducted for *Le Monde* and France Inter late in 1992 showed that 75 percent of the respondents preferred a five-year term with only one reelection permitted. An earlier SOFRES study for *Le Point*, in April 1990, found that almost 70 percent of the deputies in the Assembly favored reducing the presidential term to five years, with little variation by partisan group.

6. Maine and Nebraska have adopted legislation that assigns two electoral votes to the statewide winner, and one vote to the winner in each congressional district, of which there are two for Maine and three for Nebraska.

7. A candidate eligible to run at the second ballot may withdraw, in which case the next runner-up becomes eligible.

8. The new access rules did prevent Jean-Marie Le Pen from appearing on the ballot for the 1981 election, as he was unable to obtain the 500 necessary signatures (*L'Express*, March 20, 1992, 33). Le Pen had no such problem in 1988, and he won almost 15 percent of the first-ballot votes.

9. Strong regional support is required to win electoral votes under the U.S. presidential election system. George Wallace, a former (and future) governor of Alabama who was a third-party candidate in 1968, won less than 15 percent of the national vote total but obtained 46 electoral votes, all from southern states.

10. The U.S. Congress is normally in session for a larger proportion of the year than the French Parliament is. From 1980 through 1987, the French National Assembly sat

for an average of 122 days per year, while the U.S. House of Representatives sat for an average of 146 days and the Senate for 155.

11. Mayors, presidents of departmental councils, and presidents of regional councils are not directly elected by the voters, as U.S. governors and mayors are. In fact, the only directly elected executive office in France is the presidency. All other executive officials are either appointed (as are the prime minister and the cabinet at the national level) or chosen by elected councils. French mayors are chosen by the municipal councils, presidents of departmental councils (*conseils généraux*) are selected by those councils, and presidents of regional councils are chosen by the regional councils themselves. Top-level French politicians who go the route of multiple-office holding must cultivate their parties, keep attuned to several electorates, and master the art of coalition building within whatever conciliar arenas they aspire to lead.

12. The deprivation is less severe for ministers than for backbenchers. Ministers must resign their seats in parliament in any case, so they may retain two significant non-parliamentary elective offices. The offices of choice, since the restrictions went into effect, have been those of deputy or senator, mayor, president of a general council, and membership on a municipal council. Seats on the departmental councils rank lower. The least attractive posts are seats on the regional councils (even their presidencies) and the European Parliament (Dolez 1991). Chaban-Delmas, for example, abandoned the presidency of his regional council when required to cut back on his elective positions. The only top-tier political leader who chose to remain president of a regional council was Valéry Giscard d'Estaing, who had never been mayor of a sizable city. The limitation is enforced only after a member of Parliament has been elected to more than two restricted offices; members are not ineligible to run for more offices than they can legally accept. This allows the parties to attract votes by presenting big names as candidates for regional or European elections even though those leaders plan to resign immediately, if elected (Garraud 1992, 40; *L'Express*, June 3, 1993, 7; see also Mény 1987).

13. This point was not lost on Reydellet (1979, 746–48) or Becquart-Leclercq (1983, 1989).

14. Multiple-office holding also increases (within limits) the incomes of those who practice it (*La France des Régions*, 1986, 89 and *Le Monde*, August 19–20, 1990).

15. During the eighteenth century, seven U.S. senators and at least one member of the House of Representatives served simultaneously in statewide or county offices (Senate 1989), but the practice seems to have ceased early, either because of state constitutional or legislative prohibitions, or simply custom, encouraged by the distances between the nation's capital and the capitals of its increasingly far-flung states. In 1891, David B. Hill, who was a contender for the Democratic party's presidential nomination, became known as the "governor-senator" (Bass 1961, chap. 7) because he was elected to the U.S. Senate while he was governor of New York, but he did not assume his Senate seat until a year later, after the expiration of his term as governor. That was prior to the enactment of the Seventeenth Amendment (in 1917) providing for direct popular election of senators. Huey Long was elected to the Senate in 1930, while he was governor of Louisiana, but he too did not take up his Senate seat immediately, but rather waited for the expiration of his gubernatorial term. The only pure twentieth century U.S. practitioner of multiple-office holding that I have been able to uncover is the legendary

James Michael Curley, who served both in the House of Representatives and on the Boston city council in 1911 (Beatty 1992, 119).

16. The large number of French towns, each of which has an elected council, means that there are about five times more French local officeholders, controlling for population, than there are in the United States.

Chapter 2

1. The literature on U.S. presidential elections is enormous; we will cite only a handful of works here. Asher (1992) and Polsby and Wildavsky (1991) contain useful synthetic analyses. Historical statistics and some commentary appear in *Presidential Elections Since 1789* (1991). Abramson, Aldrich, and Rohde (1990) is an excellent overall account of the 1988 U.S. election. There are rich documentary accounts of four of the five French presidential elections to date in *Notes et Etudes Documentaires*, No. 3283 (April 19, 1966), Nos. 4201–4203 (July 7, 1975), Nos. 4647–4648 (December 21, 1981), and No. 4865 (1988). A. Duhamel (1987) and Duhamel and Jaffré (1987) are lively French preelectoral discussions of the background to the 1988 election in France and the potential candidates. A postelectoral English language discussion of the French election appears in Gaffney (1989). Boy and Mayer (1993) is the English translation of a collective work by French scholars on French electoral behavior, based on a postelectoral survey conducted in 1988.

2. John B. Anderson ran as an independent candidate in 1980, but he won less than 7 percent of the votes.

3. The U.S. president appoints far fewer such people than the French president does. Except in unusual circumstances, the vice president serves throughout the entire presidential term, and in recent decades two-term U.S. presidents have named the same vice president for both elections. French presidents normally appoint more than one prime minister: de Gaulle appointed three (two of whom became presidential candidates); Pompidou appointed two (one of whom ran for the presidency); and Giscard d'Estaing appointed two prime ministers, who competed against each other for the presidential prize. François Mitterrand named seven prime ministers between his first election in 1981 and the summer of 1993, two of whom were in cohabitation situations, and one of whom (Chirac) ran against Mitterrand unsuccessfully in 1988.

4. Georges Pompidou died in 1974, during the fifth year of his only term as president.

5. Agnew's resignation was part of a deal permitting him to plead no contest to a single lesser charge of income tax evasion, for which he was given a light sentence involving no imprisonment.

6. Michel Debré, de Gaulle's first prime minister, from 1959 to 1962, ran as the candidate of the Gaullist old guard in 1981, but he had been out of the limelight for a long time and fared poorly.

7. The only two-time loser who became a major-party candidate for a third time in the United States was William Jennings Bryan, who ran unsuccessfully in 1896, 1900, and 1908.

8. In doing so, he was emulating Georges Pompidou, who first staked his claim to becoming de Gaulle's successor by announcing, while on a trip out of the country, that he would run for the presidency if de Gaulle did not.

Chapter 3

1. French scholars followed these U.S. political developments with considerable interest. See, in particular, Gaxie (1982), Grunberg (1985, 419–26), and Lancelot (1985, 408–11).

2. The actual comparison was between French voters from 1967 to 1968, and U.S. voters from 1956 to 1958, and from 1958 to 1960. Those were years when net aggregate electoral stability was atypically high for France and low for the United States, so some caution is called for in generalization from the findings, but the underlying message that constancy of partisan choice requires constancy of partisan offerings is irrefutable.

3. This does not mean that every party had an equal probability of winning the support of the voters who were not already attached to a particular party. For many people who did not identify with a discrete party, certain other parties—notably the Communist party—might be pariahs. Still other people might be guided by their religious outlook, or a sense of left-right location, or sympathy for certain social groups (workers, small business). But for those people, the electoral problem included the far from trivial task of identifying which of the large array of contending parties most closely matched whatever more general, politically relevant orientation they might have.

4. For the contrary view, see Lewis-Beck (1984, 428–33, 447). Charlot (1986, 6) reports the results of a series of French surveys purporting to measure the incidence of party identification. Most employed the interview method of giving the respondents a list of parties from which to choose and produce characteristically inflated results. Charlot does not report the question wording, but consistency on that score is essential. French researchers measured "partisan proximity" in 1978 and 1988 with the question: "Voici une liste de partis ou mouvements politiques. Pouvez-vous me dire duquel vous vous sentez le plus proche, ou, disons, le moins éloigné?" [Here is a list of parties or political movements. Can you tell me the one you feel closest to or, let us say, the least distant from?] The incidence of valid selections was about 85 percent in both years. Strength of partisan attachment was also measured in identical terms in the two surveys. See Capdevielle, Dupoirier, and Ysmal (1981, 19–33) and Haegel (1993). For additional considerations concerning problems of ascertaining party identification in France, see Converse and Pierce (1986, chap. 3, n. 7).

5. In order to eliminate the possibility that interviewers might translate unintelligible reports of partisan attachments into some credible version, Converse and Pierce contracted for special interviewer training for their surveys in the late 1960s. Resource limitations ruled out special interviewer training for the 1988 study, but the printed questionnaires used by the interviewers contained this special instruction, alongside the question relating to party identification, and printed in large, conspicuously bold face type: "Enquêteur: Ne Rien Suggérer. Noter de façon très précise ce que vous dit l'interviewé même si ce n'est pas le nom d'un parti." [Interviewer: Do not suggest anything. Note down exactly what the respondent tells you even if it is not the name of a party.]

6. Converse's calculations were based on a turnover model that assumed that the probability of a person acquiring a partisan attachment was .8 if the person was raised in a partisan family and only .5 if the person was reared in an apolitical family. Those conditional probabilities had been empirically determined for both France and the United States during the 1950s (Converse 1969).

7. A literal application of Converse's turnover model, taking the 30 year lapse between 1958 and 1988 as a single generation, and assuming that the incidence of party identification in 1958 was 53 percent, produces a 1988 level of 66 percent, somewhat lower than our reported incidence. But given changing patterns of familial political socialization during recent decades (Percheron 1989) we should not be surprised that party identifications would accumulate at a somewhat faster rate than Converse's model assumes.

8. These matters are spelled out in detail in Converse and Pierce (1986, chap. 3).

9. Percheron (1989, 84) reports that between 1975 and 1989, there was a "dédrama-tisation" of politics within the family: "Political choices moved out of everyone's secret garden, away from the domain of silence."

10. Levels of political interest do fluctuate in any case, but here we are comparing identical measures taken at postelectoral surveys, and the difference between them is enormous by comparison with the fluctuations in the series of comparable U.S. measures taken from 1952 to 1978 (Miller, Miller, and Schneider 1980, 308).

11. There is some room for debate over what is a "discrete party." For 1967, we included references to "Gaullist" and "Giscardian" in the partisan inventory; for 1988 we excluded references to leaders. For both years, we have excluded references to left-right locations and to groups that are clearly not parties.

12. See Converse and Pierce (1986, 91–93) for a comparison of the fractionaliza-tion of the French party system of the late 1960s with that of the party systems of the United States, Great Britain, and the Netherlands at more or less the same time period.

13. On the general question of the criteria for establishing age categories for polit-ical analysis, see Percheron (1988).

14. Except for the group aged from 18 through 20 in 1988, not shown separately in figure 3.1, among whom less than 63 percent identified with a party.

15. But not, however, among the very youngest. Among the thin population slice aged 18 to 20, right-wing identifiers outnumber leftists, perhaps because they include the children of the most right-wing 1988 cohort.

16. The protest movements in the United States during the 1960s had a different kind of effect on the distribution of partisanship. Jennings and Markus (1984) found that the main political difference between graduating high school students in 1965 and their parents was that the former were less likely to identify with *any* party, a difference that endured into the early 1980s. But, as the comparison between children and parents con-notes, that was essentially a generational effect, without any marked resonance among other age groups. A graphing of the proportion of persons in the United States having a party identification (i.e., excluding leaners and independents) in 1988, by annualized age, shows no cliff connecting two plateaus of different heights. Of course, the protest movement in the United States did not have the magnitude, breadth of social support, ideological inspiration, concentration, and explosiveness that characterized the French upheaval of May 1968.

17. See Schlesinger and Schlesinger (1990) for a discussion of how French parties adapt to the exigencies and opportunities of the two-ballot electoral system.

18. The only exception was that 40–49-year-old identifiers felt closer to their par-ties than the 50–59-year-olds, largely because of the strength of right-wing partisan attachments within the "founding generation."

19. The other countries examined were Australia, Canada, the Netherlands, the United Kingdom, and the United States (where inequality grew the most from 1979 to 1986).

20. During the same period, France was also wracked by a succession of scandals. One, involving the distribution of contaminated blood to hemophiliacs during the mid-1980s, was particularly damaging. Most, however, related to kickbacks on government contracts that were used to finance the political parties. All the major parties were to some extent implicated in these activities, but the revelations were especially harmful to the Socialists, who had been more prone to moralizing than other groups. The overall result, however, was to discredit politicians generally, much as the disclosure of the extent to which U.S. congressmen exploited check-writing privileges from the House of Representatives' bank (and, to a lesser extent, the privileges of the House post office) threw them into disrepute in the United States just prior to the 1992 congressional elections.

Chapter 4

1. With the advent of the French Fourth Republic, which abandoned the two-ballot electoral system and adopted a list system of proportional representation for the popularly elected legislative chamber, Goguel no longer emphasized the stark distinction between movement and order. He was among the first to recognize that new political forces had emerged that strained the political categories of the Third Republic. The Communist party, which advocated a very different kind of movement than the other leftist parties, divided the left for more than 15 years. The early postwar Mouvement Républicain Populaire (MRP) stood on both sides of Goguel's political divide, as it was a Catholic party led by politicians who considered themselves to be socially and economically more advanced than many of their secular opponents. Finally, the political appeal of Charles de Gaulle was anchored in traditionally rightist territory, but it extended into historically leftist regions as well (northern France in particular), and the general was not only resented by most traditional right-wing leaders but actively detested by the Vichyites, whose symbolic leader—Marshal Pétain—had put a price on his head during the war.

2. I know that because I tried. In an early textbook on French politics (Pierce 1968, 1973) I made a conscious effort to avoid using the words *left* and *right* without defining them. I succeeded in doing so, but it was difficult.

3. Limited questionnaire time prevented us from eliciting the perceived left-right locations of three minor leftist candidates and of Antoine Waechter, the ecologist candidate. For analytical purposes, we scored the three leftists at 2 and Waechter at 3.87. See appendix B for details about the left-right scoring of the candidates and parties.

4. In 1976, the study also included a measure of left-right orientation, which correlated (r) with liberal-conservative positions at .446.

5. *Left* was the sixth most frequently used noun in François Mitterrand's official campaign television broadcasts during the presidential election campaign of 1981 (Charlot 1975, 240).

6. These are the mean perceptions reported by respondents who themselves had a valid location on the same scale. There is virtually no difference in the results if we base

them on all respondents who volunteered a candidate's location even if they did not report one for themselves.

7. We will pursue this issue of directional perceptions further in chapter 5, in connection with specific issue positions as well as broad ideological locations.

8. In this brief discussion, we ignore mass assignments of the candidates to the midpoint of the relevant scale.

9. The U.S. NES survey includes a probe for eliciting a liberal-conservative location from respondents who had indicated that they hadn't thought much about the matter when asked for what we refer to above as their spontaneous reply. We have not included the responses to the probe.

10. At the same time, it must be remembered that the base measures from which the U.S. and French summary variables are constructed differ, so direct comparisons of the frequencies on the two scales are of limited utility.

Chapter 5

1. The questions take this typical form: "Some people feel it is important for us to try to cooperate more with Russia, while others believe we should be much tougher in our dealing with Russia."

"Where would you place yourself on this scale, or haven't you thought much about this?"

"And where would you place _____ on this scale?"

2. The issues included in the 1988 U.S. NES survey refer to: government spending on services, government spending for defense, government versus private health insurance, government responsibility for providing jobs and a good standard of living, cooperation with Russia, equal rights for women, and two questions relating to government help for, in one case, "blacks and other minorities" and, in the other case, simply for "blacks."

3. The elementary school teacher's union obligingly raised the issue of subsidies for religious schools before the first-ballot vote (*Le Monde*, February 2, 1988), but the issue did not play a major role during the campaign.

4. After Mitterrand's election to the presidency in 1981, and the triumph of his Socialist party at the ensuing legislative election, a large number of industrial and financial enterprises were nationalized. In 1986, the right-wing parties regained a parliamentary majority and, under the leadership of Premier Jacques Chirac, undertook a major program of reprivatization.

5. Women's rights is the only U.S. issue in our battery for which the proportion of respondents without opinions is as small as it is for the French religious schools and immigration issues.

6. The measure of party identification used here is not the simple "two-party" analogue of the standard U.S. party identification measure that we employed in chapter 4,
but rather the full-fledged measure of left-right party identification that is described (but
not actually employed) in the same chapter. The two-party variant, however, produces
very similar, if not identical results. The measure of political interest is based on a
simple additive scale combining nothing more than degree of interest in the electoral
campaign and degree of interest in politics.

7. The main difference between these results, based in part on a party-specific
left-right party identification variable, and those that emerge when we employ the
two-party party identification variable, is that in the latter case the advantage of party
identification over simple left-right location widens considerably at all three levels of
political interest for the public sector issue, while the greater importance of left-right
positioning over party identification becomes more marked for the immigration issue
among the most interested voters.

8. There is one exception among twelve observations.

9. The issues are listed in n. 2 above. The two questions relating to government help
for minorities were each asked of half the sample, so we have combined their responses
in order to maintain the same sample size across all seven issues.

10. Resource and time constraints prevented us from including all nine French presidential candidates, but the four we did include received 85 percent of the votes cast at
the first ballot.

11. Converse and Pierce (1986, chap. 9) reported a similar relationship between
political involvement and the incidence of mass linkages between issues and parties, and
between issues and legislative candidates, for France in 1967.

12. Earlier, we combined two U.S. questions relating to minorities, each of which
was asked only of half the sample electorate, in order to enlarge the sample base. There
is no need to do so for this analysis, so we employ the two questions separately.

13. For correlational purposes, the U.S. preferred candidate variables were coded
1 for Bush, 2 for no candidate or a tie between Bush and Dukakis, and 3 for Dukakis.
The French coding is more complicated, and rests on the perceived left-right locations
of the candidates, as discussed in chapter 4. Each candidate was assigned his mean left-
right location, and where there were ties, the mean was taken of the left-right locations
of the candidates involved. Missing data were excluded from the proximity variable and
counted as a four-candidate tie for the directional variable.

Chapter 6

1. Most of the election results that are broadcast on election eve and reported in the
press in the wake of a U.S. election are compiled by the News Election Service, which
is jointly supported by the major television networks and wire services (Lewis 1991).
The vote totals reported in the annual volumes of *The World Almanac and Book of Facts*
(New York: Pharos Books) derive from the News Election Service. Another private organization, the Elections Research Center, has compiled a series of U.S. election statistics
under the title *America Votes*, of which 20 volumes have appeared. The series, which
began in 1956, has been published under different auspices at different times; it is cur-
rently published by Congressional Quarterly. Many of the vote totals that are published

in the annual volumes of the *Statistical Abstract of the United States* (Washington, D.C.: U.S. Department of Commerce, Bureau of the Census) derive from *America Votes*. Election results have also been reported every two years since the early 1970s in the *Almanac of American Politics*, originally authored by Michael Barone, Grant Ujifusa, and Douglas Matthews, and more recently only by Barone and Ujifusa (Washington, D.C.: National Journal). There are marginal differences in the results for any given constituency produced by these organizations (and the Clerk of the House), most of which are caused by differences in the dates at which the state and other returns were consulted. The Clerk of the House reported some 150,000 fewer votes for George Bush and Michael Dukakis in 1988 than either *America Votes* or the News Election Service (which were little more than 1,000 votes apart), a relatively small difference for an electorate of more than 90 million people.

2. Actually, three different estimates of the voting age population are made: a short-term projection that is published early in the electoral year, a postcensal estimate based on the previous census and published a year after the election, and an intercensal estimate based on the two bracketing censuses and published after the following census. There is sometimes considerable variation on the state level between these different estimates. The third type is qualitatively the best, but it is also the last to be published. On all these points, see Passel (1990).

3. Confidence in our estimated differential of 10 to 15 percent is strengthened by the finding of Wolfinger and Rosenstone (1980, 88) that "if every state had registration laws in 1972 as permissive as those in the most permissive states, turnout [in the United States] would have been about 9 percentage points higher in the presidential election." In 1972, the official turnout rate was some 5 percentage points higher than the 1988 rate of 50.1 percent.

4. On July 2, 1992, President George Bush vetoed a bill, labeled the "motor-voter bill," that would have required states, beginning in 1994, to register people to vote when they applied for a driver's license, renewed it, or changed the address on the license, as well as to permit voters to register by mail and to provide registration forms at various social service offices. On May 20, 1993, President Bill Clinton signed virtually the same bill into law.

5. Among the merits of Schonfeld and Toinet 1975 is their insistence that French voter registration procedures are not really less restrictive than those employed in the United States.

6. An excellent and convenient summary of the U.S. registration procedures, by state, appears in Hancock 1992.

7. Crewe (1981, 249) writes that "the United States, true to its liberal and Protestant tradition, is the only country where the individual elector is not automatically registered by the authorities but must take the initiative himself." The voter is not automatically registered in statist and largely Catholic France either.

8. The use of mobile registration units is authorized, but there are no data about their numbers and frequency of use.

9. Someone purged from a registration list in France must appeal either within 24 hours of receiving notice or between January 11 and January 20, and the appellant appears before a judge. The U.S. norm for objecting to notice is 30 days, and the procedures are administrative.

10. For a special consideration affecting the turnout of black voters in the United States in 1988, see chapter 9.

Chapter 7

1. We do have mass perceptions of the issue positions of the French Communist party, and we considered including those as applicable also to André Lajoinie, the Communist party's candidate (as the mass perceptions of the issue positions of the other candidates and of their respective parties are virtually identical), but we decided against the move for two reasons. First, the Communist party split prior to the election and there was a dissident communist candidate (Pierre Juquin) along with the official Communist party candidate (André Lajoinie). Secondly, given the numerous ties among the preferred candidates on an issue basis (see table 5.4) when taking only four candidates into account, to include a fifth, minor candidate, would complicate the structure of preferences disproportionately to the utility of doing so.

2. We do not mean that a measure is necessarily more valid because it has more predictive power; we mean only that in trying to assess the relative importance of various factors in the vote, one should not handicap any factor by representing it in a weaker form than necessary.

3. That shift is counterintuitive, as the candidate evaluation scores are, like the party identification scores and the original candidate choice variable, expressed in terms of mean left-right candidate locations. We would, therefore, expect the alteration we made in the dependent variable to produce a smaller coefficient for the candidate evaluation variable.

4. The Listhaug, MacDonald, and Rabinowitz team make no distinction between left-right locations (MacDonald, Listhaug, and Rabinowitz 1991) or liberal-conservative positioning (Rabinowitz and MacDonald 1989) and other, more conventional issues, but rather include them in their summations of scores for their issue batteries.

5. There are complex and powerful models that are designed to take these interactions into account from the start. Among these, the "dynamic simultaneous equation model" of Markus and Converse (1979) is probably the most efficient and complete, but it requires panel data, which is not available to us for France in 1988. See also Markus 1982.

6. Recall that our two long-term independent variables had scaling ranges of 1 to 7 (for left-right location) and 1.75 to 6.66 (for left-right party identification) respectively. The four short-term independent variables each had a range of 3.11 to 6.62. The four candidates represented on the dependent variable were scored at 3.11, 4.79, 5.55, and 6.62 respectively.

7. The cutting points on the scale of predicted values were the following: Mitterrand (less than 3.94); Barre (from 3.94 to 5.16); Chirac (from 5.17 to 6.09); and Le Pen (more than 6.09).

8. With the exception of the Le Pen anomaly, the predictions generated by our overall model survive comparison with those Converse and Pierce (1986, 323–24) produced with the model they deployed for the French legislative elections of 1967. There are too many differences in detail between the Converse-Pierce model and the one reported here for us to insist on specific proportions; the main point is that to the extent that the mod-

els are similar they produce similar results. The strongest form of the Converse-Pierce model represented long-term forces alone, as expressed by party identification, left-right location, position on a Gaullism dimension and position on a clericalism dimension, including only voters having a party identification and substituting mean scores for voters without one or more of the other attributes. That model correctly predicted more than 75 percent of the votes for the four main party groups of the era, the specific prediction rates of which varied from 80 percent to 52 percent. When we strip our present model down to only two variables, party identification and left-right location, it accurately predicts 80 percent of the cases, but the specific prediction rate for Le Pen remains at a mere 40 percent.

9. The Converse and Pierce (1986) findings concerning the relative status of party identification and left-right positioning in the French context of 1967 have been challenged by Fleury and Lewis-Beck (1993a). See also the comment by Converse and Pierce (1993) and the subsequent rejoinder by Fleury and Lewis-Beck (1993b).

10. In 1984, the preelectoral interviews were conducted between September 5 and November 5, while the postelectoral interviews were carried out in more condensed fashion, with almost all of them completed by December 12.

11. For an analysis of such thwarted voters, see chapter 9.

12. Between the two ballots of the 1988 election, candidate and Prime Minister Chirac's government negotiated the release of French hostages held in Beirut and employed military force in New Caledonia.

Chapter 8

1. Prior to the 1988 U.S. presidential election, Times Mirror, a company with vast broadcasting, television, and publishing interests, commissioned the Gallup organization to conduct a series of sample surveys that resulted in a typology of the U.S. electorate based on joint attitudinal and demographic categories (Ornstein, Kohut, and McCarthy 1988).

2. Here we prefer Axelrod's (1972) logic over that of Erikson, Lancaster, and Romero (1989), who exclude abstainers.

3. Strictly speaking, we cannot employ statistical tests with our French data, as they do not derive from a random sample. But how else can we indicate that a difference in probabilities may not be as real as it looks on its face?

4. It is by no means clear why this should be so. Our estimates show that in 1988 women were less interested than men in politics, and less likely than men to expose themselves to political information, with little reduction in the variation when controlling for education levels, which are higher, on the average, for men than for women. Almost surely, this is the result of different socialization patterns, but we do not have the data with which to examine that hypothesis. For an interesting analysis of these and other aspects of women and politics in France, see Mossuz-Lavau and Sineau 1983.

5. The denominations included in the Bush coalition were Reformation era Protestants (Lutherans, Presbyterians, and Episcopalians), as well as Methodists and Baptists outside the South.

6. See chapter 9.

7. Notably in the determination that slaves should count as three-fifths of a person for the purpose of apportioning representatives to the various states.

8. Supporters of efforts to reduce inequalities between the races in the United States often refer to "institutionalized racism." Usually, however, this refers to habitual practices and procedures within institutions that systematically operate to the disadvantage of black people, whether or not they are deliberately intended to do so (Knowles and Prewitt 1969).

9. Erikson, Lancaster, and Romero (1989) are unconcerned with internal migration; they chart only nonblack southerners.

10. The departments include the following: Alpes-de-Haute-Provence, Ariège, Aude, Bouches-du-Rhône, Corrèze, Creuse, Dordogne, Gard, Haute-Garonne, Gers, Hérault, Lot, Lot-et-Garonne, Hautes-Pyrénées, Pyrénées-Orientales, Tarn, Tarn-et-Garonne, Var, Vaucluse, and Haute-Vienne.

11. In 1969, the Pearsonian correlations (r) between religious attachment and both party identification and the first-ballot presidential vote of that year were markedly closer than they were between the same variables in 1988 (.38 and .37 vs. .31 and .27), while those between subjective class and both party identification and the vote were slightly weaker in the earlier year (.24 and .21 vs. .28 and .25).

12. The myth of a glorious but unfinished revolution came under polemical attack early in the postwar period, with Camus's criticism (1951) of what he called historical rebellion. Historians more interested in political consequences than social causes continued to undermine revolutionary romanticism, and this virtually evaporated with the collapse of the Soviet Union. The ceremonies held in France to commemorate the 200th anniversary of the Great Revolution were dominated by an astonishing historical revisionism that could find little or nothing praiseworthy in the revolutionary events (Kaplan 1993).

13. This is true also of the inner cities, but these do not appear in the Mitterrand coalition either.

Chapter 9

1. I owe this label to James F. Adams.

2. The following political leaders were included in the analysis. For 1972: only Democrats George McGovern, Shirley Chisholm, Hubert Humphrey, Henry Jackson, Edmund Muskie, and George Wallace. For 1976: Democrats Jimmy Carter, Jerry Brown, Henry Jackson, Morris Udall, and George Wallace; Republicans Gerald Ford and Ronald Reagan. For 1980: Democrats Jimmy Carter, Jerry Brown, and Edward Kennedy; Republicans Ronald Reagan, Howard Baker, George Bush, John Connally, and Gerald Ford. For 1984: Democrats Walter Mondale, John Glenn, Gary Hart, Jesse Jackson, Edward Kennedy, and George McGovern; Republicans Ronald Reagan, Howard Baker, George Bush, and Robert Dole. For 1988, Democrats Michael Dukakis and Jesse Jackson; Republicans George Bush, Robert Dole, and Pat Robertson.

3. The rationale for this decision included both the wish to remain consistent with the usage of Miller (1991) as long as there was no apparent reason not to do so and the belief that "pure" identifiers would be more likely than leaners to care about which person their party selected as its presidential candidate. The latter consideration was sus-

tained by the reports of participation in primary elections or caucuses in 1980 and 1988, the two U.S. NES surveys during the 1980s that contain the relevant data. Weak identifiers participated in the correct party primaries (or caucuses) at a rate that was some 6–7 percentage points higher than the rate for leaners.

4. In a study of U.S. primary voters who supported losers for the presidential nomination at the elections from 1968 to 1984, Southwell (1986) emphasizes 1972 and 1980 as highpoints for disgruntlement among Democrats and Republicans, respectively.

5. We have somewhat cavalierly referred to the incidence of thwarted voters, particularly in France, as calculable, but in fact it is impossible to know just how many voters are frustrated with the choices offered to them in either France or the United States. All of our estimates almost surely understate their true numbers. In France, there may be a wide choice of candidates at the first ballot, but even voters whose first-ballot choices survive into the runoff might have preferred a different candidate from the same party. And in the United States, even where there are primary elections, the preferred candidates of some voters may not compete in the primaries.

6. There is still another alternative that is regularly employed in France but that appears to be outside U.S. electoral mores: deliberately spoiling one's ballot as a mark of protest. Spoiled ballots are not counted in the United States, while they are duly recorded in France. Among our sample of the 1988 French electorate, some 2 percent of the respondents reported spoiling their ballots at the second, runoff round of voting. Every one of those respondents had voted at the first ballot for a candidate who was eliminated from the runoff. For a fuller discussion of ballot spoiling, in the context of French legislative elections, see Converse and Pierce (1986, chap. 11).

7. New York City provides for a runoff in the primary elections for mayor and a few other major city offices. The three-week lapse between the first ballot and the runoff was challenged in the courts, successfully at first but unsuccessfully on appeal, on grounds (among others) that the short period between ballots favored candidates with enough money to ensure easy access to the media over those who depended mainly on street campaigning to mobilize their supporters, and that it encouraged negative campaigning because there was so little time for candidates to mount defenses (Bullock and Johnson 1992, 80–92). The runoff ballots in the various U.S. states that employ them for primary elections usually occur two or three weeks after the first poll, although the lapse of time ranges from one week to a month (Charles S. Bullock, private communication, August 30, 1993). To my knowledge, the two-week gap between the first and second ballots has not been an issue in France.

8. A grudging endorsement, or none at all, is not necessarily a serious handicap for a finalist. Some commentators suggested that Jackson's early reservations about campaigning for Dukakis in 1988 might have helped Dukakis win votes from conservative Democrats who distrusted Jackson without costing him any support among black voters or white liberal Democrats. It is by no means certain that Chirac would have benefited from an endorsement by Le Pen in 1988. He might have lost more votes from moderates who could not tolerate Le Pen than he would have gained among Le Pen's first-ballot voters.

9. We report our estimates only starting with the 1980 election because that is when the U.S. NES began reporting voter validation data, enabling us to assess more accurately which survey respondents actually voted.

10. Recall here that when we speak of U.S. identifiers, we do not include leaners, but rather only those respondents who spontaneously declare themselves to be Democrats or Republicans.

11. A spectacular exception to that statement occurred at the presidential election of 1969, when the runoff was not clearly between a rightist and a leftist, but rather between Gaullist Georges Pompidou and centrist Alain Poher. Left-wing voters could see little or no difference between the contenders, and more than half of the thwarted voters spoiled their ballots or abstained.

12. Converse and Pierce (1992) also refer to "escape velocity," as a threshold of attachment to a party that must be crossed before a voter will depart from his or her partisan affiliation.

13. This means that we are unable to take into account here the behavior of the first-ballot supporters of leftists Pierre Boussel, Arlette Laguiller, and Pierre Juquin, or those of Antoine Waechter, the candidate of the Greens. Together, those four candidates won 8 percent of the votes cast at the first ballot.

14. The ordered logit program employed here is LIMDEP, which is copyrighted by William H. Greene, Econometric Software, Inc., Bellport, New York.

15. It is possible that left-right locations would be more significant for France if we had been able to include the voters who cast their ballots for the dropout left-wing candidates other than André Lajoinie.

Chapter 10

1. Except in the unlikely cases of a candidate winning a majority of the votes at the first ballot, or one or both of the front-runners at the first ballot choosing not to run at the second.

2. Departmental elections (called cantonal elections, because the basic electoral district was originally the *canton*) are staggered; the term is six years, but the councils of half of the departments are elected every three years. Municipal elections are held every six years. Municipal and departmental elections are normally held in March, in different years, although they have sometimes been postponed to September because of a conflicting presidential or legislative election. Regional elections have also been held in March, while the European elections are held in June.

3. Laurent (1987) uses the term "electoral nomadism."

4. For a French-U.S. comparison of cross-time voting constancy that controls for variations in electoral supply, see Converse and Pierce (1986, 42–54).

5. The Greens, however, as well as Le Pen's National Front, do not fit the left-right dimension as well as the older parties do, as we saw in chapter 7 with regard to Le Pen's presidential vote.

6. Simultaneity of presidential and congressional elections has not always been the rule in the United States. Different election dates for the president and Congress were standard in many states during the early nineteenth century. It was not until the last decade of that century that a common election date was adopted by all the then 38 states.

7. For this analysis, as in those of the preceding chapter, we consider French left-right coalitional solidarity as the equivalent of partisan consistency in the United States.

Accordingly, we group the seats won by all leftist parties into one category, and those won by the remaining candidates into the opposing category.

8. Given the nonsimultaneity of French presidential and legislative elections, panel studies would, of course, be required.

9. To establish a U.S. baseline for an earlier era, we have employed the district data for the 1950s contained in ICPSR Study No. 10. For the more contemporary period, we have established our own U.S. district data set for the 1970s and early 1980s. We have also prepared our own French district-level data set, which includes the proportion of the vote won by leftist and rightist candidates at the decisive ballot (which is the second ballot for presidential elections but either the first or the second ballot for legislative elections, depending upon at which ballot the election was decided). See appendix C for our sources.

10. The French district-level consistency correlations (*r*) for legislative voting at the decisive ballot, by time between elections, are as follows:

1986–88	(2 years)	.83
1978–81	(3 years)	.80
1962–67	(5 years)	.77
1973–78	(5 years)	.76
1967–73	(6 years)	.74
1962–73	(11 years)	.67
1967–78	(11 years)	.66
1962–78	(16 years)	.63

The correlation between these two sets of values is .977.

11. We omitted changes in the distributions of seats in France between 1986 and 1988 as a test for coattails effects because the 1986 legislative elections were held under a list system and not on the basis of single-member districts. However, the French Communist party compiled the 1986 electoral returns by 1988 districts, and that enables us to make various other 1986–1988 district-level comparisons (see app. C).

12. Edwards (1979), working before logistic regression entered the political science toolbox, employed OLS regression with the dichotomous variable of whether or not the congressional candidate of the presidential victor's party won the district seat and found modest but diminishing coattails effects from 1952 to 1968, and none in 1972. For comparative purposes, we followed his method for France in 1981 and 1988 and found more powerful coattails effects in both years than any Edwards had uncovered in the United States.

13. An analogous situation occurred earlier in the Fifth Republic. When the government adopted President de Gaulle's proposal to amend the constitution by referendum to provide for direct popular election of the president, the National Assembly voted to censure the government and de Gaulle promptly dissolved the assembly. The amendment was endorsed at the referendum of October 28, 1962, and new elections were held on November 18 and 25. Turnout at the referendum on the constitution was more than 77 percent, while at the first ballot of the legislative elections it was less than 69 percent.

14. To estimate turnout at the district level in the United States, we divided the 1980 census estimates of the voting age population for each district into the total vote cast for the two major parties in the district in 1982 and 1984. The vote totals for the winners of

uncontested seats are usually not reported, so uncontested seats had to be removed from the data set, reducing it to 365 districts. There is no such problem for France, where the turnout is officially reported. However, some French seats are uncontested at the second ballot, and inasmuch as we report the results for the decisive ballot (whether the first or the second one), some of our French entries for the legislative vote are for 0 percent or 100 percent. We reran the French regression without those districts, to create a closer match for the U.S. set, but it made little difference in the results. It naturally reduced the amount of variance explained, and it dampened the coefficients of the independent variables, but the ordering of the coefficients remained the same, and they all remained statistically significant.

15. At the municipal elections of 1983 and 1989, turnout was higher than it had been at the preceding national legislative elections.

Chapter 11

1. The U.S. states not included are those where, as in the case of Corsica for France, no interviews were held in the NES sample survey on which we are relying.

2. It is likely that the interunit variance would increase for France if we made the departments the units of analysis, as that variance appears to increase as the size of the units decreases. We cannot make a reliable test, however, as our French sample is too small to yield an adequate number of cases per department.

3. In 1912, former president Theodore Roosevelt challenged incumbent president William Howard Taft for the Republican nomination. When he failed in that bid, Roosevelt entered the race under the banner of the Progressive (or Bull Moose) party, thereby splitting the normally Republican vote. Woodrow Wilson, the Democratic candidate, won some 45 percent of the popular votes, but more than 80 percent of the electoral votes. Roosevelt won some 30 percent of the popular vote, and Taft garnered about 25 percent.

4. Ignoring the votes cast for minor candidates, these first-ballot results for France in 1974 resembled the popular vote distribution at the U.S. election of 1912, to which we have already referred. They are similar to the distribution of votes at the U.S. election of 1968, when Richard Nixon won some 44 percent of the votes (and 56 percent of the electoral votes), while Hubert Humphrey, the Democratic candidate, won almost 43 percent and third-party candidate and ex-Democrat George Wallace won almost 14 percent of the votes. Finally, the French 1974 configuration also resembled the U.S. election of 1992, which Bill Clinton won with 43 percent of the popular vote (and almost 70 percent of the electoral vote) as opposed to 38 percent for George Bush and 19 percent for Ross Perot. The three-party U.S. presidential races prior to 1992 are analyzed in Brown (1991, chap. 5).

5. The principle of equal representation for the states in the U.S. Senate has no counterpart in France, except that no department may have fewer than two deputies.

6. There is no need to go into detail concerning this counterfactual exercise, but readers may be interested to know that while the ratio of the smallest to largest U.S. state allocation of electoral votes is 1:18, it would be 1:14 for the French departments and 1:22 for the French regions. The largest 10 percent of the U.S. states control more than 30 percent of the electoral votes; the top 10 percent of French departments would control some 28 percent and the two largest French regions about 26 percent.

7. For the two elections considered, the hypothetical regional electoral college registered slightly larger majorities for the "winners" (84 percent for Mitterrand in 1974 and 61 percent for Giscard in 1981) than the departmental electoral college (77 percent and 58 percent respectively).

8. One is reminded here of the much repeated warning that with plurality rule in single-member districts, a party can win a majority of the legislative seats with barely more than 25 percent of the votes. Our experiment with a hypothetical electoral college in France in 1981 approximates that result.

Chapter 12

1. Unless one or both of those selected by the voters should choose not to run at the second ballot, in which case the next runner(s)-up would.

2. Defferre failed to win his Socialist party's support for the nomination in 1965 because he wanted to build a centrist coalition, while his party eventually favored a coalition with the Communist party.

3. See Heclo (1973) for a contrast between bureaucratic and elective leadership recruitment patterns. Schonfeld (1986) speaks of the possibility in such a top-heavy milieu of a whole generation of potential successors being skipped over completely.

4. But not because of the incumbent's appointment to the government. In that case, the legislator's seat is filled by a supernumerary, who is designated at the same time the deputy is elected.

5. The technique was exploited, if not invented, by General Boulanger in the late nineteenth century. Boulanger, who was regarded as a threat to the Third Republic by its leaders, was dismissed from the army in 1888. No longer ineligible for elective office, Boulanger took advantage of an electoral law that permitted candidates to run in more than one by-election simultaneously by turning successive clusters of by-elections into personal triumphs. Boulanger was driven into exile, and he committed suicide, but no candidate has since been permitted to run in more than one district at a time.

6. In this affair, life imitated art. An amusing novel (Duchateau 1987) about the French political elite's reaction to an announcement that President Mitterrand had been shot appeared early in 1987. One of the episodes describes Léotard and his allies within the Chirac government—known as "la bande à Léo" [Leo's gang]—discussing how to promote Léotard's presidential chances by, among other stratagems, resigning from the government. I read this book soon after it appeared, and remember my astonishment when I later read in the French press about the possibility of Léotard's resignation.

7. Soon after this episode, Noir became involved in a curious imbroglio with his son-in-law, a Lyon businessman who claimed to have bankrolled Noir's campaigns and who was indicted for alleged bribery of France's top television anchorman, among others. Noir held his parliamentary seat against an RPR challenger at the 1993 legislative elections, but the following year he came under investigation for possible misuse of public funds for earlier campaign expenditures.

8. Notably to support Pierre Mendès-France during the Fourth Republic, and to promote the presidential chances of Gaston Defferre for the election of 1965.

9. There are issues over which the RPR and the UDF have disagreed. The RPR was more skeptical of European integration and more suspicious of the United States (less

"Atlanticist") than the UDF. But these differences did not surface during the presidential elections of 1974, 1981, or 1988. If they had done so in 1988, we would have had a larger issue battery for France than we do.

10. *Economist* (March 27, 1993) highlighted the election of 46-year-old Bill Clinton to the U.S. presidency while all the main contenders for the French presidency were in their 60s or 70s, including Valéry Giscard d'Estaing and Jacques Chirac, who (like Mitterrand before them) were working their way back from earlier defeats that might well have discouraged less determined men.

11. Michel Rocard, who has figured prominently in this chapter, is a Protestant.

12. With all due qualifications, one might say that Pierre Mendès-France, who became prime minister in 1954, under the French Fourth Republic, specifically to end the then French war in Indochina, was McGovern's French counterpart.

13. Chaban's position was badly weakened early in 1972 when it became public knowledge that he had not paid any income tax for four years. His tax situation was entirely legal, but it was politically damaging for the prime minister. He tried to explain away the problem in a television appearance that was openly compared with Richard Nixon's famous "Checkers" speech, but he was obviously less successful than Nixon had been (Alexandre 1973).

14. The terminology is inspired by Williams (1964, chap. 30).

15. Skowronek (1993) similarly holds that comparison based on commonality of situation can be more useful for understanding presidential behavior than analysis resting on literal chronological succession.

16. Adams appointed Clay secretary of state, giving rise to the complaint that there had been a "corrupt bargain," although there is no evidence that any prior bargain had been struck.

17. Little is known about Jackson's early years, but he was raised and cut his political teeth in anti-Federalist territory.

References

Abramson, Paul R., John H. Aldrich, and David W. Rohde. 1990. *Change and Continuity in the 1988 Elections*. Washington, D.C.: Congressional Quarterly.

Alexandre, Philippe. 1973. *Exécution d'un homme politique*. Paris: Bernard Grasset.

Ambrose, Stephen E. 1989. *Nixon: The Triumph of a Politician 1962–1972*. New York: Simon and Schuster.

Andrews, William G. 1982. *Presidential Government in Gaullist France: A Study of Executive-Legislative Relations 1958–1974*. Albany: State University of New York Press.

L'Année politique, économique et sociale 1988. 1989. Paris: Editions du Moniteur.

L'Année politique, économique et sociale 1992. 1993. Paris: Editions Evénements et Tendances.

Asher, Herbert B. 1992. *Presidential Elections and American Politics: Voters, Candidates, and Campaigns since 1952*. 5th ed. Homewood, Ill.: The Dorsey Press.

Axelrod, Robert. 1972. Where the Votes Come From: An Analysis of Electoral Coalitions, 1952–1968. *American Political Science Review* 66:11–20.

———. 1974. Communication. *American Political Science Review* 68:717–20.

———. 1978. Communication. *American Political Science Review* 72:622–24 and 1010–11.

———. 1982. Communication. *American Political Science Review* 76:393–96.

———. 1986. Presidential Election Coalitions in 1984. *American Political Science Review* 80:281–84.

Baker, Kendall L., Russell J. Dalton, and Kai Hildebrandt. 1981. *Germany Transformed: Political Culture and the New Politics*. Cambridge, Mass.: Harvard University Press.

Bass, Herbert J. 1961. *"I am a Democrat": The Political Career of David Bennett Hill*. Syracuse, N.Y.: Syracuse University Press.

Beatty, Jack. 1992. *The Rascal King: The Life and Times of James Michael Curley 1874–1958*. Reading, Mass.: Addison-Wesley.

Becquart-Leclercq, Jeanne. 1983. Cumul des mandats et culture politique. In *Les Pouvoirs locaux à l'épreuve de la décentralisation*, ed. Albert Mabileau, pp. 207–39. Paris: Pedone.

———. 1989. Multiple Officeholding in Local and National Elective Positions. *Tocqueville Review* 9:221–41.

Boy, Daniel, and Nonna Mayer, eds. 1993. *The French Voter Decides*. Ann Arbor: University of Michigan Press.

Brown, Courtney. 1991. *Ballots of Tumult: A Portrait of Volatility in American Voting*. Ann Arbor: University of Michigan Press.

Bullock, Charles S., III, and Loch K. Johnson. 1992. *Runoff Elections in the United States*. Chapel Hill: University of North Carolina Press.

Butler, David, and Donald Stokes. 1969. *Political Change in Britain: Forces Shaping Electoral Choice*. New York: St. Martin's Press.

Calvert, Randall L., and John A. Ferejohn. 1983. Coattail Voting in Recent Presidential Elections. *American Political Science Review* 77:407–19.

Campbell, Angus. 1966. Surge and Decline: A Study of Electoral Change. In Angus Campbell et al., *Elections and the Political Order*, chap. 3. New York: John Wiley and Sons.

Campbell, Angus, Philip E. Converse, Warren E. Miller, and Donald E. Stokes. 1960. *The American Voter*. New York: John Wiley and Sons.

———. 1966. *Elections and the Political Order*. New York: John Wiley and Sons.

Campbell, Angus, and Henry Valen. 1966. Party Identification in Norway and the United States. In Angus Campbell et al., *Elections and the Political Order*, chap. 13. New York: John Wiley and Sons.

Campbell, James E. 1986. Predicting Seat Gains from Presidential Coattails. *American Journal of Political Science* 30:165–83.

———. 1987. The Revised Theory of Surge and Decline. *American Journal of Political Science* 31:965–79.

———. 1991. The Presidential Surge and its Midterm Decline in Congressional Elections, 1868–1988. *Journal of Politics* 53:477–87.

———. 1993. Surge and Decline: The National Evidence. In *Controversies in Voting Behavior*, ed. Richard G. Niemi and Herbert F. Weisberg, 3d ed., 222–40. Washington, D.C.: Congressional Quarterly Press.

Camus, Albert. 1951. *L'Homme révolté*. Paris: Gallimard.

———. 1956. *The Rebel: An Essay on Man in Revolt*. New York: Vintage Books.

Capdevielle, Jacques, Elisabeth Dupoirier, and Colette Ysmal. 1981. Tableau des électorats en mars 1978. In Jacques Capdevielle et al., *France de Gauche Vote à Droite*. Paris: Presses de la Fondation Nationale des Sciences Politiques.

Carmines, Edward G. 1991. The Logic of Party Alignments. *Journal of Theoretical Politics* 3:65–80.

Cayrol, Roland. 1988. The Electoral Campaign and the Decision-Making Process of French Voters. In *France at the Polls, 1981 and 1986: Three National Elections*, ed. Howard Penniman, 130–54. Durham, N.C.: Duke University Press.

Cerny, P. G. 1970. The Fall of Two Presidents and Extraparliamentary Opposition: France and the United States in 1968. *Government and Opposition: A Journal of Comparative Politics* 5:287–306.

Charlot, Jean. 1986. La transformation de l'image des partis politiques français. *Revue Française de Science Politique* 36:5–13.

Charlot, Monica. 1975. The Language of Television Campaigning. In *France at the Polls: The Presidential Election of 1974*, ed. Howard R. Penniman, 227–53. Washington, D.C.: American Enterprise Institute.

Code électoral. 1989. Journal Officiel de la République Française. (10 février 1989).

Cohen, J., and P. Cohen. 1975. *Applied Multiple Regression/Correlation Analysis for the Behavioral Sciences*. Hillsdale, N.J.: Lawrence Erlbaum Associates.

Converse, Philip E. 1966. The Concept of a Normal Vote. In Angus Campbell et al., *Elections and the Political Order*, chap. 2. New York: John Wiley and Sons.

———. 1969. Of Time and Partisan Stability. *Comparative Political Studies* 2:139–71.

———. 1976. *The Dynamics of Party Support: Cohort-Analyzing Party Identification.* Beverly Hills: Sage Publications.

Converse, Philip E., and Georges Dupeux. 1966a. De Gaulle and Eisenhower: The Public Image of the Victorious General. In Angus Campbell et al., *Elections and the Political Order*, chap. 15. New York: John Wiley and Sons.

———. 1966b. Politicization of the Electorate in France and the United States. In Angus Campbell et al., *Elections and the Political Order*, chap. 14. New York: John Wiley and Sons.

Converse, Philip E., and Gregory B. Markus. 1979. Plus Ça Change . . . : The New CPS Election Study Panel. *American Political Science Review* 73:32–49.

Converse, Philip E., and Roy Pierce. 1985. Measuring Partisanship. *Political Methodology* 11:143–66.

———. 1986. *Political Representation in France*. Cambridge, Mass.: The Belknap Press of Harvard University Press.

———. 1992. Partisanship and the Party System. *Political Behavior* 14:239–59.

———. 1993. Comment on Fleury and Lewis-Beck: "Anchoring the French Voter: Ideology versus Party." *Journal of Politics* 55:1110–17.

Corwin, Edward S. 1948. *The President: Office and Powers, 1787–1948. History and Analysis of Practice and Opinion.* 3d ed. New York: New York University Press.

Crewe, Ivor. 1976. Party Identification Theory and Political Change in Britain. In *Party Identification and Beyond: Representations of Voting and Party Competition*, ed. Ian Budge, Ivor Crewe, and Dennis Farlie, 33–61. London: John Wiley and Sons.

———. 1981. Electoral Participation. In *Democracy at the Polls: A Comparative Study of Competitive National Elections*, ed. David Butler, Howard R. Penniman, and Austin Ranney. Washington, D.C.: American Enterprise Institute for Public Policy Research.

Crozier, Michel. 1970. *La Société bloqué.* Paris: Editions du Seuil. Translation, *The Stalled Society.* New York: Viking Press, 1973.

Debré, Michel. 1955. Trois caractéristiques du système parlementaire français. *Revue Française de Science Politique* 5:21–48.

Denk, Charles E., and Steven E. Finkel. 1992. The Aggregate Impact of Explanatory Variables in Logit and Linear Probability Models. *American Journal of Political Science* 36:785–804.

Deutsch, Eméric, Denis Lindon, and Pierre Weill. 1966. *Les Familles Politiques: Aujourd'hui en France.* Paris: Les Editions de Minuit.

Dolez, Marc. 1991. La loi sur le cumul des mandats cinq ans après. *Le Monde*, March 27.

Duchateau, Jean. 1987. *Meurtre à l'Elysée.* Paris: Calmann-Lévy.

Duhamel, Alain. 1987. *Le Ve président.* Paris: Gallimard.

Duhamel, Olivier. 1989. Des élections enfin municipales. In *Elections Municipales 1989*, ed. Philippe Habert and Colette Ysmal, 13–14. Paris: Le Figaro/Etudes Politiques.

————. 1991. La Vᵉ bis. *L'Express*, 16–17. November 22.

Duhamel, Olivier, and Jérôme Jaffré. 1987. *Le Nouveau président*. Paris: Editions du Seuil.

Dupin, Eric. 1992. Les hauts et les bas de la décennie Mitterrand. In SOFRES, *L'état de l'opinion 1992*, ed. Olivier Duhamel and Jérôme Jaffré, 73–87. Paris: Editions du Seuil.

Duverger, Maurice. 1980. A New Political System Model: Semi-presidential Government. *European Journal of Political Research* 8:165–87.

The Economist. March 27, 1993.

Edsall, Thomas Byrne, with Mary D. Edsall. 1992. *Chain Reaction: The Impact of Race, Rights, and Taxes on American Politics*. New York: W. W. Norton and Company.

Edwards, George C., III. 1979. The Impact of Presidential Coattails on Outcomes of Congressional Elections. *American Politics Quarterly* 7:94–108.

Edwards, George C., III, with Alec M. Gallup. 1990. *Presidential Approval: A Sourcebook*. Baltimore: Johns Hopkins University Press.

Elections Législatives de Mars 1993. March 1993. *Le Monde*, Dossiers et Documents.

Erikson, Robert S., Thomas D. Lancaster, and David W. Romero. 1989. Group Components of the Presidential Vote, 1952–1984. *Journal of Politics* 51:338–46.

L'Express. November 29, 1991; March 20, 1992; April 1, 1993; June 3, 1993; July 14, 1994. Paris.

Ferejohn, John A., and Randall L. Calvert. 1984. Presidential Coattails in Historical Perspective. *American Journal of Political Science* 28:127–46.

Fiorina, Morris P. 1989. *Congress: Keystone of the Washington Establishment*. 2d ed. New Haven: Yale University Press.

Fleury, Christopher J., and Michael S. Lewis-Beck. 1993a. Anchoring the French Voter: Ideology versus Party. *Journal of Politics* 55:1100–09.

————. 1993b. *Déjà Vu* All Over Again: A Comment on the Comment of Converse and Pierce. *Journal of Politics* 55:1118–26.

Fougeyrollas, Pierre. 1963. *La Conscience politique dans la France contemporaine*. Paris: Denoël.

La France des Régions: Avec les résultats des élections 1986. *Le Monde*, Numéro spécial de Dossiers et Documents du Monde.

Gaffney, John, ed. 1989. *The French Presidential Elections of 1988: Ideology and Leadership in Contemporary France*. Aldershot, U.K. and Brookfield, Vermont: Dartmouth Publishing Company.

Gallup Opinion Index, The. 1974. No. 112, October. Princeton, N.J.: American Institute of Public Opinion.

Gallup Report, The. 1988. No. 278, November. Princeton, N.J.: The Gallup Poll, 1981–89.

Garraud, Philippe. 1992. Le kaléidoscope des candidatures et des campagnes. In *Le Vote éclaté*, ed. Philippe Habert, Pascal Perrineau, and Colette Ysmal, 33–55. Paris: Département d'Etudes Politiques du Figaro and Presses de la Fondation Nationale des Sciences Politiques.

Gaxie, Daniel. 1982. Mort et résurrection du paradigm de Michigan. Remarques sur quelques résultats récents de la sociologie des comportements politiques aux Etats-Unis. *Revue Française de Science Politique* 32:251–69.

Goguel, François. 1946. *La politique des partis sous la IIIe République*. Paris: Editions du Seuil.

———. 1981. La signification des succès de la gauche. *Le Monde*, November 9–10.

———. 1982. Encore un regard sur les élections législatives de juin 1981. *Pouvoirs* 23:135–43.

———. 1983. *Chroniques électorales*. Vol. 3. *La cinquième république après de Gaulle*. Paris: Presses de la Fondation Nationale des Sciences Politiques.

———. 1989. La vrai nature des municipales. In *Elections Municipales 1989*, ed. Phillippe Habert and Colette Ysmal, 15. Paris: Le Figaro/Etudes Politiques.

Gottschalk, Peter. 1993. Changes in Inequality of Family Income in Seven Industrialized Countries. *American Economic Review* 83:136–42.

Green, Donald Philip, and Bradley Palmquist. 1990. Of Artifacts and Partisan Instability. *American Journal of Political Science* 34:872–902.

Grunberg, Gérard. 1985. L'instabilité du comportement électoral. In *Explication du vote: Un bilan des études électorales en France*, ed. Daniel Gaxie, 418–46. Paris: Presses de la Fondation Nationale des Sciences Politiques.

Habert, Philippe, Pascal Perrineau, and Colette Ysmal. 1992. *Le Vote éclaté: Les élections régionales et cantonales des 22 et 29 mars 1992*. Paris: Département d'Etudes Politiques du Figaro and Presses de la Fondation Nationale des Sciences Politiques.

Haegel, Florence. 1993. Partisan Ties. In *The French Voter Decides*, ed. Daniel Boy and Nonna Mayer, 131–48. Ann Arbor: University of Michigan Press.

Hancock, Brian. 1992. *Fast Facts on State Registration and Election Procedures*. National Clearinghouse on Election Administration. Technical Report 2, February.

Heath, Anthony, and Roy Pierce. 1992. It was Party Identification All Along: Question Order Effects on Reports of Party Identification in Britain. *Electoral Studies* 11:93–105.

Heclo, Hugh. 1973. Presidential and Prime Ministerial Selection. In *Perspectives on Presidential Selection*, ed. Donald R. Matthews. Washington, D.C.: The Brookings Institution.

Huckfeldt, Robert, and Carol W. Kohfeld. 1989. *Race and the Decline of Class in American Politics*. Urbana: University of Illinois Press.

Inglehart, Ronald, and Hans-Dieter Klingemann. 1976. Party Identification, Ideological Preference and the Left-Right Dimension among Western Mass Publics. In *Party Identification and Beyond: Representations of Voting and Party Competition*, ed. Ian Budge, Ivor Crewe, and Dennis Farlie, 243–73. London: John Wiley and Sons.

Jacobson, Gary C. 1990. *The Electoral Origins of Divided Government: Competition in U.S. House Elections, 1946–1988*. Boulder: Westview Press.

Jennings, Jerry T. 1990. Estimating Voter Turnout in the Current Population Survey. In U.S. Department of Commerce, Bureau of the Census, *Studies in the Measurement of Voter Turnout*, 21–29. Washington, D.C.: Current Population Reports, Special Studies, P-23 No. 168.

Jennings, M. Kent, and Gregory B. Markus. 1984. Partisan Orientations over the Long Haul: Results from the Three-Wave Political Socialization Panel Study. *American Political Science Review* 78:1000–18.

Kallenbach, Joseph E. 1966. *The American Chief Executive: The Presidency and the Governorship*. New York: Harper and Row.

Kaplan, Steven L. 1993. *Adieu 89*. Paris: Fayard.

Key, V. O., Jr. 1955. A Theory of Critical Elections. *Journal of Politics* 17:3–18.

Kimberling, William. 1992. *Federal Election Statistics*. National Clearinghouse on Election Administration. Technical Report 1, February.

Kish, Leslie. 1992. Weighting for Unequal P_i. *Journal of Official Statistics* 8:183–200.

Klingemann, Hans-Dieter. 1979. Measuring Ideological Conceptualizations. In Samuel H. Barnes, Max Kaase, et al., *Political Action: Mass Participation in Five Western Democracies*. Beverly Hills: Sage Publications.

Klingemann, Hans-Dieter, and Charles L. Taylor. 1978. Partisanship, Candidates, and Issues: Attitudinal Components of the Vote in West German Federal Elections. In *Elections and Parties: Socio-political Change and Participation in the West German Federal Election of 1976*, ed. Max Kaase and Klaus von Beyme, 97–133. Beverly Hills: Sage Publications.

Knowles, Louis L., and Kenneth Prewitt, eds. 1969. *Institutional Racism in America*. Englewood Cliffs, N.J.: Prentice-Hall.

Lancelot, Alain. 1985. L'orientation du comportement politique. In *Traité de Science Politique*, ed. Madeleine Grawitz and Jean Leca, 3:367–428. Paris: Presses Universitaires de France.

———, ed. 1986. *1981: Les Elections de l'alternance*. Paris: Presses de la Fondation Nationale des Sciences Politiques.

Laponce, J. A. 1972. In Search of the Stable Elements of the Left-Right Landscape. *Comparative Politics* 4:455–75.

Laurent, Annie. 1987. Le nomadisme électoral: Le double vote du 16 mars 1986 dans le Nord-Pas-de-Calais. *Revue Française de Science Politique* 37:5–20.

Lehingue, Patrick. 1987. Les pratiques d'éclatement du vote: vote législatif et vote régional. L'exemple du département de la Somme. In *Régions: Le Baptême des urnes*, ed. Pascal Perrineau, 155–74. Paris: Pedone.

Levy, Michel. 1978. Le corps électoral. *Population et Sociétés*. February, No. 110.

Lewis, I. A. (Bud). 1991. Media Polls, the *Los Angeles Times* Poll, and the 1988 Presidential Election. In *Polling and Presidential Election Coverage*, ed. Paul J. Lavrakas and Jack H. Holley, 57–82. Newbury Park, Calif.: Sage Publications.

Lewis-Beck, Michael S. 1984. France: The Stalled Electorate. In *Electoral Change in Advanced Industrial Democracies: Realignment or Dealignment?*, ed. Russell J. Dalton, Scott C. Flanagan, and Paul Allen Beck, chap. 14. Princeton: Princeton University Press.

Light, Paul C. 1988. *Baby Boomers*. New York: W. W. Norton and Company.

Lipset, Seymour Martin. 1963. *The First New Nation: The United States in Historical and Comparative Perspective*. New York: Basic Books.

Lipset, Seymour Martin, and Stein Rokkan. 1967. *Party Systems and Voter Alignments*. New York: Basic Books.

Longley, Lawrence D., and Alan G. Braun, with a foreword by U.S. Senator Birch Bayh. 1972. *The Politics of Electoral College Reform*. New Haven: Yale University Press.

MacDonald, Stuart Elaine, Ola Listhaug, and George Rabinowitz. 1991. Issues and Party Support in Multiparty Systems. *American Political Science Review* 85: 1107–31.

Mair, Peter. 1989. The Problem of Party System Change. *Journal of Theoretical Politics* 1:251–76.

Markus, Gregory B. 1982. Political Attitudes During an Election Year: A Report on the 1980 NES Panel Study. *American Political Science Review* 76:538–60.

Markus, Gregory B., and Philip E. Converse. 1979. A Dynamic Simultaneous Equation Model of Electoral Choice. *American Political Science Review* 73:1055–70.

Massot, Jean. 1986. *La Présidence de la République en France: Vingt ans d'élection au suffrage universel 1965–1985.* Notes et Etudes Documentaires No. 4801. Paris: La Documentation Française.

Mayer, Nonna, and Annick Percheron. 1990. Les absents du jeu électoral. *Données Sociales.* Paris: INSEE (Institut Nationale de la Statistique et des Etudes Economiques), 398–401.

McNemar, Quinn. 1969. *Psychological Statistics.* 4th ed. New York: John Wiley and Sons.

Mény, Yves. 1987. Les restrictions au cumul des mandats: réforme symbolique ou changement en profondeur? *Tocqueville Review* 8:279–90.

———. 1992. *La corruption de la République.* Paris: Fayard.

Michelat, Guy, and Michel Simon. 1977. *Classe, religion, et comportement politique.* Paris: Presses de la Fondation Nationale des Sciences Politiques and Editions Sociales.

Mill, J. S. 1946. *On Liberty and Considerations on Representative Government.* Oxford: Basil Blackwell.

Miller, Warren E. 1991. Party Identification, Realignment, and Party Voting: Back to the Basics. *American Political Science Review* 85:557–68.

Miller, Warren E., Arthur H. Miller, and Edward J. Schneider. 1980. *American National Election Studies Data Sourcebook 1952–1978.* Cambridge, Mass.: Harvard University Press.

Mitofsky, Warren J., and Martin Plissner. 1988. Low Voter Turnout? Don't Believe It. *New York Times*, November 10.

Mitra, Subrata. 1988. The National Front in France—A Single-Issue Movement? *West European Politics* 11:47–64.

Le Monde. October 14, 1969; February 2, 1988; June 8, 1989; June 28, 1990; June 12, 1992. Paris.

Morin, Jean. 1983. Un Français sur dix ne s'inscrit pas sur les listes électorales. *Economie et Statistique.* Paris: INSEE (Institut National de la Statistique et des Etudes Economiques), February, No. 152.

———. 1987. La participation électorale. *Données Sociales.* Paris: INSEE (Institut Nationale de la Statistique et des Etudes Economiques), 606–10.

Mossuz-Lavau, Janine, and Mariette Sineau. 1983. *Enquête sur les femmes et la politique en France.* Paris: Presses Universitaires de France.

New York Times. November 10, 1988; November 5, 1992.

Notes et Etudes Documentaires. April 19, 1966. *Textes et documents relatifs à l'élection présidentielle des 5 et 19 décembre 1965.* Paris: La Documentation Française, No. 3283.

―――. July 7, 1975. *Textes et documents relatifs à l'élection présidentielle des 5 et 19 mai 1974*. Paris: La Documentation Française, No. 4201–4203.

―――. December 21, 1981. *Textes et documents relatifs à l'élection présidentielle des 26 avril et 10 mai 1981*. Paris: La Documentation Française, No. 4647–4648.

―――. 1988. *Textes et documents relatifs à l'élection présidentielle des 24 avril et 8 mai 1988*, ed. Didier Maus. Paris: La Documentation Française, No. 4865.

Ornstein, Norman J. 1985. The Elections for Congress. In *The American Elections of 1984*, ed. Austin Ranney, 245–76. Durham: Duke University Press.

Ornstein, Norman J., Andrew Kohut, and Larry McCarthy. 1988. *The People, the Press, and Politics: The Times Mirror Study of the American Electorate*. Reading, Mass.: Addison-Wesley.

Parodi, Jean-Luc. 1971. Sur deux courbes de popularité. *Revue Française de Science Politique* 21:129–51.

―――. 1983. Dans la logique des élections intermédiaires. *Revue Politique et Parlementaire* 903:42–71.

―――. 1989. Une élection intermédiaire précoce. In *Elections Municipales 1989*, ed. Philippe Habert and Colette Ysmal, 6–7. Paris: Le Figaro/Etudes Politiques.

―――. 1992. La double consultation de mars 1992. A la recherche d'un modèle. In *Le Vote éclaté*, ed. Philippe Habert, Pascal Perrineau, and Colette Ysmal, 269–85. Paris: Département d'Etudes Politiques du Figaro and Presses de la Fondation Nationale des Sciences Politiques.

Passel, Jeffrey S. 1990. Effects of Population Estimates on Voter Participation Rates. In U.S. Department of Commerce, Bureau of the Census, *Studies in the Measurement of Voter Turnout*, 31–63. Washington, D.C.: Current Population Reports, Special Studies, P–23, No. 168.

Percheron, Annick. 1986. Les absents de la cène électorale. In *Mars 1986: La drôle de défaite de la gauche*, ed. E. Dupoirier and G. Grunberg, 139–47. Paris: Presses de la Fondation Nationale des Sciences Politiques.

―――. 1988. Classes d'âge en question. *Revue Française de Science Politique* 38:107–24.

―――. 1989. Peut-on encore parler d'héritage politique en 1989? In *Idéologies, partis politiques et groupes sociaux*, ed. Yves Mény, 71–88. Paris: Presses de la Fondation Nationale des Sciences Politiques.

Phillips, Kevin. 1991. *The Politics of Rich and Poor: Wealth and the American Electorate in the Reagan Aftermath*. New York: HarperCollins Publishers.

Pierce, Roy. 1968. *French Politics and Political Institutions*. New York: Harper and Row.

―――. 1973. *French Politics and Political Institutions*. 2d ed. New York: Harper and Row.

―――. 1991. The Executive Divided Against Itself: Cohabitation in France, 1986–1988. *Governance* 4:270–94.

Pierce, Roy, and Philip E. Converse. 1989. Attitudinal Roots of Popular Protest: The French Upheaval of May 1968. *International Journal of Public Opinion* 1:221–41.

―――. 1990. Attitudinal Sources of Protest Behavior in France: Differences between Before and After Measurement. *Public Opinion Quarterly* 54:295–316.

Pierce, Roy, and Thomas R. Rochon. 1988. The French Socialist Victories of 1981 and the Theory of Elections. In *France at the Polls, 1981 and 1986: Three National Elections*, ed. Howard R. Penniman, 179–95. Durham, N.C.: Duke University Press.

Polsby, Nelson W., and Aaron Wildavsky. 1991. *Presidential Elections: Contemporary Strategies of American Electoral Politics*. 8th ed. New York: Free Press.

Presidential Elections Since 1789. 1991. 5th ed. Washington, D.C.: Congressional Quarterly.

Rabinowitz, George, and Stuart Elaine MacDonald. 1989. A Directional Theory of Voting. *American Political Science Review* 83:93–121.

Rae, Douglas. 1967. *The Political Consequences of Electoral Laws*. New Haven: Yale University Press.

Reydellet, Michel. 1979. Le cumul des mandats. *Revue du Droit Public et de la Science Politique* 95:693–768.

Schlesinger, Joseph A., and Mildred Schlesinger. 1990. The Reaffirmation of a Multiparty System in France. *American Political Science Review* 84:1077–1101.

Schonfeld, William R. 1986. Le RPR et L'UDF à l'épreuve de l'opposition. *Revue Française de Science Politique* 36:14–29.

Schonfeld, William R., and Marie-France Toinet. 1975. Les abstentionnistes ont-ils toujours tort? La participation électorale en France et aux Etats-Unis. *Revue Française de Science Politique* 25:645–76.

Servan-Schreiber, Jean-Jaques. 1967. *Le Défi américain*. Paris: Denoël. Translation, *The American Challenge*. New York: Atheneum, 1968.

Shively, W. Phillips. 1972. Party Identification, Party Choice, and Voting Stability: The Weimar Case. *American Political Science Review* 66:1203–25.

Shugart, Matthew Soberg, and John M. Carey. 1992. *Presidents and Assemblies: Constitutional Design and Electoral Dynamics*. Cambridge: Cambridge University Press.

Siegfried, André. 1913. *Tableau politique de la France de l'Ouest sous la Troisième République*. Paris: Colin.

———. 1930. *Tableau des partis en France*. Paris: Bernard Grasset.

———. 1948. Les problèmes de la nomenclature politique. In Fondation nationale des sciences politiques, Centre d'études scientifiques de la politique intérieure, *Colloque de sociologie électorale*. Paris: Domat-Montchrestien.

Skowronek, Stephen. 1993. *The Politics Presidents Make: Leadership from John Adams to George Bush*. Cambridge, Mass.: The Belknap Press of Harvard University Press.

Sondages. 1952. *Revue française de l'opinion publique*. No. 3. Numéro Spécial.

———. 1965. *Revue française de l'opinion publique*. No. 4. Numéro Spécial.

Southwell, Priscilla L. 1986. The Politics of Disgruntlement: Nonvoting and Defection among Supporters of Nomination Losers, 1968–1984. *Political Behavior* 8:81–95.

Stanley, Harold W., William T. Bianco, and Richard G. Niemi. 1986. Partisanship and Group Support Over Time: A Multivariate Analysis. *American Political Science Review* 80:969–76.

Stanley, Harold W., and Richard Niemi. 1991. Partisanship and Group Support, 1952–1988. *American Politics Quarterly* 19:189–210.

Statistical Abstract of the United States: 1991. U.S. Bureau of the Census. Washington, D.C.: 1991.

Thomassen, Jacques. 1976. Party Identification as a Cross-National Concept: Its Meaning in the Netherlands. In *Party Identification and Beyond: Representations of Voting and Party Competition*, ed. Ian Budge, Ivor Crewe, and Dennis Farlie, 63–79. London: John Wiley and Sons.

U.S. Senate. 1989. *Biographical Directory of the United States Congress, 1774-1989* 100th Cong., 2d sess, S. Doc. 100-34.

Verba, Sidney, and Norman Nie. 1972. *Participation in America: Political Democracy and Social Equality.* New York: Harper and Row.

Williams, Philip M. 1964. *Crisis and Compromise: Politics in the Fourth Republic.* London: Longmans.

Wolfinger, Raymond E., and Steven J. Rosenstone. 1980. *Who Votes?* New Haven: Yale University Press.

Index

Page references to tables and figures are identified by t and f, respectively.

drive for U.S. presidency, 25–26
election and reelection, 186
resignation, 20, 226–27
role in Republican party, 171
Noir, Michel, 222
Nonvoters. *See* Turnout

Ornstein, Norman, 187

Parodi, Jean-Luc, 185, 196, 197, 203
Partisanship. *See* Party identification
Party identification
  defined, 31–34
  France
    alignment (1988), 57–60
    change in incidence of, 40–43
    compared to ideological location,
      80–83
    in first-ballot electoral choice
      model, 123–33
    fractionalization index, 47
    incidence and composition, 42–49
    incidence by age, 49–50, 58
    left-right identification by age,
      50–55
    left-right locations, 34–36, 73–74,
      125–30, 134–38
    measurement, 42–44, 73–74
    as predictor of electoral choices, 63
    in run-off ballot electoral choice
      model, 133–43
    scalar representation, 35–36, 61–65
  intergenerational transmission, 43–45,
    48–50
  relation to issue positions, 79–83
  theory, 33–34
  United States
    by age, 52–53
    categories and shifts, 36–37
    changes in distribution (1950s–80s),
      38–39
    direction by year of birth (1900–58),
      52–53
    in electoral choice model, 133–43
    incidence and political composition,
      36–39

measurement of, 36
with split-ticket voting, 184–90
stability of, 175–76
See also Voter perceptions
Party solidarity, U.S., 172–75, 189–90
  See also Coalition solidarity in France
Party system
  France, 11–12, 15, 40–41
    left-right party classification, 61–73,
      243–45
    pseudo-two-party, 46–47, 50, 59, 174
    regionalism of, 160–61
    role in choice of presidential candi-
      dates, 216
    simplification and stabilization,
      41–42, 46–47
  United States
    nominating conventions, 10
    regionalism of, 160–61
    two-party, 9–10, 15, 175
  See also Party identification
Perception. *See* Voter perceptions
Percheron, Annick, 60, 102, 103, 104
Perot, Ross, 10, 17, 22, 222, 223
Perrineau, Pascal, 184, 200
Phillips, Kevin, 163
Pierce, Roy, 5, 19, 32, 34, 35, 36, 40, 42,
  43, 54, 57, 62, 63, 64, 65, 67, 68,
  75, 79–81, 138, 147, 178, 179, 204
Plissner, Martin, 101
Poher, Alain, 23–24
Polarization
  according to social class in France and
    United States, 148–52, 161–64
  around gender, 152–54
  around issues, 77–79
  around religion in France, 149–52
  around voter preferences, 205–9
  measure of (eta), 204–5
  voter perceptions of candidates' degree
    of, 86–88
Political interest
  growth in France of, 45–46
  and issue positions, 81t, 85t
  marais in France, 63
  turnout, 117t